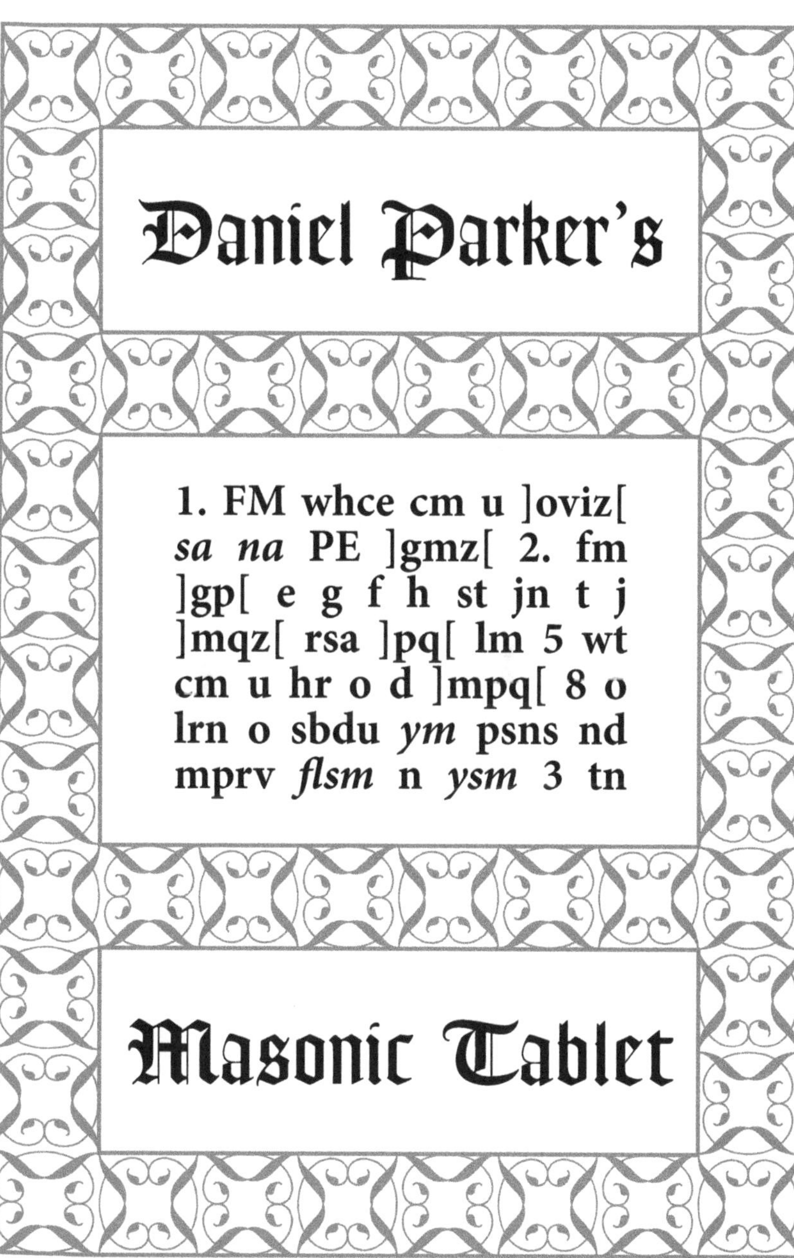
Daniel Parker's
1. FM whce cm u]oviz[
sa na PE]gmz[2. fm
]gp[e g f h st jn t j
]mqz[rsa]pq[lm 5 wt
cm u hr o d]mpq[8 o
lrn o sbdu ym psns nd
mprv flsm n ysm 3 tn
Masonic Tablet

Daniel Parker's MASONIC TABLET

A History, Decryption, and Facsimile of America's First Cipher Ritual

cptd mg brs nd *swlf* 7 hw d u no ursif]p
on ftn trd]cma[nv dnd nd m wlng o b trd
ym obn 1 hw shl i no u o b a n 4 y a crt
rft *stnp* f *ym* ntnc 1 wt r sns 2 rt *s/gn*
prp . 3 pls o gv *em* e sn f n *Pe* . (rss nd gvs
t hs o e *ytnp* f *ym* obn tt i wd rthr hv *ym*
thn o rvl e *stres* f *erf ysm* nl]qmp[fly .
n fndly r]cmz[bry *prg* wrb ;a br *yam* no
a n e *xl* . 7 pls o gv ur lft *dnh* br e *nkt*
nd gv t) A gvs B e *prg* . B *sys* wt s tt A i

Arturo de Hoyos, 33°, Grand Cross, K.Y.C.H.

Grand Archivist and Grand Historian

Past Master, McAllen Lodge No. 1110, AF&AM of Texas

Westphalia Press

Daniel Parker's MASONIC TABLET: A History, Facsimile, and Reproduction of America's First Cipher Ritual

Westphalia Press

An imprint of Policy Studies Organization
1367 Connecticut Avenue NW
Washington, D.C. 20036
info@ipsonet.org

ISBN: 978-1-63723-531-7

Daniel Gutierrez-Sandoval, Executive Director
PSO and Westphalia Press

For

R.·.W.·. Daniel Gardiner, PM, 32°
Grand Secretary of the Grand Lodge, AF&AM of Montana

Who has a "Master's Grip" on the development of American Craft ritual, who understood the importance of Parker's text in Masonic history, and who encouraged me in this work, proofread my text, and made helpful suggestions.

and

Kent Logan Walgren (1947–2003)
Masonic Bibliographer Extraordinaire

Whose friendship and love of Masonic books and history will always be dear to my memory, and who worked with me to identify the various editions of Parker's Masonic Tablet.

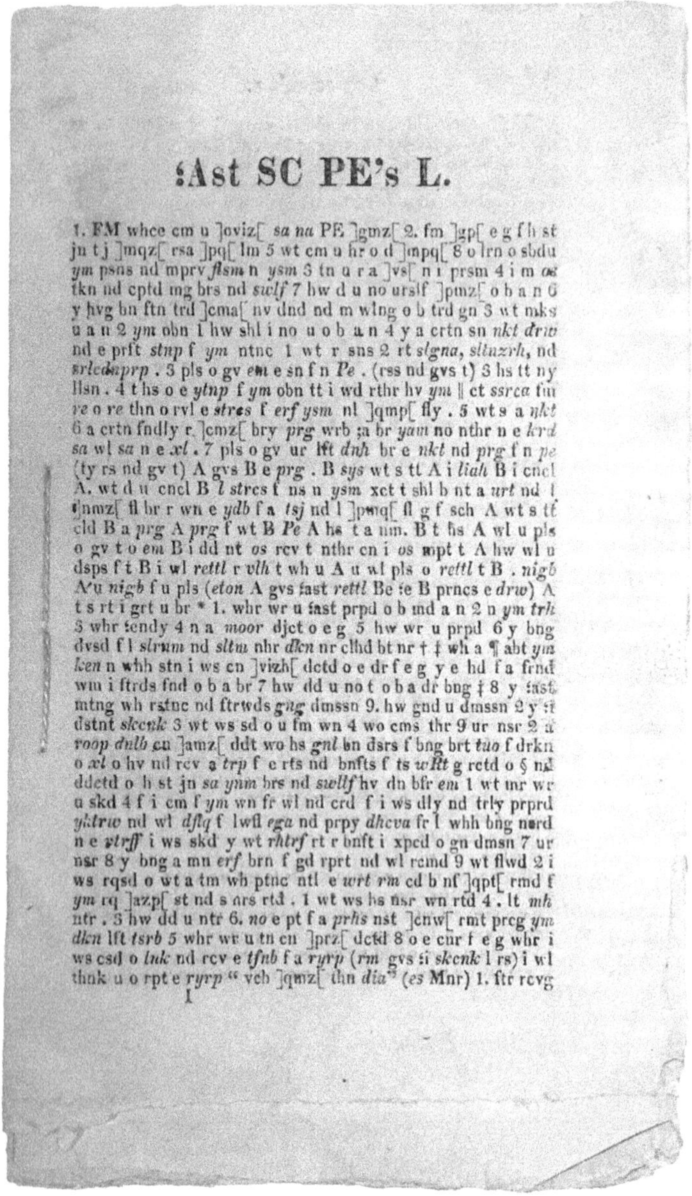

:Ast SC PE's L.

1. FM whce cm u]oviz[sa na PE]gmz[2. fm]gp[e g f h st
jn t j]mqz[rsa]pq[lm 5 wt cm u hr o d]mpq[8 o lrn o sbdu
ym psns nd mprv flsm n ysm 3 tn u r a]vs[n i prsm 4 i m os
tkn nd cptd mg brs nd swlf 7 hw d u no urslf]pmz[o b a n 6
y hvg bn ftn trd]cma[nv dnd nd m wlng o b trd gn 3 wt mks
u a n 2 ym obn 1 hw shl i no u o b a n 4 y a crtn sn nkt drw
nd e prft stnp f ym ntnc 1 wt r sns 2 rt signa, sltuzrh, nd
srlcdnprp . 3 pls o gv em e sn f n Pe . (rss nd gvs t) 3 hs tt ny
llsn . 4 t hs o e ytnp f ym obn tt i wd rthr hv ym ‖ ct ssrca fm
re o re thn o rvl e stres f erf ysm nl]qmp[fly . 5 wt s a nkt
6 a crtn fndly r]cmz[bry prg wrb ;a br yam no nthr n e krd
sa wl sa n e xl . 7 pls o gv ur lft dnh br e nkt nd prg f n pe
(ty rs nd gv t) A gvs B e prg . B sys wt s tt A i liah B i cncl
A. wt d u cncl B l strcs f ns n ysm xct t shl b nt a urt nd l
ȷnmz[fl br r wn e ydb f a tsj nd l]pmq[fl g f sch A wt s tf
cld B a prg A prg f wt B Pe A hs t a nm. B t hs A wl u pls
o gv t o em B i dd nt os rcv t nthr cn i os mpt t A hw wl u
dsps f t B i wl rettl r vlh t wh u A u wl pls o rettl t B . nigb
A'u nigb f u pls (eton A gvs fast rettl Be :e B prncs e drw) A
t s rt i grt u br * 1. whr wr u fast prpd o b md a n 2 n ym trh
3 whr :endy 4 n a moor djct o e g 5 hw wr u prpd 6 y bng
dvsd f l slrum nd sltm nhr dkn nr clhd bt nr † ‡ wh a ¶ abt ym
ken n whh stn i ws cn]vizh[dctd o e dr f e g y e hd f a frnd
wm i ftrds fnd o b a br 7 hw dd u no t o b a dr bng ‡ 8 y :ast
mtng wh rstnc nd ftrwds gng dmssn 9. hw gnd u dmssn 2 y :i
dstnt skcnk 3 wt ws sd o u fm wn 4 wo cms thr 9 ur nsr 2 a
roop dnlb cn]amz[ddt wo hs gnl bn dsrs f bng brt tuo f drkn
o xl o hv nd rcv a trp f e rts nd bnfts f ts wRt g rctd o § nd
ddctd o h st jn sa ynm brs nd swllf hv dn bfr em 1 wt mr wr
u skd 4 f i cm f ym wn fr wl nd crd f i ws dly nd trly prprd
yktrw nd wl dflq f lwfl ega nd prpy dhcva fr l whh bng nerd
n e vtrff i ws skd y wt rhtrf rt r bnft i xpcd o gn dmsn 7 ur
nsr 8 y bng a mn erf brn f gd rprt nd wl rcmd 9 wt flwd 2 i
ws rqsd o wt a tm wh ptnc ntl e wrt rm cd b nf]qpt[rmd f
ym rq]azp[st nd s nrs rtd . 1 wt ws hs nsr wn rtd 4 . lt mh
ntr . 3 hw dd u ntr 6. no e pt f a prhs nst]cnw[rmt prcg ym
dkn lft tsrb 5 whr wr u tn cn]prz[dctd 8 o e cnr f e g whr i
ws csd o lnk nd rcv e tfnb f a ryrp (rm gvs :i skcnk l rs) i wl
thnk u o rpt e ryrp " vcb]qmz[thn dia" (es Mnr) 1. ftr rcvg

I

First edition of the Rev. Daniel Parker's *Masonic Tablet* (New York, 1822)

CONTENTS

PREFACE

In August 1992 I visited the Ezra A. Cook Publishing Company in Chicago. The business, which was at 6604 West Irving Park Road, was a storefront, with a warehouse portion in the back. The onsite manager (and sole employee present) was Shirley Gustafson, a friendly, even jovial, person, who enticed me to travel from my home in McAllen, Texas, to visit the Chicago store, by telling me that their uncataloged warehouse portion held many old Masonic books, including manuscripts and rituals, which I could peruse and purchase.

The company was originally founded in 1867 by Ezra Asher Cook (1841–1911) as a printing office specializing in engraving, lithography, and blank books.[1] Its most enduring legacy, however, was as a publisher and distributor of anti-Masonic works and "exposures." Ezra A. Cook, who was "unalterably opposed to secret societies," was a founding member of the National Christian Association, which opposed oath-bound fraternities and societies. His wife, Elizabeth Maria Blanchard Cook, was the daughter of Jonathan Blanchard (1811–1892), who became the founder and first president of Wheaton College (Illinois). Blanchard, an anti-Mason from his youth,[2] was the driving force behind the National Christian Association. With his son-in-law they published *The Christian Cynosure*,[3]

1. Cook, a Civil War veteran, was wounded in 1864 at the battle of Drury's Bluff, Virginia, and mustered out a few months later. He started his stationary business in December 1867 with offices on La Salle Street, which were completely destroyed in the great fire of 1871. He rebuilt his "spacious and commodious establishment" on Wabash Avenue, and earned a reputation as "a clear-headed business man, honorable and fair in all transactions." See Charles M. Clark, *The History of the Thirty-Ninth Regiment Illinois Volunteer Veteran Infantry, (Yates Phalanx.) in the War of the Rebellion. 1861–1865* (Chicago: Veteran Association of the Regiment, 1889), 324; *Origin, Growth, and Usefulness of the Chicago Board of Trade: Its Leading Members, and Representative Business Men in Other Branches of Trade. An Epitome of Chicago's History and the Prominent Points of Interest* (New York: Historical Publishing Company, 1885–86), 349.

2. Clyde S. Kilby, *A Minority of One* (Grand Rapids, Mich.: William B. Eerdmans Publishing Co., 1959), 168.

3. "In the 1930s, The Cynosure's management passed from interdenominational circles to Christian Reformed Church (CRC) hands, although its anti-order emphasis remained. During the 1950s, the NCA's advisory council included pulpit luminaries such as V. Raymond Edman, president of Wheaton College; Evan Welsh, Chaplain, Wheaton College; and A. W. Tozer, pastor

each issue of which carried advertisements for Cook's anti-Masonic publications. Among the more (in)famous titles offered were William Morgan's *Illustrations of Masonry by One of the Fraternity* (1826), and the exposures of ex-Masons like Edmond Ronayne (1832–1911)[4] and Jacob O. Doesburg (1838–1904).[5] Jonathan Blanchard, and his son Charles, introduced and annotated some of Cook's books.

By the 1980s, when I learned of Ezra A. Cook Publishers, their glory days had long since passed. The name had been sold as an imprint to the Charles T. Powner Company, which offered titles under both names.[6] A native of Sardinia, Indiana, Charles Tracy Powner (1854–1920) was a Past Master of Concordia Lodge No. 476, Greensburg, Indiana, and a Royal Arch Mason.[7] In 1903 he moved to Chicago to manage a book company, and he soon opened a chain of his own bookshops, which he called the "House of a Million Books."[8] Powner, assisted by his son, Willard Earl Powner (1887–1960), who was also possibly

and author. Eventually the Lodge's influence diminished and an array of post-1950s ills emerged; consequently The Cynosure's circulation waned. Bidding its readers a grateful farewell, the paper folded in 1983." < *https://archon.wheaton.edu/?p=creators/creator&id=64* >

4. Ronayne was a Past Master of Keystone Lodge No. 639, Chicago. His ritual of the Blue Lodge was so accurate it was used by members to learn their work before the Grand Lodge printed an official text. His interesting autobiography was published as *Ronayne's Reminiscences: A History of his Life and Renunciation of Romanism and Freemasonry* (Chicago: Free Methodist Publishing House, 1900).

5. Doesburg was a Past Master of Unity Lodge No. 191, Holland, Michigan, and served as Secretary of his lodge just before his departure. A pharmacist, he sometimes permitted the lodge to meet at his business. *See History of Ottawa County, Michigan: With Illustrations and Biographical Sketches of Some of Its Prominent Men and Pioneers* (Chicago: H. R. Page & Co., 1882), 86.

6. I am unsure when Powner acquired Cook's titles. *The American Book Trade Directory*, vol. 1 (New York: R. R. Bowker, 1915) does not list Ezra A. Cook at all, although it includes Powner's "Antiquarian Book Store." Volume 2 (1919) lists "Cook (E. A.)" as a publisher identified in the 1918 *Publisher's Weekly*, and gives Cook the same physical address as Powner, while volume 3 (1922) lists "Cook, (Ezra A.) Publisher, Inc.," again with the same address as the "Antiquarian Book Store (C. T. Powner)." Later editions of the *American Book Trade Directory* read "Cook, Ezra A., Inc. Pubns. Acquired by Charles T. Powner. . . ."

7. Charles T. Powner served as Master of Concordia Lodge No. 476, during the 1896–97 year, and was also a member of Burney Lodge No. 341, Knights of Pythias. See *Proceedings of the Seventy-fifth Annual Meeting of the M.W. Grand Lodge of Free and Accepted Masons of the State of Indiana, held at Indianapolis, May 26 and 27, A. D. 1896, A. L. 5896.* (Indianapolis: Sentinel Printing Co., 1896), 53; Lewis Albert Harding, ed., *History of Decatur County, Indiana: Its People, Industries and Institutions* (Indianapolis, Indiana: B. F. Bowen, 1915), 308, 318. In 1894 Powner, an enthusiastic Mason, greeted Grand Master Frank E. Gavin's visit to Greensburg by presenting a talk, "Why I am a Mason." See *Indianapolis Journal*, Sunday, June 3, 1894, 2. "Former Teacher Dies Suddenly—Aged 66 Years Made Fortune in Book Business," *Greensburg Daily News*, December 31, 1920.

8. Samuel Putnam, *Powner's "The House of a Million Books" A Retrospective 1908–1925* (Chicago: W. E. Powner, 1925).

a Royal Arch Mason,[9] maintained the business until the elder Powner moved to Tucson, Arizona, and later to Los Angeles, where he died. Willard—who went by "W. E. Powner"—remained in Chicago and formed the affiliate P.R.C. Publications, with a partner,[10] which continued to reprint Masonic exposures. The younger Powner also printed books on a variety of other topics, including mysticism, spiritism, card-playing, chess, and even bartending. The company's Masonic advertisements disingenuously stated they had "continuously served the Craft since 1867." In addition to Masonic exposures, their publications catalogs included cipher rituals printed by themselves and others (*King Solomon and his Followers* and *Ecce Orienti*), some titles from the Macoy Publishing and Masonic Supply Company, and used copies of well-known works, such as Albert Pike's *Morals and Dogma*, and Albert G. Mackey's *Encyclopedia of Freemasonry*.

At the time I visited Ezra A. Cook storefront I was about three and a half years into my project to reverse-engineer Pike's *Morals and Dogma*,[11] and I hoped I might find some useful texts. True to her word, Shirley led me to the warehouse and I carefully picked through the stacks, gathering two large boxfuls of items for purchase. Among them was a small, twenty-eight-page, unbound, uncut, string-tied cipher ritual which I had never seen before. From the paper and typeface, it appeared to have been printed in the early nineteenth century. Excited with my finds I hand-carried the cipher and a couple of other rare items on my flight home. I did not know it then, but I had just purchased one of the rarest Masonic ciphers in existence: the first edition, first printing of the first Masonic cipher ritual printed in the United States!

I soon discovered what I believed was a reference to the cipher in a Charles T. McClenachan's *History of the Most Ancient and Honorable Fraternity of Free*

9. "W. E. Powner," a member of Park Lodge No. 213 (Chicago), was exalted a Royal Arch Mason in 1912. *Proceedings of the Grand Royal Arch Chapter of the State of Illinois, Sixty-third Annual Convocation Held at Chicago, October 24–25, 1912, A.I. 2442* (Springfield, Illinois, 1912), 164.

10. W. E. Powner listed his business partner as C. E. Reed in the *Certified List of Domestic and Foreign Corporations for the Year 1943* (Illinois: Office of Secretary of State), 1808. Hence, I suspect that the letters "P. R. C." may be the initials of "Powner, Reed, and Cook." They often used the Ezra A. Cook Publishing imprint for Masonic titles, but the books were also copyrighted by Charles T. Powner Publishing, or P.R.C. Publications. By 1958 W. E. Powner hired D. H. Sass as his business manager and buyer. In 1960, the year of W. E. Powner's death, Sass appears as the sole proprietor of the Charles T. Power Co., an "Affiliate of PRC Publications." This ended the Powner family publishing legacy. See *American Book Trade Directory* (1958), 182; *The Standard Advertising Register* vol. 48 (1960), 642.

11. Arturo de Hoyos, *Albert Pike's Morals and Dogma: Annotated Edition* (Washington, D.C: Supreme Council, 33°, 2011).

and Accepted Masons in New York from its Earliest Date (1892), where I learned that Daniel Parker, of Kingston, New York, printed a "Masonic Tablet" in 1822. Although I managed to read a portion of the cipher, I did not attempt to decrypt its full contents. A few months later, in January 1993, my friend Kent L. Walgren of Salt Lake City coincidentally sent me a photocopy of a work called *Morgan Confirmed* (1827).[12] I say coincidentally, because Kent was not aware that I had purchased the cipher. *Morgan Confirmed* was a reprint of the *Masonic Tablet* with a (somewhat faulty) decryption of the cipher, and Kent's notes revealed he also knew about Parker and his cipher. In conversation Kent called it the "Ast ritual"—alluding to the first words of the text. At the back of *Morgan Confirmed* was a cipher key, used to decrypt the text. The following month, in February 1993, I attended the "Masonic Week" events in Washington, DC, when I stopped by the House of the Temple to continue my research for my *Morals and Dogma* project. While looking through the library's stacks I found a bound copy of a different edition of Parker's *Masonic Tablet* which also included a second section on the York Rite's degrees, as well as two cipher keys. I made a copy, and forwarded one to Kent, who was working on his bibliography of American Masonic imprints.[13] In addition to bibliographic details, Kent listed the locations of known surviving copies of the books in his bibliography. He informed me that, at the time, my copy was the only known copy of the first edition.[14] While he cataloged Masonic libraries throughout the country we worked together to identify the various known editions of Parker's work.

As the years passed I eventually decrypted the *Masonic Tablet*, and in 2001 I completed a draft edition, which included a brief biography about Parker. I sent a copy to Kent, who noted that my work was the first time that all of Parker's text had been decrypted. The draft's biography of Parker became the basis for a

12. Edward Hickes, *Morgan Confirmed: or The Secrets of Freemasonry Made Known to all the World: Being An authentic and true History, by the Masons Themselves, of All Their Transactions, Signs, Ceremonies, Formalities of Initiation, Expulsion, Proceedings, &c. &c. Obtained by the Possession of a Key to a Masonic Document; which Key and Document are herewith published; and are of such a nature that any Person can, by use of them, understand immediately, and can practice all that the most accomplished Freemason can do: Confirming All the unfortunate Morgan has written on the Subject; and furnishing much additional and interesting Matter* (New York: Printed for the author, 1827).

13. Kent Logan Walgren, *Freemasonry, Anti-Masonry and Illuminism in the United States, 1734–1850: A Bibliography* 2 vols. (Worcester, Mass.: American Antiquarian Society, 2003).

14. In 2011 the library of the Supreme Council, 33°, NMJ, acquired two copies of the first edition. See < *https://nationalheritagemuseum.typepad.com/library_and_archives/2011/09/rare-ast-ritual-given-to-library.html* >

paper I delivered to Quatuor Coronati Lodge No. 2076 (London) in June 2018,[15] and the latter was used to prepare the introduction to this book. From 2001 until his unfortunate early passing in 2003, Kent and I continued to discuss Parker's editions, making a few conclusions which came too late to be included in his published bibliography. We lamented that, at the time, we were likely the only people who cared about the imprint. That would change five years after Kent's passing when I briefly discussed Parker's *Masonic Tablet* in my reprint of David Bernard's *Light on Masonry* (1829).[16] I didn't know it at the time, but Bro. Daniel Gardiner (now R.W. Grand Secretary of the Grand Lodge of Montana) paid particular attention to my introduction to that reprint. Fortunately, Bro. Daniel developed a keen interest in and understanding of the evolution of American Masonic ritual, and he worked to decrypt the Blue Lodge portion of Parker's text from a copy of the book from the Grand Lodge of Massachusetts. When I learned of his interest we mutually shared our decryptions. After I told Bro. Daniel I was preparing the present book for publication he graciously offered to proof my decryption. His eagle eyes saved me from numerous grammatical errors, inconsistencies, and occasional humorous typos and blunders. His contributions made this a better book, and I am grateful to have had his help.

It should be noted that although this text purports to describe ritual practices in New York in 1822, it does not reflect current usages. Following the anti-Masonic period of 1826–42 the rituals in all American states underwent changes and refinement, some of which are quite significant. Such being the case, this text may be only helpful in giving us glimpse into the remote past.

15. Arturo de Hoyos, "An American Masonic Odyssey: The Revd Bro. Daniel Parker and His *Masonic Tablet*," *Ars Quatuor Coronatorum* 131 (2018), 181–223.

16. Arturo de Hoyos, *Light on Masonry: The History and Rituals of America's Most Important Masonic Exposé* (Washington, DC: Scottish Rite Research Society, 2008).

INTRODUCTION

Prior to the mid-nineteenth century, most American grand lodges did not enforce ritual uniformly and individual lodges enjoyed some freedom of doing things their own way, so long as there was a general agreement in the major features, especially in the "modes of recognition" (signs, tokens, and words).[1] The language was somewhat less formal, and some American lodges preserved archaic expressions and/or practices. For example, Benjamin W. Case, a physician who was made a Mason in 1796, in Newport, Rhode Island, recalled that during the initiation of an Entered Apprentice Mason there was an attempt made "to frighten or alarm the candidate ... by making noises, shuffling on the floor, throwing sticks down and directing the candidate to step high."[2] Similarly, the *Edinburgh Register House* (1696), *Chetwode Crawley* (ca. 1700), and *Arlie* (1705) manuscripts all stated that during the initiation there were a "great many ceremonies to frighten" the candidate. Dr. Case also remarked that generally, "The oaths, forms of initiation, and manner of working in lodges were similar to those laid down in a book called *Jachin and Boaz*, until about the time of the publication of Webb's Monitor in 1802." He added when he again attended those same lodges about 1810 he "found material alterations in the ceremonies and

1. "The Grand Lecturer of New York informs us, notwithstanding all this discussion, that he found, during the last year, no less than five different systems of work and lectures existing in that State, and that four of them prevailed in a single lodge—so that, until the labor began, the brethren did not know which particular system was to be the order of the evening." —Philip C. Tucker, G.M. of Vermont, *Address of the Grand Master, 1859*

2. Testimony of Benjamin W. Case, in *Report of the Committee Appointed by the General Assembly of the State of Rhode-Island and Providence Plantations to Investigate the Charges in Circulation Against Freemasonry and Masons in Said State: Together with the Official Documents and Testimony Relating to the Subject* (William Marshall, State Printer, 1832), 76. In 1817 Case was elected Master of St. John's Lodge No. 1, New Port, Rhode Island, but following a controversy the Grand Lodge declared the election void. Case and his followers acted schismatically and declared themselves "free and independent from the Grand Lodge." He took the lodge's "papers, records and jewels" which were finally reacquired from his heirs in 1858 by Bro. Nathan Hammett Gould. During the "Morgan affair" Case was editor of the *Anti-Masonic Rhode Islander. Weekly, Newport*, established April 29, 1829, although the paper died within six months from lack of funds.

oaths in the lodges; changes were introduced, which were not in use at the time of my initiation." With the exception of exposés, very few printed testimonies exist regarding the nature of early American ritual. Perhaps the most important is Daniel Parker's *Masonic Tablet* of 1822. The text, which provides the first full description of American Craft ritual, is largely unknown and, prior to the current work, it had never been completely deciphered and printed.

AMERICA'S FIRST MASONIC GUIDEBOOK

In order to appreciate the context of America's first printed cipher ritual it's helpful to briefly rehearse some history which, during this period, largely revolved around the man who endeavored to codify American craft ritual. As Dr. Case noted, the changes in ritual coincided with the appearance of "Webb's Monitor." *The Freemason's Monitor or Illustrations of Masonry in Two Parts* (Albany, 1797; 2nd ed., 1802), by Thomas Smith Webb[3] (1771–1819), was the first guidebook to American Freemasonry and exerted a tremendous stabilizing influence on the ritual. Webb, a Boston native, was initiated in Rising Sun Lodge, Keene, New Hampshire, at age nineteen, on December 24, 1790, then passed and raised three days later, on St. John's Day.[4] Contrary to what has been recently written, he was not "a regular attendee at the lodge during his brief sojourn in Keene"[5] but rather the lodge records show that he "discontinued, July 6, 1791, was admitted again August 13, 1791, and again withdrew March 7, 1792."[6] As a youth he apprenticed in a print shop, and in 1793, he and *a partner* opened a wallpaper ("paper staining") business in Hartford, Connecticut,[7] but Webb dropped out "almost immediately, or else acted as a partner in absentia."[8] In November of that year he moved to Albany, New York, where he joined Union Lodge No. 1, and established another wallpaper business[9] with Henry Spencer (1748–1823), a bookbinder and

3. In the first edition Webb simply identified himself as "A Royal Arch Mason."

4. Henry Leonard Stillson and William James Hughan, *History of the Ancient and Honorable Fraternity of Free and Accepted Masons, and Concordant Orders* (Boston and New York: Fraternity Publishing Co.; London: George Kenning, 1891), 599.

5. Robert G. Davis, *The Mason's Words: The History and Evolution of the American Masonic Ritual* (Guthrie, OK: Building Stone Publishing, 2013).

6. Henry W. Rugg, *History of Freemasonry in Rhode Island* (E. L. Freeman & Son, State Printer, 1895), p. 283.

7. Richard C. Nylander, et al., *Wallpaper in New England* (Society for the Preservation of New England Antiquities, 1986), 21.

8. Phyllis Kihn, "Zecheriah Mills: Paper Hanging Manufacturer of Hartford, 1793–1816," in *Bulletin of the Connecticut Historical Society*, 26 (January 1961): 1, 21.

9. Margaret Coffin, *Borders and Scrolls: Early American Brush-Stroke Wall Painting 1790–1820*

Thomas Smith Webb, author of *The Freemason's Monitor or Illustrations of Masonry* (1797). Charles T. McClenachan, *History of the Most Ancient and Honorable Fraternity of Free and Acepted Masons inNew York* (New York: Grand Lodge, 1892), 2: frontispiece.

bookseller.[10] The title page of Webb's book states that it was printed "for *Spencer and Webb," but the printer's name is not identified.*[11]

The inspiration for Webb's book and ritual was largely twofold. The first was William Preston's *Illustrations of Masonry* (1772). In July 1796 the Albany bookstore of John Barber and Solomon Southwick (a Freemason) offered Preston's work for sale, and Webb must have quickly secured a copy. Webb's second source was the well-known exposé *Jachin and Boaz* (1762). Webb, who had a liberal education and some skill at writing, borrowed both from Preston's title and content and used *Jachin and Boaz* (in print in the United States since 1774), for the ritualistic structure. According to tradition Webb also learned ritual from John Hanmer, an Englishman who was a member of Preston's Lodge of Antiquity No. 1, though this is unproven. Although the story has been oft-repeated, Hanmer's identity and original membership in Craft Masonry remains a bit of a mystery.

Southwick, who became one of Webb's students, later remarked he had "obtained possession of a printed copy of the very identical edition of Jachin and Boaz, out of which he was himself taught the first three degrees of Masonry, by the late Thomas S. Webb, author of the Masonic Monitor, and during his lifetime regarded by the fraternity as an infallible oracle, in their '*sublime*' mysteries."[12] Webb possibly revised the Craft ritual as he worked on his *Monitor*, since David Vinton may have transcribed the Webb work around 1798.[13] It is known

(Albany Institute of History and Art; SUNY Press, 1986), 20.

10. Hannah French, "Early American Bookbinding by Hand," in Hellmut *Lehmann-Haupt, ed. Bookbinding in America: Three Essays*. Rev. *ed.* (New York: R. R. Bowker, 1967), 99; *Vermont History, Volumes 42–43* (Vermont Historical Society, 1974): 290; J. Munsell, *Annals of Albany* vol. 8 (Albany: J. Munsell, 1857): 93.

11. Henry Spencer's brother Thomas (1752–1840) was also an Albany bookseller, who did business with printer Solomon Southwick (1773–1839), a Freemason, and later prominent anti-Mason. Webb's printer may have been John McDonald, who sold his business to Joseph Fry and Henry C. Southwick (brother of Solomon) in 1798. The Fry and Southwick print shop was on Market Street, as was the Spencer and Webb business. Henry C. Southwick, also a Mason, would be appointed printer of the Grand Lodge of New York, in 1820. See J. Munsell, *Annals of Albany* vol. 8 (Albany: J. Munsell, 1857), 334; Charles Thompson McClenachan, *History of the Most Ancient and Honorable Fraternity of Free and Accepted Masons in New York, from the Earliest Date: Embracing the History of the Grand Lodge of the State, from Its Formation in 1781* [...] (New York: Published by the Grand Lodge, 1888), 324.

12. *National Observer* 2, no. 44, whole no. 122 (Albany, May 23, 1828): [4]. Spaulding also tells the story in his book *A Solemn Warning Against Free-Masonry. Addressed to the Young Men of the United States* (Albany: Geo. Galpin, Office of the National Observer, 1827), 71.

13. "The Vinton notes compare in some respects very nearly with yours; in others, they differ very materially. They are not properly notes so much as full reading. They are full of signs and contracted words, but he did not seem to have even learned the idea of the cypher in which yours

William Preston, author of *Illustrations of Masonry* (1772). Albert G. Mackey et al., *Encyclopedia of Freemasonry and Kindred Sciences* (Chicago, Toronto, New York, London: Masonic History Co., 1929), s.v. Preston, William.

that Benjamin Gleason became Webb's student around 1801–1802, and that he thought so highly of Webb's revisions that he urged the Grand Lodge of Massachusetts to adopt it. On June 24, 1805 Gleason wrote:

> A sanction from the Grand Lodge of Massachusetts is presumed, a uniform and exemplary mode of work and lecturing will soon succeed the present mutilations and informalities—and Free-Masonry thus rendered glorious, will in due time be "a Name and a Praise throughout the Earth."[14]

Accordingly, Grand Master Isaiah Thomas appointed Gleason to be "Grand Lecturer and Instructor," with the power to correct the "rude, imperfect, and in many instances, erroneous Lectures and modes of work" throughout the Commonwealth.[15] This began a concerted effort to promote Webb's ritual throughout the United States, which story is itself is too long and involved to rehearse at this time.

On the other hand there were others, including Minnesota Grand Master A. T. C. Pierson, who were neither enamored with Webb nor enchanted by his work:

> [S]uch was his wonderful Masonic experience had in—Keene, N. H., 1792–5, that he made a perfect ritual. "Great is Diana." A laboring man—poor, with a growing family, no Masonic publications in that day except Preston and the constitutions of Jachin and Boaz, much of his work he took from the latter, and yet with all his cares, he got up a perfect work. Again, Webb, in changing and altering Preston's lectures, left out the most beautiful and instructive part, and destroyed much of the symbolism of the degrees.[16]

and others is written. The history of them is about this: vinton was one of the earliest of webb's pupils; he went South, lectured, and was the author of one funeral ode, 'Solemn Strikes the Funeral Chime.' He taught in North Carolina, and to some few Lodges furnished a copy of his lectures. He died in Bowling Green, Kentucky, and was buried by the Masons. After his death, in his trunk was found this copy of notes and some other papers which told who and what he was. His teachings are probably those of webb's teachings. It is supposed this copy was made about 1798." W. B. Langridge, October 19, 1866, to Samuel Willson, in *Proceedings of the Grand Lodge of Illinois, of Ancient, Free and Accepted Masons, at the Twenty-seventh Grand Annual Communication, Held at Springfield, Oct. 1st and 2d, A.L. 5867* (Springfield: H. G. Reynolds & Son, 1867), 175.

14. Benjamin Gleason, *A Masonic Address, &c. Pronounced Before the Brethren of Mount Moriah Lodge, at Reading, on the anniversary of St. John the Baptist, June 24th, A.L. 5805* (Boston: A Newell, 1805), 12.

15. *Proceedings of the Most Worshipful Grand Lodge of Ancient Free and Accepted Masons of the Commonwealth of Massachusetts* [...] *1792–1815* (Cambridge: Press of Caustic-Claflin Co., 1905), 283.

16. A. T. C. Pierson, St. Paul, Minnesota, February 12, 1863, to James Fenton, Detroit, Michigan, quoted in James Fenton, *An Address Delivered at Masonic Hall, Detroit, March 13, 1863* (Detroit: Free Press Steam Power Press Printing House, 1863), 10.

Whatever the merits or failings of Webb's ritual, such is the power of the printed word that he now sits firmly enthroned in the pantheon of the fraternity. Webb served as Grand Master of Rhode Island in 1813–14, and became the founder of what is called the "York Rite" in the United States.

Much of the Webb-form ritual was preserved and promulgated by a variety of published monitors, while the secret portions were enciphered in his student's manuscript books; but it would take about twenty-five years, from the first publication of the Webb's book, until someone came upon the idea of *printing* a cipher ritual as a companion volume.

Daniel Parker

The Rev. Daniel Parker was an imposing figure standing "over six feet in height, powerfully made and of great strength." Born in Washington, Connecticut, on June 22, 1774, he was the eldest son of Amasa Parker (a Revolutionary War veteran) and Deidamia Parmelee. He entered Yale in 1797, but left before the end of his freshman year, and joined the next class in sophomore year.[17] While at Yale he was admitted to the Linonian Society, which was founded to promote "'Friendship and Social Intercourse,' as well as the cultivation of literature."[18] In 1799 he married Anna Fenn, the daughter of Col. Thomas Fenn, a "distinguished Revolutionary veteran," and they had two sons and one daughter.

Parker studied theology and began preaching as a Congregational minister in 1801 in the small parish of Ellsworth Society, in Sharon, Connecticut. He accepted a calling and was ordained in 1802,[19] and in 1806 he received an *ad eundem* Master's degree from Williams College. While acting as a minister in Ellsworth "he established, and had charge of, an academy at that place, which acquired a high reputation."[20] The success of his academy (one of the first female boarding schools in the United States[21]) and the time it required led Parker to request a demission from his church calling. The church, unhappy with his avocation, would only grant his dismissal after a trial.[22] In June 1812 he attended

17. Franklin B. Dexter, *Biographical Sketches of the Graduates of Yale College with Annals History. Vol. V. June 1792—September, 1805* (New York: Henry Holt and Co., 1911), 331–34.

18. *A Catalogue of the Linonian Society, of Yale College: founded September twelfth, 1753* ([New Haven:] Hitchcock & Stafford, 1841), 1, 27.

19. *The Connecticut Evangelical Magazine*, Vol. 3 (Hartford: Hudson & Goodwin, 1802), 39.

20. William Hunt, *The American Biographical Sketch Book* (New York: Nafis & Cornish, 1849), 117.

21. Henry Reed, the Cincinnati *Gazette*, quoted in *Supplement to the Courant. Published Every Other Week as a Part of the Connecticut Currant,* 34 (Hartford, Saturday, April 3, 1869): 9, 67.

22. Daniel Parker, *Proscription Delineated; or a Development of Facts Appertaining to the*

his last meeting of General Association of Connecticut, and in March 1813 he was dismissed as a Congregational minister.[23] As a result of hardships which partially resulted from the War of 1812, and other financial problems,[24] he was forced into bankruptcy in 1814, as were many other Americans.

Following his bankruptcy Parker hoped to make fresh start. In March 1816 he moved his family to Greenville, Green County, New York, where he served a principal of the new Greenville Academy (attended by Martin Van Buren, later American President). The academy's act of incorporation was signed February 27, 1816, by Daniel D. Tompkins, who was then governor of the State of New York, and Sovereign Grand Commander of the Supreme Council, 33°, Northern Masonic Jurisdiction. Parker served as principal of Greenville Academy until 1817, and was also a member of the Greenville literary institution.[25]

Unfortunate hardships followed Parker to New York. The Litchfield, Connecticut, North Association for Ministers filed charges against him in August 1817 for fraud and falsehood, accusing him of misusing his ministerial certificate which had been suspended.[26] It has been suggested that his persecution was at least partially due to his prominent Masonic membership.[27] He defended his character in a 290-page book entitled *Proscription Delineated*,[28] and in a 140-page follow-up

Arbitrary and Oppressive Proceedings of the North Congregationalist Association of Lichfield, County, in Relation to the Author (Hudson: Stone and Cross, 1819), 26; Dexter, *Biographical Sketches* [...] (1911), 5:332. Parker and his prosecutor in the trial, Dr. Lyman Beecher, were former classmates. In his autobiography the latter accused Parker of neglecting his calling: "There was a man by the name of P— settled at Sharon who went into everything but the work of the ministry—speculated, borrowed money at bank, and got aground." Charles Beecher, ed., *Autobiography, Correspondence, etc. of Lyman Beecher, D.D.* 2 vols. (New York: Harper & Brothers, 1865), 1:454.

23. *Proceedings of the General Association of Connecticut June 1812* (Hartford: Peter B. Gleason & Co., 1812), 12; B. B. Edwards, *The American Quarterly Register* (Boston: Perkins & Marvin, 1832), 4:319; Giles Frederick Goodenough, ed., *A Gossip About a Country Parish of the Hills and Its People* (Amenia, NY: Times Press, 1900), 14.

24. Goodenough, ed., *A Gossip* [...] (1900), 16.

25. Daniel Parker, *A New-Year's Discourse, Delivered Before the Members of the Literary Institution in Greenville , Green County, the 1st of January 1817* (Catskill, [N.Y.]: M. Croswell & Son, [1817]); Benjamin Franklin Hough, *Historical and Statistical Record of the University of the State of New York: During the Century from 1784 to 1884. With an Introductory Sketch by David Murray* (Albany, NY: Weed, Parsons & Co., 1885), 634.

26. The Congregation's position was detailed in Joseph Harvey, *A Reply to the Statements of Mr. Daniel Parker: In a Late Publication, Entitled "Proscription Delineated."* (Hartford, Conn.: Peter B. Gleason and Company, 1819); Dexter, *Biographical Sketches* [...] (1911), 5:332.

27. Dexter, *Biographical Sketches* [...] (1911), 5:334.

28. Daniel Parker, *Proscription Delineated; or a Development of Facts Appertaining to the Arbitrary and Oppressive Proceedings of the North Congregationalist Association of Lichfield, County,*

called *A Complete Refutation.*[29] In 1818 he moved to Hudson, New York, where he served until 1819 as the principle of the Hudson Academy,[30] when he moved to Kingston. In 1823 Parker was employed to take charge of the Kingston Academy, and was paid a base salary of $300 per annum (approximately $154,000 income value in 2016[31]), which position he held until September 1826.[32]

Parker had strong academic and literary interests, and later published a book on arithmetic.[33] It is said that towards the end of his life Rev. Parker became interested in the mystic doctrines of Emanuel Swedenborg.

The Freemason

Rev. Parker was initiated in into Freemasonry in Connecticut "several years before [he] entered upon the ministry." This may have been around 1795, when he turned twenty-one, five or six years before he started preaching. His Masonic membership records have not been discovered, but at the grand lodge session of May 17, 1815, just a month shy of his forty-first birthday, he was appointed charter Master of a new lodge.

> The petition from the brethren in Sharon, praying for the establishment of a new Lodge in that town, continued from the last Grand Communication, was introduced, and the consideration thereof resumed. The committee appointed to examine the Master elect, reported, that they made the examination as directed, and found him well qualified. After a full discussion, and the hearing of a remonstrance, the petition was granted, and a charter ordered to be issued, by the name of "Hamilton Lodge, No. 54"—Bro. Daniel Parker to be first Master, and the Wardens appointed as per petition.[34]

in Relation to the Author (Hudson: Stone and Cross, 1819).

29. Daniel Parker, *A Complete Refutation of the Reply of Mr. Joseph Harvey to Proscription Delineated* (New-York: Wiley & Halsted, 1820).

30. Franklin Benjamin Hough, *Historical and Statistical Record of the University of the State of New York: During the Century from 1784 to 1884* (Albany: Weed, Parsons & Co., Printers), 664.

31. According to *measuringworth.com* (accessed August 25, 2016).

32. Nathaniel Bartlett Sylvester, *History of Ulster County, New York: With Illustrations and Biographical Sketches of its Prominent Men and Pioneers* (Philadelphia: Everts & Peck, 1880), 1:216.

33. Daniel Parker, A.M., *The Improved Arithmetic: newly arranged and clearly illustrated, both theoretically and practically, to meet the exigencies of the student in the acquisition of the nature and science of numbers; and also to aid the accountant in all arithmetical computations, relative to business transactions; designed for the use of academies, schools, and counting-houses* (New York: J. & J. Harper, 1828).

34. E. G. Storer, ed., *Record of Freemasonry in the State of Connecticut, with a Brief Account of its Origin in New England, and the Entire Proceedings of the Grand Lodge, from its First Organization, A.L. 5789* (New Haven: Henry B. Storer, Printer, 1859), 266. In his published defense Parker referred to himself as a Past Master. See *Proscription Delineated* (1819), 92.

In 1815 and 1816, owing to financial burdens and his recent move to New York, Worshipful Bro. Parker was unable to attend the grand communications of the Grand Lodge of Connecticut, and Hamilton Lodge sent a proxy. The following year no officer was present and the lodge was found delinquent "for non-attendance and not making returns."[35]

Bro. Parker was also active in the Captitular (Holy Royal Arch) Masonry, and in 1813 he was appointed to a grand chapter committee to examine the proficiency of officers elect.[36] In the same year he petitioned the grand chapter for a charter to establish a Royal Arch chapter in Kent. This was approved, and he presided as high priest of the new Hamilton Chapter No. 14 in 1814–15.[37] In 1814 he also served as grand secretary, *pro tempore*, of the Grand Royal Arch Chapter of Connecticut and was a part of the committee assigned to find a new grand secretary.[38] In 1815 at the installation of the officers of Meridian Chapter No. 15, Royal Arch Masons, Canaan, he delivered a discourse on Psalm 133:1 ("Behold, how good and how pleasant it is for brethren to dwell together in unity. . . .") which he later published.[39]

The New York Mason

Parker's residence in New York was during one of its most exciting periods. De Witt Clinton, grand master of the Grand Lodge of New York from 1806–20, oversaw the Erie Canal project of 1817–25, which was one of the country's most ambitious feats of engineering. Albany had recently seen the publication of Webb's *The Free-Mason's Monitor*, and during 1813–15 a Supreme Council of the Ancient and Accepted (Scottish) Rite was established in New York City.

Kingston Lodge No. 23 was chartered by the Grand Lodge of New York in August 1808. In 1820, "Immediately after this [June 24, St. John's Day] anniversary

35. Hamilton Lodge No. 42 surrendered its charter to the Grand Lodge in 1838, and had it restored in 1873. The lodge ultimately surrendered its charter in 1997, and the members were assigned to Montgomery Lodge No. 13 (originally chartered by the Grand Lodge of Massachusetts in 1783).

36. Joseph K. Wheeler, ed., *Records of Capitular Masonry in the State of Connecticut: with a Brief History of the Early Grand Chapters, and the Proceedings of the Grand Chapter, from its Organization, A.D. 1798* (Hartford, CT: Press of Wiley, Waterman & Eaton, 1875), 59.

37. Wheeler, ed., *Records of Capitular Masonry in the State of* Connecticut (1875), p. 57, 59, 64, 66, 69; Samuel Green, ed., *The Connecticut Annual Register and United States Calendar for the Year of our Lord 1815* (New London, CT, 1815), 79.

38. Wheeler, ed., *Records of Capitular Masonry in the State of* Connecticut (1875), 63.

39. Daniel Parker, *A Discourse, Delivered at Canaan, March 23, 1815, at the Installation of Meridian Chapter* (Hartford [CT]: Peter B. Gleason & Co., Printers, 1815).

the number of the lodge was changed from 23 to 20, and by a resolution of the lodge the charter under which it was working was forwarded to the Grand Lodge for the necessary change." Parker likely affiliated with Kingston lodge soon after his move, and in 1824 he acted as lodge orator at that year's St. John's Day anniversary.[40] It is not known if he was among the members of his lodge which greeted the visiting Marquis de Lafayette at nearby Red Hook, in September 1824.

Parker's interest in the Royal Arch continued in New York. In 1817 he and two other Royal Arch Masons were granted a charter "to hold a Chapter at New Durham, County of Greene, by the name of Friendship Chapter, No. 65," and the following year he attended the Grand Royal Arch Chapter of New York in Albany, as its representative.[41] While serving as High Priest of Friendship Chapter Parker was also listed as a subscribing purchaser of Salem Town's *A System of Speculative Masonry* (1818).[42] Still suffering from financial hardships, the following year he applied through his chapter for assistance from the Grand Chapter, which request was denied, although he was given $50 as a charitable donation.[43]

In 1820 Parker may have run afoul of the Grand Royal Arch Chapter of New York, causing them to adopt a resolution regarding the conferral of the Order of the High Priesthood. They noted that it was improper to confer the degree of High Priest upon any companion who had not been regularly elected to that office by a legally constituted Chapter of Royal Arch Masons.

> *Whereas*, It is represented to this Grand Chapter that some Companions attempt, or pretend, to confer that degree on those who are not entitled to receive the same, therefore
>
> *Resolved*, That this Grand Chapter does expressly prohibit every Royal Arch Mason under this jurisdiction, who has not been regularly elected High Priest from receiving the said degree of High Priest, or any degree purporting to be the degree of High Priest, from every person or persons

40. Nathaniel Bartlett Sylvester, *History of Ulster County, New York: With Illustrations and Biographical Sketches of its Prominent Men and Pioneers* (Philadelphia: Everts & Peck, 1880). 1:266.

41. *Proceedings of the Grand Chapter of Royal Arch Masons of the State of New York, from its Organization, in 1798, to 1867, Inclusive. Volume I. 1798–1853* (Buffalo: Published by Order of the Grand Chapter, 1871), 136, 141.

42. Salem Town, *A System of Speculative Masonry, in its Origin, Patronage, Dissemination, Principles, Duties, and Ultimate Designs, Laid Open for the Examination of the Serious and Candid: Being a Course of Lectures, Exhibited Before the Grand Chapter of the State of New-York, at their Annual Meetings, Held in Temple Chapter Room, in the City of Albany* (Salem, NY: Dodd and Stevenson, 1818), 255.

43. *Proceedings of the Grand Chapter of Royal Arch Masons of the State of New York* [...] *Volume I. 1798–1853* (1871), 146–47.

> whatever; and all Companion Royal Arch Masons are expressly forbidden to confer or attempt to confer the said degree, or any degree purporting to be such, on any Companion not entitled to receive the same, on pain of expulsion.
>
> Resolved, That the Grand Secretary transmit a copy of the foregoing resolution to every Chapter under this jurisdiction, and also Comps. Joseph H. Ellis, of Otsego County, and Daniel Parker, of Hudson.[44]

The *Masonic Tablet, or Free-Mason's Circular*

Nothing exists to show when Parker conceived his idea to create a cipher-text of Masonic ritual, and nothing suggests that he did so with malicious intent. Indeed, its text reveals it as nothing more or less than a supplement to Webb's *Free-Mason's Monitor*. Parker's work supplied the missing esoteric content, with included frequent notes to "see Monitor." It is not known what the members of his lodge thought about it, although they notified the Grand Lodge of its availability on December 4, 1822.

> A Communication was received from Kingston Lodge, No. 20, informing the Grand Lodge that a printed work, as a help to the memory, called the "Masonic Tablet," was being advertised and sold by the Rev. Daniel Parker, to whom the Grand Secretary had written, condemning the same. The Communication of the Grand Secretary was approved by the Grand Lodge, which added that it decidedly condemned the use of all books or manuscripts, the support or tendency of which was to elucidate and explain Freemasonry.[45]

Although one person reported that he had seen the *Masonic Tablet* as early as 1820 (quoted later in this article), there is nothing else to support this date. In any case, it is noteworthy that the Grand Lodge, which also overlooked the Webb manuscript ciphers, took no action against Parker other than to generally condemn the work, while Peter Ross' history of New York Masonry called it a "perfectly harmless book."[46] Understandably, the *Masonic Tablet* must have pleased some Masons while simultaneously angering others. Although it certainly facilitated learning ritual, its publication was strictly a breach of obligation.

44. *Proceedings of the Grand Chapter of Royal Arch Masons of the State of New York* [...] *Volume I. 1798–1853* (1871), 172.

45. Charles T. McClenachan, *History of the Most Ancient and Honorable Fraternity of Free and Accepted Masons in New York from its Earliest Date*, 2 vols. (New York: Published by the Grand Lodge, 1892), 2:351.

46. Peter Ross, *A Standard History of Freemasonry in the State of New York* (New York and Chicago: Lewis Publishing Co., 1899), 282.

EDITIONS OF PARKER'S CIPHER

Parker's text was available in three versions—Craft, Chapter, or both. The ritual was protected by employing a simple cipher which utilized five tactics to conceal the ritual: (1) letter and/or number substitution, (2) omission of letters, (3) inclusion of meaningless letters between backward brackets, numbers and punctuation marks, (4) spelling words backwards, and (5) inclusion of simple foreign words. The cipher is sometimes referred to as the "Ast ritual"—an allusion to the first line on the document. The heading of the first page of the Craft Ritual reads " :Ast SC PE's L," which deciphers as "[Fir]st S[e]c[tion] E[ntered] [A] p[prentice]'s L[ecture]," and the Chapter page begins "TP OS TCL," meaning "P[as]t [Master']s L[e]ct[ure]."

Lacking publication information, identifying the various editions was achieved by textual analysis, and comparing types of paper and binding. During the 1990s I worked with my very dear and late friend Kent Logan Walgren to identify the editions, the results of which were published in Walgren's masterful *Freemasonry, Anti-Masonry and Illuminism in the United States, 1734–1850: A Bibliography* (2003).[47] Subsequent to completing his bibliography however, but prior to publication, we agreed on some minor refinements which are not reflected in the printed text. In the following descriptions Walgren's catalog numbers are used to identify the editions. There were at least three Craft editions of the *Masonic Tablet* printed ca. 1822.

The first edition, untitled and string tied, measured 20×12 cm., with 28 pages (Walgren #2038). At the time the bibliography was published I owned the only known copy of the first printing, but a second copy was subsequently discovered and donated to the Scottish Rite Masonic Museum and Library of the Supreme Council, 33°, Northern Masonic Jurisdiction, in Lexington, Massachusetts.[48]

The second edition, untitled and string tied, was retypeset and measured 17×10 cm., with 44 pages (Walgren #2039).

The third edition, untitled and string tied, was identical to the second, with the addition of a five page key to the cipher (Walgren #2040). A posthumously-printed version of the third edition appeared about ca. 1845, measuring 15.5×9.5 cm, with 88 pages, and included the key to the cipher. This edition was hardbound in either green or brown blind-stamped cloth (Walgren #4630).

47. Kent Logan Walgren, *Freemasonry, Anti-Masonry and Illuminism in the United States, 1734–1850: A Bibliography* 2 vols. (Worcester, MA: American Antiquarian Society, 2003).

48. *http://nationalheritagemuseum.typepad.com/library_and_archives/daniel-parker/*

The fourth edition, string tied, ca. 1824, measuring 19.5 × 13 cm., was retypeset, with the addition of the new title *The Free-Mason's Circular*, with 33 pages. It was originally believed that this edition dated to ca. 1840 (Walgren #4206). This edition accidently omits parts of two lines on page 8, which were restored in a second, corrected, printing, which may have appeared in late 1824, or early 1825 (not in Walgren). As will be discussed later, the second printing was deciphered into plaintext during America's anti-Masonic episode under the title *Morgan Confirmed* (1827).

The Capitular edition, also untitled, appeared ca. 1822, measured 17 × 10 cm., with 19 pages, and included a 12-page key to the cipher. It includes rituals of the Past Master, Most Excellent Master, and Royal Arch Mason.

To enable the reader to see the simplicity and security of Parker's cipher, I have decrypted a portion of the first catechism below. Note that in the original *Masonic Tablet* the text runs together, but it is here broken apart into sentences for ease of comparison.

Masonic Tablet – Cipher Text	Masonic Tablet – Plain Text
:Ast SC PE's L	**First Section Entered Apprentice's Lecture**
1. FM whnc cm u]oviz[*sa na* PE]gmz[	[Q] From whence came you as an Entered Apprentice?
2. fm]gp[e g f h st jn t j]mqz[rsa]pq[lm	[A] From the lodge of holy St. John at Jerusalem.
5 wt cm u hr o d]mpq[	[Q] What came you here to do?
8 o lrn o sbdu *ym* psns nd mprv *flsm* n *ysm*	[A] To learn to subdue my passions and improve myself in Masonry.
3 tn u r a]vs[n i prsm	[Q] Then you are a Mason I presume?
4 I m os tkn nd cptd mg brs nd *swlf*	[A] I am so taken and accepted among Brothers and Fellows.
7 hw d u no urslf]pmz[o b a n	[Q] How do you know yourself to be a Mason?
6 y hvg bn ftn trd]cma[nv dnd nd m wlng o b trd gn	[A] By having been often tried, never denied and my willingness to be tried again.
3 wt mks u a n	[Q] What makes you a Mason?
2 *ym* obn	[A] My obligation.
1 hw shl I no u o b a n	[Q] How shall I know you to be a Mason?
4 y a crtn sn *nkt drw* nd e prft stnp f *ym* ntnc	[A] By a certain sign, token, word, and the perfect points of my entrance.
1 wt r sns	[Q] What are signs?
2 rt slgna, sltnzrh, nd *srlcdnprp*	Right angles, horizontals, and perpendiculars.

The cipher for the Capitular degrees differed from those of the Craft, perhaps intended to safeguard them from those who had not yet obtained them. Questions and answers are not separated by numbers, as with the Symbolic Degrees, but use italicized letters. Letter substitutions compounded the difficulty in deciphering, e.g., *q* = *a*, *z* = *I* (the personal pronoun), *j* = *i* (or sometimes has no meaning in a word), while other letters and/or combinations had other meanings, e.g, *o* = *Master*, *.t* = *to*, *v* = *and*, *yn* = *then*, *ys* = *this*, *qt* = *that*, *zm* = *am*, some of which is seen in the following brief example of the first lines.

PT OS TCL	**Past Master's Lecture**
E r u q pt o	[Q.] Are you a Past Master?
P z hv t. hnr .t eb	[A.] I have the honor to be.
A hw rrjvd u .t yt hnr	[Q.] How arrived you at that honor?
D bi e bng dli lcjtd .t prjsd vr q rgli cnjstd m f frr v acjd gs	[A.] By being duly elected and installed to preside over a regularly constituted lodge of Free and Accepted Masons.
I bi wm wr u nsjtld	[Q.] By whom were you installed?
B bi mi prjdcjeer n ffc	[A.] By my predecessor in office.

The Chapter cipher also employed abbreviations and modifications of Latin, e.g., *bon* (good), *cap* (chapter) *prim* (first), *bi, bis* (two, twice), *ter, terd, trig* (three, third), *quotr* (fourth), *qunq* (fifth), *sep* (seventh), *dec, decsx* (ten, tenth), *leg* (reads), *nov* (new), *nox* (night), *sic* (so, thus), *terr* (ground), *vid* (see).

Minding your Ps and Qs

Typesetting the *Masonic Tablet* must have an extremely difficult task. Since the text could not be read by the typesetter, he was obliged to carefully set the type in what seemed like a random order. With such a small typeface we expect occasional letter confusion, and indeed, we see such things as a confusion of "c" for "e," and "m" for "w." We also sporadically find letters out of place, such as "drrd" for "rdrd" (ordered), and "*prsh*" for "*prhs*" (sharp). Recalling that italicized type is to be read backwards, we find "*wyfrg*" rather than "wyfrg" (wayfaring), and "eh" rather than "*eh*" (he). There are two errors, however, which can only be understood by examining the second edition (reproduced in this book): (1) the entire fifth line from the bottom of page 13 is inverted, and (2) the first two lines of page 18 properly belong on page 20. In each case the errors take up the length of a line in the second edition, although subsequent editions carried over these errors. However, because the new text blocks were a different size the anomalies were inexplicable without seeing the second edition. There are only occasional footnotes, indicating errors, in the decrypted ritual. I opted to highlight only a few which I considered particularly noteworthy.

The Grand Chapter Reacts

Because the *Masonic Tablet* included the rituals of Capitular Masonry, the Grand Chapter of Royal Arch Masons of the State of New York also had cause to investigate the matter. The detailed reports of the Grand Chapter, which describe Parker's odyssey, reveal that he was afforded due process when his troubles began in February 1823.

Livingston Billings, a Past Master of Sullivan Lodge No. 272, and member of Sullivan Chapter No. 65, and Benjamin Chamberlain, of Washington Chapter No. 29, brought a complaint the Grand Chapter of Royal Arch Masons of the State of New York:

> A complaint was made by Comp. Livingston Billings against Comp. Daniel Parker, P.·. H.·. P.·. of a Chapter under the jurisdiction of this Grand Chapter, which was referred to a Committee, which reported as follows:
>
> It appears to your Committee that, within the last year, Comp. Parker, has procured to be published and had offered publicly for sale, certain printed pamphlets purporting to be the lectures on the several degrees in Masonry. Your Committee are of opinion that such publication is a violation of every principle of Masonry, and subversive of the best interests thereof. Your Committee have prepared resolutions which they deem proper to be adopted in the premises, which they beg leave to submit.
>
> 1. *Resolved*, That the Grand Secretary cite the said Daniel Parker to appear before the Grand Chapter on the first day of the nest annual meeting, to show cause why he should not be expelled for unmasonic conduct in the premises. And further, that the Grand Secretary furnish said Parker with a copy of these resolutions.
>
> 2. *Resolved*, That it shall not be lawful for any Companion or Brother under the jurisdiction of this Grand Chapter, to write, print, or publish, or cause to be written, printed, or published, any book or books, or anything on the subject of Masonry, without the permission and approbation of the Grand Council.
>
> 3. *Resolved*, That the Grand Secretary transmit a copy of these resolutions to every Subordinate Chapter under the jurisdiction of this Grand Chapter, and a like copy to each Grand Chapter in the United States.
>
> L. Billings,
> B. Chamberlain.[49]

49. *Proceedings of the Grand Chapter of Royal Arch Masons of the State of New York* [...] *Volume I. 1798–1853* (1871), 208.

The following year (February 5, 1824) the committee reported.

> The Committee appointed to investigate the case of Comp. Daniel Parker, High Priest elect of a subordinate Chapter at Kingston, reported as follows:
>
> That they have given the subject that attention which the circumstances under which they were compelled to act would permit. It is with deep regret that your Committee are compelled to state their conviction, that the said Comp. Daniel Parker, by a series of reprehensible conduct as a Mason, has rendered himself a dangerous member of our fraternity and wholly undeserving of its benefits, its honors, or its confidence. It has satisfactorily appeared to your Committee, after a patient examination of a number of brethren, some of whom occupy and adorn the highest stations in the gift of then order, that Comp. Parker has not only expressly violated one of the most important of our Masonic obligations, by printing and publishing, or causing to be printed and published, a work calculated to expose some of the mysteries which bind together and preserve our fraternity; but, in order to find a more ready and profitable market, he has added to his perfidy a series of falsehoods in regard to the opinions of his work entertained by some of our most eminent officers. * * * * With these facts before them, the Committee cannot hesitate as to the course that ought to be pursued. Comp. Parker cannot be allowed, while laboring under charges or imputations like these, to mingle in fellowship with our brethren—much less to preside as the head of a subordinate Chapter, whose motto is "Holiness to the Lord." Your Committee therefore recommend the adoption of the following resolutions:
>
> *Resolved*, That Comp. Daniel Parker, recently elected High Priest of Mount Horeb Chapter, No. 75, at Kingston, be, and he is hereby suspended, not only as the presiding officer of said Chapter, but as a member of our fraternity.
>
> *Resolved*, That the aforesaid Daniel Parker be cited to appear before this Grand Chapter on the first day of its session, to be held in February, 1825, to show cause, if any he has, why he should not be expelled.
>
> *Resolved*, That the Grand Secretary, under the direction of the Grand Council, be instructed to prepare charges and specifications, upon which the foregoing report and resolutions are founded, and serve a copy of the same upon the said Daniel Parker.
>
> All of which is respectfully submitted,
>
> By order of the Committee,
>
> WILLIAM L. STONE,
>
> *Chairman.*[50]

50. *Proceedings of the Grand Chapter of Royal Arch Masons of the State of New York* [...] *Volume I. 1798–1853* (1871), 208.

A family illness prevented Parker from attending the February 1825 meeting. At the meeting of February 8, 1826, while Parker served as High Priest of Mount Horeb Chapter, it was reported:

> That the Grand High Priest has had an interview with Comp. Parker on the subject of his tracts, as he calls them, and by referring to a letter from the said Parker, which accompanies this report, dated Jan. 30th, 1826, to Comp. Ames, it will be perceived that he admits the substance of the charges against him, and justifies his conduct. The Grand Chapter will therein discover the reasons which he urges in his defence. The Grand Council are in possession of his tract with explanations, which it is unnecessary to detail in this report.

The report was received and referred to a select committee. On February 10, 1826, the committee reported:

> That they deemed the publication of the tract alluded to in said charges and which the said Parker, in the letter accompanying the report, admits he has published, a direct violation of the long established usages of the fraternity. The Committee have also perused the letter in which the said Parker justifies the said publication, and cannot forebear giving it as their decided opinion that the language it contains is highly indecorous and insulting to the Grand Council; and that said Comp. Parker ought to be suspended or expelled from all participation in the benefits of Masonry.
>
> Whereupon, it was
>
> *Resolved*, that Daniel Parker, High Priest of Mount Horeb Chapter, No. 75, be and he is hereby expelled from this Grand Chapter, and from all the communication with the Chapter and Mark Lodges under the jurisdiction of the same.[51]

Parker's conduct, which was deemed "reprehensible," resulted in his expulsion from the Fraternity only a few months before Morgan disappeared. In a letter to John Quincy Adams, William L. Stone, author of *Letters on Masonry and Anti-Masonry* (1832),[52] cited Parker's case in reference to the so-called Masonic "penalties" to demonstrate that expulsion is the only true penalty of the Fraternity.

> The truth is, that a simple expulsion from a lodge, or chapter, with a public advertisement of the fact, is the only penalty, for any offence, which the Masons, previously to the Morgan outrage, have ever, to my

51. *Proceedings of the Grand Chapter of Royal Arch Masons of the State of New York* [...] *Volume I. 1798–1853* (1871), 239, 257.

52. William L. Stone, *Letters on Masonry and Anti-Masonry, Addressed to the Hon. John Quincy Adams* (New York: O. Halsted, 1832).

> knowledge, considered themselves authorized to inflict. As an illustration of this assertion, I may perhaps be excused for stating a case in point. No longer than the year 1824,—only two years before the Morgan outrage—I myself introduced a resolution into the Grand Chapter, requiring the Grand Priest of a subordinate chapter to show cause why he should not be expelled. The accusation was the same as that for which Morgan died, viz: the writing and revealing of Masonic secrets. The charge was investigated, *and he was expelled*. He is yet a living witness that his throat was not cut across, nor his tongue torn out by its roots, nor his body buried in the rough sands of the sea.[53]

"Morgan" was, of course, William Morgan, author of *Illustrations of Masonry by One of the Fraternity* (1826), the most infamous of the American Masonic exposés. The story of Morgan's disappearance, and the turbulent period which followed, has often been told and need not be recited again here. Suffice it to say that his disappearance, following a boast to publish an exposure of Masonic ritual, precipitated an anti-Masonic episode which swept the United States from 1826 to 1842.

In about the year 1825 Parker moved to New York City, where he worked as a teacher. It is not known if there were any bitter feelings on his part, but Stone noted that *someone*, who must have been Rev. Parker, met with William Morgan at a hotel. If true, Morgan may have been influenced by the *Masonic Tablet:*

> He [Morgan] was at a Masonic hotel in this city, for a short time, in the course of that year, and was often closeted with a man of considerable talents, and some scholarship, who had been expelled from the fraternity the preceding year, for a breach of his Masonic faith, in writing and exhibiting certain Masonic matters that were then supposed to be unwritten. Parts of his manuscripts had been shown by Morgan to his friends....[54]

We last hear of Parker about nine years later. During an outbreak of cholera which began in August 1834,[55] we discover that he was again preaching. "He was urged to leave the city until the alarm was over, but declined, saying it was his duty to remain and care for his parishioners, whatever might be the consequences. He died at his post on September 26, [1834], in his 61st year..."[56]

53. William L. Stone, *Letters on Masonry and Anti-Masonry, Addressed to the Hon. John Quincy Adams* (New York: O. Halsted, 1832), 80.

54. Stone, *Letters on Masonry and Anti-Masonry*, 130.

55. "Cholera in New York," *North River Times* Vol. 1 (Haverstraw, NY, 22 August 1834), No. 1.

56. Dexter, *Biographical Sketches* (1911) 5:333.

Morgan Confirmed

The story of the *Masonic Tablet/Free-Mason's Circular* does not end with Parker's death. Although it was prepared as an aide-mémoire, it was perhaps inevitable that it would be used as a witness to describe the rituals of the fraternity during the "Morgan Affair"—an anti-Masonic period in American history which lasted from 1826–42. In brief, this period was named for William Morgan, of Batavia, New York, who disappeared in September 1826, after he boasted of his intent to print an exposé of Masonic rituals for the public. It was presumed he was "murdered by the Masons," which set off an anti-Masonic excitement which grew rapidly and burned so furiously that the fraternity was nearly extinguished in the United States. In 1827, the year following Morgan's disappearance, a second, corrected edition of *The Free-Mason's Circular* (ca. 1824–25), was reprinted and decrypted by "Edward Hickes" under the title *Morgan Confirmed: or the Secrets of Freemasonry Made Known to all the World . . . Obtained by the Possession of a Key to a Masonic Document* (1827).[57] In his introduction Hickes, about whom nothing can be found, claimed to be Mason, yet his decryption includes several errors, which make his claim questionable.

"The Mason's own book"

Unaware that *Morgan Confirmed* had been published, in May 1831, the "Anti-masonic State Convention of the Massachusetts," held at Faneuil Hall, Boston, noted that it had acquired a copy of a cipher ritual, which they referred to as "the Mason's own book." From the context, and the extracts which were printed, it is easily identified as Parker's work. At that time it was resolved that a committee

> examine a pamphlet herewith presented, believed to have been designed and published in cypher, by Masons, as a guide for Masters of Lodges to procure uniformity of the working of the first three degrees in Masonry, and that they report to this Convention how far the same confirms the disclosures, that have been made, touching the first three degrees, together with their opinions on such other original Masonic documents as may be presented for their consideration.[58]

57. *Morgan Confirmed: or The Secrets of Freemasonry Made Known to all the World: Being An authentic and true History, by the Masons Themselves, of All Their Transactions, Signs, Ceremonies, Formalities of Initiation, Expulsion, Proceedings, &c. &c. Obtained by the Possession of a Key to a Masonic Document; which Key and Document are herewith published; and are of such a nature that any Person can, by use of them, understand immediately, and can practice all that the most accomplished Freemason can do: Confirming All the unfortunate Morgan has written on the Subject; and furnishing much additional and interesting Matter* (New York: Printed for the author, 1827).

58. *An Abstract of the Proceedings of the Antimasonic State Convention of Massachusetts. Held*

William Morgan, author of *Illustrations of Masonry by One of the Fraternity* (1826), David Bernard, *Light on Masonry* (Utica, NY: William Williams, 1829), frontispiece.

The committee, having discharged it duty, the following was reported:

Mr Hallett, from the Committee on a Pamphlet in character and cypher, &c. presented a Report, which was read and laid on the table. A part of the accompanying pamphlet was read, as transcribed from the original.

The Committee to whom-was referred a pamphlet published in characters and cypher, purporting to be a publication put forth by adhering Masons, beg leave to

REPORT.

That the pamphlet in question, which is herewith presented as a part of this Report, is without title or date, and consists of an ingeniously devised system of short hand, by omitting consonants, inverting their order and the occasional use of arbitrary signs, with other guards against detection, sufficient to render the decyphering of the work hardly possible, without the aid of the disclosures that have been made of the lectures and obligations of the three first degrees, which are fully comprised in this publication. It therefore might have been put forth, at the time it is believed to have been devised, with perfect confidence that through it the secrets of Masonry could not become intelligible to the world, though your Committee infer from certain references to the devisers of this and similar systems of rendering the masters of lodges bright Masons, that it was not seconded with approbation by the higher orders of the Fraternity.

The evidence on which the Committee found their belief that this pamphlet contains original Masonry in the three first degrees, as administered in the New England lodges, is circumstantial, but of a nature that must convince every candid mind. Such circumstantial evidence is as conclusive as positive testimony, and on it rests the proof of the origin of the most celebrated works of antiquity, and in a great degree, the authority of the Scriptures themselves.

Your Committee have the fact, that this pamphlet was the property of an adhering Mason, a citizen of Providence, R[hode]. I[sland]. who died at sea, and that it was found among his papers after his decease, several years before the abduction of William Morgan, and of course before Antimasonry bad an existence. This fact might be directly substantiated, but from the circumstance that it requires a presentation to the public of the names of females, who would naturally shrink from such an exhibition. Independent of this fact, the internal evidence of age, in the appearance of the type, letter, &c. a criterion by which a printer or antiquarian would fix the age of a work with very tolerable accuracy, is entirely satisfactory, that the origin of the publication must be carried back to a period often, fifteen

in Faneuil Hall, Boston, May 19 & 20, 1831. (Boston: Office of the Boston Press, for the Publishing Committee, 1831), 27.

and perhaps twenty years. It could also be shown that a Past Master of a lodge in Rhode Island, a warm adhering Mason, has repeatedly admitted, on examination of the work, that he had seen it in the lodge, over which he presided, in 1820, and that he believed it to be genuine Masonry, as it was administered in that lodge, but that no person, not a Mason, would ever be the wiser for it. We have also satisfactory evidence of the fact, that another copy of this work is in the possession of an adhering Mason, of Newport, R. I. by whom it has been shown to gentlemen in that town, and pronounced by him to be genuine Masonry, devised for the purpose of enabling Masters of lodges, to whom alone the Key was entrusted, to perform the ceremonies and administer the oaths with accuracy and uniformity. Your Committee therefore, on every principle of evidence, are satisfied of the fact that this work was published several years before any inquiry had been made in this country, affecting the character of Freemasonry.

Having thus fixed the period of publication, beyond the origin of the present investigations into Masonry, it is obvious that the book in question must have been published from one of two motives—Either by adhering Masons for the purpose of affording aid in delivering the lectures and administering the oaths, and thereby producing uniformity in the work of the lodge room—or, that it was published by the enemies of Masonry, for the purpose of disclosing the secrets of the Order.

The last of these grounds is wholly untenable from the consideration that had the author of the work intended to disclose the real or pretended secrets of the order, he never would have been at the' labor and expense of publishing it in a form as unintelligible to the uninitiated as were the symbols and devices which had already been published and approved by masonic chapters and lodges.— To disclose the secrets of Masonry, out of the lodge room, could not therefore, by any plausible construction, have been the design of a publication so carefully shrouded in mystery, as to render it a sealed book to the uninitiated.

The only possible conclusion then to arrive at, is that the work was designed and published by Masons, and for the use of Masons. The Committee challenge a refutation of this position by the advocates of the Order, for which purpose the work in question is offered to the examination of members of the Fraternity. That the work has not been generally known by Masons, (excepting perhaps, Masters of Lodges) is presumed from the fact that your Committee have met with no seceding or other Mason, not a Master of a lodge, who professes any acquaintance with the cypher. One seceder, a Past Master of a lodge in Rhode Island, has recognized the work as a guide by which Masonic oaths were administered, and Masters of lodges brightened in their duties.

A strong evidence of the authenticity of this work, has been derived by testing the effect of a repetition of its oaths upon adhering Masons. Many

> who have sheltered themselves behind the slightest variation in terms, to deny the whole obligation as cited from Bernard, in peremptory phrase, have shrunk from the test of the oath when presented to them from what your Committee would designate by way of distinction, "The Masons Own Book" in no instance within our knowledge, has an adhering Mason denied the terms of the oaths as transcribed from this book. Should it be objected to the authenticity of this book, that its publication by Masons, would be a violation of the Entered Apprentices oath, not to cut, carve, print, &c. the answer is plain, that the same obligation would apply with equal forte to the Monitor of Webb, the Chart of Jeremy L. Cross, and the whole collection of Masonic Mirrors, Charts and Emblems, published under the express sanction of the highest Masonic bodies in this country.
>
> Having thus fairly established the Masonic origin and authenticity of this work, the next is, what does it disclose, and how do the statements here given by adhering Masons correspond with those given by seceding Masons? On this point the work in question is entirely satisfactory and conclusive, as will be seen by a translation, herewith presented, of the three first lectures in the three first degrees. It will be found that while every substantial point in the obligation, is here expressly confirmed, there are repeated variations in language and arrangement, from the disclosures made by other sources of information, such as must inevitably occur, in oral repetitions, for which the Masters of different lodges rely upon memory alone.
>
> * * * * *
>
> The Committee would here close their suggestions with the remark that in their opinion the work they have examined fully and circumstantially establishes the fact that the three first degrees of the Order are faithfully revealed to the world, by seceding Masons, and that the information of the disclosures in these degrees, by this evidence drawn from Masonic authority, is strong collateral evidence that the disclosures made by them of the advanced degrees, are equally correct. The fact that Masons and their adherents deny to this day that the secrets of the three first degrees are before the public, while their own Book, in their own figures and devices convicts them of misrepresentation, furnishes fair ground for the belief that they are equally disingenuous and reckless in denying the truth of the disclosures in the advanced degrees.[59]

Although the report ended with a remark that a "correct translation of the three first Lectures, comprised in the pamphlet" was submitted to the convention, the decryption was curiously not included in the published report. The

59. *An Abstract of the Proceedings of the Antimasonic State Convention of Massachusetts* [...] (1831), 46–48.

reason for the omission was soon discovered by the "Committee Appointed by the General Assembly of the State of Rhode-Island and Providence Plantations to Investigate the Charges in Circulation Against Freemasonry." In contradistinction to the "Antimasonic State Convention of the Massachusetts," which used Parker's cipher to condemn the fraternity, the committee appointed by the State of Rhode Island discovered that it vindicated the character of local Masons. The Rhode Island committee found that Parker's ritual text, which was prepared for Masonic use, did not include the objectionable language or "falsified forms" contained in exposés which had been prepared for the public. The Rhode Island committee confirmed what Masons—and honest ex-Masons—had said: "infamous interpolations"[60] had been added to ritual exposés to prejudice the public against the fraternity.

> There is one curious piece of documentary evidence, proving the correctness and truth of the constructions and explanations, given by Masons, of their Masonic obligations, which has been inadvertently furnished by those who now insist upon a totally different understanding of those obligations; such an one as would render them highly criminal. In the published proceedings of an antimasonic assemblage, held in Boston in May last, we find the following entry, viz: "On motion of B. F. Hallett, Esq. of R. I. it was resolved that Messrs. Hallett, Whalley and Pike, of Suffolk, be a committee to examine a pamphlet herewith presented, believed to have been designed and published in cypher, by Masons, as a guide for masters of lodges," &c. &c. And shortly afterwards, among the same proceedings, is to be found the report or that committee. More than one half of that report is occupied in establishing the fact that the said pamphlet in cypher is a genuine Masonic work, and "contains *original Masonry, in the three first degrees as administered in the New England lodges.*" This fact they pronounce to be conclusively substantiated by such kind of evidence as that on which *"rests"* to use their own language, *"the proof of the origin of the most celebrated works of antiquity, and, in a great degree, the authority of the scriptures themselves."* They therefore, "by way of distinction," they say, designate this book by the title of "the Mason's Own Book." In another part of the report they say, "we have also satisfactory evidence of the fact, that another copy of this work is in the possession of an adhering Mason in Newport, R. I." It happens that this last mentioned copy is now in possession of this committee; and has been identified by the testimony of one of the witnesses, (Doct. B. W. Case,) who had been in possession of both the copies; that which was carried to Boston, as well as this. Dr. Case obtained

60. Arturo de Hoyos, *Light on Masonry: The History and Rituals of America's Most Important Masonic Exposé* (Washington, DC: Scottish Rite Research Society, 2008), 76–77.

> this book from Capt. Howland, a Mason, and afterwards loaned it to the chairman of this committee, whom he also favored with a key or translation of a considerable portion of it, with which, for a clue, the rest is easily decyphered. The committee before mentioned, after assuring the Boston assembly that "the information developed is doubtless highly important," conclude as follows, viz: "Annexed to this report, is a correct translation of the three first lectures comprised in the pamphlet under consideration, all which is submitted for the disposition of the convention." But it seems that, that *convention* did not think proper to make any other disposition of the highly important translation, than to suppress it; for it is not to be found among the *published* proceedings of that body; and we do not understand that it ever has been made public. The reason of this attempted concealment and suppression of that important document is now obvious. It appears that the oaths given in that book in cypher, are the same as those proved to be used by Masons in Rhode Island; almost word for word the same as those used in Newport; and wholly falsifying the forms contained in Bernard and Allyn's books, so far as they differ from the Rhode Island forms; not one of the obnoxious clause* introduced in those books being found in "*The Mason's own book.*"[61]

Additionally, the Rhode Island committee concluded that a literal interpretation of the symbolic penalties was both inappropriate and unjustified, and suggested that "obnoxious and criminal clauses" were inserted into popular exposés "to serve the purposes of corrupt politicians."[62]

PARKER'S CIPHER LEGACY

As noted earlier, the third edition of the *Masonic Tablet* was reprinted ca. 1845, soon after the Morgan affair died out. Coinciding with a renewed interest in the fraternity, Parker's rituals were likely responsible for inspiring the explosion of printed cipher rituals during the mid-to-late nineteenth century, the first of which was another untitled work, which began with the header *O a* □ *E.A.* (Walgren #4696), meaning "Opening a lodge of Entered Apprentices." This first new cipher, which included the ritual for New Hampshire, was likely printed about 1843. It was much simpler than Parker's cipher, merely employing the first

61. *Report of the Committee Appointed by the General Assembly of the State of Rhode-Island and Providence Plantations to Investigate the Charges in Circulation Against Freemasonry and Masons in Said State: Together with the Official Documents and Testimony Relating to the Subject* (Providence: William Marshall, State Printer, 1832), 26.

62. *Report of the Committee Appointed by the General Assembly of the State of Rhode-Island* [...] (1832), 28.

letter of each word. Its layout was somewhat similar, but improved and, like Parker's, included notes to refer to the printed monitors, which it supplemented.

Within the next quarter decade American Masonry witnessed a proliferation of printed ciphers, the most successful were entitled *Ecce Orienti* and *King Solomon and his Followers*, which included the unique ritual work for several of the American grand lodges. Although these ciphers were also frowned upon, some grand lodges have subsequently embraced them as unofficial, and in some case, official guides to the ritual. But that, is another story.

Daniel Parker's

The *Masonic Tablet*

Deciphered

First Section, Entered Apprentice's Lecture

[Q.] From whence came you as an Entered Apprentice?

[A.] From the lodge of holy St. John at Jerusalem.

[Q.] What came you here to do?

[A.] To learn to subdue my passions and improve myself in Masonry.

[Q.] Then you are a Mason I presume?

[A.] I am so taken and accepted among Brothers and Fellows.

[Q.] How do you know yourself to be a Mason?

[A.] By having been often tried, never denied and my willingness to be tried again.

[Q.] What makes you a Mason?

[A.] My obligation.

[Q.] How shall I know you to be a Mason?

[A.] By a certain sign, token, word, and the perfect points of my entrance.

[Q.] What are signs?

[A.] Right angles, horizontals, and perpendiculars.

[Q.] Please to give me the sign of an Entered Apprentice?

[A.] (*Rises and gives it.*)

[Q.] Has that any allusion?

[A.] It has, to the penalty of my obligation, that I would rather have my throat cut across from ear to ear than to reveal the secrets of Freemasonry unlawfully.

[Q.] What is a token?

[A.] A certain friendly or Brotherly grip whereby one Brother may know another in the dark as well as in the light.

[Q.] Please to give you left hand Brother the token and grip of an Entered Apprentice?

(*They rise and give it.*) *A gives B the grip. B says:*

[Q.] What is that?

[A.] I hail.

[A.] *B.* I conceal.

[Q.] *A.* What do you conceal?

[A.] *B.* All secrets of Masons in Masonry except it shall be unto a true and lawful Brother or within the body of a just and lawful lodge of such.

[Q.] *A.* What is that called?

[A.] *B.* A grip.

[Q.] *A*. Grip of what?

[A.] *B*. Entered Apprentice.

[Q.] *A*. Has it a name?

[A.] *B*. It has.

[Q.] *A*. Will you please to give it to me?

[A.] *B*. I did not so receive it, neither can I so impart it.

[Q.] *A*. How will you dispose of it?

[A.] *B*. I will letter or halve it with you.

[Q.] *A*. You will please to letter it?

[A.] *B*. Begin.

[Q.] *A*. You begin, if you please?

(*Note: A gives first letter, B second, B pronounces the word.*)

[A.] It is right. I greet you Brother B—.

[Q.] Where were you first prepared to be made a Mason?

[A.] In my heart.

[Q.] Where secondly?

[A.] In a room adjacent to the lodge.

[Q.] How were you prepared?

[A.] By being divested of all minerals and metals, neither naked nor clothed, barefoot nor shod, hoodwinked with a cable-tow about my neck, in which situation I was conducted to the door of the lodge by the hand of a friend whom I afterwards found to be a Brother.

[Q.] How did you know it to be a door, being hoodwinked?

[A.] By first meeting with resistance and afterwards gaining admission.

[Q.] How gained you admission?

[A.] By three distinct

[2]

knocks.

[Q.] What was said to you from within?

[A.] Who comes there?

[Q.] Your answer?

[A.] A poor blind candidate who has long been desirous of being brought out of darkness to light, to have and receive a part of the rights and benefits of this Right Worshipful lodge, erected to God and dedicated to holy St. John as many Brothers and Fellows have done before me.

[Q.] What more were you asked?

[A.] If I came of my own free will and accord, if I was duly and truly prepared, worthy and well qualified, of lawful age and properly avouched for; all which being answered in the affirmative I was asked by what further right or benefit I expected to gain admission.

[Q.] You answer?

[A.] By being a man, free born, of good report and well recommended.

[Q.] What followed?

[A.] I was requested to wait a time with patience until the Right Worshipful Master could be informed of my request and his answer returned.

[Q.] What was his answer when returned?

[A.] Let him enter.

[Q.] How did you enter?

[A.] On the point of a sharp instrument piercing my naked left breast.

[Q.] Where were you then conducted?

[A.] To the center of the lodge, where I was caused to kneel and receive the benefit of a prayer.

(*Master gives three knocks, all rise.*)

[Q.] I will thank you to repeat the prayer?

[A.] "Vouchsafe thine aid." (*See Monitor*)

[Q.] After receiving the benefit of the prayer, what were you then asked?

[A.] In whom I put my trust.

[Q.] Your answer?

[A.] In God.

[Q.] What followed?

[A.] My trust being in God, I was taken by the right hand, bid to rise, follow my leader and fear no danger.

[Q.] Where were you then conducted?

[A.] Once around the lodge to the Junior Warden in the south, where the same questions were asked and the like answers returned as at the door.

[Q.] How did the Junior Warden in the south dispose of you?

[A.] He ordered me to pass on to the Senior Warden in the west, where the same questions were asked and the like answers returned as before.

[Q.] How did the Senior Warden in the west dispose of you?

[A.] He ordered me to pass on to the Right Worshipful Master in the east, where the same questions were asked and the like answers returned as before.

[Q.] How did the Right Worshipful Master in the east dispose of you?

[A.] He ordered me to be reconducted to the Senior Warden in the west, who taught me to advance by one upright regular step, my feet forming the right angle of an oblong square, my body erect towards the east.

[Q.] What did the Right Worshipful Master then do with you?

[A.] He made me a Mason.

[Q.] How?

[A.] In due form.

[Q.] What is that due form?

[A.] By kneeling on my naked left knee, my right forming a square, my body erect, my left hand supporting the Holy Bible, square and compass, my right covering the same; in which due form I received the oath or obligation of an Entered Apprentice.

Master gives three knocks (All rise).

[Q.] I will thank you to repeat the oath or obligation?

[A.] I W

[3]

H, of my own free will and accord, in the presence of Almighty God and this Right Worshipful lodge, erected to Him and dedicated to holy St. John, do hereby and hereon most solemnly and sincerely promise and swear that I will always hail, forever conceal and never reveal any of the secret arts, parts or points of the mysteries of Freemasonry to any person under the canopy of heaven except it shall be unto a lawful Brother or within the body of a just and lawful lodge of such, nor unto him or them until by due trial, strict examination or by the lawful information of a Brother I shall have found him or them to be as justly and lawfully entitled to the same as I am myself. I furthermore promise and swear that I will not write them, print, cut, carve, mark, paint, stain or engrave them on any thing moveable or immovable whereby a letter, figure or character may become legible or intelligible so that the secrets of the Craft may at any time be unlawfully obtained. All this I do most solemnly and sincerely promise and swear with a firm and fixed resolution to perform the same without any equivocation, mental reservation, self reservation, or secret evasion of mind in me whatever, binding myself under no less penalty than that of having my throat cut across, *etc.*

[Q.] After receiving the oath or obligation of Entered Apprentice, what were you then asked?

[A.] What I most desired.

[Q.] Your answer?

[A.] Light.

[Q.] Did you receive it?

[A.] I did.

[Q.] How?

[A.] By the order of the Right Worshipful Master with the assistance of the Brethren.

[Q.] On being brought to light what were the first things presented to your view?

[A.] Three great lights in Masonry, assisted by the help of three lesser.

[Q.] What are the three great lights in Masonry?

[A.] The Holy Bible, square and compass.

[Q.] What are their moral assistants?[1]

[A.] The Holy Bible is given us to be the rule and guide of our faith, the square to square our actions, and the compass to keep us within due bounds with all mankind but more especially a Brother.

[Q.] What are the three lesser lights in Masonry?

[A.] The sun, moon and Master of the lodge.

[Q.] Why are they said to be the three lesser lights in Masonry?

[A.] Because as the sun rules the day and the moon governs the night so ought the Right Worshipful Master to endeavor to rule and govern his lodge with equal regularity.

[Q.] By what are they represented?

[A.] By three burning tapers placed in a triangular form in the lodge, south, west, east.

[Q.] After these lights were explained to you, what did you next observe?

[A.] The Right Worshipful Master approaching me from the east, under the due guard and sign of an Entered Apprentice, who presented me with his right hand in token of his brotherly-love and friendship, and with it the grip and word of an Entered Apprentice; bid me rise, go and salute the Junior and Senior Wardens as such.

[Q.] After saluting the Junior and Senior Wardens as an Entered Apprentice, what did you next observe?

1. "wt r tr mrl sss." This may be an error for "What are their moral uses?" The *Freemason's Circular* changed this to "wh d th mrl tch" (What do they morally teach?).

[A.] The Right Worshipful Master approaching me from the east a second time, who presented me with a lamb skin or white leather apron which he informed me was an emblem of innocence and the badge of a Mason; more ancient than the Golden Fleece or Roman Eagle, more honorable than the Star or Garter, or any other order that could be conferred on me at

[4]

that time or any future period by king, prince, potentate, or any other person except he be a Mason, which he hoped I would wear with equal pleasure to myself and honor to the fraternity, bid me step to the Senior Warden in the west who taught me to wear it as an Entered Apprentice.

[Q.] How should an Entered Apprentice wear his apron?

[A.] With the top turned up.

[Q.] After being taught to wear your apron as an Entered Apprentice what were you then informed of?

[A.] That agreeably to an ancient custom in all regular and well governed lodges I was requested to deposit something of a metallic kind, not for its value alone but that it might be laid up among the records in the archives of the lodge as a memorial that I was there made a Mason. But on strict examination I found myself entirely destitute.

[Q.] How were you then disposed of?

[A.] I was ordered to be reconducted to the place from whence I came, there to be invested of what I had been divested of and in due time returned to the lodge for further information.

[Q.] After being invested of what you had been divested and on returning to the lodge, where were you first conducted?

[A.] To the Northwest corner where I was taught to say, Right Worshipful Master, Wardens and Brethren of this Right Worshipful lodge, I return you my hearty and sincere thanks for the honor you have conferred on me in making me a Mason and admitting me a member of this ancient and honorable institution.

[Q.] Where were you then placed as the youngest Entered Apprentice?

[A.] In the Northeast corner of the lodge, my feet forming a square, my body erect to the right hand of the Right Worshipful Master, who was then pleased to say that I there stood as a just and upright Mason, and gave it to me strongly in charge ever to walk and act as such.

[Q.] What did the Right Worshipful Master then present you with?
[A.] The working tools of an Entered Apprentice.
[Q.] What are they?
[A.] The twenty-four inch gauge and common gavel.
[Q.] I would thank you to explain the use of the twenty-four inch gauge?
[A.] The twenty-four inch, *etc.* (*see Monitor*).
[Q.] I would thank you to explain the use of the common gavel?
[A.] The common gavel is an instrument, *etc.* (*see Monitor*).

Second Section of Entered Apprentice's Lecture.

You have satisfied me, Brother A., as to the manner and method of your initiation into this degree but, as there appears to be many singularities made use of on this occasion, I wish to know why you were caused to submit to them in the first place.

[Q.] Why were you divested of all minerals and metals?

[A.] For two reasons: first, in order that I should carry nothing offensive or defensive into the lodge with me.

[Q.] Second reason?

[A.] Because at the

[5]

building of king Solomon's temple, there was not heard the sound of axe, hammer, or any tool of iron.

[Q.] How could the building of such stupendous magnitude as king Solomon's temple be erected without the use of iron tools?

[A.] Because the stones were all hewed, squared, marked, and numbered in the quarries where they were raised. The timber was fallen and prepared in the forests of Lebanon and carried on floats by sea to Joppa, and from thence conveyed to Jerusalem, where they were set up with wooden mauls prepared for that purpose. And, when the whole building was completed, its several parts fitted to that exact nicety that they had more the appearance of the handy work of the Supreme Architect of the Universe than that of human hands.

[Q.] Why were you neither naked nor clothed?

[A.] Because Masonry regards no man for his worldly wealth or honors. It was therefore to signify that it was the internal, and not the external, qualifications of a man that should recommend him to be made a Mason.

[Q.] Why were you neither barefoot nor shod?

[A.] It was in conformity to an Israelitish custom adopted by Masons, and we read in the book of Ruth it was the manner in former times concerning redeeming and changing that, to confirm all things, a man plucked off his shoe and gave it to his neighbor. This was testimony in Israel. This, therefore, we do, on these solemn occasions, as a token of our sincerity and a pledge of our fidelity in the business we were then about, thereby signifying that we renounce our own wills in all matters as it regards the secrets of Free Masonry, and become obedient to the laws of our ancient institution.

[Q.] Why were you hoodwinked, with a cable-tow about your neck?

[A.] For several reasons: first, as I was then in darkness as it regarded the secrets of Free Masonry, so should I endeavor to keep all the world in future, until they should become as justly and lawfully by them as I was then about to do.

[Q.] Second reason?

[A.] That my heart might be taught to conceal, before my eyes should discover, the beauties of Masonry.

[Q.] Third reason?

[A.] That, had I refused to submit to the forms and ceremonies made use of at my initiation, and thereby been thought unworthy of being taken by the hand as a Brother, I might, by the assistance of the cable-tow, have been led out of the lodge, without discovering the form thereof.

[Q.] Why were you caused to give three distinct knocks at the door?

[A.] For two reasons: first, to alarm the lodge and inform the Right Worshipful Master that there was a candidate prepared for initiation.

[Q.] Second reason?

[A.] It was to remind me of a certain text in scripture: Ask, and ye shall receive; seek, and ye shall find; knock, and it shall be opened unto you.

[Q.] How did you apply that text of scripture to your then situation?

[A.] I asked the recommendation of a friend to be made a Mason; I sought admission through that recommendation; I knocked at the door of the lodge, and it became

[6]

open unto me.

[Q.] Why were you received on the point of a sharp instrument piercing your naked left breast?

[A.] It was to remind me as that was an instrument of torture to my flesh, so might the recollection thereof be to my conscience, should I ever presume to reveal the secrets of Freemasonry unlawfully.

[Q.] Why were you conducted to the center of the lodge and there caused to kneel and receive the benefit of a prayer?

[A.] Because no person should ever enter upon any great or important undertaking without first invoking a blessing of Deity.

[Q.] Why were you asked in whom you put your trust?

[A.] Because, agreeable to the laws of our ancient institution, no atheist could be made a Mason. It was therefore necessary that I should profess my belief in Deity, otherwise no obligation would be binding upon me.

[Q.] Why were you taken by the right hand, bid to rise, follow your leader, and fear no danger?

[A.] Because at that time I could neither foresee nor prevent danger, it was therefore to signify that I was then in the hands of a true and trusty friend, in whose fidelity I might with safety confide.

[Q.] Why were you conducted once around the lodge to the Junior Warden in the south?

[A.] That all the Brethren might see I was duly prepared.

[Q.] Why were you caused to meet with those several obstructions at the Junior and Senior Wardens, and the Right Worshipful Master's in the east?

[A.] Because there were guards placed at the south, west, east entrances of king Solomon's temple.

[Q.] For what purpose were guards placed in these several stations?

[A.] To see that none passed or repassed but such as were duly qualified, agreeable to which custom I was caused to meet with these several obstructions, in order that I might be duly examined before I could be made a Mason.

[Q.] Why were you caused to kneel on your naked left knee, and not your right or both, when you received the oath or obligation of an Entered Apprentice?

[A.] Because the left is said to be the weakest side of a man's body. It was therefore to signify that it was the weakest part of Masonry that I was then entering upon, being that of an Entered Apprentice.

[Q.] Why were you caused to lay your naked right hand, and not your left or both, upon the Holy Bible, square, and compass when you received the oath or obligation of an Entered Apprentice?

[A.] Because the right hand was said by our ancient Brethren to be the seat of fidelity. They had a deity whom they worshipped by the name of Fides, who is sometimes represented by two right hands joined together, and at others by two human figures holding each other by the right hand. The right hand, therefore, we make use of on this great and solemn occasion to testify in the strongest manner the sincerity of our intentions in the business we were then engaged.

[Q.] Why were you presented with a lamb skin or white leather apron, and why is that said to be an emblem of innocence?

[A.] Because the lamb, *etc.* (*see Monitor*)

[Q.] Why were you requested to deposit something

[7]

of a metallic kind in the lodge?

[A.] It was to remind me that my then extremely poor and pennyless situation should be a striking lesson to me, should I ever after meet a friend, but more especially a worthy Brother, in the like situation then I should consider it my duty to contribute liberally to his relief, so far as I could do it without injury to myself.

[Q.] Why were you placed in the Northeast corner of the lodge as the youngest Entered Apprentice?

[A.] Because in all operative Masonry the first stone of every building is usually placed in the northeast corner. It was therefore necessary that I should be placed in that station, being the youngest Entered Apprentice, to be near the Right Worshipful Master, there to receive those first instructions on which I should build my future moral and Masonic edifice.

Thus Endeth the Second Section.

Third Section [of] Entered Apprentice's Lecture.

You have satisfied me as to the manner and mode of your initiation into this degree, and the reasons why you were caused to submit to the several singularities made use of on that occasion, but you have not yet informed me what makes a lodge or by what a lodge is governed.

[Q.] In the first place, I wish to know, what makes a lodge?

[A.] A certain number of Masons, duly assembled, with the Holy Bible, square, compass, and a warrant or charter empowering them to work.

[Q.] Where did our ancient Brethren usually assemble?

[A.] On a high hill, or in a low vale.

[Q.] Why on a high hill or in a low vale?

[A.] The better to observe the approach of cowans and eaves-droppers ascending or descending.

[Q.] What form is a lodge?

[A.] Oblong.

[Q.] How long?

[A.] From east to west.

[Q.] How broad?

[A.] From between the north and south.

[Q.] How high?

[A.] From the earth to the heavens.

[Q.] How deep?

[A.] From the surface of the earth to the center.

[Q.] Why is a lodge said to be so long, so broad, so high, and so deep?

[A.] It is to denote the universality of Masonry, and that a Masons' charity should be equally extensive.

[Q.] Very great.[2] What supports this vast fabric?

[A.] Three great pillars.

[Q.] What are they called?

[A.] Wisdom, Strength, and Beauty.

[Q.] Why is it necessary there should be wisdom, strength, and beauty to support a lodge?

[A.] Because it is necessary there should be wisdom, to contrive, strength, to support, and beauty, to adorn, all great and important undertakings.

2. *vry gt.* This comment is anomalous, and does not occur in other contemporary rituals.

[Q.] By whom were they represented?

[A.] By the Right Worshipful Master, Senior and Junior Wardens.

[Q.] Why were they said to represent the pillars of Wisdom, Strength, and Beauty?

[A.] The Right Worshipful Master represents the pillar of Wisdom, it being

[8]

supposed that he has Wisdom to rule and govern his lodge. The Senior Warden represents the pillar of Strength, it being his duty to pay the craft their wages, if any truly be due, and see that none go away dissatisfied, harmony being the Strength and support of all societies, but more especially this of ours. The Junior Warden represents the pillar of Beauty, it being his duty to call the craft from labor to refreshment at the hour of high twelve, which is the Beauty and glory of the day.

[Q.] What is the covering of a lodge?

[A.] A clouded canopy or starry heaven, where all good Masons hope at last to arrive.

[Q.] By what means?

[A.] By the help of a ladder.

[Q.] What is that ladder called?

[A.] The theological ladder, which Jacob, in his vision, saw ascending from earth to heaven.

[Q.] How many principle rounds has this ladder?

[A.] Three.

[Q.] What are they called?

[A.] Faith, hope, and charity.

[Q.] Why so?

[A.] Because it is necessary we should have faith in God, hope in immortality, and charity to all mankind.

[Q.] Which of these three are the greatest?

[A.] The third, charity.

[Q.] Why so?

[A.] Because our faith may be lost in sight; our hope, in fruition; but charity extends beyond the grave, through the boundless realms of eternity.

[Q.] What are the ornaments of a lodge?

[A.] The mosaic pavement, the indented tessel, and blazing star.

[Q.] What are they?

[A.] The mosaic pavement is a representation of the ground floor of king Solomon's temple; the indented tessel is that beautiful tessellated border or skirting that surrounded it, with the blazing star in the center, which is commemorative of that beautiful star which appeared to guide the wise men from the east to the place of our Saviors' nativity.

[Q.] How do you moralize them?

[A.] The Mosaic Pavement is emblematical of human life, which is chequered, *etc.* (*see Monitor*).

[Q.] How many Lights have you in an Entered Apprentice's lodge?

[A.] Three.

[Q.] How are they placed?

[A.] East, west, and south.

[Q.] Have you none in the north?

[A.] None.

[Q.] Why not?

[A.] Because king Solomon's temple was placed so far north of the ecliptic that the sun nor moon at their meridian height could dart no rays into the north part of it. And as Masonry first rose in the east, and spread to the west, so we Masonically term the north a place of darkness.

[Q.] What is the furniture of a lodge?

[A.] The Holy Bible, square, and compass.

[Q.] To whom do they belong?

[A.] The Holy Bible, to God; the square, to the Master; and the compass to the craft.

[Q.] Why are they thus dedicated?

[A.] The Holy Bible we dedicate to God, it being the inestimable gift of God to man, and on it we obligate a new admitted Brother; the square to the Master, it being the proper Masonic emblem of his office, and is constantly to remind him of the duty he owes to the lodge over which he is appointed to preside; the compass to the craft, for, by a due attention to its use, we are taught to regulate our

[9]

desires, and keep our passions within due bounds.

[Q.] How many jewels have you in an Entered Apprentice's lodge?

[A.] Six: three movable, and three immovable.

[Q.] What are the three movable jewels?

[A.] The square, level, and plumb.

[Q.] What do they morally teach?

[A.] The square, morality; level, equality; and the plumb, rectitude of life.

[Q.] What are the immovable jewels?

[A.] The rough ashlar, the perfect ashlar, and the trestle board.

[Q.] What are they?

[A.] The rough ashlar is a stone taken from the quarry in its rude and natural state. The perfect ashlar is a stone made ready by the hands of the workmen, to be adjusted by the working tools of a Fellow Craft; and the trestle board is for the Master to draw his designs upon.

[Q.] How do you moralize them?

[A.] By the rough ashlar, *etc.* (*See Monitor*)

[Q.] How is a lodge situated?

[A.] Due east and west.

[Q.] Why so?

[A.] For several reasons: first, because the sun, the beauty and glory of the day, rises in the east, and sets in the west.

[Q.] Second reason?

[A.] Because all arts and sciences as well as Masonry first rose in the east and spread to the west.

[Q.] Third reason?

[A.] Because all churches and chapels are, or ought to be, so situated.

[Q.] Why are all churches and chapels so situated?

[A.] Because that was the situation of king Solomon's temple.

[Q.] And why was king Solomon's temple so situated?

[A.] Because after Moses had been instrumental in conducting the children of Israel through the Red Sea, when pursued by pharaoh and his host, he there, by Divine command, erected a tabernacle which he placed due east and west to perpetuate the memory of that miraculous east wind by which their mighty deliverance was wrought. This tabernacle was an exact model of king Solomon's temple, for which reason this and every regular and well governed lodge is, or ought to be, so situated.

[Q.] To whom were lodges dedicated in ancient times?

[A.] To king Solomon.

[Q.] Why to king Solomon?

[A.] Because he was our first Most Excellent Grand Master.

[Q.] To whom are lodges dedicated in modern times?

[A.] To Saint John the Baptist and Saint John the Evangelist.

[Q.] Why to those two?

[A.] Because they were important Christian patrons of Masonry and, since their time, there is represented in every regular and well governed lodge a certain point within a circle (*see Monitor*).

[Q.] What are the tenets of your profession as a Mason?

[A.] Brotherly-love, relief and truth.

[Q.] I will thank you to explain the tenet of brotherly-love.

[A.] By the exercise of brotherly-love, *etc.* (*see Monitor*).

[Q.] I will thank you to explain the tenet of relief.

[A.] To relieve the distressed, *etc.* (*see Monitor*).

[Q.] I will thank you to explain the tenet of truth.

[A.] Truth is a Divine attribute, *etc.* (*see Monitor*).

[Q.] You informed me that I should know you to be a Mason by a certain sign, token, word, and the perfect points of your entrance. The former you have explained to me, but not the latter, the points. I wish to know what they are, and how many

[10]

there are.

[A.] There are four: the guttural, the pectoral, the manual, and the pedal.

[Q.] What do they further allude to?

[A.] To the four cardinal virtues, which are, temperance; fortitude, prudence, and justice.

[Q.] I will thank you to explain the cardinal virtue of temperance.

[A.] *Candidate rises with the due guard of an Entered Apprentice, and says*: Temperance is that due restraint, *etc.* (*see Monitor*) *with this addition*: "and which would consequently subject him to the first penalty of his obligation: that of having his throat cut across, *etc.* which alludes to the guttural."

[Q.] I will thank you to explain the cardinal virtue of fortitude.

[A.] Fortitude is that noble and steady purpose of the mind (*see Monitor*) *with this addition*: and which was emblematically represented on his first admission into the lodge, by being received on a sharp instrument piercing his naked left breast, which alludes to the pectoral.

[Q.] I will thank you to explain the cardinal virtue of prudence.

[A.] Prudence teaches us to regulate our lives and actions (*see Monitor*) *with this addition:* ever bearing in mind that memorable period when his left knee was bare bent, his right forming a square, his body erect, his left hand supporting the Holy Bible, square, and compass, his naked right hand covering the same, which alludes to the manual.

[Q.] I will thank you to explain the cardinal virtue of justice.

[A.] Justice is that standard or boundary of right, *etc.* (*see Monitor*) *with this addition:* ever remembering the time when he was placed in the north-east corner of the lodge as the youngest Entered Apprentice, his feet forming a square, his body erect at the right hand of the Right Worshipful Master, who was then pleased to say that he there stood as a just and upright Mason, and gave it to him strictly in charge ever to walk and act as such, which alludes to the pedal.

[Q.] With what did Entered Apprentices serve their Masters in ancient times, and what ought they to in modern?

[A.] With freedom, fervency, and zeal.

[Q.] By what are they represented?

[A.] By chalk, charcoal, and clay.

[Q.] Why do chalk, charcoal, and clay represent freedom, fervency, and zeal?

[A.] Because there is nothing more free than chalk, for on the slightest touch it will leave a trace behind; there is nothing more fervent than charcoal, which, when well lighted will cause the most obdurate metals to yield; and there is nothing more zealous than clay, or our mother earth which is constantly employed for man's use, and at the same time reminding us that, as from it we came, so unto it we must all return.

Thus Endeth the Entered Apprentice's Lecture.

[II]

First Section in the Fellow Craft's Lecture.

[Q.] Brother, will you be off, or from?

[A.] I will be from.

[Q.] From what?

[A.] From the degree of an Entered Apprentice to that of a Fellow Craft.

[Q.] Then you are a Fellow Craft, I presume?

[A.] I am. Try me.

[Q.] How will you be tried?

[A.] By the square.

[Q.] Why by the square?

[A.] Because that is one of the working tools of my profession.

[Q.] What is a square?

[A.] An angle of ninety degrees, or the fourth part of a circle.

[Q.] What induced you to become a Fellow Craft?

[A.] In order that I might obtain wages, the better to support myself, and assist all worthy distressed Fellow Craft.

[Q.] Where was you made a Fellow Craft?

[A.] In the body of a just and lawful lodge of Fellow Crafts, duly assembled, and lcgally constituted.

[Q.] Where was you prepared to be made a Fellow Craft?

[A.] In a room adjacent to the lodge.

[Q.] How were you prepared?

[A.] By being divested of all minerals and metals, neither naked nor clothed, barefoot nor shod, hoodwinked, with a cable-tow twice around my naked right arm.

[Q.] Why had you a cable-tow twice around your naked right arm?

[A.] It was to denote as a Fellow Craft that I was under a double tie to the fraternity.

[Q.] Where were you then conducted?

[A.] To the door of the lodge by the hand of a Brother, where I was caused to give three distinct knocks.

[Q.] To what do those three distinct knocks allude?

[A.] To the jewels of a Fellow Craft.

[Q.] What are they?

[A.] The listening ear, the instructive tongue, and faithful breast.

[Q.] I will thank you to explain them.

[A.] The listening ear receives the sound from the instructive tongue, and the sacred mysteries of Freemasonry are safely guarded in the repository of a faithful breast.

[Q.] What was said to you from within?

[A.] Who comes there, repeated.

[Q.] Your answer?

[A.] A Brother who has justly and lawfully served his time as an Entered Apprentice, and now seeks for further light in Masonry, by being passed to the degree of a Fellow Craft.

[Q.] What more were you asked?

[A.] If I came of my own free will and accord, if I was duly and truly prepared, worthy and well qualified, if I had made the necessary proficiency in the preceding degree, and properly vouched for; all which being answered in the affirmative, I was asked by what further right or benefit I expected to gain admission.

[Q.] Your answer?

[A.] By the benefit of a pass.

[Q.] Did you give that pass?

[A.] I did not, but my conductor gave it for me.

[Q.] Please to give it to your left hand, Brother.

[A.] (*They rise and give it:* Sh—) It is right. I greet you Brother Sh—.

[Q.] What followed?

[A.] I was requested to wait a time with

[12]

patience until the Right Worshipful Master could be informed of my request, and his answer returned.

[Q.] What was his answer, when returned?

[A.] Let him enter.

[Q.] How did you enter?

[A.] On the angle of the square, presented to my naked right breast, which was to teach me that the square of truth and virtue should be a rule and guide of all my transactions through life.

[Q.] Where were you then conducted?

[A.] Twice around the lodge, to the Junior Warden in the south, where the same questions were asked, and the like answers returned as at the door.

[Q.] How did the Junior Warden in the south dispose of you?

[A.] He ordered me to pass on to the Senior Warden in the west, where the same questions were asked, and the like answers returned, as before.

[Q.] How did the Senior Warden in the west dispose of you?

[A.] He ordered me to pass on to the Right Worshipful Master in the east, where the same questions were asked, and the like answers returned as before.

[Q.] How did the Right Worshipful Master in the east dispose of you?

[A.] He ordered me to be reconducted to the Senior Warden in the west, who taught me to advance, by two upright regular steps, my feet forming the right angle of an oblong square, my body erect towards the east.

[Q.] What did the Right Worshipful Master then do with you?

[A.] He made me a Fellow Craft.

[Q.] How?

[A.] In due form.

[Q.] How is that due form?

[A.] By kneeling on my right knee, my left forming a square, my body erect, my right hand covering the Holy Bible, square, and compass, and my left supported on the square, in which due form I received the oath or obligation of a Fellow Craft.

(*Master gives three knocks. All rise*) I will thank you to repeat that oath.

I, L. M., of my own, *etc.* (*introduce the name of the degree, and is the same as the oath of an Entered Apprentice*). I furthermore promise and swear, I will answer all lawful signs and tokens that may be sent or given unto me from a true and lawful Fellow Craft, or from the body of a just and lawful lodge of such, if within the first angle or square of my work. (*Note: at the building of king Solomon's temple, the Fellow Crafts had certain angles or squares marked out for them to work in, and they were under no obligation to attend any sign or token given them beyond that angle or square.*) That I will aid and assist all worthy distressed Fellow Crafts, so far as I can do it without injury to myself. All this I do most solemnly and sincerely, promise and swear, with a firm and fixed, *etc.* (*as in the Entered Apprentice's oath, as far as the penalty*) than that of having my left breast cut open, my heart plucked from thence, and that given as a prey to the beasts of the fields, and fowls of the air, so help me God, *etc.*

[Q.] After receiving the oath or obligation of a Fellow Craft, what were you then asked?

[A.] What I most desired.

[Q.] Your answer?

[A.] More

[13]

light.

[Q.] Did you receive it?

[A.] I did.

[Q.] How?

[A.] By order of the Right Worshipful Master, with the assistance of the Brethren.

[Q.] On being brought to light, what did you then discover more than you had done before?

[A.] One point of the compass bare, the other being hidden, which was to signify as a Fellow Craft that I had received light as yet but partially.

[Q.] After these things were explained to you, what did you next observe?

[A.] The Right Worshipful Master approaching me from the east, under the due guard and sign of a Fellow Craft who presented me his right hand in token of a continuance of his Brotherly-love and friendship, and with it the pass, token of a pass, grip and word of a Fellow Craft, bid me rise, go and salute the Junior and Senior Wardens as a Fellow Craft.

[Q.] What did you next observe?

[A.] The Right Worshipful Master in the east, who ordered me to be reconducted to the Senior Warden in the west, who taught me to wear my apron as a Fellow Craft.

[Q.] How should a Fellow Craft wear his apron?

[A.] With the top turned down.

[Q.] After being taught how to wear your apron as a Fellow Craft, how were you then disposed of?

[A.] I was ordered to be reconducted to the place from whence I came, there to be invested of what I had been divested of, and, in due time, returned to the lodge for further information.

Thus Endeth the First Section of the Fellow Craft's Lecture.

Second Section of Fellow Craft's Lecture.

[Q.] How many kinds of masonry are there?

[A.] Two: operative and speculative.

[Q.] What is meant by operative masonry?

[A.] By operative masonry we allude, *etc.* (*See Monitor*)

[Q.] What is meant by speculative Masonry?

[A.] By speculative Masonry we learn to subdue the passions, *etc.* (*See Monitor*)

[Q.] Have you ever wrought?

[A.] I have in speculative masonry only, but our ancient Brethren wrought in operative as well as speculative.

[Q.] Where did our ancient Brethren usually work?

[A.] At the building of king Solomon's Temple and other stately edifices.

[Q.] How many days in the week did they work?

[A.] Six.

[Q.] Did they not work on the seventh?

[A.] They did not.

[Q.] Why not?

[A.] Because in six days God created the heavens and the earth and rested on the seventh. The seventh day, therefore, our ancient Brethren consecrated as a day of rest from their labors, thereby enjoying frequent opportunities of contemplating <the glorious works of creation and of adoring their Great Creator.

[Q.] Did they receive any wages?

[A.] They did.

[Q.] What?>[3]

[A.] Corn, wine, and oil.

[Q.] Where did they receive them?

[A.] In the middle chamber of king Solomon's Temple.

[Q.] How gained you your way thither?

[A.] Through a porch.

[Q.] In passing through this porch, did you observe anything worthy of your attention?

[A.] I did. Two great pillars. One on the right and the other on the left.

[Q.] What is the one on the right

3. The text between the angled brackets, from "and of adoring their great creator" to "what," all appear on the same line, which is accidently inverted.

[14]

called?

[A.] B—.

[Q.] What is the one on the left called?

[A.] J—.

[Q.] What does the one on the right denote?

[A.] Strength.

[Q.] What does the one on the left denote?

[A.] To establish.

[Q.] What do they both together allude to?

[A.] To a certain text in scripture, "In strength will I establish this, mine house, forever."

[Q.] What were these pillars?

[A.] They were molten or cast brass.

[Q.] Where were they cast?

[A.] On the clayey ground between Succoth and Zarthan, where all the holy vessels of the temple were cast.

[Q.] By whom were they cast?

[A.] By Hiram Abiff, the widow's son of the tribe of Napthali.

[Q.] Were these pillars hollow or solid?

[A.] They were hollow.

[Q.] For what purpose?

[A.] As a safe repository for the records in the archives of the lodge, against inundations and conflagrations.

[Q.] How high were these pillars?

[A.] Thirty-five cubits each.

[Q.] Were they adorned with anything?

[A.] They were, with two chapiters, one on the top of each, of five cubits, making in the whole forty cubits high.

[Q.] Were these chapiters adorned with anything?

[A.] They were, with lily work, network, and pomegranates.

[Q.] What do they denote?

[A.] Peace, unity, and plenty.

[Q.] Why so?

[A.] Because the lily, from its purity and the remote situation in which it usually grows, denotes peace; the network, from the intimate connection of its several parts, denotes unity; and the pomegranate, from the exuberance of its seeds denotes plenty.

[Q.] Were these chapiters adorned with anything further?

[A.] They were, with two balls or pommels, one on the top of each, representing the globes.

[Q.] What are the globes?

[A.] Two artificial spherical bodies, on the convex surface of which are represented the countries, seas, and various parts of the earth, the planetary revolutions, face of the heavens, and other important particulars.

[Q.] How were they distinguished?

[A.] The sphere with the parts of the earth delineated on its surface is called the terrestrial globe, and that with the constellations and other heavenly bodies is called the celestial globe.

[Q.] In going your way to the middle chamber, did you observe anything further worthy of your notice?

[A.] I did: a flight of winding stairs, consisting of three, five and seven steps.

[Q.] To what does the number three allude?

[A.] To the three principle officers of the lodge: Right Worshipful Master, Senior and Junior Wardens.

[Q.] To what do they further allude?

[A.] To our three ancient Grand Masters, Solomon, king of Israel, Hiram, king of Tyre, and Hiram Abiff.

[Q.] To what does the number five allude?

[A.] To the five orders in architecture, which are the Tuscan, Doric, Ionic, Corinthian, and Composite.

[Q.] To what do they further allude?

[A.] To the five senses of human nature, which are hearing, seeing, feeling, smelling, and tasting.

[Q.] Which of these are the most essential to us as Masons?

[A.] The three first: hearing, seeing, and feeling.

[Q.] Why so?

[A.] Because by hearing, we hear the word; by seeing, we see the sign; and by feeling, we feel the grip, whereby one Brother may know another in the dark, as in the light.

[Q.] To what does the number seven allude?

[A.] To the seven liberal arts and sciences, which are: grammar,

[15]

rhetoric, logic, arithmetic, geometry, music, astronomy.

[Q.] Where were you then conducted?

[A.] To the outward door of the middle chamber of king Solomon's Temple, which I found guarded by the Junior Grand Warden who demanded of me the pass and token of the pass of a Fellow Craft.

[Q.] Did you give that pass?

[A.] I did.

[Q.] Please to give it to your left hand Brother.

[A.] (*They rise and give it:* Sh—.)

[Q.] The word is right, please to pass.

[Q.] What does this word denote?

[A.] Plenty (*in Hebrew*)

[Q.] How is it represented?

[A.] By a field of corn growing near a waterfall.

[Q.] From whence did this word originate?

[A.] It was in consequence of a quarrel between Jephthah, Judge of Israel, and the Ephramites (*Judges, 21st chapter*). The Ephramites had long been a turbulent and rebellious people, whom Jephthah had endeavored to subdue by lenient measures, but without effect. They being highly incensed at not being called in to share the rich spoils of the Ammonitish war, gathered together a mighty army. Jephthah also gathered together the men of Gilead, gave them battle, and put them to flight. And, in order to make his victory more complete, he placed guards at the several passages of Jordan, and commanded them, "If any should come that way say unto them. 'Say now Sh—.'" But they being of a different tribe could not frame to pronounce the word right, and said S—, which trifling defect proved them to be enemies and cost them their lives. And there fell at that time forty and two thousand; since when Sh— has been established as the pass word to be given before we can gain admission into any regular and well governed lodge of Fellow Crafts.

[Q.] Where was you then conducted?

[A.] To the inner door of the middle chamber of king Solomon's Temple, which I found guarded by the Senior Grand Warden, and who demanded of me the grip and word of a Fellow Craft.

[Q.] Did you give it?

[A.] I did.

[Q.] Please to give it to your left hand Brother.

[A.] (*They rise and give it without any division.*)

[Q.] It is right. Please to enter.

[Q.] On entering the middle chamber of king Solomon's Temple, what were the first things presented to you?

[A.] The working tools of a Fellow Craft.

[Q.] What are they?

[A.] The plumb, square, and level.

[Q.] What do they morally teach?

[A.] The plumb is an instrument, *etc.* (*see Monitor*).

[Q.] What was your attention further directed to?

[A.] To the letter G, which is the initial of geometry, or the fifth science, on which Masonry is principally founded.

[Q.] What is meant by geometry?

[A.] By geometry, *etc.* (*see Monitor*).

[Q.] To what does the letter G further allude? (*Gives three knocks, all rise.*)

[A.] To the sacred namc of Dcity, to whom all should, with reverence, bow (*here the whole lodge bow*) from the youngest Entered Apprentice in the Northeast corner of the lodge, to the Right Worshipful Master in the chair.

Thus Endeth the Fellow Craft's Lecture.

Ceremony of closing this degree is the same as the Entered Apprentice's except the name of the degree: two knocks. Fellow Craft's lodge is always closed sine die. It is always considered as a special lodge.

[16]

First Section of Master Mason's Lecture.

[Q.] Will you be off or from?

[A.] From.

[Q.] From what?

[A.] From the degree of a Fellow Craft to that of a Master Mason.

[Q.] Then you are a Master Mason, I presume? (Brother Senior Warden, are you a Master Mason?)

[A.] I am.

[Q.] What induced you to become a Master Mason?

[A.] In order that I might obtain Master's wages, the better to support myself, and to assist all worthy distressed Master Masons, their widows and orphans.

[Q.] Where were you made a Master Mason?

[A.] In the body of a just and lawful lodge of Master Masons, duly assembled, and legally constituted.

(*Note: These questions and answers are necessary questions and answers between the Master and Senior Warden in commencing the opening of a Master's lodge. In opening, the Master then asks:* How many compose such a lodge? *Answer is,* Three, five, seven, or more.)

[Q.] Where were you prepared to be made a Master Mason?

[A.] In a room adjacent to the lodge.

[Q.] How were you prepared?

[A.] By being divested of all minerals and metals, neither naked nor clothed, barefoot nor shod, hoodwinked, with a cable-tow three times around my naked body.

[Q.] Why had you a cable-tow three times around your body?

[A.] It was to signify that as I advanced in Masonry, my obligations became more and more binding on me.

[Q.] Where were you then conducted?

[A.] To the door of the lodge by the hand of a Brother where I was caused to give three distinct knocks.

[Q.] To what do these three distinct knocks allude?

[A.] To the jewels of a Master Mason.

[Q.] What are they?

[A.] Friendship, morality, and brotherly-love.

[Q.] What was said to you from within?

[A.] Who comes there, thrice repeated.

[Q.] Your answer?

[A.] A Brother who has justly and lawfully served his time as an Entered Apprentice, been passed to the degree of a Fellow Craft, and now seeks for further light in Masonry by being raised to the sublime degree of a Master Mason.

[Q.] What more were you asked?

[A.] If I came of my own free will and accord, if I was duly and truly prepared, worthy and well qualified, if I had made the necessary proficiency in the preceding degree, and properly avouched for, all which being answered in the affirmative, I was asked by what further right or benefit I expected to gain admission.

[Q.] Your answer?

[A.] By the benefit of a pass.

[Q.] Did you give that pass?

[A.] I did not, but my conductor gave it for me.

[Q.] Please to give it to your left hand Brother.

[A.] (*They rise and give it: T—*)

[Q.] [It] is right. I greet you, Brother T—.

[Q.] Who was T— ?

[A.] He was an ingenious workman in various metals and brother to Jubal, the inventor of music, or the sixth science.

[Q.] What followed?

[A.] I was requested to wait a time with patience until the Right Worshipful Master could be informed of my request and his answer returned.

[Q.] What was his answer when

[17]

returned?

[A.] Let him enter and be received in due form.

[Q.] How were you received?

[A.] On the points of the compass extended to my naked breasts, which was to signify that as the vital principle of life lay within the breast, so were the most valuable tenets of Masonry contained within the points of the compass, which are friendship, morality, and brotherly-love.

[Q.] Where were you then conducted?

[A.] Three times around the lodge, to the Junior Warden in the south, where the same questions were asked and the like answers returned as at the door.

[Q.] How did the Junior Warden in the south dispose of you?

[A.] He directed me to pass on to the Senior Warden in the west, where the same questions were asked and like answers returned as before.

[Q.] How did the Senior Warden in the west dispose of you?

[A.] He directed me to pass on to the Right Worshipful Master in the east, where, *etc.*

[Q.] What did the Right Worshipful Master then demand from you?

[A.] From whence I came.

[Q.] Your answer?

[A.] From the west.

[Q.] What more did he demand.

[A.] Whither I was traveling.

[Q.] Your answer?

[A.] Towards the east.

[Q.] What more did he demand?

[A.] What I was in pursuit of.

[Q.] Your answer?

[A.] That which was lost, which by my own endeavors, and his assistance, I hoped to obtain.

[Q.] What more did he demand?

[A.] What I alluded to.

[Q.] You answer?

[A.] To the secrets of a Master Mason.

[Q.] How did the Right Worshipful Master then dispose of you?

[A.] He ordered me to be reconducted to the Senior Warden in the west, who taught me to advance by three upright regular steps, my feet forming a square, my body erect towards the east.

[Q.] What did the Right Worshipful Master then do with you?

[A.] He made me a Master Mason.

[Q.] How?

[A.] In due form.

[Q.] What is that due form?

[A.] By kneeling on my naked knees, my body erect, my hands covering the Holy Bible, square and compass, in which due form I received the oath, or obligation, of a Master Mason.

(*Master gives three knocks. All rise.*)

I will thank you to repeat that oath or obligation.

(*The Master kneels and takes off his hat opposite to the candidate. In giving the obligation, the Deacons hold the rods over the head*[4] *of the candidate*)

4. Although the text reads "hds"—which suggests "hands"—the ceremonies state the Deacons "hold the rods over the candidate's head" (hld e rds vr e cnds hd).

I, M. E., of *etc.*, I furthermore promise and swear, that I will answer all lawful signs and summonses that may be given or sent unto me from a just and lawful Master Mason, or from the body of a just and lawful lodge of such, if within the length of my cable-tow; that I will aid and assist all worthy distressed Master Masons, their widows and orphans, so far as I can do it without injury to myself or family; that I will keep a Brother's secrets as my own, when given in charge as such, murder and treason excepted, and that left to my own discretion; that I will abide by and support the bylaws of the lodge of which I may become a member, the constitution of the Grand Lodge under which the same is holden, and the general regulations of Masonry. I furthermore promise and swear, that I will not be at the making of a woman a Mason, a young man

[18]

[5]under age, an old man in his dotage, an atheist, a madman, or a fool, knowing them to be such; that I will not wrong a Brother, nor deprive him of his good name, nor suffer it to be done by others, if within my power to prevent it, but will apprize him of all approaching danger, so far as it shall come to my knowledge; that I will not violate the chastity of a Brother's wife, daughter, sister, or mother, knowing them to be such; that I will not give the Master Mason's word, except on the five points of fellowship, and not above my breath, unless absolute necessity shall require it. All this, I do most solemnly and sincerely, *etc.*, binding myself under no less penalty, than that of having my body severed in two, my bowels taken from thence, and burned to ashes, and these ashes scattered to the four winds of heaven, my body quartered and placed on the four cardinal points of the universe, so that there be no more remembrance had of me among men or Masons forever. So help me God, and keep me steadfast, in this, my Master Mason's oath or obligation.

[Q.] After receiving the oath or obligation of a Master Mason, what were you then asked?

[A.] What I most desired.

[Q.] Your answer?

[A.] More light.

[Q.] Did you receive it?

[A.] I did.

5. At this point I omit the two lines belonging to the top of p. 20 (see the introduction).

[Q.] How?

[A.] By order of the Right Worshipful Master, with the assistance of the Brethren.

[Q.] After being brought to light, what did you then discover more than you had done before?

[A.] Both points of the compass bare, which was to signify that I never should lose sight of the moral application of that useful implement, for by a due attention to its use, we are taught to regulate our desires, and keep our passions within due bounds with all mankind, but more especially a Brother.

[Q.] After these things were explained to you, what did you next observe?

[A.] The Right Worshipful Master approaching me from the east, under the due guard and sign of a Master Mason, who presented me with his right hand in token of a continuance of his brotherly-love and friendship, and with it the pass, and the token of a pass, of a Master Mason, and bid me rise, go and salute the Junior and Senior Wardens as such.

[Q.] After saluting the Junior and Senior Wardens as a Master Mason, what did you next observe?

[A.] The Right Worshipful Master in the east, who ordered me to be reconducted to the Senior Warden in the west, who taught me to wear my apron as a Master Mason.

[Q.] How should a Master Mason wear his apron?

[A.] With the left corner tucked up.

[Q.] After being taught to wear your apron as a Master Mason, how were you then disposed of?

[A.] I was ordered to be reconducted to the place from whence I came, there to be invested of what I had been divested, and in due time returned to the lodge for further information.

[*Note: Before the candidate goes out, the Master gives him the following charge:*

Master: Brother A, before we can proceed any further with you in this solemn ceremony, it will be necessary for you to travel, in order to convince the Brethren of your fidelity and fortitude. In the course of your travels, you may meet with ruffians, who will endeavor to extort from you the

[19]

secrets of a Master Mason. Some will go so far, Brother A, as even to threaten to take your life. But you must be prepared even to lay down your life, rather than to reveal any of the secrets of Freemasonry that have been committed to you. Therefore, on your firmness, fidelity, and fortitude, rest our future favors.]

Conduct the candidate to the preparative room.

Thus Endeth the First Section of the Master Mason's Lecture.

Second Section of Master's Lecture.

[Q.] You have satisfied me as to the manner and mode of your entrance into this degree, but you have not yet informed me what a Master Mason's lodge represents, nor have you explained to me the origin or historical part of this degree. In the first place, I wish to know what a Master Mason's lodge represents?

[A.] The Sanctum Sanctorum, or Holy of Holies, of king Solomon's Temple.

[Q.] After being reinvested of what you had been divested, and on returning to the lodge, where were you first conducted?

[A.] To the Northeast corner of the lodge, where I was caused to kneel, and hear the Master Mason's prayer repeated.

(*Note: A cushion is placed on the floor, between the altar and the Master's throne, in the Northeast side of the lodge. The Senior Deacon receives the candidate at the door, advancing towards this cushion, saying,* "It was the daily custom of our Grand Master Hiram Abiff, at the hour of high twelve," *etc. See second section of the work in this degree.*)

(*Note: Again, while the candidate is investing himself with his clothing, the Master appoints the assassins, who are stationed, south, west, east; likewise, three Fellow Craft representing the twelve; also the wayfaring man, with a cain* [sic] *and pack on his back. Master gives three knocks. All rise.*)

[Q.] I will thank you to repeat that prayer.

[A.] "Thou, O God, knowest our downsitting," *etc.* (*see Monitor*).

[Q.] After hearing the Master Mason's prayer repeated, what followed?

[A.] I then rose and was conducted to the south door, where I was accosted by a Fellow Craft, who demanded of me at three several times the secrets of a Master Mason, or he would take my life. But, on my third refusal, he struck me on the throat with the 24 inch gauge.

[Q.] Where were you then conducted?

[A.] To the west door, where I was accosted by a Fellow Craft, who in like manner demanded of me at three several times the secrets of a Master Mason, or he would take my life. But, on my third refusal, he struck me on my right breast with a square.

[Q.] Where were you then conducted?

[A.] To the east door, where I was accosted by a Fellow Craft, who in like manner demanded of me at three several times the secrets of a Master Mason, or he would take my life. But, on my third refusal, he smote me on the head with the common gavel, or setting maul which

[20]

<felled me at his feet.

[Q.] Whom did you represent?

[A.] Our Grand Master, Hiram Abiff, who was slain when the temple was near its completion.

[Q.] Was his death>[6] premeditated?

[A.] It was.

[Q.] By whom?

[A.] By fifteen Fellow Craft, who, seeing the temple near its completion, were fearful they should not be able to obtain Master Mason's wages when traveling into foreign countries, entered into a horrid conspiracy to extort from our Grand Master Hiram Abiff the secrets of a Master Mason, or to take his life. But twelve of them, fearing the evil consequences, were struck with horror at the atrocity of the crime, and recanted. But the other three, who were Jubela, Jubelo, Jubelum, being more hardened in villainy, were determined to put their murderous designs into execution, and accordingly placed themselves at the south, west, and east entrances of the temple.

[Q.] At what time did this happen?

[A.] At the hour of high twelve, when the Craft were called from labor to refreshment.

[Q.] How came he alone at this time?

6. Between the angled brackets are the two lines which were misplaced at p. 18.

[A.] It was the daily custom of our Grand Master Hiram Abiff, at the hour of high twelve, when the Craft were called from labor to refreshment, to go into the temple to view the work, to see if there could be any improvement made there for its utility or ornament, and also to draw designs on his trestle board for the Craft to pursue their labors. After which, he entered the Sanctum Sanctorum, or Holy of Holies, there to offer up his adoration and prayers to the true and living God for the sins of the people.

[Q.] What followed?

[A.] After performing this pious ceremony, he then arose and attempted to go out of the south door of the temple, which he found guarded by Jubela, who demanded of him at three several times the secrets of a Master Mason, or he would take his life. But, on his third refusal, he struck him across the throat with the twenty-four inch gauge.

[Q.] What followed?

[A.] He then attempted to make his escape out of the west door of the temple, which he found guarded by Jubelo, who demanded of him at three several times the secrets of a Master Mason, or he would take his life. But, on his third refusal, he struck him on his right breast with a square, which caused him to stagger and reel.

[Q.] What followed?

[A.] He then endeavored to make his escape out of the east door, which he found guarded by Jubelum, who in like manner demanded of him at three several times the secrets of a Master Mason, or he would take his life. But, on his third refusal, he smote him on [his] head with a common gavel or setting maul, which felled him lifeless at his feet.

[Q.] What did they then do with the body?

[A.] They buried it in the rubbish of the temple at low twelve, or twelve at night, when they agreed to meet to consult what further to do with it.

[Q.] Did they meet agreeably to appointment?

[A.] They did.

[Q.] What did they then do with the body?

[A.] They carried it a westerly course from the temple, and buried it at the brow of a hill called Mount Moriah, and at the head of the grave transplanted a sprig of cassia, so that if occasion should require, they themselves might know where to find it. Then, for fear of detection, they endeavored to make their escape out of the kingdom.

[Q.] What followed?

[21]

[A.] Confusion in the temple.

[Q.] What caused this confusion?

[A.] By our Grand Master Hiram Abiff being missing.

[Q.] How long had he been missing?

[A.] Since the hour of high twelve of yesterday.

[Q.] How did they know him to be missing?

[A.] By there being no designs drawn on his trestle board for the Craft to pursue their labors.

[Q.] What did king Solomon then order?

[A.] He ordered the Senior Grand Warden to cause the inner apartments of the temple to be searched, and also the roll of the workmen to be called.

[Q.] Was this done agreeably to his order?

[A.] It was.

[Q.] What was the Senior Grand Warden's report?

[A.] That the inner apartments of the temple had been searched without effect, and also the roll of the workmen had been called, and there appeared to be three Fellow Crafts missing, who were Jubela, Jubelo, Jubelum, and from the similarity of their names, they appeared to be Brethren and men of Tyre.

[Q.] What did king Solomon then inform the Senior Grand Warden?

[A.] That there had appeared before him twelve Fellow Crafts, clothed in white aprons and white gloves, in token of their innocence, and imploring his pardon, and informed him that they twelve, and three others, seeing the temple near its completion, were fearful they should not be able to obtain Master Mason's wages when traveling into foreign countries, entered into a horrid conspiracy to extort from our Grand Master Hiram Abiff the secrets of a Master Mason, or to take his life. But, they twelve, fearing the evil consequences, were struck with horror at the atrocity of the crime, and recanted; but they were fearful that the other three had put their murderous designs into execution.

[Q.] What did king Solomon then order?

[A.] He ordered the Senior Grand Warden to cause these twelve Fellow Crafts to be sent out: three east, three west, three north, and three south, in search of our Grand Master Hiram, and the deserters from the temple.

[Q.] Were they sent out agreeably to his order?

[A.] They were.

[Q.] What was the Senior Grand Warden's report on their return?

[A.] That three of them, traveling on the coast of Joppa, met a wayfaring man of whom they inquired if he had seen any workmen from the temple pass that way. He informed them that he had seen three, inquiring for a passage to Ethiopia, but, not being able to obtain one, they had returned back into the country.

[Q.] What did king Solomon then inform the Senior Grand Warden?

[A.] That it was of the highest importance that our Grand Master Hiram Abiff should be found. He therefore ordered the Senior Grand Warden to cause these twelve Fellow Crafts to be sent out again, in the same directions, and with this injunction: that if they did not succeed in finding the body of our Grand Master Hiram Abiff, or the deserters from the temple, they themselves should be deemed murderers, and suffer accordingly.

[Q.] Were they sent agreeably to his orders?

[A.] They were.

[Q.] What was the Senior Grand Warden's report on their return?

[A.] That one of them, traveling a Westerly course from the temple, had occasion to ascend a hill

[22]

called Mount Moriah at the brow of which one of them, being more weary than the rest, sat down to refresh himself and, on rising, he accidentally took hold of a sprig of cassia, which coming up easily, the ground being recently removed, had the appearance of a grave, which excited his suspicion. On which, he hailed his Brethren; and while contemplating on the spot, they heard exclamations from the adjacent clefts, accusing and excusing each other.

[Q.] What were these exclamations?

[A.] The first exclaimed, "Oh, that I had my throat cut," *etc.*, that appeared to be the voice of Jubela; the second exclaimed Jubelo; the third exclaimed, "I am worse than you both: it was I that deprived him of life. Oh, that I had my body," *etc.*, "ere I had been the means of the death of so good and great a man as our Grand Master Hiram." On which they immediately rushed in upon them, seized them and bound them, and carried them up to the city.

[Q.] What did king Solomon then order?

[A.] He ordered the Senior Grand Warden to cause them to be sent up before him.

[Q.] Were they sent up agreeably to his order?

[A.] They were.

[Q.] What did king Solomon then order?

[A.] He ordered the Senior Grand Warden to cause them to be taken without the gates of the city, and there severally executed, agreeably to the imprecations from their own mouths.

[Q.] Was this done agreeably to his order?

[A.] It was.

[Q.] What did king Solomon then order?

[A.] He ordered the Senior Grand Warden to cause the twelve Fellow Crafts to be sent out to the place where the weary Brother sat down to rest and refresh himself, and search for the body of our Grand Master Hiram Abiff, and, if found, to search for the secrets of a Master Mason, and see if they could be found on or about the body, or a key to them.

[Q.] Were they sent out agreeably to his order?

[A.] They were.

[Q.] What was the Senior Grand Warden's report on their return?

[A.] That they had found the body.

[Q.] Where?

[A.] At a westerly course from the temple, at the brow of a hill, called Mount Moriah, that they had made search for the secrets of a Master Mason, but they were not to be found on or about the body, nor a key to them.

[Q.] What did king Solomon then inform the Senior Grand Warden?

[A]. That the Master Mason's word was lost.

[Q.] What did king Solomon then order?

[A.] He ordered the Senior Grand Warden to take suitable assistance and go out with him to endeavor to raise the body of our Grand Master Hiram Abiff for a more decent interment.

[Q.] Did they go out agreeably to his order?

[A.] They did.

[Q.] How did king Solomon order the body to be raised?

[A.] By the grip of an Entered Apprentice.

[Q.] What was the Senior Grand Warden's report?

[A.] That he could not, for the flesh was putrid, and slipped.

[Q.] How did he then order the body raised?

[A.] By the grip of a Fellow Craft, which he informed him was the same.

[Q.] How did he then order the body raised?

[A.] By the strong grip or lion's paw, and on the five points

[23]

of fellowship, and the first word that should be spoken after the body was thus raised should be a substitute for the Master Mason's word until future ages should find the right.

[Q.] What was the first word spoken after the body was thus raised?

[A.] —

[Q.] What are the five points of fellowship?

[A.] Foot to foot, knee to knee, breast to breast, hand to back, cheek to cheek, with mouth to ear.

[Q.] What do they denote?

[A.] Foot to foot denotes that we should never hesitate to go a foot out of our way to assist a Brother; knee to knee denotes that we should remember a Brother in our devotions; breast to breast that we should keep our Brother's secrets as our own, when given to us as such, murder and treason excepted, and that left to our own discretion; hand to back denotes that we should endeavor to support a Brother when falling; cheek to cheek, with mouth to ear, the way in which the Master Mason's Word is given.

[Q.] What is the introductory clause of your obligation as a Master Mason?

[A.] That I will always hail, forever conceal, and never reveal, *etc.* (*see obligation*).

[Q.] How many points have you in your obligation as a Master Mason?

[A.] Eight: four positive, and four negative.

[Q.] What is the first positive point?

[A.] That I will answer all lawful signs and summons, *etc.* (*see obligation*)

[Q.] What is the second positive point?

[A.] That I will aid and assist, *etc.* (*see obligation*)

[Q.] What is the third positive point?

[A.] That I will keep a Brother's secrets, *etc.* (*see obligation*)

[Q.] What is the fourth positive point?

[A.] That I will abide by and support, *etc.* (*see obligation*)

[Q.] What is the first negative point?

[A.] That I will not be at the making, *etc.* (*see obligation*)

[Q.] What is the second negative point?

[A.] That I will not wrong a Brother, *etc.* (*see obligation*)[7]

[Q.] What is the fourth negative point?

[A.] That I will not give the Master Mason's word, *etc.* (*see obligation*)

[Q.] What is the penalty of your obligation as a Master Mason?

[A.] That I would rather have my body severed, *etc.* (*see obligation*)

[Q.] What are the working tools of a Master Mason?

[A.] All the implements of Masonry indiscriminately, but more especially the trowel.

[Q.] I will thank you to explain the trowel.

[A.] The Trowel is an instrument, *etc.* (*see Monitor*).

Thus Endeth the Master Mason's Lecture.

Note: After presenting the Working Tools to the candidate, the Master reads the charge and says, This charge, Brother A., it was my duty as presiding officer of this lodge to communicate to you, not doubting but you will let the excellent precepts therein contained have their due with you in all your transactions through life. *The Master then bows to the candidate and says,* Brother Senior Deacon, you will please to furnish Brother A. with a convenient seat in the lodge, as a worthy Master Mason. *All sit; pause one minute.*

[24]

Ceremony of Opening Apprentices Lodge.

Master: Brethren, please to clothe.

Master goes up to the east and says, Brother Senior Warden, you will please to approach the east and receive your jewels.

Master says: With pleasure I present unto you with the jewels of your office.

Master then calls Brother Junior Warden in order, then Treasurer, Secretary, and Deacons.

(*All silent for one minute*).

Master sits down, gives one knock, and says, Please to come to order. (*All rise.*) Brethren, we are about opening a lodge of Entered Apprentices, in which I will thank you for your assistance and attention.

7. The third negative point is not in the text.

Master: Brother Senior Warden, you will please to satisfy yourself that all present are Masons.

Senior Warden rises and says, I am satisfied, Right Worshipful Master, that all present are Masons.

Master: You will please to call the Brethren to order as Entered Apprentices, reserving yourself for the last.

Senior Warden: Brethren, please to come to order as Entered Apprentices.

(*Give due guards as Entered Apprentices*).

Senior Warden sits down. Master gives one knock and says (*Junior Deacon rises*), Brother Junior Deacon, the first care of a Mason?

Junior Deacon: To see the lodge duly tyled, Right Worshipful.

Master: You will please to perform that part of your duty, and inform the Tyler that we are about opening a lodge of Entered Apprentices, that he sees the door is tyled accordingly.

Junior Deacon goes to the door, gives three distinct knocks, and says, Brother Tyler, we are about opening a lodge of Entered Apprentices. You will please to see the door is tyled accordingly.

Tyler answers, So mote it be.

Junior Deacon returns to his place and says, We are tyled, Right Worshipful.

Master: How are we tyled, Brother?

Junior Deacon: By a Mason without the door, armed with a proper implement of his office.

Master: The Tyler's place?

Junior Deacon: At the door, with a drawn sword in his hand.

Master: His duty there?

Junior Deacon: To observe the approach of cowans and eavesdroppers ascending or descending, and see that none pass or repass without permission from the Right Worshipful Master.

Master gives two knocks (*Officers rise*) *and says*, Brother Senior Warden, from whence came you as an Entered Apprentice?

Senior Warden: From the lodge of holy Saints John at Jerusalem.

Master: What came you here to do?

Senior Warden: To learn to subdue my passions, and improve myself in Masonry.

Master: Then you are a Mason, I presume?

Senior Warden: I am so taken and accepted among Brothers and fellows.

Master: Where were you made a Mason, Brother?

Senior Warden: In the body of a just and lawful lodge of Masons, duly assembled, and legally constituted.

Master: How many compose such a lodge?

Senior Warden: Three, five, seven, or more.

Master: When the lodge consists of seven, who compose it?

Senior Warden: Right Worshipful Master, Senior and Junior Warden, Treasurer and Secretary, Senior and Junior Deacons.

Master: The Junior Deacon's place in the lodge?

Senior Warden: At the Senior Warden's right.

Master: Your duty there, Brother Junior Deacon?

Junior Deacon: To carry messages from the Senior Warden in the west, to the Right Worshipful Master in the east, or elsewhere about the lodge as he may direct; also, to see the lodge duly tyled.

Master: The Senior Deacon's place in the Lodge?

Junior Deacon: At the Right Worshipful Master's right.

Master: Your duty there, Brother Senior Deacon?

Senior Deacon: To carry orders from

[25]

the Right Worshipful Master in the east, to the Senior Warden in the west, or elsewhere about the lodge as he may direct; also, to introduce all visiting Brethren.

Master: [The] Secretary's place in the lodge?

Senior Deacon: At the Right Worshipful Master's left.

Master: Your duty there, Brother Secretary?

Secretary: To observe the will and pleasure of the Right Worshipful Master; to record the proceedings of the lodge; to receive all monies, and pay them over into the hands of the Treasurer.

Master: The Treasurer's place in the lodge?

Secretary: At the Right Worshipful Master's right.

Master: Your duty there, Brother Treasurer?

Treasurer: To receive all monies from the hands of the Secretary; to keep a just and regular account of the same; and pay them out at the will and pleasure of the Right Worshipful Master, with the consent of the Brethren.

Master: The Junior Warden's station in the lodge?

Treasurer: In the south, Right Worshipful.

Master: Your duty in the south, Brother Junior Warden?

Junior Warden: As the sun is in the south at its meridian height, which is the beauty and glory of the day, so stands the Junior Warden in the south, to call the Craft from labor to refreshment, and from refreshment to labor, at the will and pleasure of the Right Worshipful Master.

Master: The Senior Warden's station in the lodge?

Junior Warden: In the west, Right Worshipful.

Master: Your duty in the west, Brother Senior Warden?

Senior Warden: As the sun sets in the west to close the day, so stands the Senior Warden in the west, to assist the Right Worshipful Master in closing the lodge; to pay the Craft their wages, if any there be due, and see that none go away dissatisfied; harmony being the strength and support of all societies, but more especially this of ours.

Master: [The] Master's station in the lodge?

Senior Warden: In the east, Right Worshipful.

Master: His duty there?

Senior Warden: As the sun rises in the east to open and adorn the day, so stands the Right Worshipful Master in the east, to open his lodge, in due time set the Craft to work, and give them proper instructions.

Master gives three knocks and rises with the lodge, and says, Brother Senior Warden, you will please to take notice, it is my direction that a lodge of Entered Apprentices be now opened, and stand open for the space of one hour, for the dispatch of business. You will please to report the same to the Junior Warden in the south, that the Brethren may have due notice thereof, and govern themselves accordingly.

Senior Warden: Brother Junior Warden, you will please to take notice it is the Right Worshipful Master's will and pleasure that a lodge of Entered Apprentices be now opened for the space of one hour for the dispatch of business. You will please to report the same to the Brethren that they may have due notice thereof and govern themselves accordingly.

Junior Warden: Brethren, you have heard the will and pleasure of the Right Worshipful Master. You will please to take due notice thereof, and let it be accordingly so done.

Master: Together, Brethren.

(*All give the due guard and sign of Entered Apprentice.*)

Master gives one knock. (*answered by Senior and Junior Warden*) *and says* 133*d Psalm, with his hat off, then says,* I declare the lodge of Entered Apprentices duly opened for the dispatch of business (*all sit down silently for one minute*).

Master: Brother Secretary, you will please to read the proceedings of the last lodge.

(*He rises and reads.*)

Master: Brethren, if the proceedings of the last lodge meet

[26]

your approbation, you will please to signify it by the usual sign of an Entered Apprentice.

(*They give it*)

Master: They are approved. Brother Secretary, you will please to record that the proceedings of the last lodge were read and approved.

Master: Brother Senior Warden, have you any particular business in the west before the lodge of Entered Apprentices?

Senior Warden: I know of nothing in the west, Right Worshipful.

Master: Have you anything in the south, Brother Junior Warden?

Junior Warden: I know of nothing in the south, Right Worshipful.

Master: What is your pleasure, Brethren?

Brother: I will propose, Right Worshipful, that we commence the lectures in this degree.

Master gives one knock. Brethren, please to come to order (*all silent one minute*).

Ceremony of Closing the Entered Apprentice's Lodge.

Master: Have you any further business in the west before this lodge of Entered Apprentices, Brother Senior Warden?

Senior Warden: I know of nothing further in the west, Right Worshipful.

Master: Anything further in the south, Brother Junior Warden?

Junior Warden: I know of nothing further in the south, Right Worshipful.

Master: Has any Brother anything to offer for the good of Masonry, but more especially for this lodge? If not, we will proceed to close.

(*Silence one minute*).

Master gives one knock. Junior Deacon rises.

Master: Brother Junior Deacon, the last as well as the first care of a Mason?

Junior Deacon: To see the lodge duly tyled, Right Worshipful.

Master: You will please to perform that part of your duty, and inform the Tyler we are about to close this lodge of Entered Apprentices, and that he sees the door tyled accordingly.

Junior Deacon goes to the door (as in opening) of the lodge, and gives the alarm, and returns to his place and says, We are tyled, Right Worshipful.

Master: How are we tyled, Brother?

Junior Deacon: By a Mason without the door, armed with the proper implement of his office.

Master: The Tyler's place?

Junior Deacon: At the door, with a drawn sword in his hand.

Master: His duty there?

Junior Deacon: To observe the approach of cowans and eavesdroppers, ascending or descending, and see that none pass or repass without permission from the Right Worshipful Master.

Master gives two distinct knocks (the officers rise) and says, Brother Senior Warden, at the opening of this lodge, you informed me that you was a Mason, made in the body of a just and lawful lodge of Masons duly assembled and legally constituted. How many compose such a lodge?

Senior Warden: Three, five, seven, or more.

Master: When a lodge consists of seven, who compose it?

Senior Warden: Right Worshipful Master, Senior and Junior Wardens, Treasurer and Secretary, Senior and Junior Deacons.

Master: The Junior Deacon's place in the lodge?

Senior Warden: At the Senior Warden's right.

Master: Your duty, Brother Junior Deacon?

Junior Deacon: To carry messages from the Senior Warden in the west, *etc.* (*Note: Here the officers all tell their respective duties, the same as in opening, up to the Master*).

Master

[27]

gives three knocks, all rise with the Master, and says, Brother Junior Warden, please to take notice it is my direction that this lodge of Entered Apprentices be now closed, and stand closed, until our next regular meeting, unless sooner called on some special emergency, of which due notice will be given. You will please to report the same to the Senior Warden in the west, that the Brethren may have due notice thereof, and govern themselves accordingly.

Junior Warden: Brother Senior Warden, you will please to take notice it is the Right Worshipful Master's will and pleasure that this lodge of Entered Apprentices be now closed, and stand closed, *as above.*

Senior Warden: Brethren, you have heard the will and pleasure of the Right Worshipful Master. You will please to take due notice thereof, and let it be accordingly so done.

Master: Together, Brethren. (*All give due guard and sign of Entered Apprentice*) *after which Master gives one knock, answered by the Junior and Senior Wardens. He then takes off his hat and says*, Brother Junior Warden, how should Masons meet?

Junior Warden: On the level, Right Worshipful.

Master: How should they part, Brother Senior Warden?

Senior Warden: On the square, Right Worshipful.

Master takes off hat and says, So may we ever meet and part, my Brethren. I declare this lodge of Entered Apprentices duly closed, and may the blessing of God rest upon us, and all regular good Masons.

Brethren all response: So mote it be.

Master takes off his jewel and says, The Brethren will please to deposit their jewels in the east.

Ceremony of Opening a Lodge of Fellow Crafts

Master: Brother Senior Warden, you will please to satisfy yourself that all present are Fellow Crafts.

Senior Warden rises and looks around the lodge, says, I am satisfied, Right Worshipful, that all present are Fellow Crafts.

Master: Please to call the Brethren to order as Fellow Crafts, reserving yourself for the last.

Senior Warden: You will please to come to order as Fellow Crafts

(*Note: They put the right hand on the left breast and the Senior Warden sits down*).

Master: (*Gives one knock. Junior Deacon rises*). Brother Junior Deacon, the first care of a Fellow Craft?

Junior Deacon: To see the lodge is duly tyled.

(*Note: The Junior Deacon having told his duty*) *The Master gives two knocks, and officers rise.*

Master: Brother Senior Warden, are you a Fellow Craft?

Senior Warden: I am. Try me.

Master: How will you be tried?

Senior Warden: By the square.

Master: Why by the square?

Senior Warden: Because that is one of the working tools of my profession.

Master: What is a square?

Senior Warden: An angle of ninety degrees, or the fourth part of a circle.

Master: What induced you to become a Fellow Craft?

Senior Warden: In order that I might obtain wages, the better to support myself and assist a worthy distressed Fellow Craft.

Master: Where were you made a Fellow Craft?

Senior Warden: In the body of a just and lawful

[28]

lodge of Fellow Crafts, duly assembled and legally constituted.

Master: How many compose such a lodge?

Senior Warden: Three, five, seven, or more.

Master: When a lodge consists of five, who compose it?

Senior Warden: Right Worshipful Master, Senior and Junior Wardens, Senior and Junior Deacons.

Master: The Junior Deacon's place in the lodge?

Senior Warden: At the Senior Warden's right.

Master: Your duty there, Brother Junior Deacon?

Junior Deacon: To carry messages from the Senior Warden in the west, *etc.*
(*The officers tell their respective duties up to the Master as in preceding degree.*)

Master (*gives three knocks and all rise*), *and he says*, Brother Senior Warden, you will please to take notice it is my direction that this lodge of Fellow Crafts be now opened, and stand open, for the space of one hour, for the dispatch of business. You will please to report the same to the Junior Warden in the south, that the Brethren may have due notice thereof, and govern themselves accordingly.

Senior Warden: Brother Junior Warden, you will please to take notice it is the Right Worshipful Master's will and pleasure that a lodge of Fellow Crafts be opened in this place for the space, *etc., as above.*

Junior Warden: Brethren, you have heard the will and pleasure of the Right Worshipful Master. You will please to take due notice thereof, and govern yourselves accordingly.

Master: Together, Brethren. (*All give due guard and sign of Fellow Craft*); *gives two knocks*. I declare this lodge of Fellow Crafts duly open for the dispatch of business.

Master: Anything in the west, Brother Senior Warden?

Senior Warden: Nothing in the west, Right Worshipful.

Master: Anything in the south, Brother Junior Warden?

Junior Warden: Nothing in the south, Right Worshipful.

Master: What is your pleasure, Brethren?

Brother: I propose that we receive the lectures in this degree.

(*Note: The ceremony of closing a Fellow Craft's lodge is the same as the Entered Apprentice's, except the name of the degree, two knocks, etc.*).

Ceremony of Opening a Lodge of Master Masons.

Master: Brother Senior Warden, you will please to satisfy yourself that all present are Master Masons.

Senior Warden examines and reports: I am satisfied, Right Worshipful, that all present are Master Masons.

Master: Brother Senior Warden, please to call the Brethren to order as Master Masons, reserving yourself for the last.

(*Note: When the Master gives two knocks in opening, he asks the Senior Warden the brackets of the first section of the lectures. Each officer tells his duty as in the preceding degrees, up to the Master.*)

Master (*Gives three knocks. All rise*): Brother Senior Warden, have you ever traveled?

Senior Warden: I have, Right Worshipful.

Master: Whither?

Senior Warden: From west to east, and from east to west again.

Master: What were you in pursuit of?

Senior Warden: That which was lost.

Master: What do you allude to, Brother Senior Warden?

Senior Warden: To the secrets of a Master Mason.

Master: Do you possess them?

Senior Warden: I do not, Right Worshipful, but I have a substitute.

Master: Brother Senior Warden, you will please to take

[29]

notice it is my direction that the substitute for the Master Mason's word be sent up into the east, attended with its due guards and signs.

Master says, Brethren, you will please to form.

(*The Senior Deacon forms one line on the right of the Master; the Junior Deacon forms the left line, leaving an avenue; the Brethren facing the center. The Senior Deacon goes to the west, to the head of his line; the Junior Deacon to the west, to the head of his. The Senior Warden descends from his station, past the Senior Deacon, the Senior Deacon turning to the right. Thus Senior Warden and Senior Deacon then commence, from the due guard and sign of an Entered Apprentice, up to the grand sign of a Master, and then on the five points. The Senior Deacon gives the Senior Warden the Master's word; the Senior Deacon then turns to the first Brother on his line, and the same ceremony is pursued through the line, up to the Master. The proper Brother giving the last word, the Junior Deacon proceeds with the Senior Warden in the same manner as the Senior Warden had done, and pursues with his line. The Senior and Junior Deacons, after having received the word respectively, follow up their respective lines with their rods to see that each Brother gives the word and signs correctly. In the left line was a vacancy for the Junior Warden to step in and fill the space in the line. When the word has arrived to his vacancy* [*he*] *gives the word, and goes back to his station. The Master descends from his throne and gives the word to the last Brother on each line, right and left, then returning to his throne. The Brethren remain standing.*

Master says, Brother Senior Warden, the substitute for a Master Mason's word has come up into the east correctly. You will please to take notice it is my direction that a lodge of Master Masons be now opened, and stand open, *etc., as in other degrees.*

Senior Warden says as in other degrees, except the name of the degree.

Junior Warden says as in other degrees.

Master says, Together, Brethren, *and gives all the signs up to the Master; then gives three distinct knocks, answered by the Senior and Junior Wardens, and declares*, This Master's lodge to be duly opened, for the dispatch of business. (*All sit*)

The Master consults the officers and Brethren as in former degrees.

Ceremony of Closing Master Mason's Lodge.

Master: Brother Senior Warden, have you any further business in the west before this lodge of Master Masons?

Senior Warden: I know of nothing further in the west, Right Worshipful.

Master: Have you any further business in the south, Brother Junior Warden?

Junior Warden: I know of nothing further in the south, Right Worshipful.

Master: What is your pleasure, Brethren? If there is no further business before the lodge of Master Masons, we will proceed to close it. (*Pause one minute*) *Master gives one knock; Junior Deacon rises.* Brother Junior Deacon, the last as

[30]

well as the first care of a Master Mason?

Junior Deacon: To see the lodge duly tyled, Right Worshipful.

Master: You will please to perform that part of your duty, and inform the Tyler that we are about to close this lodge of Master Masons, and that he sees the door tyled accordingly.

Junior Deacon goes to the door, gives three distinct knocks; answered by the Tyler; opens the door and says, Brother Tyler, we are about closing this lodge of Master Masons. You will please to see the door tyled accordingly.

Tyler shuts the door and returns to his place and says, We are duly tyled, Right Worshipful.

Master: How are we tyled, Brother?

Junior Deacon: By a Master Mason without the door, armed with the proper implement of his office.

Master: The Tyler's place?

Junior Deacon: At the door, with a drawn sword in his hand.

Master: His duty there?

Junior Deacon: To observe the approach of cowans and eavesdroppers, ascending or descending, and to see that none pass or repass without permission from the Right Worshipful Master.

Master (*Gives two knocks. Officers rise.*) Brother Senior Warden, at the opening of this lodge, you informed me that you was a Master Mason, made in the body of a just and lawful lodge of Master Masons, duly assembled and legally constituted. How many compose such a lodge?

Senior Warden: Three, five, seven, or more.

Master: When a lodge consists of three, who compose it?

Senior Warden: Right Worshipful Master, Senior and Junior Wardens.

Master: The Master's station in the lodge?

Senior Warden: In the east, Right Worshipful.

Master: His duty there?

Senior Warden: As the sun rises in the east to open and adorn the day, *etc.*

(*Master gives three Knocks; all rise. Master lifts his hat and bows to the Senior Warden*). Brother Senior Warden, have you ever traveled?

Senior Warden: I have, Right Worshipful.

Master: Whither?

Senior Warden: From west to east, and from east to west again.

Master: What were you in pursuit of?

Senior Warden: That which was lost.

Master: What do you allude to?

Senior Warden: The secrets of a Master Mason.

Master: Do you possess them, Brother Senior Warden?

Senior Warden: I do not, Right Worshipful, but I had a substitute, which I sent up into the east.

Master: Brother Senior Warden, you will please to take notice, it is my direction that the substitute of a Master Mason's word be returned into the west, there to be deposited until further called for, attended with its due guards, through the Deacons only.

(*Note: The Senior and Junior Deacons go before the throne in the east. The Master descends and stands between them, fronting the Senior Deacon. They go through the due guards and signs, from Entered Apprentice up to Master Mason. The Senior Deacon then gives the Master's word on the five points of fellowship to the Master, after which, Senior Deacon bows to Master and goes through the same ceremony with the Senior Warden, and Senior Warden gives the word to the Senior Deacon. During this time, the Junior Deacon is communicating the signs and Master's word to the Right Worshipful Master. Junior Deacon bows, and goes to the west to Senior Warden and goes through the same ceremonies with the Senior Warden, receiving the word from the Senior Warden. All take their stations.*)

Senior Warden says, The substitute for the Master Mason's word has been returned into the west correctly, Right Worshipful, there to be deposited until further called for agreeably to your orders.

Master (*bows to the Junior Warden and says*): Brother Junior Warden, please to take notice, it is my direction that this lodge of Master Masons be now closed, and stand closed, until our next regular

[31]

communication, unless sooner called on some special emergency, of which, due notice will be given. You will please to report the same to the Senior Warden in the west, that the Brethren may have due notice thereof, and govern themselves accordingly.

Junior Warden (*bows to the Senior Warden, and says*): Brother Senior Warden, you will please to take notice: it is the Right Worshipful Master's will and pleasure, *as above, etc.*

Senior Warden: Brethren, you have heard the will and pleasure of the Right Worshipful Master. You will please to take due notice thereof, and let it be accordingly so done.

Master: Together, Brethren. (*Gives all the signs, from Entered Apprentice to Master Mason*). *Gives three separate knocks, answered by the Junior and Senior Wardens, takes off his hat and says*, Brethren, I declare this lodge of Master Masons duly closed.

Examination of a Visiting Brother in the Tyler's Room.

Committee appointed by the Right Worshipful Master of three, of which no one wears a jewel. They assemble in the Tyler's room. The Tyler has reported Brother A from Lodge at place, etc.

Master: Are there any Brethren in the lodge who can avouch for Brother *A*? Brothers *B*, *C*, and *H*, you are appointed a committee to go out and examine Brother *A*.

(*They take a Bible with them*). *Tyler introduces them to Brother A.*

Committee: Brother *A*, we are happy to see you. We understand you wish to take a seat with us.

A: I do, sirs, if it is agreeable.

Committee: It is our usual custom in this lodge, sir, to demonstrate the Tyler's oath, or obligation. Have you any objection, sir, to take such an oath?

A: I have not.

Committee: Present the Holy Bible. Please to repeat your name, and say after me, I, *A*, of my own free will and accord, in the presence of Almighty God, and these gentlemen, do hereby, and hereon, most solemnly and sincerely swear, that I have been regularly initiated an Entered Apprentice, passed to the degree of a Fellow Craft, and raised to the sublime degree of a Master Mason, in a true and lawful lodge of Free and Accepted Masons, and never have been stood suspended, or expelled therefrom, according to the best of my knowledge. So help me God, and keep me steadfast in this, my Tyler's oath or obligation.

Committee: Have you anything whereby you can satisfy us that you are a Mason?

A: I have, sirs: signs, tokens, and words.

Committee: Give us some signs.

(*Gives the due guard and sign of an Entered Apprentice, etc., etc.*).

The committee return and report: Right Worshipful, we are satisfied that Brother *A*, from the lodge at *place*, is a Brother Master Mason.

[32]

Ceremony of Calling to Refreshment.

Master gives two knocks. Brother Treasurer, the Junior Warden's station in the lodge?

Treasurer: In the south, Right Worshipful.

Master: Your duty in the south, Brother Junior Warden?

Junior Warden: As the sun, *etc.*

Master: Brother Junior Warden, what is [the] clock?

Junior Warden: High twelve, Right Worshipful.

Master gives three knocks: Brother Senior Warden, you will please to take notice, it is my direction that the Craft be now called from labor to refreshment for a short space of time. You will please to report, *etc.*

Senior Warden: Brother Junior Warden, you will please to take notice, it is the Right Worshipful Master's will and pleasure, [*etc.*]

Junior Warden: Brethren, you have heard the will and pleasure, *etc.*

Master: Together, Brethren (*gives signs, three knocks*). I declare the Craft duly called to refreshment. Brother Junior Warden, the Craft is now under your direction. You will please to see they are duly refreshed.

[Ceremony of Calling to Labor]

To call to labor, Master gives one knock: Brethren, please to come to order. *All sit silent; gives two knocks. The officers rise*: Brother Treasurer, the Junior Warden's station in the lodge?

Treasurer: In the south, Right Worshipful.

Master: Your duty in the south, Brother Junior Warden?

Junior Warden: As the sun, *etc.*

Master: Brother Junior Warden, what is the clock?

Junior Warden: One hour past meridian, Right Worshipful.

Master: It is time the Craft are called to labor. *Gives three knocks, all rise.* Brother Senior Warden, you will please to take notice, it is my direction that the Craft be now called from refreshment to labor. You will please to report, *etc.*

Senior Warden: Brother Junior Warden, you will please to take notice, it is the Right Worshipful Master's will and pleasure that the Craft be called from refreshment to labor. You will please to report the same to the Brethren, *etc.*

Junior Warden: Brethren, you have heard the will and pleasure, *etc.*

Master: Together, Brethren. *Gives signs, gives knocks.* I declare the Craft duly called to labor for the dispatch of business.

Work in Entered Apprentice.

Note: When the candidate is prepared and brought to the door, the committee gives one knock, as a private signal that they are now at the door. Master gives one knock, and says, Ask and you shall receive; *one knock,* Seek and you shall find; *one knock,* Knock, and it shall be opened unto you.

The committee then gives the regular alarm: three knocks.

Master says, Brother Junior Deacon, Please to attend the alarm.

Junior Deacon goes to the door, answers the alarm, opens the door, and says, Who comes there, *etc., as in First Section of Lecture. Junior Deacon returns to his place.*

Master: Brother Junior Deacon, what occasions the alarm?

Junior Deacon: A poor blind candidate, *etc., the same as at the*

[33]

door. After the questions and answers are through between the Master and Junior Deacon, Master gives three knocks (all rise) and says, Brethren, you have heard the occasion of the alarm at the door in the ceremonies now about to be performed. I will thank you for your assistance and attention. Brother Senior Deacon, you will receive the candidate on the point of a sharp instrument presented to his naked left breast, and inform him as this is an instrument of torture, *etc.* (*See second section of lecture.*)

After this ceremony, the Senior Deacon takes the candidate under the arm and approaches towards the east, saying, No person should ever enter upon any great or important undertaking without first invoking the blessing of Deity.

Here a cushion is placed between the altar and the throne. They kneel.

Master says, Let us pray. Vouchsafe thine aid, *etc.* (*see Monitor*) *After prayer, the Master descends from the throne, puts his right hand on the candidate's head, and says*, In whom do you put your trust?

Answer: In God.

Master: Your trust being in God, arise, follow your leader, and fear no danger.

Senior Deacon rises, goes around the lodge whence to the Junior Warden in the south, where he makes a regular alarm.

Junior Warden: Who comes there?

Senior Deacon: A poor blind candidate, *etc., as at the door.* (*See first section of lecture.*)

Senior Deacon then passes on to the Senior Warden in the west, where the same ceremony is performed as before, and from thence to the Right Worshipful Master (see first section) when he is ordered to be reconducted to the Senior Warden, who causes him to advance by one upright regular step, his feet forming the right angle of an oblong square, his body erect towards the east; then kneels at the altar.

Master kneels opposite the candidate, takes off his hat, and repeats the obligation.

During this ceremony, the Brethren form a circle around the altar, all standing silent.

The Senior and Junior Deacons hold their rods over the candidate's head in the form of an arch.

After the obligation, Master rises and says, Brother A, what do you most desire?

Answer: Light.

Master then repeats the three first verses of the first chapter of Genesis, and says, In humble imitation of this august command, I say, let this, our Brother, see the light by which Masons work. Together, Brethren!

One clap of the hands is given. Master says, Brother A, on being brought to light, the first things that are presented to your view are the three great lights in Masonry, assisted by the help of the three lesser. *Here he explains the lights as in the first section of lecture.*

Here the work follows as in lecture, first section, vizt., the word and grip of Entered Apprentice. Master approaching from the east second time—presenting lamb skin, etc., as in first section of lecture to the conclusion.

The candidate is now ordered out to be invested etc., and returning to the Northeast corner of the lodge. See lecture first section, as a just and upright Mason, *etc. The Master then presents the working tools and explains their uses, and then reads the charge.*

[34]

Ceremony and Work in Fellow Craft Lodge

Candidate is divested of all minerals and metals, neither naked nor clothed, barefoot nor shod, hoodwinked, with a cable-tow twice around the naked right arm; and, thus prepared, is conducted to the door of the lodge and gives three distinct knocks.

Master says, Brother Junior Deacon, you will please to attend the alarm.

Junior Deacon goes to the door, answers the alarm, opens the door, and says, Who comes there?

Repeated here the same questions and answers as before. See first section in lecture. Junior Deacon returns to his place.

Master: What occasions the alarm at the door?

Junior Deacon: Brother A, who has justly and lawfully served his time as an Entered Apprentice, *etc. The same questions and answers as at the door.*

Master gives three knocks, all rise: Brethren, you have heard, *etc.* I will thank, *as in Entered Apprentice's work.* Brother Senior Deacon (*who advances before the throne*), after reminding the candidate of the manner in which he was received in the preceding degree, you will receive him on the angle of the square (*presenting it to him*), and inform him that the square of truth and virtue should be the rule and guide of all his transactions through life. Let him enter.

Senior Deacon then goes to the door and says, Let him enter. *After which he says*, Brother A, when you were received into the lodge of Entered Apprentices, you entered on the point of a sharp instrument presented to your naked left breast. You now enter this lodge of Fellow Crafts on the angle of the square, *etc. as above*. You will follow your leader.

He goes twice around the lodge, to the Junior Warden in the south, where the same etc., as at the door, and directs him to pass on to the Senior Warden in the west, and thence to the Right Worshipful Master in the east, as before; then reconducted to the Senior Warden in the west, who taught me to advance[8] *by two upright, etc., as in first section of lecture. At the first step candidate salutes the Right Worshipful Master with the due guard and sign of an Entered Apprentice.*

Master then descends to the altar, and says, Brother A, before we can proceed any further with you in this solemn ceremony, it will be necessary for you to take the oath or obligation, whereby you will bind yourself to keep inviolably the secrets of this degree.

The Master then orders the Senior Warden to cause the candidate to kneel on his naked right knee, his left forming a square, etc., as in lecture. Master kneels opposite. Brethren form a circle around the altar, the Deacons placing their rods in the form of an arch. Master gives the obligation; after which, Master rises and says, Brother A, what do you most desire?

Answer: More light.

Master: Brethren, I will thank you to assist me in bringing this, our Brother, to see more light in Masonry. Together, Brethren! (*Gives three claps of hands*) Brother A, on being brought to light in this degree, what you now discover more than you have before is one point of the

[35]

compass bare, the other being hidden, which is to signify as a Fellow Craft that you had received light as yet but partially.

Master then says, Brother [A],[9] I now approach you, from the east, under

8. *Who taught me to advance.* The change to first person suggests that Parker had the lecture (catechism) in mind.

9. The cipher mistakenly reads "Brother B."

the due guard, and sign, of a Fellow Craft, *then gives him the grip and word of a Fellow Craft. The work follows as in lecture, first section.*

The Second Section

When the candidate is dressed, the committee approach the door and give a regular alarm.

Master says, Brother Junior Deacon, please to attend the alarm.

Junior Deacon goes to the door, returns, and says, Right Worshipful Master, the candidate is ready to be admitted.

Master: Brother Senior Deacon, you will please to receive the candidate.

Senior Deacon goes to the door and says, Let him enter, *takes him by the hand, and says*, It was an ancient custom for all regular worthy Fellow Crafts to be received and recorded in the middle chamber of king Solomon's temple. In going their way thither, they had to pass through a porch, at the entrance of which were two great pillars, one on the right, and the other on the left. The second, on the right, called Jachin, and the first, on the left, Boaz.

Here the two pillars are chalked out on the floor, together with the flight of winding stairs, drawn in such a manner as to bring the seven steps opposite the Junior Warden. See lecture second. After the explanation of the pillars and stairs, the Senior Deacon and candidate arrive at the Junior Warden and give a regular alarm.

The Junior Warden rises and says, Who comes there?

Senior Deacon answers, Brother A, who has justly and lawfully *etc., as at the door on first entrance, the same questions and answers.*

Junior Warden demands the pass word of a Fellow Craft. It is given. He says, It is right. From whence did this word originate?

Senior Deacon: It was in consequence of a quarrel between Jephthah, Judge of Israel, and the Ephraimites. *Judges, 12th Chapter.* The Ephraimites, *etc. See second section, lecture.*

After which, the Junior Warden says, It is well. It is my direction that you pass on to the inner door of the temple, which you will find guarded by the Senior Grand Warden, who will demand of you the grip and word of a Fellow Craft.

They pass on to the Senior Warden, make a regular demand, he rises and says, Who comes there? Who comes there?

Senior Deacon answers, Brother A, who wishes to be received and recorded in the middle chamber of the temple as a worthy Fellow Craft.

Senior Warden: Please to give me the grip and word of a Fellow Craft.

Candidate gives it.

Senior Warden: The word is right. Please to enter.

They pass on towards the east, past the altar.

Master rises and says, You are now received and recorded in the middle chamber of king Solomon's temple as

[36]

a worthy Fellow Craft. I will now, with pleasure, present you the working tools of a Fellow Craft, which are the plumb, square, and level. *The Master now explains them (see Monitor).*

After this, the Master says, I will now direct your attention to the letter G (*points to the carpet*). *Master says*, This letter G, Brother A, is the initial of geometry, or the fifth science, on which Masonry is principally founded. By Geometry, *etc.* (*see Monitor*). This letter G further alludes to the sacred name of Deity (*Master gives three knocks, all rise and bow to the sacred name of Deity*) to whom all should, *as in second section, lecture, and the conclusion.*

Master then reads the charge, after which, he says, This charge, Brother A, it is my duty to communicate to you, not doubting that you will let the excellent precepts therein contained have their due weight upon you in all your transactions through life.

Thus Endeth the Work in Fellow Craft Lodge.

Work in the Master Mason's Degree.

The candidate is prepared by being divested etc., as in the other degrees, with a cable-tow three times around his naked body. The committee then make the alarm at the door, as in the preceding degrees.

Master: Brother Junior Deacon, see what occasions the alarm at the door.

Junior Deacon attends the alarm and inquires, Who comes there? Who comes there?

Committee: Brother A, who has justly and lawfully served his time as an Entered Apprentice, been passed to the degree of a Fellow Craft, and now seeks for further light in Masonry by being raised to the sublime degree of a Master Mason.

After the several questions and answers, the Junior Deacon returns to his place.

Master: Brother Junior Deacon, what occasions the alarm at the door?

Junior Deacon answers as at the door.

Master gives three knocks, all rise: Brethren, you have heard the occasion of the alarm at the door in the ceremonies now about to be performed. I will thank you for your assistance and attention. Brother Senior Deacon (*he advances before the throne*), after reminding the candidate of the manner in which he was received into the preceding degrees, you will receive him on the points of this sharp instrument, extended to his naked breasts, which signifies that as the vital principle of life lies within the breasts, so are the most valuable secrets of Masonry contained within the points of the compass, which are friendship, morality, and brotherly-love. Let him enter.

Junior Deacon goes to the door and says, Let him enter, *and adds*, Brother A, when you were received into the degree of Entered Apprentice, you entered on the point of a sharp instrument of torture to your flesh, which, you were informed, the recollection thereof might be to you should you ever presume to

[37]

reveal the secrets of Free Masonry unlawfully. When you entered a lodge of Fellow Crafts, you were received on the angle of the square, and informed that the square of truth and virtue should be the rule and guide of all your transactions through life. You now enter this lodge of Master Masons on the points of the compass, extended, *etc., as above*. You will follow your leader. *Goes three times around the lodge.*

Junior Warden knocks once as he passes the first time, answered by the Senior Warden and Right Worshipful Master; second round to Junior Warden, Senior Warden, and Right Worshipful Master, knocks twice; and the third round, three times each. During this ceremony, the Master reads: Remember thy Creator, *etc. Ezekiel, 12th Chapter (see Monitor). After the third round, makes an alarm at the Junior Warden in the south. Here the same questions and answers as at the door. He passes to the Senior Warden the same, thence to the Right Worshipful Master. The same questions and answers, after which the Master says*, From whence come you?

Answer: From the west.

Master: Whither are you traveling?

Answer: To the east.

Master: What are you in pursuit of?

Answer: That which was lost, which, by my own endeavors, with your assistance, I hope to obtain.

Master: It is well.

The Master then orders him to be conducted to the Senior Warden in the west, who teaches him to advance by three upright regular steps, his feet forming a square, and his body erect to the east, saluting the Master on the first and second degrees. The Master descends, and gives the obligation in due form. See lecture.

Master then rises, and says, Brother A, what do you most desire?

Answer: More light.

Master says, Brethren, I will thank you to assist me in bringing this our Brother to light.

All give three times three.

Master says, Brother, on being brought to light in this degree, what you now discover more than you had done before is both points of the compass bare, which signifies that you never should lose sight of the moral application of that useful implement for, by a due attention to its use, we are taught to regulate our desires, and keep our passions within due bounds with all mankind, but more especially a Brother.

Master then gives him the due guards, signs, grip, and pass word, and orders him to go and salute the Junior and Senior Wardens.

The candidate then approaches the east, and receives the following charge: Brother A, before we can proceed any further with you in this solemn ceremony, it will be necessary for you to travel, *etc.*

See the conclusion of the first section of the lecture in this degree.

Conduct the candidate to the preparation room.

[38]

Second Section

While the candidate is out, the Master appoints the three assassins, three Fellow Crafts representing the twelve, and the wayfaring man. They take their respective stations. When the candidate is clothed, he comes in blindfolded.

After a regular alarm, Master orders the Senior Deacon to receive him and conduct him towards the Northeast corner of the lodge, saying, It was the daily custom of our Grand Master, *etc. See second section of lecture, down to place when he arrives at the cushion. He kneels.*

Master gives three knocks, and says, Let us pray. "Thou, O God," *etc.* (*see Monitor*).

Senior Deacon then rises, goes on towards the south, saying, "After performing this pious duty, he then rose and attempted to go out at the south door."

Here the candidate is seized by Jubela, who says, Who comes here?

Senior Deacon: Your Grand Master, Hiram Abiff.

Jubela: The very man I have been waiting for. Give me the secrets of a Master Mason.

Senior Deacon: This is not a proper time to demand these secrets. Wait with patience, and in due time you shall receive them as justly and lawfully as I have done.

Jubela: Talk not of time, place, or patience, but instantly give me the secrets of the Master Mason, or I will take your life.

[*Senior*][10] *Deacon*: This is not a proper time, or place.

Jubela: Talk not of time, nor place, I say, *and then strikes him across the throat.*

Senior Deacon then goes on to the west, where he endeavored[11] *to make his escape out the west door. Here he was*[12] *attacked by Jubelo. Here the same questions and answers are given as before. Jubelo strikes him with the square.*

Senior Deacon then goes to the east gate, where he is seized by Jubelum, and the same questions and answers are given, with this addition the Senior Deacon says, The temple is now near its completion, and all those who are found worthy shall receive them as justly and lawfully as I have done.

Jubelum: What? Still persist? Then die!

Here the work follows like the lectures.

After the Fellow Crafts carry the body off and make their escape, confusion ensues. Assassins go into the south west corner of the lodge.

Master gives one knock, and says, Brother Senior Warden, what occasions all this confusion?

Senior Warden says as in lecture. In the second confusion, after orders are given to call the roll of the workmen, the three Fellow Crafts go up to the Master and confess their

10. Parker has "Junior Deacon."

11. The past tense suggests that the ritual was reconstructed from the lecture.

12. See above note.

guilt. Work the same as in lecture. Every time the Fellow Crafts are sent out and return, there is confusion.

Master gives one knock, and calls on the Senior Warden, who answers as in lecture.

When the body is raised, it is done in the north west corner of the lodge. The Brethren form a circle around the candidate, and the Senior Warden raises him on the five points of fellowship, and gives him the word. The Brethren and

[39]

officers all return to their places and sit down.

The Senior Deacon conducts the candidate to the throne, when the Right Worshipful Master rises and reads to him the following history.

Sacred history informs us that it was determined in the councils of infinite wisdom that a temple should be founded in Jerusalem, which should be erected to God, and dedicated to His holy name. The high honor and distinguished privilege of performing this sacred service was denied to David, king of Israel, because, as the Scriptures inform us, "He was a man of blood," and during almost the whole period of his reign he was agitated and distracted by the tumultuous confusion of war.

We learn also, from the same source, that the God of Israel promised David that, "Out of his loins he would raise up a seed to serve him." This divine and memorable promise was afterwards fulfilled in the person of Solomon, and in the splendid and unexampled career of his prosperity.

After David was gathered to the land of his fathers, and the last honors paid to his memory, Solomon ascended the throne and wielded the scepter of Israel, peace reigned within its borders, and all the children of Israel looked forward with particular satisfaction for the display of that wisdom which was destined to amaze and astonish the world.

In the second month of the fourth year of his reign, Solomon commenced the building of the temple which, agreeable to divine command, was to be erected to God, and dedicated to His holy name, the curious workmanship of which was calculated to excite the wonder and astonishment of all succeeding ages. Josephus informs us that, for the space of seven years, during which period the temple was erected, it did not rain, except in the night season, when the Craft were called from labor to refreshment, so that the work was not the least impeded in its progress, a striking proof of the care and protection of divine providence.

About this period, Solomon received a congratulatory letter from his particular friend, Hiram, king of Tyre, in which he offered him every assistance in his power, and manifested a strong disposition to participate, at least in some feeble degree, in these high honors which seemed to cluster around the throne of Solomon.

The building of the temple thus progressing with the assistance of Hiram, king of Tyre, and under the immediate inspection and direction of Hiram Abiff, the widow's son, the temple was well-nigh completed when several of the Craft, for the purpose of obtaining greater wages in foreign lands, became

[40]

the assassins of the Grand Master Hiram, and thus, for a short period, the completion of the temple was impeded.

You, Brother A, have this evening represented our Grand Master Hiram Abiff, the chief architect in the building of king Solomon's temple, as has been just remarked. He was assassinated near the completion of this superb edifice, and his death was seldom equaled, and probably never excelled.

A conspiracy was formed against his life by fifteen Fellow Crafts, who, seeing the work nearly accomplished, were fearful they should not be able to obtain Master Mason's wages when traveling in foreign countries, entered into a horrid conspiracy to extort from our Grand Master Hiram Abiff the secrets of a Master Mason, or to take his life. But twelve of them, dreading the evil consequences, were struck with horror at the atrocity of the crime, and recanted; the other three, who were Jubela, Jubelo and Jubelum, being more hardened in villainy, were determined to put their murderous designs into execution, and accordingly placed themselves at the south, west, and east entrances of the temple at the hour of high twelve, when the Craft were called from labor to refreshment.

It was the daily custom of our Grand Master Hiram Abiff, at this hour, to go into the temple to view the work, and see if there could be any improvement made, either for its utility or ornament, and also to draw designs on his trestle board, for the Craft to pursue their labors, after which, he entered the

Sanctum Sanctorum, or Holy of Holies, there to offer up his adorations and prayers to the true and living God for the sins of the people.

After performing this pious duty, he rose and attempted to go out at the south door, which he found guarded by Jubela, who demanded of him it three several times, in a barbarous manner, the secrets of a Master Mason, or he would take his life.

After some altercation, he made his escape and endeavored to pass out at the west door, which he found guarded by Jubelo, who in like manner demanded of him it three several times, the secrets of a Master Mason, and here a scuffle ensued.

He then endeavored to make his escape out of the east door, which he found guarded by Jubelum, who in like manner demanded it three several times the secrets of a Master Mason, but on his third refusal he smote him on the head with a common gavel, or setting maul, which felled him lifeless at his feet.

They then buried the body in the rubbish of the temple, until low twelve, or twelve at night, when they agreed to meet and consult what further to do with it. They met agreeably to appointment and agreed to carry the body a westerly course from the temple, and buried it at the brow of a hill called Mount Moriah, in a grave six feet long, and six feet deep. At the head of the grave they transplanted a sprig of cassia, that if occasion required, they might know where to find it, and then, for fear of detection, endeavored to make their

[41]

escape out of the kingdom.

The next day king Solomon heard of the confusion, repaired to the temple, and inquired the cause. The Senior Grand Warden then informed him that our Grand Master Hiram Abiff was missing, that he had not been seen since the hour of high twelve of yesterday. king Solomon ordered the Senior Grand Warden to cause the inner apartments of the temple to be searched, and also a roll of the workmen to be called, which being done the Senior Grand Warden informed him that the inner apartments of the temple had been searched, without effect, and also a roll of the workmen had been called, and there appeared to be three Fellow Crafts missing, who were Jubela, Jubelo, Jubelum, and from the similarity of their names, they appeared to be Brethren and men of Tyre.

King Solomon informed the Senior Grand Warden that there had appeared before him twelve Fellow Crafts, clothed in white aprons, and with gloves, in token of their innocence, and imploring his pardon, and informed him that they twelve, with three others, had entered into a horrid conspiracy to extort from our Grand Master Hiram Abiff the secrets of a Master Mason, or take his life, but they had recanted.

King Solomon then ordered the Senior Grand Warden to cause the twelve Fellow Crafts to be sent out three east, three west, three north, and three south, and search for our Grand Master Hiram, and also for the deserters from the temple.

They were sent out accordingly, and three of them traveling on the coast of Joppa met a wayfaring man, of whom they inquired if he had seen any workmen from the temple. He informed them that he had seen three, inquiring for passage into Ethiopia; but, not being able to obtain one, they had returned back into the country.

The Fellow Crafts returned to the city and reported. king Solomon observed it was of the highest importance that our Grand Master Hiram should be found, ordered the Fellow Crafts to be sent out again in the same directions.

They were accordingly sent out, and traveled for fifteen days, when three of them ascending a hill called Mount Moriah, one of them being weary and almost exhausted, sat down to rest and refresh himself. On rising, he accidentally caught hold of a sprig of cassia, which, coming up easily, the ground having been recently removed, had the appearance of a grave, which excited his suspicion, on which he hailed his Brethren and, while contemplating on the spot, they heard exclamations from the adjacent cliffs, accusing and excusing each other, which appeared to be the voices of the three assassins, or deserters from the temple.

Here, Brother A, is the origin of the three penalties. Jubela exclaimed, "Oh, that I had my throat cut across," *etc.*, ere I had been accessory to the death of our Grand Master Hiram. Jubelo exclaimed, "Oh, that I had had my left breast" cut ere, *etc.* Jubelum exclaimed, I am worse than you both. It was I that deprived him

[42]

of life. "Oh, that I had my body severed," *etc.*, on which they immediately rushed upon them, bound them, and carried them up to the city.

King Solomon ordered them to be sent up before him, which was accordingly done, and there confessed their guilt. He then ordered them to be taken without the gates of the city, and there severally executed agreeably to the imprecations from their own mouths. This was done under the direction of the Senior Grand Warden.

King Solomon then ordered him to send out the three Fellow Crafts to the place where the weary Brother sat down to rest and refresh himself, in search of the body of our Grand Master Hiram and, if found, to search for the secrets of a Master Mason, and see if they can be found on or about the body, or a key to them.

They went out, made search, and returned and reported that they had found the body on a westerly course from the temple, at the brow of a hill called Mount Moriah, in a grave six feet long and six feet deep, dug due west and east; that they had made search for the secrets of a Master Mason, but they were not to be found on or about the body, nor a key to them.

King Solomon then exclaimed the Master Mason's word is lost. He then requested the Senior Grand Warden to take suitable assistance and go out with him and endeavor to raise the body of our Grand Master Hiram for a more decent interment. They went out in procession and, on arriving at the grave, king Solomon lamented the fate of his worthy and particular friend, and exclaimed, Alas, poor Hiram! and wept bitterly.

After some pause he ordered the Senior Grand Warden to endeavor to raise the body of our Grand Master Hiram by the grip of an Entered Apprentice. He tried and could not, the flesh being putrid and slipped. He then endeavored to raise it by the grip of a Fellow Craft, which gave way in the same manner.

King Solomon then ordered the Senior Grand Warden to endeavor to raise the body by the strong grip, or lion's paw, and on the five points of fellowship, and the first word that should be spoken after the body was thus raised should be the substitute for the Master Mason's word, until future ages should find the right.

He accordingly raised the body on the five points of fellowship, and the first word that was spoken was by the Senior Grand Warden, who exclaimed ________.[13] This being the first word is consequently the substitute of a Master Mason. This word is neither Greek, Hebrew, nor English. This is the origin of this word, and the strong grip.

When the Fellow Crafts were sent out to the grave, on seeing the body, they involuntarily found their hands in this position, to keep off the effluvia

13. The open parenthesis symbol appears here to indicate the substitute word.

which rose from the corpse that had been buried already fifteen days, and is thus called the due guard.

On looking into the grave, and finding the body in such a horrid and mangled condition, they exclaimed, raising their arms, O Lord, our God, which is called

[43]

the grand sign of a Master Mason. Whenever you see this sign, it is your duty to repair to their assistance or, when you hear these words exclaimed in the night, when the sign cannot be seen, you will repair to his relief.

The five points of fellowship are foot to foot, knee to knee, breast to breast, hand to back, cheek to cheek, with mouth to ear. Foot to foot denotes we should never hesitate to go out of our way to assist a Brother; knee to knee denotes that we should remember a Brother in our devotions; breast to breast, that we should keep a Brother's secrets as our own, when given to us in charge as such, murder and treason excepted; hand to back, that we should endeavor to support a Brother when falling; cheek to cheek, with mouth to ear, is the manner in which the Master's word is given. You will please to give me that word as you received it from the Senior Warden (*they give it*).

[The Master's Carpet][14]

The Master then returns to his place, and says, Brother A, I would inform you that our Grand Master Hiram Abiff was buried three several times: first, in the rubbish of the temple; second, at the brow of the hill called Mount Moriah; third, under the Sanctum Sanctorum, or Holy of Holies.

king Solomon ordered a marble monument to be erected to the memory of so humble and distinguished an architect. On it was a virgin, weeping; before her, a book, open; in her left hand, an urn; in her right hand, a sprig of cassia. Behind her stood Time, with his hands enfolded in the ringlets of her hair.

The virgin, weeping, denotes the temple unfinished; the book, open, denotes that the life and death of our Grand Master Hiram are on perpetual record; the urn denotes that his ashes were safely deposited; the sprig of cassia,

14. The Master's Carpet lecture was delivered by the Worshipful Master in the east. While speaking he would point out the various symbols of the degree on a painted cloth (the "carpet"), or printed chart, which hung on the wall.

the timely discovery of his grave; Time, behind her, with his hands enfolded in the ringlets of her hair, denotes that, although our Grand Master was dead and the temple unfinished, yet time, patience, and perseverance accomplish all things.

The ninth, and last class of emblems,[15] are the gavel, the spade, the coffin, and the sprig of cassia: the gavel, with which our Grand Master Hiram was slain; the spade, which dug his grave; and the coffin, that received his remains. These, to the thinking mind, cause serious reflections. But, when we look forward to the sprig of cassia which bloomed at the head of his grave, it reminds us of that better and immortal part, which will survive the grave. It being the inspiration of that Supreme Intelligence whom we all adore and being the nearest resemblance of that Great Deity that pervades all nature, and informs us that we shall never, never, never die.

History Finished.

Master then proceeds thus: I now present you with the working tools of a Master Mason, which are all the implements of Masonry indiscriminately, but more especially, the trowel.

He then reads the charge, after which he says, This charge, Brother A,

[44]

it was my duty to communicate to you, not doubting but you will let the excellent precepts therein contained have their due weight upon you in all your transactions through life.

Master says, Brother Senior Deacon, please to furnish Brother A with a convenient seat in the lodge as a worthy Master Mason.

(*Note: For further instruction, the candidate is referred to the Holy Bible, Josephus, Villalpandus, Scott, Pennell, Anderson, and many other authors on Masonry, from whom he will receive much instruction.*)

15. Parker omits the first eight classes of emblems, which appeared in such works as Jeremy Ladd Cross's *The True Masonic Chart; or Hieroglyphic Monitor* (New Haven, Conn., 1819).

[*The Masonic Tablet: Captitular Degrees*]

Past Master's Lecture.

[Q.] Are you a Past Master?

[A.] I have the honor to be.

[Q.] How arrived you at that honor?

[A.] By being duly elected and installed to preside over a regularly constituted lodge of Free and Accepted Masons.

[Q.] By whom were you installed?

[A.] By my predecessor in office.

[Q.] What were the previous ceremonies at your installation?

[A.] I was conducted to the altar where I was caused to kneel and receive the oath or obligation of this degree.

[Q.] I will thank you to repeat the oath or obligation.

[A.] I A.B. of my own free will and accord, in the presence of Almighty God and this worshipful lodge of Past Masters, erected to Him and dedicated to Holy Saints John, do hereby and hereon most solemnly and sincerely promise in addition to my former obligations, that I will always hele, forever conceal and never reveal this degree of a Past Master which I am now about to receive to any in the world, except it be to a true and lawful Brother Past Master or any elected to fill the chair of a Master's lodge or in the body of a just and lawful lodge of Past Masters nor unto him or them until by strict trial, due examination or the lawful information of a Brother I shall have found him or them to be as justly and lawfully entitled to the same as I am myself. I furthermore promise that I will answer all lawful signs and summons that may be given or sent unto me from a true and lawful Past Master or from the body of a just and lawful lodge of such if within the length of my cable-tow; that I will aid and assist all worthy and distressed Past Masters, their widows and orphans in preference to any other persons, so far as I can do it without injury to myself and family; that I will rule and govern the lodge over which I am appointed to preside agreeably to the ancient customs, usages and laws of the Institution; that I will abide by and support the bylaws of the lodge, the constitution of the Grand Lodge under which the same is holden, and the general regulations of Masonry; I furthermore promise that I will not rule and govern the lodge over which I am appointed to preside in an arbitrary manner; that I will not preside over this or any other lodge without giving a lecture or part of a lecture, or if within my power causing the same to be done; that I will not wrong this lodge or suffer it to be done by others if in my power to prevent it knowingly, but will apprise them of all approaching danger so far as it shall come to my knowledge; all this I do most solemnly and sincerely promise without any equivocation, mental reservation or evasion of mind in me whatever, binding myself under no less penalty than that of having my tongue cleaved, so that I shall no longer be able to pronounce the word of this degree, so help me God and keep me steadfast in this my oath or obligation of a Past Master.

[Q.] After receiving the oath or obligation of a Past Master what did you observe?

[A.] The Right Worshipful Master approaching me from the east under the due guard and sign of a Past Master, who presented me his right hand in token of his continuance of brotherly-love and friendship, and with it the grip and word of a Past Master, and bid me go and salute the Senior and Junior Wardens as such.

[Q.] How were you then disposed of?

[A.] I was taken by the right hand by the Master of Ceremonies and conducted before the throne where I was caused to give my assent to certain ancient charges as contained

[2]

in the book of Constitutions.

[Q.] What followed?

[A.] I was then taken by the right hand and arm by my predecessor in office and conducted near to the chair for installation, where I had the honor of receiving a Masonic salute from the lodge, my predecessor exclaiming, "Brethren, behold your Master."

[Q.] What are the duties of a Past Master?

[A.] To rule and govern his lodge agreeably to the ancient constitutions, usages and laws of the Institution.

[Q.] What is the further duty of a Past Master?

[A.] It is the further duty of a present or Past Master to preside at all festivals, Installations and dedications of lodges, at the laying of cornerstones, of all churches, chapels, and other stately edifices.

[Q.] What further duties are required of a present or Past Master?

[A.] It is the duty of a present or Past Master to repair to the house of mourning at the decease of a worthy Brother, there to consult with his friends, take charge of the funeral ceremony at lodge, form a procession and attend the solemn ceremonies at the grave.

[Q.] Have you any signs in this degree?

[A.] I have.

[Q.] Please to give me the first.

[A.] (*He rises and gives the due guard.*)

[Q.] What is that called?

[A.] The due guard of a Past Master.

[Q.] To what does that allude?

[A.] To the penalty of my obligation; that I would rather have my tongue cleaved than reveal the secrets of this degree unlawfully.

[Q.] Please to give me the next sign?

[A.] (*The next Brother rises and gives it, crossing all penalties.*)

[Q.] What is that called?

[A.] The grand sign of a Past Master.

[Q.] To what does that sign allude?

[A.] To the penalties of my former obligations.

[Q.] Please to give your left hand Brother the grip and word of a Past Master.

[A.] (*They rise and give it.*)

[Q.] It's right. I greet you Brother G—. (*G is hard.*) To what does that word allude?

[A.] To the title of a Past Master.

[Q.] What is the title of a Past Master?

[A.] Right Worshipful.

(Master rises and takes the Brother by the right hand and says, "I greet you Right Worshipful Brother _____.")

(Thus endeth the Past Master's lecture.)

Ceremony of Opening a Past Master's Lodge

Past Masters may be made in a Mark Mason's Lodge, or rather the Mark Lodge is not closed but the Past Masters' is opened up in it. [*The*] *Right Worshipful now takes off his jewel and says,* Brother Senior Warden, I have important business to attend to, and I must go if the Brethren will excuse it.

Senior Warden says: Right Worshipful, if you leave us there will be no one to preside over the lodge.

Right Worshipful says: I cannot tarry, my business is urgent.

Senior Warden says: If you will have the goodness to preside until we can elect a Master, Right Worshipful, you will oblige us.

Right Worshipful says: If you will be expeditious I will.

He returns and says: Brethren, you will please to bring in your votes for a Master.

(*The votes are before prepared for the Candidate.*)

He is duly elected. On being informed he is much surprised. The Senior Warden then receives him and conducts him, or the Master of Ceremonies does it by the order of the Senior Warden, and conducts him to the altar where he receives the obligation. He is then installed in due form. He is then conducted to the Chair. The Brethren are then ordered by the Master of Ceremonies to form a procession and salute the new Master. This being done some of the Brethren make a disturbance.

Some of the Brethren say: Right Worshipful, I wish you would call the Brethren to order.

He knocks two or three times and says, Brethren, come to order.

They do not attend.

He is requested again to call to order, but being confused does not give his order correctly. Some of the Brethren inform him to give but one knock. He does this and all is [in] order.

(*But one Candidate can be brought in at a time. After all are received the charge is given.*)

[3]

The Lodge may close in due form, or in the Mark Master's degree. (*The jewels in a Past Masters lodge may be the same as in the Mark Masters degree.*)

Most Excellent Master's Lecture

[Q.] Brother, are you a Most Excellent Master?
[A.] I have been received and acknowledged as such.
[Q.] Where were you received?
[A.] In a regularly constituted lodge of Most Excellent Masters.
[Q.] How gained you admission?
[A.] By six distinct knocks at the door.

[Q.] What was said to you from within?

[A.] Who comes here?

[Q.] Your answer?

[A.] Brothers A, B and C (*as may be*) who have justly and lawfully served their time as Entered Apprentices, been passed to the degree of Fellow Crafts, raised to the sublime degree of Master Masons, been invested with the degree of Mark Master, been duly elected and installed Past Masters and now wish for further promotion by being received and acknowledged as Most Excellent Masters.

[Q.] What more were you asked?

[A.] If I came of my own free will and accord, if I was worthy and well qualified, duly and truly prepared, if I had made the necessary proficiency in the preceding degrees and properly vouched for, all which being answered in the affirmative I was asked by what further right or benefit I expected to gain admission.

[Q.] Your answer?

[A.] By the benefit of a pass.

[Q.] Did you give it?

[A.] I did not, but my conductor gave it for me.

[Q.] Please to give it to your left hand Brother.

[A.] (*They rise and give it.*)

[A.] It is right, I greet you Brother G—.

[Q.] To what does that word allude?

[A.] To the title of a Past Master, the honor I then sustained.

[Q.] Did this gain you admission?

[A.] It did.

[Q.] How were you then disposed of?

[A.] I was conducted six times around the lodge to the altar, where I was caused to kneel and receive the oath or obligation of a Most Excellent Master.

[Q.] I will thank you to repeat that oath.

[A.] I, A.B., of my own free will and accord, in the presence of Almighty God and this lodge of Most Excellent Masters, erected to Him and dedicated to holy Saints John, do hereby and hereon, in addition to my former obligations, most solemnly and sincerely promise that I will always hele, forever conceal and never reveal this degree of Most Excellent Master which I am now about to receive to any of an inferior degree, or to any in the world, except it be to a true and lawful Most Excellent Master or in the body of a just and lawful lodge of Most Excellent Masters nor unto him or them until by strict trial, due examination or the lawful information of a Most Excellent Master I shall have found him or them to be as justly and lawfully entitled to the same as I am myself. I furthermore promise that I will answer all lawful signs and summons that may be given or sent unto me from a true and lawful Most Excellent Master or from the body of a just and lawful lodge of such if within the length of my cable-tow; that I will aid and assist all worthy and distressed Most Excellent Master's, their widows and orphans in preference to any other persons, so far as I can do it without injury to myself or family; that I will abide by and support all the laws, rules and regulations of a Most Excellent Masters lodge, the constitution, laws and edicts of the Grand Chapter of the State, under which the same is holden, and the General Grand Chapter of the United States; that I will dispense light and knowledge to a Most Excellent Masters Lodge so far as I can do it according to the best of my abilities; I furthermore promise that I will not conduct in a manner derogatory to the honor I now sustain, or to the name by which I am about to be called which is that of a Most Excellent Master; all this I do most solemnly and sincerely promise

[4]

with a firm and fixed resolution to keep and perform the same, without any equivocation, mental reservation or evasion of mind in me whatever, binding myself under no less penalty than that of having my breast torn, *etc.* and my above to rot, so help me, *etc.*

[Q.] After receiving the oath or obligation of a Most Excellent Master what did you then observe?

[A.] The Right Worshipful Master approaching me from the east under the due guard and sign of a Most Excellent Master who presented me his right hand in token of a continuance of his brotherly-love and friendship and with it the grip and word of a Most Excellent Master.

[Q.] Have you any signs in this degree?

[A.] I have.

[Q.] Please to give me the first?

[A.] (*He gives the due guard.*)

[Q.] What is that called?

[A.] The due guard of a Most Excellent Master.

[Q.] To what does that allude?

[A.] To the penalty of my obligation, that I would rather have my breast, *etc.*, than reveal the secrets of this degree unlawfully.

[Q.] Please to give me the next sign?

[A.] (*He rises and gives it.*)

[Q.] What is that called?

[A.] The grand sign of a Most Excellent Master, or sign of admiration.

[Q.] To what does that allude?

[A.] To the grand sign and exclamation as given by the Most Excellent Masters when the keystone was placed on the royal arch of king Solomon's temple.

[Q.] Please to give your left hand Brother the grip and word of a Most Excellent Master.

[A.] (*He rises and gives it.*)

[Q.] It is right. I greet you Brother R——. To what does that word allude?

[A.] To the title of a Most Excellent Master, the character I now have the honor to sustain.

[Q.] Have you any other signs?

[A.] I have.

[Q.] Please to give me the next.

[A.] (*He rises and gives it. Grip covering all grips.*)

[Q.] What is that called?

[A.] The grand token of a Most Excellent Master.

[Q.] To what does it allude?

[A.] To all the grips of my former degrees, or the grip of all grips.

(Thus endeth the Most Excellent Master's lecture.)

Ceremony of Opening a Most Excellent Master's Lodge

The officers the same as in the Mark and Past Master's degrees, and the St. John the same. The Master of Ceremonies may commence in the Mark Master's degree, and continue through the Past Master's and Most Excellent Master's degrees.

Right Worshipful says: Brother Senior Warden, please to satisfy yourself that all present are Most Excellent Masters.

Senior Warden: I am satisfied, Right Worshipful, that all present are Most Excellent Masters.

Right Worshipful: Please to call the Brethren to order as Most Excellent Masters, reserving yourself to last.

Senior Warden: Brethren, please to come to order as Most Excellent Masters.

(*They come to order with the due guard of a Most Excellent.*)

The Senior Warden sits down.

Right Worshipful gives three knocks. Senior Overseer or Junior Deacon rises.

Right Worshipful says: Brother Senior Overseer, are we tyled?

Senior Overseer: I will go and see, Right Worshipful.

(*He goes out the door and gives twice three and is answered by the Tyler. He returns to his place and says*:) We are tyled, Right Worshipful.

Right Worshipful says: How?

Senior Overseer says: By a Most Excellent Master without the door, armed with the proper implements of his office.

(*The same questions and answers follow with the officers as in the three degrees.*)

Right Worshipful gives twice three (*all rise*) *and he says*, Brother Master of Ceremonies, you will please to form the Brethren in order, for opening a Most Excellent Master's lodge.

Brother Master of Ceremonies says: Brethren, you will please to form in due order around the altar.

(*The Brethren form in order around the altar, kneeling on the right knee, the left forming a square, right arms over the left, leaving an opening at the east, west, and north, for the officers.*)

Brother Master of Ceremonies says, The Brethren are now in due order for opening a lodge of Most Excellent Masters.

Right Worshipful says, Brothers Senior and Junior Wardens, will you have the goodness to assist me in opening a lodge of Most Excellent Masters?

(*The Right Worshipful Master, Senior and Junior Wardens descend to the altar in their several places and the*

[5]

Right Worshipful Master reads the twenty-fourth Psalm, stands after reading. The officers kneel with their Brethren, locking arms. All give twice three in silence, or balance twice three, when all rise. Right Worshipful Master, Senior and Junior Wardens go to their respective stations. Right Worshipful reads the one hundredth and twenty-second Psalm.)

Right Worshipful then says: Brother Senior Warden, please to take notice it is my direction that a Most Excellent Masters lodge be now opened and stand open for the dispatch of business until closed again. By my order you will be pleased to report the same to the Junior Warden in the north, that the Brethren may have due notice thereof and govern themselves accordingly.

Senior Warden says, Brother Junior Warden, you have heard the direction of the Right Worshipful Master. You will please to take due notice thereof and let it be accordingly so done.

Right Worshipful says: Together Brethren (*and gives all the signs from the Entered Apprentice up to the Most Excellent Master's degree, then gives twice three knocks, not answered by the Senior and Junior Wardens, and declares the lodge to be opened.*)

Work in the Most Excellent Master's Degree

Receive as many candidates at once as you please. The Master of Ceremonies and Junior Overseer go out.

Master of Ceremonies returns and says, Right Worshipful, the candidates are ready.

(*The Junior Overseer makes the alarm at the door.*)

Right Worshipful says: Brother Senior Overseer, please to attend to the alarm.

Senior Overseer goes to the door, gives twice three knocks. He is answered by the Junior Overseer. He opens the door and says, Who comes here?

He is answered inside as in lecture by Junior Overseer, Brothers A, B, and C, who have been regularly, *etc. and the password is given. Senior Overseer returns to his place.*

Right Worshipful says: What occasions this the alarm at the door, Brother Senior Overseer?

Senior Overseer answers: Brothers A, B, and C, who have been regularly *etc.*, as at the door, and gives the password.

Right Worshipful gives three knocks, all rise and he says, Brothers Masters, you will please to receive the candidates and conduct them six times around the lodge.

Right Worshipful reads 2 Chronicles 6:24 passage. The candidates step in the west and face the east and give the Right Worshipful a new sign, every degree beginning with the Entered Apprentice, up to the sixth degree. When they stop the Right Worshipful Master descends to the altar and gives the obligation. After the obligation the Right Worshipful Master presents them with the password; first, the Past Master's word, then the Most Excellent Master's word. They rise and he orders them to salute the Junior and Senior

Wardens as Most Excellent Masters. Right Worshipful Master takes his place (there is now a confusion).

Right Worshipful Master gives three knocks and rises with the lodge and inquires, What occasions all this confusion?

Senior Warden says the craftsmen are at a stand, that a keystone is wanting before they can finish their work; that none of them received orders to make it, the workmen had nothing further to do without your orders.

Right Worshipful says: Such a stone has been made and finished, no doubt agreeable to the original design of the temple. You will therefore take notice that it is my order that inquiry be made of the Overseers if any stone of that shape (*pointing to the mark on the arch*) has been presented for inspection.

Senior Warden orders the Master of Ceremonies to inquire. The Master of Ceremonies goes up to them who are now assembled; they inform him there was a stone prepared, but it not having the mark of any of the craft thereon, and they not knowing its use agreed to heave it over among the rubbish.

Right Worshipful says: It is my order that strict search be made for it in and about the temple, among the

[6]

rubbish.

They all look about for it and the candidate finds it. A procession is then formed by the Master of Ceremonies. They pass around the lodge three times, singing "All Hail to the Morning," conducted by the Master of Ceremonies. The candidate carries the stone the third time, they halt at the arch. The ceremonies now begin, they stop singing. The candidate then places the keystone in the arch. They all step back and give the grand sign and word. The Right Worshipful now descends with the Junior and Senior Wardens, and explains to them they origin of the sign (they return again). The Master of Ceremonies orders the procession formed again. They go around the lodge three times more and finish the singing. The first of the last three rounds Brethren take off their aprons and place them upon the altar; second time around, their jewels.

(*Most Excellent Master's lodge closed after the manner of opening. The Master of Ceremonies forms the Brethren around the altar kneeling on the left knee, the right forming a square, and left arms over the right; then close in due form.*)

Royal Arch Lecture[16]

First section, first lesson

[Q.] Are you a Royal Arch Mason?

[A.] I am that I am.

[Q.] How shall I know you to be a Royal Arch Mason?

[A.] By three times three and under a living arch.

[Q.] Where were you made a Royal Arch Mason?

[A.] In a regularly constituted Chapter of Royal Arch Masons.

[Q.] How many make a regularly constituted Chapter?

[A.] Nine Royal Arch Masons, consisting of the High Priest, King, and Scribe, Captain of the Host, Royal Arch Captain, Principal Sojourner, and the three officers of the veils.

[Q.] Whom do the three first represent?

[A.] Those three ancient Brethren who came past the Grand Council at Jerusalem and held their meetings in the tabernacle.

[Q.] Whom do the three latter represent?

[A.] Haggai, Joshua, and Zerubabbel. They were the three worthies who first brought to light the principal secrets of this degree after they had been buried in darkness from the death of our Grand Master Hiram Abiff. At the erection of the second temple at Jerusalem and as a reward for their merits were advanced to be the three officers of the veils.

[Q.] How many were there?

[A.] Four.

[Q.] What were their colors?

[A.] Blue, purple, scarlet, and white.

[Q.] What does the color of blue denote?

[A.] It is an emblem of friendship, and as such is characteristic of a Master's lodge.

[Q.] What does the purple denote?

[A.] It being composed of blue and red, is therefore placed between the first and third veils of those colors to denote the intimate connection that subsists between this emblematic degree and Ancient Craft Masonry.

[Q.] What does the scarlet denote?

16. This section begins at a normal paragraph break, and is not offset.

[A.] That fervency and zeal which ought to actuate all Royal Arch Masons as the principal characteristic of this degree.

[Q.] What does the white denote?

[A.] That purity of intention and rectitude of conduct which ought to govern all those who seek to gain admission into the sacred sanctuary or Holy of Holies.

[Q.] Where were those veils placed?

[A.] At the outside of the tabernacle.

[Q.] Why there?

[A.] To serve as a covering for the tabernacle, and a stall for the Masonic degrees.

[Q.] Why were guards placed there?

[A.] To take special care that none passed except such as were duly qualified, as none were allowed to [the] presence of the Grand High Priest and King, but the descendants of the Twelve Tribes of Israel.

[Q.] How did the children of Israel make themselves known to the guards?

[A.] By the same words and sign as were given to Moses when he was commanded to lead the children of Israel out of the land of Egypt and out of the house of bondage.

(Thus Endeth the First Section)

Second Section

[Q.] Where were you prepared for your exaltation to this degree?

[A.] In a place

[7]

representing the outer court of the tabernacle.

[Q.] How were you prepared?

[A.] By being divested of my outer apparel, my arms and breasts bare, hoodwinked, slipshod, with a cable-tow seven times around my body, accompanied by two worthy Brethren with like qualifications with myself, in which situation we were conducted to the door of the lodge by the hand of a Companion, where we were caused to give seven distinct knocks.

[Q.] To what do those seven distinct knocks allude?

[A.] To the seventh degree of Masonry on which we were about to enter.

[Q.] What was said to you from within?

[A.] [*blank*]

[Q.] Your answer?

[A.] Three worthy Brethren who have justly and lawfully served their times as Entered Apprentices, passed to the degree of Fellow Crafts, raised to the sublime degree of Master Masons, been advanced to the degree of Mark Masters, been duly qualified and installed Past Masters, been received and acknowledged as Most Excellent Masters, and now wish for further promotion by being exalted to the sublime degree of Royal Arch Masons.

[Q.] What more were you asked?

[A.] If we came of our own free will and accord, if we were worthy and well qualified, duly and truly prepared, if we had made the necessary proficiency in the preceding degrees, and properly vouched for, all of which being answered in the affirmative we were asked by what further right or benefit we expected to gain admission.

[Q.] Your answer?

[A.] By the benefit of a pass.

[Q.] Did you give that pass?

[A.] We did not, but our conductor gave it for us.

[Q.] Please to give it to your left hand Companion.

[A.] (*They rise and give it.*)

[Q.] It is right. I greet you Brother R—. To what does that pass allude?

[A.] To the title of a Most Excellent Master, the character we then sustained.

[Q.] What followed?

[A.] We were requested to await a time with patience until the Captain of the Host could be informed of our request and his answer returned.

[Q.] What was his answer when returned?

[A.] Let them enter and be received in due form.

[Q.] How were you received?

[A.] Under a living arch.

[Q.] Why under a living arch?

[A.] It impresses upon our minds that the principal secrets of this degree should never be communicated except under the living arch.

(Thus Endeth the First Lesson of the Second Section.)

Second Lesson

(First round)

[Q.] How were you then disposed of?

[A.] We were conducted once around the court of the tabernacle, then were caused to kneel and invoke the blessing of God.

[Q.] I will thank you to repeat that prayer.

[A.] (*They rise and he repeats:*) "Supreme Architect..." (*see Monitor*).

(Second round)

[Q.] After performing this pious duty how were you then disposed of?

[A.] We were conducted again around the court of the tabernacle, where we were met by the Captain of the Host, who demanded from us who we were and what were our intentions.

[Q.] Your answer?

[A.] We are three worthy Brethren who have justly and lawfully served our times as Entered Apprentices, been passed to the degree of Fellow Crafts, raised to the sublime degree of Master Masons, advanced to the degree of Mark Master, been duly elected and installed Past Masters, been received and acknowledged Most Excellent Masters, and now wish for further payment by being exalted to the sublime degree of Royal Arch Mason.

[Q.] What was then said to you?

[A.] We were informed that on pursuing our intentions we should be under the necessity of passing those disagreeable and rugged paths which all regular Royal Arch Masons had travelled before us, but before we proceeded further it would be necessary for us to kneel in due form and receive the oath or obligation of this degree.

[8]

[Q.] (*Gives seven distinct knocks, all rise.*) I will thank you to repeat that oath.

[A.] I A. B., of my own free will and accord, in the presence of Almighty God, and this Excellent Chapter of Royal Arch Masons, erected to Him and dedicated to Holy St. John, do hereby and hereon, in addition to my former obligations, most solemnly and sincerely promise that I will always hele, forever conceal, and never reveal any of the secret arts, parts or points, of the mysteries of Freemasonry appertaining to this degree of a Royal Arch Mason, to any person under the canopy of heaven except it shall be to a true and lawful Royal Arch Mason or within the body of a just and regularly constituted Chapter of such or unto him or them until by strict trial due examination or the lawful information of a Companion Royal Arch Mason I shall have found him or them to be as justly and lawfully entitled to the same as I am myself. I furthermore promise that I will answer all lawful signs and summonses that may be given or sent unto me from a true and regular Royal Arch Mason or from a regularly constituted Chapter of such if within the length of my cable-tow; that I will aid and assist all worthy distressed Royal Arch Masons, their widows and orphans, in preference to any other persons, so far as I can do it without injury to myself and family; that I will abide by and support all the laws, rules, and regulations of the Chapter of which I may become a member, the constitution, laws, and edicts of the Grand Chapter of the State under which the same is holden, and the General Grand Chapter of the United States; that I will keep a Companion Royal Arch Mason's secrets as my own, when given to me in charge as such, murder and treason excepted, and they left to my own discretion; that I will support the cause of a Companion Royal Arch Mason, right or wrong, so far as to deliver him out of imminent danger; I further promise that I will not draw the blood of a Companion Royal Arch Mason in anger, knowing him to be such; that I will not be at the opening of a Chapter unless there are nine regular Royal Arch Masons present, including the Tyler; nor will I be at the exaltation of more or less than three at one and the same time; that I will not explain the key or characters of this degree to any person, except it be to a regular Royal Arch Mason; that I will not give the grand Royal Arch Mason's word except in the presence of three regular Royal Arch Masons, we first agreeing by three times three, and under a living arch. All this I do most solemnly and sincerely promise with a firm and fixed resolution to perform the same without any equivocation, mental reservation or secret evasion of mind in me whatever, binding myself under no less penalty than that of having the, *etc*. So help me, *etc*.

(Third Round)

[Q.] After receiving the oath or obligation of a Royal Arch Mason, how were you then disposed of?

[A.] We were conducted around the outer court of the tabernacle, where was exhibited to us a symbol of a burning bush.

[Q.] Why was a symbol of a burning bush exhibited to you at your exaltation?

[A.] To impress upon our minds that the words and signs following were of a divine institution, and as such sacredly be received by the children of Israel, and by them transmitted to their posterity as marks by which they might make themselves known and be distinguished by each other ever after.

[Q.] What followed?

[A.] A representation of the destruction of king Solomon's temple.

[Q.] By whom was it destroyed?

[A.] By Nebuchadnezzar, king of Babylon, who in the eleventh year of the reign of Zedekiah, king of Judah, besieged the city, destroyed the temple, took away all the holy vessels thereof, the two brazen pillars, and the remnant of the people that escaped the sword carried he away captive to Babylon, where they

[9]

remained servants to him and his successors until the reign of Cyrus, king of Persia.

[Q.] Of what duration was their captivity?

[A.] Seventy years.

[Q.] By whom were they liberated?

[A.] By king Cyrus of Persia, who in the eleventh year of his reign issued his proclamation saying, "Thus saith Cyrus, king of Persia" (*reads second, see Monitor*).

[Q.] Whom did you then represent?

[A.] Three children of Israel returning from the Babylonian captivity.

[Q.] In this situation what answer did you make to the officers of Cyrus as contained in his proclamation?

[A.] Being doubtful as to the reception we should meet with from our Brethren, we said "When we shall come unto our Brethren, and shall say unto them the God of our Fathers has sent us unto you, and they shall say unto us, What is His name? What shall we say unto them?"

[Q.] Your answer?

[A.] I Am That I Am. And thus shall you say unto the children of Israel, I Am hath sent us unto you.

(Thus Endeth the Second Lesson of the Second Section.)

(Fourth Round)

[Q.] Did you pursue your journey?

[A.] We did, through hard and rugged paths.

[Q.] What did those hard and rugged paths represent?

[A.] The journey of the children of Israel in the wilderness.

[Q.] Did you meet with any obstructions?

[A.] We did, with several.

[Q.] Where did you meet with them first?

[A.] At the first veil of the tabernacle where, on making the regular demand, we heard the master thereof exclaim, "Who dares approach this first veil of our sacred tabernacle?" He supposing an enemy to be near alarmed his Companions who, when assembled, demanded "Who comes here?"

[Q.] Your answer?

[A.] Three weary sojourners, who have come up to help aid and assist in rebuilding the House of the Lord, without hope of fee or reward.

[Q.] What were you then asked?

[A.] From whence we came.

[Q.] What were you then informed?

[A.] That by an order of the Grand Council then sitting at Jerusalem, made in consequence of difficulties that had arisen among the workmen by the introduction of strangers, none were admitted to help, aid, and assist, in this so noble and glorious an undertaking, but the descendants of the Twelve Tribes of Israel; it was therefore necessary that we should be more particular in tracing our genealogy, and demanded of us who we were.

[Q.] Your answer?

[A.] We are of your own Brethren and kindred, children of the captivity, who have been regularly initiated as Entered Apprentices, been passed to the degree of Fellow Crafts, raised to the sublime degree of Master Masons, advanced to the degree of Mark Masters, received and acknowledged as Most Excellent Masters at the completion of the temple, were at the destruction thereof by *Nebuchadnezzar, king of Babylon, who in the eleventh year of the reign of Zedekiah, king of Judah, besieged the city, destroyed the temple, took away all the holy vessels thereof with the two brazen pillars, and the remnant of the people that escaped the sword, carried them away captive to Babylon where they remained servants to him and his successors until the reign of Cyrus King of Persia, by whose orders they are now liberated, and have come up to help, aid, and assist in this so noble and glorious an undertaking.*

[Q.] What more were you asked?

[A.] By what further right or benefit we expected to gain admission.

[Q.] Your answer?

[A.] By the benefit of a pass.

[Q.] What was that pass?

[A.] I Am That I Am. I Am hath sent us unto you.

[Q.] Did this gain you admission?

[A.] It did.

[Q.] What was then said to you?

[A.] Good men and true we must have been, or thus far could not have come. Further we could not go without his word, sign, and word of exhortation.

[Q.] What was his word?

[A.] I Am That I Am. I Am hath sent us unto you. Shem, Ham, and Japhet.

[Q.] What was his sign?

[A.] It was in imitation of that as

[10]

given to Moses when he was commanded to cast his rod upon the ground, and it became a serpent; and on taking it up it became a rod in his hand as before.

[Q.] What was his word of exhortation?

[A.] It was explanatory of that sign, and as contained in the book of Moses, Exodus 4:1-10 verse.

(Thus Endeth the Third Lesson of the Second Section.)

(Fourth Lesson of the Second Section. Fifth Round.)

[Q.] Where did you meet with the next obstruction?

[A.] At the second veil of the tabernacle where, on making the regular demand, we heard the master thereof exclaim, "Who dares approach this second veil of our sacred tabernacle? Who comes here?"

[Q.] Your answer?

[A.] Three weary sojourners, who have come up to help aid and assist in rebuilding the House of the Lord, without hope of fee or reward.

[Q.] What was then said to you?

[A.] We were asked by what further right or benefit we expected to gain admission.

[Q.] Your answer?

[A.] By the benefit of a word, sign, and word of exhortation, as given us by the Master of the First Veil.

[Q.] Did this gain you admission?

[A.] It did.

[Q.] What was then said to you?

[A.] Good men and true we must have been, or thus far could not have come. Further we could not go without his word, sign, and word of exhortation.

[Q.] What was his word?

[A.] I Am that I Am. I Am hath sent us unto you. Shem, Ham, and Japhet; Shem, Japhet and Adoniram.

[Q.] What was his sign?

[A.] It was in imitation of that as given to Moses when he was commanded to put his hand into his bosom, and it became leprous as snow, and placing his hand into his bosom again it became as his other flesh.

[Q.] What was his word of exhortation?

[A.] It was explanatory of that sign, and as contained in the book of Moses, Exodus 4:1-10 verse (*see Monitor*).

(Thus Endeth the Fourth Lesson of the Second Section)

(Fifth Lesson of the Second Section. Sixth Round)

[Q.] Where did you meet with the next obstruction?

[A.] At the third veil of the tabernacle where, on making the regular demand, we heard the master thereof exclaim, "Who dares approach this third veil of our sacred tabernacle? Who comes here?"

[Q.] Your answer?

[A.] Three weary sojourners, who have come up to help, aid, and assist in rebuilding the House of the Lord, without hope of fee or reward.

[Q.] What was then said to you?

[A.] We were asked by what further right or benefit we expected to gain admission.

[Q.] Your answer?

[A.] By the benefit of a word, sign, and word of exhortation, as given us by the master of the first and second veils.

[Q.] Did these gain you admission?

[A.] They did.

[Q.] What was then said to you?

[A.] Good men and true we must have been, or thus far could not have come. Further we could not go without his word, sign, word of exhortation, and signet.

[Q.] What was his sign?

[A.] It was in imitation of that as given to Moses when he was commanded to take the water from the river and poor it upon the dry ground, and the water which he took from the river became as blood upon the dry ground.

[Q.] What was his word of exhortation?

[A.] It was explanatory of that sign, and is contained in the book of Moses, Exodus 4:10 verse.

(Seventh Round)

[Q.] Where did you meet with the next obstruction?

[A.] At the fourth veil of the tabernacle where, on making the regular demand, we heard the master thereof exclaim, "Who dares approach this fourth veil of our sacred tabernacle, where incense burns day and night upon the holy altar? Who comes here?"

[Q.] Your answer?

[A.] Three weary sojourners, who have come up to help aid and assist in rebuilding the House of

[11]

the Lord, without hope of fee or reward.

[Q.] What were you then asked?

[A.] From whence we came.

[Q.] Your answer?

[A.] From Babylon.

[Q.] What were you then informed?

[A.] That by an order of the Grand Council then sitting at Jerusalem, made in consequence of the difficulties that had arisen among the workmen by the introduction of strangers, none were allowed to help, aid, and assist, in this so noble and glorious an undertaking but the descendants of the Twelve Tribes of Israel; it was therefore necessary that we should be more particular in tracing our genealogy, and demanded of us who we were.

[Q.] Your answer?

[A.] We are of your own Brethren and kindred, children of the captivity, who have been regularly initiated as Entered Apprentices, been passed to the degree of Fellow Crafts, raised to the sublime degree of Master Masons, advanced to the degree of Mark Masters, received and acknowledged as Most Excellent Masters at the completion of the temple, were at the destruction thereof by Nebuchadnezzar, king of Babylon, who in the eleventh year of the reign of Zedekiah, king of Judah, besieged the city, destroyed the temple, took away all the holy vessels thereof with the two brazen pillars, and the remnant of the people that escaped the sword, carried them away captive to Babylon where they remained servants to him and his successors until the reign of Cyrus King of Persia, by whose orders they are now liberated, and have come up to help, aid, and assist in this so noble and glorious an undertaking.

[Q.] What more were you asked?

[A.] By what further right or benefit we expected to gain admission.

[Q.] Your answer?

[A.] By benefit of the words, signs, and words of exhortation, as given us by the Masters of the first, second, and third veils, and the signet.

[Q.] Did these gain you admission?

[A.] They did.

[Q.] By whom were you received?

[A.] By the Royal Arch Captain, who conducted us into the presence of the High Priest, King, and Scribe, who were then sitting in Grand Council, by whom we were examined as it respected our skill in the preceding degrees; which meeting their approbation we were asked what part of the building we were willing to undertake.

[Q.] Your answer?

[A.] That we were inclined to undertake any part, even the most servile in promoting so noble and glorious an undertaking.

[Q.] What followed?

[A.] We were presented with the working tools and informed that from the specimens we had given of our skill in the preceding degrees no doubt could be entertained of our ability to perform any part, even the most difficult, but as it was necessary that the rubbish should be removed from the easternmost part of the ruins in order to lay the foundation of the second temple we were directed to commence our opperations there, and it was given us strictly in charge to observe and preserve everything of value as no doubt many models of excellence lay buried there which, if brought to light, would be of essential service to the fraternity.

[Q.] What followed?

[A.] We repaired to the place as directed and wrought four days without discovering anything of importance except passing several pillars in the different orders of architecture. The fifth day we came to what we at first supposed to be an impenetrable rock, but one of my Companions, striking with a crow, we observed it returned a hollow sound, at which we redoubled our assiduity and, after removing more of the rubble, we found it resembled the top of an arch, on the vertex of which was a stone of singular form, and on it certain mysterious characters which, from the length of time it had been buried, were now nearly effaced.

[Q.] What followed?

[A.] We, with some difficulty, raised it and night drawing on us we repaired with it to the presence of the High Priest, King, and Scribe, who were then sitting in Grand Council, for its

[12]

examination.

[Q.] What was your opinion of this stone?

[A.] That it was the keystone of a Mark Master Mason, and from the place in which it was found would no doubt lead to further discoveries of importance to the Craft, on which we were asked if we were willing to penetrate this arch in quest of further treasures.

[Q.] You answer?

[A.] That no doubt the task would be attended with difficulty and danger, that we were willing to undertake that even at the hazard of our lives.

[Q.] What followed?

[A.] We repaired to the place and, after moving several of the stones in order to widen the aperture, one of the Companions fastened a cable-tow seven times around my body; and it was agreed that if I should find the place offensive, either offensive to health or sight, I should shake it on the right as a signal for ascending, and if should wish to descend still further I should shake it on the left. In this manner I descended.

[Q.] What followed?

[A.] After some search I found in the recess of the arch three jewels. The place now becoming offensive in consequence of the moist air, that had been long confined there, I gave the signal and ascended.

[Q.] What followed?

[A.] We repaired with them to the presence of the High Priest, King, and Scribe, who were then sitting in Grand Council, for their examination.

[Q.] What was their opinion of this treasure?

[A.] That they were the jewels of our three ancient Grand Masters: Solomon king of Israel, Hiram king of Tyre, and Hiram Abiff, and from the place in which they were found no doubt would lead to still further discoveries of importance to the Craft, on which we were asked if we were willing to penetrate this arch in quest of further treasures, with an assurance that our merits should not go unrewarded.

[Q.] What followed?

[A.] We repaired to the place and I descended as before. The sun was now at its meridian height which directed its reflecting rays in at the innermost recesses of the arch, which enabled me to discover in the easternmost part thereof a pedestal of singular form overlaid with gold, and on its sides and top were certain mysterious characters.

[Q.] What followed?

[A.] Availing myself of this treasure I gave the signal for ascending; the vertical rays of the sun now darting full in my face, I involuntarily found my hand in this position, to guard my eyes from the intense light and heat.

[Q.] What followed?

[A.] We repaired with it to the presence of the High Priest, King, and Scribe, who were then sitting in Grand Council, for its examination.

[Q.] What was their opinion of this treasure?

[A.] That it was the Ark of the Testimony, but not knowing the characters on its sides and top ordered it to be opened.

[Q.] What were its contents?

[A.] A pot, a rod, and a Book of the Law, in which were deposited a key to those characters, and in which it was written, "I Am that I Am, and God spoke unto Moses," *etc.*

[Q.] What was their opinion of the contents?

[A.] That the pot was the pot of manna, which Moses by divine command laid up in the ark of the covenant of the miraculous manner by which the children were supplied with that article while traveling through the wilderness, and the rod was the rod of Aaron which budded and blossomed and brought forth fruit in a day, and which was also laid up in the side of the ark of the covenant, as a memorial of the appointment of the Levites to the Priesthood.

[Q.] How were those characters explained?

[A.] Those on its sides composed the names of out three ancient Grand Masters, and those on its top that great and sacred name which I am not authorized to give but in the manner I received it.

[Q.] How were your merits received?

[A.] The High Priest, King, and Scribe descended from their throne and

[13]

invested us with the principal secrets of this degree.

[Q.] How were those secrets communicated?

[A.] The Grand Royal Arch Word, in the presence of three Royal Arch Masons; we first agreeing by three times three, and under a living arch, and that great and sacred name in a reverential manner.

Officers in a Royal Arch Chapter

with their Jewels and Clothing and Titles

High Priest, King, Scribe, Captain of the Host, Royal Arch Captain, Principal Sojourner, three officers of the veils, and Tyler. High Priest wears a white robe, red velvet miter, with a triangle on front, a breastplate of twelve brilliant stones of various colors representing the Twelve Tribes of Israel, suspended from the neck, by crimson velvet, a Master's jewel, and carries a mallet. King wears a purple crown and robe, carries a scepter and wears the Senior Warden's jewel. Scribe wears a white turban or bonnet, a scarlet robe and carries a roll of paper; he wears the Junior Warden's jewel. Captain of the Host wears the Master Overseer's jewel which is a yellow metal and carries a sword. Royal Arch Captain wears the Senior Overseer's jewel, a yellow metal and sword. Principal Sojourner wears the Junior Overseer's jewel, a yellow metal and carries a rod. The Masters of the Veils carry swords, and the Master of the scarlet has a signet suspended from a button. Tyler wears two crossed swords and carries a sword. Furniture is the Ark of the Covenant, being a box of yellow color; name on the top is God in Masonic characters, and on the sides Solomon king of Israel, Hiram king of Tyre, and Hiram Abiff, in Masonic characters, containing a pot of manna in a small box, a small rod, and the Book of the Law. In the book is a key on chart folded, and in the box are Master Masons' jewels: three squares with blue ribbons. Tools are a crow, spade, and pickaxe.

Ceremony of Opening a Royal Arch Chapter

High Priest gives three knocks. Captain of the Host answers.

High Priest: Are all present Royal Arch Masons, Companion?

Captain of the Host: We are, Most Excellent.

High Priest: Are all the avenues to the temple guarded and secure?

Captain of the Host: I will send and see, Most Excellent.

Captain of the Host orders the Principal Sojourner to do it. Principal Sojourner goes to the door and gives three and one. Tyler answers. Principal Sojourner then assents to the Captain of the Host that it is guarded.

The Captain of the Host says, The avenues to the temple are secure, Most Excellent.

High Priest gives twice three knocks.

Royal Arch Captain rises and says: Companions, it is our Most Excellent High Priest's will and pleasure that you form in order for opening a Royal Arch Chapter.

They all assemble around the altar, kneel upon the right knee, interlinking hands right over left, in fellowship. East left open for the High Priest, King, and Scribe.

The Royal Arch Captain says: [We] are now in order for opening.

Most Excellent High Priest, King, and Scribe rise. High Priest reads 2 Thessalonians 3:6–17 verse. The Grand Council then descends to the altar, join hands, balance three times in silence; all rise from triangles and open a Royal Arch Chapter. High Priest, King, and Scribe then return to their places and the Companions take their places.

High Priest says: Excellent Companion King, please to take notice it is my direction that this Royal Arch Chapter be now opened and stand open until closed again by my order. You will please to report the same to Excellent Companion Scribe, that the Companions may have due notice thereof and govern themselves accordingly.

King says: It is the direction of the Most Excellent High Priest that a Royal Arch Chapter be now opened and stand open until closed again by his order. You will please to

[14]

report the same to the Companions that they may have due notice thereof and govern themselves accordingly.

The Scribe says: Companions, you have heard the direction of the Most Excellent High Priest. You will take due notice thereof and let it be accordingly so done.

High Priest says: Together, Companions.

All the signs are given from Entered Apprentice to the Royal Arch.

The High Priest then gives twice three and one knocks, and declares, This Royal Arch Chapter to be duly open for the dispatch of business. Companion Secretary, please to read the proceedings of the last Chapter.

Secretary reads. High Priest then calls for a vote approved by the Entered Apprentice sign.

Ceremony of Closing a Royal Arch Chapter

High Priest: Is there any further business, Excellent Companion King, before this Council?

King: I know of nothing further, Most Excellent.

High Priest: Do you know of anything further, Excellent Companion Scribe?

Scribe: I know of nothing further, Most Excellent.

High Priest gives three knocks: Companion Captain of the Host, are all the avenues to the temple guarded and secure?

Captain of the Host: I will send and see, Most Excellent.

Principal Sojourner goes, gives three and one at the door; Tyler answers.

Captain of the Host returns and says, We are secure, Most Excellent.

The High Priest gives twice three and one.

Royal Arch Captain rises, and says, Companions, it is our Most Excellent High Priest's will and pleasure that you form in order for closing.

They form around the altar as before, kneel on the left knee, linking hands left over right, Royal Arch Captain stationed at the foot of the altar afront the Council and says, Most Excellent, we are now in order for closing.

High Priest says: Excellent Companions King, and Scribe, will you assist us in closing this Royal Arch Chapter?

Council descends, and kneels, then repeats the following prayer, By the wisdom of the Supreme High Priest may we be, *etc.* (*See Monitor*).

After this prayer they link hands, balance three times three, all rise from triangles, after which all front the altar and the High Priest says, Excellent Companion King, you will please to take notice it is my will and pleasure that this Chapter of Royal Arch Masons be now closed and stand closed, until convened again by my order. You will please to report the same to the Scribe, that the Companions may have due notice thereof, and govern themselves accordingly.

King says: Excellent Companion Scribe, you will please to take notice it is the direction of our Most Excellent High Priest that this Chapter of Royal Arch Masons be now closed and stand closed until convened again by his order. You will please to report the same to the Companions that they may have due notice thereof and govern themselves accordingly.

The Scribe says: You have heard the direction of the Most Excellent High Priest. You will please to take due notice thereof, and let it be accordingly so done.

High Priest says: Together, Companions. *Gives all signs from the Entered Apprentice up and from the Royal Arch downward. Gives twice three and one and says*, Excellent Companion Scribe, how should we meet?

Scribe says: On the level.

High Priest says: How should we part, Excellent Companion King?

The King says: On the square.

High Priest says: So may we meet and part. Companions, I declare this Chapter duly closed.

Work in the Royal Arch Degree

After the Chapter is duly opened the candidates being prepared as in lecture they make a regular demand by twice three and one. Captain of the Host orders the Royal Arch Captain to attend the alarm.

Royal Arch Captain goes and answers the alarm and demands, Who comes here?

The Principal Sojourner conducts the Candidates and says, Three worthy Brethren, who have justly and lawfully served their times as Entered Apprentices, *etc.* (*as in the lecture*), and now wish for further promotion by being exalted to the sublime degree of Royal Arch Mason.

After giving the password they are admitted; they are then

[15]

conducted by the Principal Sojourner through the living arch. The Brethren form interlinking hands during this round. The Principal Sojourner repeats the following in Isaiah 4:16 verse; after passing around the first time they are stopped in the west by the Principal Sojourner, and caused to kneel and receive the benefit of a prayer as follows, Supreme Architect of Universal Nature, *etc.* (*see Monitor*).

(Second Round)

They are conducted the second time around at the same place under the arch. The candidates now meet the Captain of the Host, who demands of them who they are, from whence they came, and what are their intentions.

The Principal Sojourner answers: They are three worthy Brethren, who have been regularly initiated Entered Apprentice Masons (*as at door*), by being exalted to the sublime degree of Royal Arch Masons.

Captain of the Host says: It is well. In pursuing your intentions you will be under the necessity of passing through those disagreeable rugged paths which all Royal Arch Masons have travelled. But before you proceed any further it will be necessary for you to kneel and receive the oath or obligation of this degree.

Candidates receive it from the Captain of the Host.

(Third Round)

The candidates rise and go around the third time. As they are travelling the Principal Sojourner repeats the following in Exodus 3:1–7 verse. The candidates arrive at the bush at the words Moses, Moses, *and are unblinded. When Moses hides his face, they are blinded again. If there is time read 2 Chronicles 36:11–20 verse. Now the destruction of the temple commences, clashing of swords near the candidates making great tumult, etc. After which they are taken captive and carried into another room.*

The following is read by the Principal Sojourner while they are in captivity, the candidates being still blinded, Psalm 140:1–2 and 3, or either of them. After this is read the Captain of the Host goes to the door, opens it and reads the following in the hearing of the candidates, Ezekiel 1:1–3 verse.

After he has finished reading, Principal Sojourner says, I will go up, *and turns to the candidates and says*, Will you? *They answer*, Yes.

Principal Sojourner says to the Captain of the Host, How shall we be able to pass the guards?

Captain of the Host says: By these words you shall be able to pass, 'I Am That I Am. I Am hath sent us unto you.'

(Fourth Round)

The Principal Sojourner conducts them around the fourth time as before over rugged paths, they are then conducted to the first veil, where they give six distinct knocks, twice three.

The Master of the Veil exclaims, Who comes here? Who dares approach this first veil of the sacred tabernacle? (*same alarm*)

The candidates are now blinded but see not but the blue veil. The guards all assemble in the first veil and inquire the cause. The Master of the Veil informs them that it was indicative of the approach of enemies.

The veil is then drawn and the three Masters present their swords to the breasts of the candidates with a stamp, Who comes here?

Principal Sojourner says: Three weary sojourners who have come up to help, aid, and assist rebuilding the House of the Lord, without the hope of fee or reward.

Master of the Veil says: From whence came you?

Principal Sojourner: From Babylon.

Master of the Veil says: By an order of the Grand Council, now sitting at Jerusalem, made in consequence of difficulties that had arisen among the workmen by the introduction of strangers, none were allowed to help, aid, and assist, in this so noble and glorious an undertaking but the descendants of the twelve tribes of Israel. It is therefore necessary that you should be more particular in tracing your genealogy. We therefore wish to know who you are.

Principal Sojourner says: We are of your own Brethren and kindred, children of the captivity, who have been regularly initiated as Entered Apprentices, been passed to the degree of Fellow Crafts, raised to the sublime degree of Master Masons, advanced to

[16]

the degree of Mark Master, been received and acknowledged as Most Excellent Masters at the completion of the temple, were at the destruction thereof by Nebuchadnezzar, king of Babylon, who in the eleventh year of the reign of Zedekiah, king of Judah, besieged the city, destroyed the temple, took away all the holy vessels thereof with the two brazen pillars, and the remnant of the people that escaped the sword, carried them away captive to Babylon where they remained servants to him and his successors until the reign of Cyrus King of Persia, by whose orders they are now liberated, *and have come up to help, aid, and assist in this so noble and glorious an undertaking.*

Master of the Veil says: By what further right or benefit do you expect to gain admission?

Principal Sojourner says: By benefit of a pass.

Master of the Veil says: Please to give us this pass.

Principal Sojourner: I Am That I Am. I Am hath sent us unto you.

Master of the Veil says: Good men and true you must have been, or thus far could not have come. Further you could not go without my word, sign, and word of exhortation. My word is this: "I Am that I Am. I Am hath sent us unto you. Shem, Ham, and Japhet." My sign is in imitation of that given to Moses when he was commanded to cast his rod upon the ground, and it became a serpent; and on taking it up it became a rod in his hand as before. The word of exhortation is explanatory of this sign, and as contained in the book of Moses, Exodus 4:1-10 verse.

(Fifth Round)

The candidates are again conducted around the Chapter and arrive at the purple, where they make a demand as at the first veil by twice three knocks.

Master of the Veil: Who dares approach this second veil of our sacred tabernacle? Who comes here?

Principal Sojourner: Three weary sojourners, who have come up to help, aid, and assist in rebuilding the House of the Lord, without hope of fee or reward.

Master of the Veil: By what further right or benefit do you expect to gain admission?

Principal Sojourner: By the benefit of a word, sign, and word of exhortation, given us by the Master of the First Veil.

Master of the Veil: Please to give them to us.

Principal Sojourner gives them all as he received them.

Master of the Veil: Good men, *etc.* My word is "I Am That I Am. I Am hath sent us unto you. Shem, Ham, and Japhet; Shem, Japhet and Adoniram." My sign is in imitation of that as given to Moses when he was commanded to put his hand into his bosom, and it became leprous as snow, and placing his hand into his bosom again it became as his other flesh. My word of exhortation is explanatory of this sign, and is contained in the book of Moses, Exodus 4:1-10 verse.

(Sixth Round)

The candidates arrive at the scarlet or third veil, where they make a regular demand by twice three knocks.

Master of the Veil: Who dares approach this third veil of our sacred tabernacle? Who comes here?

Principal Sojourner: Three weary sojourners, *etc.*

Master of the Veil: By what further right, *etc.*

Principal Sojourner: By the benefit of the words and signs and words of exhortation as given us by the Master of the Veil.

[*Master of the Veil*:] Please to give them to us.

Principal Sojourner gives them all.

Master of the Veil: Good men and true, *etc.* Further you cannot go without my sign, word of exhortation, and signet. My sign is in imitation of that as given to Moses when he was commanded to take the water from the river and poor it upon the dry ground, and the water which he took from the river became as blood upon the dry ground. My word of exhortation is explanatory of this sign, and is contained in the book of Moses, Exodus 4:1-10. This is the signet.

(Seventh Round)

During this round of the candidates the following is read by the High Priest: Haggai

[17]

2:1-23, *and ends with* "as a signet, for I have chosen thee." *At the same time the candidates arrive at the white veil or fourth veil. Principal Sojourner makes the alarm as before by twice three.*

Royal Arch Captain: Who dares approach this fourth veil of our sacred tabernacle, where incense burns day and night upon the holy altar?

Principal Sojourner: Three weary sojourners, etc.

Royal Arch Captain: Who are you and from whence came you?

Principal Sojourner: From Babylon.

Royal Arch Captain: By an order of the Grand Council then sitting at Jerusalem, *etc.* (*as at the first veil*).

Principal Sojourner: We are of your own Brethren and kindred, children of the captivity, *etc.* (*as at the first veil*).

Royal Arch Captain: By what further right or benefit, *etc.*

Principal Sojourner: By the benefit of the words and signs as given us by the Masters of the first, second, and third veils, and the signet.

Royal Arch Captain: Please to give us the pass.

Principal Sojourner: I Am That I Am, *etc. etc. etc.*

Royal Arch Captain: What signs have you?

Principal Sojourner: The first was we see the rod, *etc.*, at the second, the leper's hand, *etc.*, at the third was the water poured upon the dry ground, *etc.*, and here is the signet of Zerubabbel. By these signs and words we have passed through the veils.

Royal Arch Captain: I am satisfied. Good men and true you must have been or thus far could not have come. I will now with pleasure introduce you before the Grand Council in the tabernacle. (*He then conducts them before the Grand Council and says*:) Most Excellent High Priest, King, and Scribe, I have the pleasure of introducing three weary Brethren who were captives in Babylon. They have proved themselves to be regular descendants of the Twelve Tribes of Israel, and have satisfied us as to the legal manner in which they have gained admission in to the holy tabernacle, by giving us the regular signs, words, and tokens; and here, Most Excellent, is the signet of our worthy Companion Zerubabbel. I know it well.

(*To the candidates*:) Have you wrought in the several degrees in the temple, and been advanced legally and regularly?

Principal Sojourner: We have, Most Excellent.

High Priest: Please to give us the signs in the preceding degrees.

(*They give them.*)

High Priest: At the commencement of your journey did you meet with any difficulties in going your way thitherward?

Principal Sojourner: We did, Most Excellent.

High Priest: Where did you receive the first pass word?

Principal Sojourner: From the Captain of the Host.

High Priest: What was that pass word?

Principal Sojourner: I Am That I Am. I Am hath sent us unto you.

High Priest: Have you examined them through the veil, Companion Royal Arch Captain?

Royal Arch Captain: I have, Most Excellent.

High Priest: Good men and true you must have been, or thus far could not have come. We are pleased with you, and you all merit our approbation. What part of the building are you willing to undertake?

Principal Sojourner: We are willing to undertake any part, Most Excellent; even the most servile in the performance of so noble and glorious an undertaking.

High Priest then presents them with a crowbar, a spade, and a pickaxe, and says, From the specimens you have exhibited in the preceding degrees, no doubt can be entertained in our minds of your ability to perform any part, even the most difficult. But it is necessary to remove the rubbish from the easternmost part of the ruins of the temple. You will therefore commence your preparations there, and we give it to you strictly in charge to observe and preserve everything of value which may be found as no doubt many models of excellence lie buried there which, if brought to light, will prove of essential service to the Craft.

(*Candidates bow and go out. High Priest reads Zechariah* 4:6–10 *verse. Candidates return and say*:)

Principal Sojourner: We wrought four days at the easternmost part of the ruins without making any discoveries of importance except

[18]

passing by the ruins of several pillars in the different orders of architecture. But the day being the fifth day, still pursuing our labors, we came to what we at first supposed an impenetrable stone, but one of my companions striking it with a crow, we observed it returned a hollow sound, at which we redoubled our assiduity, and after removing more of the rubbish we found it resembled the top of an arch, on the vertex of which was a stone of singular form, with which some difficulty we raised, and upon it found certain characters which by length of time are now nearly effaced. Night drawing on we concluded to repair with it before your Most Excellent Council. (*Gives the stone to the High Priest, who receives it.*)

High Priest: This was no doubt an elegant piece of work in its design (*shows it to the King and Scribe*). What are your opinions, Excellent Companions King and Scribe?

They say: It is our opinion that this must have been the keystone of a Mark Master Mason.

High Priest: It must be so. It is valuable. (*He then passes it over his eyes and dedicates it.*) Holiness to the Lord! (*High Priest then gives it to the King, who does the same, and then to the Scribe.*)

High Priest: This stone, from the place in which it was found, will no doubt lead to still further discoveries. Are you willing on the morrow to penetrate this arch in quest of further treasures?

Principal Sojourner: It is probable the task will be attended with difficulty and danger, yet we are willing, Most Excellent, even at the hazard of our lives, to promote so noble and glorious an undertaking.

High Priest: You will repair to the same place and work diligently and cautiously.

(*Candidates bow and go out. Again return.*)

Principal Sojourner: Most Excellent, on repairing to the place agreeably to your order we removed several of the stones to widen the aperture. My Companions fastened a cable-tow seven times around my body to assist me in descending the arch, and it was agreed that if I should find the place offensive, either to health or sight, I should shake it on the right side, as a token for ascending; and should I wish to descend still further, I should shake it on the left. In this manner I descended and after some search found those three jewels tied together. The place then becoming offensive by reason of the moist air, which had for a long time been confined there, I gave the signal and ascended. I have now repaired with them before this Most Excellent Council for your examination. (*He gives them to the High Priest*)

High Priest examines them and says, These were the jewels of our ancient Grand Masters, Solomon king of Israel, Hiram king of Tyre, and Hiram Abif. They are precious and valuable relics. (*They dedicate them.*)

High Priest: Are you willing again to penetrate this arch in quest of further treasures? You may be assured your merits shall not go unrewarded.

Principal Sojourner: However difficult and dangerous the task, Most Excellent, we are willing to hazard our lives in promoting so noble and glorious an undertaking.

High Priest: You will then repair to the same place again and be particular in your researches.

(*They bow and go out again. Return with the ark.*)

Principal Sojourner: Most Excellent, we repaired to the arch again, agreeably to your orders, and after removing several more of the stones I again descended as before. The sun had now risen at its meridian height and darted his refulgent rays in the innermost recess of the arch, so that I was enabled to discover in the easternmost part thereof a pedestal of singular form, overlaid with pure gold, on the sides and top of which are certain mysterious characters.

Aveiling myself of this treasure, I gave the signal, and ascending, the vertical sun darting its rays full in my face, I involuntarily found my hand in this position, to defend my eyes from

[19]

its intense light and heat. We have now repaired with this valuable curiosity before the presence of this Most Excellent Grand Council for your inspection (*He gives the ark to the High Priest*).

High Priest: This is something most precious and valuable.

King: It is indeed. What characters are those on the sides and top?

Scribe: It will open, will it not?

High Priest: This must be the ark of the testimony. Let us endeavor to open it. (*He opens it*)

High Priest: Here is a rod.

King: Here is a box.

Scribe: Here is a book likewise. (*He opens the book.*) What is this? It must be a key to those words on its sides and top.

High Priest: Let us read it. (*He opens the book and reads John 1:1–5, and Deuteronomy 31:24–26, and Exodus 25:21, and Exodus 16:31–34, and Numbers 17:10, and Hebrews 9:2–5, and Exodus 2:3.*)

(*The High Priest then lays down the book and opens the golden pot of manna. They all taste of it; High Priest, King, and Scribe consult together.*)

High Priest says: Companions, it is the opinion of this Most Excellent Council that this is the Ark of the Covenant; that this is the pot of manna which Moses, by divine command, laid up in the side of the Ark of the Covenant as a memorial of that miraculous manner in which the children of Israel were supplied with that article in the wilderness; that the rod was the rod of Aaron which budded, blossomed, and brought forth fruit in a day, and which was also laid up in the Ark [of] the Covenant as a memorial of the appointment of the Levites to the Priesthood. Those characters on the sides of the ark are the names of the three ancient Grand Masters, and this is the Book of the Law, written by Moses; this is the key to the characters. On the top of this ark is that great and sacred name which I am not authorized to give but in the manner in which I shall communicate it to you, my worthy Companions, as a reward for your fidelity and fortitude.

(*The High Priest places the contents in the ark again, closes it, and says:*) This ark is a sacred and valuable memorial of the goodness of God. We will therefore dedicate it to Him in due form. (*They all dedicate it.*)

The Companions now stand before the throne. The High Priest, King, and Scribe descend and communicate the Grand Secret Word of a Royal Arch Mason—the High Priest, Royal Arch Captain and one Candidate; the King, Captain of the Host, and one Candidate; the Scribe, Principal Sojourner and one Candidate. After which the High Priest communicates the signs and reads the charge of the word: The first syllable is Hebrew, the second is Samaritan, and the third is Chaldean, and each syllable signifies the sacred word in the respective language, and thus comes three times three. The Samaritan language is the Masonic language, or the key language of Royal Arch Masons.

THE MASONIC TABLET

CRAFT RITUAL

(Kingston, New York, 1822)
Facsimile

:Ast SC PE's L.

1. FM whce cm u]oviz[*sa na* PE]gmz[2. fm]gp[e g f h st jn t j]mqz[rsa]pq[lm 5 wt cm u hr o d]mpq[8 o lrn o sbdu *ym* psns nd mprv *flsm* n *ysm* 3 tn u r a]vs[n i prsm 4 i m *os* tkn nd cptd mg brs nd *swlf* 7 hw d u no urslf]pmz[o b a n 6 y hvg bn ftn trd]cma[nv dnd nd m wlng o b trd gn 3 wt mks u a n 2 *ym* obn 5 hw shl i no u o b n 4 y a crtn sn *nkt drw* nd e prft *stnp* f *ym* ntnc 1 wt r sns 2 rt *slgna, sltnzrh,* nd *srlcdnprp* . 3 pls o gv *em* e sn f n *Pe* . (rss nd gvs t) 3 hs tt ny llsn . 4 t hs o e *ytnp* f *ym* obn tt i wd rthr hv *ym* ‖ ct *ssrca* fm *re* o *re* thn o rvl e *strcs* f *erf ysm* nl]qmp[fly . 5 wt s a *nkt* 6 a crtn fndly r]cmz[bry *prg* wrb :a br *yam* no nthr n e *krd* s: wl *sa* n e *xl* . 7 pls o gv ur lft *dnh* br e *nkt* nd *prg* f *pe* (ty rs nd gv t) A gvs B e *prg* . B *sys* wt s tt A i *liah* B i cncl A. wt d u cncl B *l strcs* f ns n *ysm* xct t shl b nt a *urt* nd l]nmz[fl br r wn e *ydb*▪ *tsj* nd l]pmq[fl g f sch A wt s tt cld B a *prg* A *prg* f wt B *Pe* A hs t a nm. B t hs A wl u pls o gv t o *em* B i dd nt *os* rcv t nthr cn i *os* mpt t A hw wl u dsps f t B i wl *rettl* r *vlh* t wh u A u wl pls o *rettl* t B . *nigb* A u *nigb* f u pls (*eton* A gvs :ast *rettl* Be :e B prncs e *drw*) A t s rt : grt u br * 1. whr wr u :ast prpd o b md a n 2 n *ym trh* 3 whr :endy 4 n a *moor* djct o e g 5 hw wr u prpd 6 y bng dvsd f l *slrnm* nd *sltm* nhr *dkn* nr clhd bt nr † ‡ wh a ¶ abt *ym ken* n whh stn i ws cn]vizh[d:td o e dr f e g y e hd f a frnd wm i ftrds fnd o b a br 7 hw dd u no t o b a dr bng ‡ 8 y :ast mtng wh rstnc nd ftrwds *gng* dmssn 9. hw gnd u dmssn 2 y :i dstnt

1

!AST SC PE'S L,

dstnt *skcnk* 3 wt ws sd o u fm wn 4 wo cms thr 9 u
nsr 2 a *roop dnlb* cn]amz[ddt wo hs *gnl* bn dsrs f
bng brt *tuo* f drkn o *xl* o hv nd rev a *trp* f e rts nd
bnfts f ts *wRt* g rctd o § nd ddctd o h st jn *sa ynm* brs
nd *swllf* hv dn bfr *em* 1 wt mr wr u skd 4 f i cm f *ym*
wn fr wl nd crd f i ws dly nd trly prprd *yhtrw* nd wl
dflq f lfwl *ega* nd prpy *dhcva* fr l whh bng nsrd n e
vtrff i ws skd y wt *rhtrf* rt r bnft i xpcd o gn dmsn 7
ur nsr 8 y bng a mn *erf* brn f gd rprt nd wl rcmd 9
wt flwd 2 i ws rqsd o wt a tm wh ptnc ntl e *wrt rm* cd
b nf]qpt[rmd f *ym* rq]azp[st nd s nsr rtd . 1 wt ws
hs nsr wn rtd 4 . lt *mh* ntr . 3 hw dd u ntr 6. *no* e pt
f a *prks* nst]cnw[rmt prcg *ym dkn* lft *tsrb* 5 whr wr
u tn cn]prz[dctd 8 o e cnr f e g whr i ws csd o *lnk*
nd rcv e *tfnb* f a *ryrp* (*rm* gvs !i *skcnk* l rs) i wl thnk u
o rpt e *ryrp* " vch]qmz[thn *dia* " (*es* Mnr) 1. ftr recvg
e *tfnb* f e *rypr* wht wr u tn *skd* 2 . n wm i pt *ym* trst
3 . ur nsr . 4 . n § 5 wht flwd 6. *ym* trst bng . n § i
. ws tkn y e rt *dnh* bd o rs flw *ym* ldr nd fr *on* dgr 7.
whr wr u tn cndd . 8 wncc rnd e g o e jn . n e S. whr
e sm qs]avt[tns wr skd nd e lk nsrs]pqz[rtd . s t e
dr 8 . [illegible]dd e jn n e S. dsps f u . 4 *eh* drd *em* o ps *ne*
o e *sn* [illegible] e W whr e sm qs]pm[tns wr skd nd e lk
nsrs]maz[rtd . s bfr 3 hw dd e sn ne W dsps f u . 2 *eh*
drrd *em* o ps *n* o e *wRt rm* n e E . whr e sm qs]pna[
tns wr skd nd e lk nsrs]poz[rtd . s bfr 9 . hw dd e
wRt rm . n e E dsps f u . 6 h rdrd *em* o b rcndd o e sn
n e W . we tht *em* o dvnc y !a prt rgr *pts ym* ft frg e
rt ngl f n blng *rqs ym ydb* rct . twds e E . 1 . Wt dd
e *wRt rm* tn d wh u 2 h md *em* a n 3 hw . 6 n du *mrf*
5 wt s tt du *mrf* . 8 y *glnk no ym dkn* lt *en ym* rt frmg
a *rqs* ym *ydb* rct *ym* lt hnd sptg e h b *rqs* nd *sspmc ym*
rt cvg e sm n whh du *mrf* i rcd e *tho* r *nbo* f . n P.E .
rm gvs ! *i skcnk* (l rs) i wl tk u o rpt e *tho* r obn . i W

ſAST SC PE'S L.

H f *ym* wn *erf* wl nd crd. n e prsnc f *ytml* § nd ts wRt g rcd o hm nd dcd o h st jn d hry nd hrn mt sly nd sncy prs nd *rws* tt i wl *syl lah* frvr *lcnc* nd nr rvl ny f e *trcs* rts *stp* r *stnp* f e ms]qzp[trs f *erf ysm* o ny prn ndr e *ypnc* f *nvh* xpt t sl b nt a lfl br r wn e *ydb* f a *tsj* nd lfl g f sch nr . nt hm r tm ntl y du trl stt xnm r y e lfl nfrmn f a br i sl hv *dnf* hm]pm[r tm o b *sa* jtly nd lfl nltd o e sm *sa* i *ma flsm* . i frhr prs nd *rws* tt i wl nt rt tm *trp, tc vrc. krm tnp* stn r *vgn* tm *no* ny tg mbl r mmbl wry a *rttl, rfg* r chr *yam* bcm lgl r ntgl *os* tt e *stres* f e *tfrc yam* t ny tm b nlfly btnd l ts i d mt sly nd sncry prs nd rws wh a *mrf* nd *txf* rs]pagg[ln o pr*mf* e sm wtt ny *nvq* mnl rsrn slf rsvn r *trcs* vsn f *dnm* n *em* wtvr bndg mslf ndr *on* ls *ytnp* tn tt f hvg *ym* ‖ *tc ssrc* et 1 ftr rcvg e *tho* r obn f Pe . wt wr u tn skd 2 wt i mst dsrd & ur nsr 4 *xl* 5 dd u rcv t 6 i dd 7 hw 8 y e rdr f e *wRt mr* wh e stnc f e bn 9 . n bng brt o *xl* wt wr e ſast tgs prsd o ur vw. 6 ſi gt *sxl* n *ysm* sstd y e hp f ſi lsr 7 wt r e ſi grt *sxl* n *ysm* 4 e h b *rqs* nd *sspmc* 3 wt r tr mrl sss 2 e h b s gvn s o b e rl nd gd f r fth e *rqs* o *rqs* r ctns nd e *sspmc* o kp . s wn du bnds wh l mkd bt mr sply a br . 1 wt r e ſi lsr *sxl* n *ysm* 2 e *nus nm* nd *rm* f e g 3 wy r ty sd o b e ſi lsr *sxl* n *ysm* 4 bcs s e *nus* rls e *yd* nd e *nm* gvns e *tn os* ogt e *wRt rm* o ndr o rl nd gvn s g wh ql rglty 5 y wt r ty rprstd 6 . y ſi bng *srpt* plcd n a *rlgrt mrf* n e g *s w e* 7 ftr ts sxl wr xpd o u wt dd u *txn* bsv. 8 e *wRt rm* ppchg *em* fm e E ndr e du *drg* nd sn f n *Pe* wo prsd *em* wt s rt *nd* n *nkt* f s bry lv nd frdsp nd wh t e *prg* nd wd f n *Pe* bd *em* rs *og* nd slt e j nd sn s sch. 9 ftr sltg e j nd sns n P.e wt dd u *nxt* bsv. 2 e *wRt rm* ppcg *em* fm e E a ſe tm wo prsd *em* wh a *bml nks* r wt *rhtl nrp* whh *eh* nfrnd *em sw* n mbm f ncnc nd e bg f a n mr nct tn e gln flc r]qrmz[*nmr lgE* mr hn]arz[rbl tn e *rts* r *rtrg* r ny thr rdr tt cd b cn]pz[frd n *ew* t

:ED SC F PE'S L:

tt tm r t ny ftr prd y *gnk* prnc ptnt r ny thr *nsrp xpt eh* b a n wh eh hpd i wd wr wh ql plsr o *flsm* nd m o e fr]ovn[trny bd *em pts* o e sn n e W. wo tht *em* o wr t s n Ep. 3 hw sd n *Ep* wr s *nrp* 6 wh e *pt* trnd *pu* 7 ftr bng tht o wr ur *nrp* s an *P.e* wt wr u tn nfmd f. 5 tt grby o n ncnt csm n l rgr nd wl gvd gs i *sw* rqsd o dpt smg f e mtlc *dnk* nt fr]brvm[ts vlu ln *tb* tt t mt b ld *pu* mng e rcds n e rcvs f e g s a mmrl tt i *sw* tr md a n *tb* n stt xcmn i *dnf flsm* ntry dstt 1 hw wr u tn dspd f 4 i *sw* rdd o b rcndd o e plc fm wnc i cm tr o b nvsd f wt i hd bn]paz[dvsd f nd n du tm rtd o e g fr frtr nfmn . 3 ftr bng nvsd f wt u hd bn dvsd nd n rtrng o e g whr wr u :ast cndd . 2 o e *Wn* crnr whr i *sw* tht o *ys* wRt *rm* ns nd bn f ts *wRt* g i rtn u *ym* rty nd sncr *sknht* fr e nr u v cnfd n *em* n mkg *em* a n nd dmng *em* a *rbm* f ts mct nd nbl nstn . 7 whr wr u tn plcd s e yngst *Pe* 8 n e *En* crnr f e g *ym* ft fng a rqs ym *ydb* rct t e rt *hnd* f e wRt *rm* wo *sw* tn plsd to *ys* tt i tr std *sa* a jst nd prt n nd gv t o *em* stngy n *grhc* vr o *klw* nd ct *sa* sch. 5 wt dd e *wRt rm* tn prsnt u wh 4 e wrkg tls f *na Pe* 7 wt r ty 8 e :e o *hcn* gg nd cmn *lvg* 3 i wd tk u o xpn e *esu* f e : eo *hcn* gg 4 e :eo *hcn* et (*es* mnr) 1 i wl tk u o xpn e *esu* f e cmn *lvg* 2 e cmn *lvg* s *na* nstrmt et (*es* mnr.)

:Ed SC F PE's L.

1. U hv stsfd *em* br A *sa* o e mnr nd md f ur ntn nt ts dgr *tb sa* tr prs o be *ynm* sng]prz[lrts md *esu* f n ts ccsn i *hsw* o no wy u wr csd o sbmt o tm n e :ast plc wy wr u dvd f l *slrnm* nd *sltm* 2 fr :e rsns :ast n rdr tt i sd cry nog fnsv r dfnsv nt e g wh *em* 3 :ed rsn 4 bcs t e

Bldg f *gnk* sns *lpmt* tr *ws tn* rd e *dns* f x mr r ny *lt* f rn 5 hw cd e bldg f sch st]gm[pnds mg]rst[ntd *sa gnk* sns *lmpt* be rcd wht e *esu* f rn *slt* 6 bcs e *snst* wr l *dwh drqs dkrm* nd nbd n e qrs whr ty wr rsd e *rbmt sw* fln nd ppd n e *strf* f *nbl* nd crd n *stlf* y *aes* o *pj* nd fm tnc cnvd o *mlsrj* whr ty wr st *pu* wk wdn *slw* ppd fr tt prps nd wn e whl bldg *sw* cmpd ts svl *strp* fd o tt xt nct tt t hd mr e prnc f e ndy wrk f e spm rctt f e nvrs tn tt f umn nds . 3 wy wr u nhr *dkn* nr clhd 4 bcs *ysm* rgds *on* mn fr s wrldy wlh r nrs t *sw* thrfr o sgnf tt t *sw* e ntrl nd nt e xtrl ql]paz[fctns f a mn tt sd rcmd hm o b md a n . 5 wy wr u nhr bt nr † 6 t *sw* n cnfrmt o *na* srltsh csm dpd y ns nd w *dr* n e *kb* f *htr* t *sw* e mnr n frmr ts cn]snz[crng rdmg nd chn]pg[gg tt o cnfm l tgs a mn plkd ff hs *ohs* nd gv t o hs nhbr ts *sw* a tstmny n srl ts thfr w d n ts smn csn *sa* a *nkt* f r snct nd a plg f r fdlt n e bsn w wr tn bt thrb sg]beg[nfg tt w rnc r wn wls n l mtrs *sa* t rgds e *strcs* f *erf ysm* nd bcm bdnt o e *swl* f r nct nstn. 3 wy wr u ‡ w a ¶ bt ur *kcn* 4 fr svl rsns *!ast sa* i *sw* tn n drkn *sa* t rgdd e *strcs* f *erf ysm os* sd i ndvr o kp l e wld n ftr ntl ty sd bcm *sa* jlty nd lfly y tm *sa* i *sw* tn bt o d . 1 *!end* rsn 2 tt *ym* rt mt b tht o cncl bfr ym *sye* sd *rvcsd* e bts f *ysm* 3 !id rsn 4 tt hd i *dsfr* o sb]pag[mt o e fms nd cr]qua[mns md *esu* f t *ym* ntn nd thrb hv bn tht nwhty o b tkn y e *dnh sa* a br i mt y e stnc f e ¶ hv bn ld *tu* f e g wtt dsrvg e fm trf 7 wy wr u csd o gv !i dstnt *skcnk* t e dr. 8 fr !e rsns *!ast* o lrm e g nd nfm e *wRt rm* tt tr *sw* a cndt ppd fr ntn . 1 !end rsn 4 t *sw* o rmd *em* f a crtn xt n *rtprcs ks* nd *ey* sl rcv sk nd *ey* sl *dnf kcn* ndt sl b *dnp* nt u 3 hw d u ply tt xt f *rtprcs* o ur tn stn. 4 i *dks* e rcm]quaz[ndn f a frnd o b md a n i sgt dmsn th tt rcmn]oviz[dn i *dkcnk* t e dr f e g nd t bcm

1*

56 ED SC F PE'S L.

pn nt *em 5* wy wr u rcd pn e pnt f a *prhs* nst]qm[rmt prcng ur *dkn* lft *tsrb* 6 t *sw* o rmd *em sa* tt *sw na* nst]ovec[rmt f trtr o *ym hslf os* mt e rcln thrf b o *ym* cncnc sd i vr prsm o rvl e scts of *erf ysm* nlfy . 7 wy wr u cndd o e cnr f e g nd tr csd o *lnk* nd rcv e *tfnb* f a *ryrp* 2 bcs *on* prsn sd vr ntr pn ny gt r mpt ndertkg wtt ast nvkg a *gnslb* f *ytd* 3 wy wr u *dks* n wm u pt ur trst 4 bcs grbl o e *swl* f r ncnt nstn *on tshta* cd b md a n ft ws thrfr ncsr tt i sd prs *ym* blf n *ytd* thrws *on* obn wd b bndg pn *em 5* wy wr u tkn y e rt *dnh* bd o rs flw ur ldr nd fr *on* dnr . 6 bcs t tt tm i cd nhr frs nr prvnt dnr t ws thrfr o sgnf tt i ws tn n e *sdnh* f a tr nd trst frnd n wse fdlt i mt wh sft cnfd 7 wy wr u cndd wnce and e g o e jn n e s . 8 tt l e bn mt *es* i ws dly prprd 9 wy wr u csd o mt wh tse svl bst]piz[rctns t e j nd sns nd e *wRt rm* n e E . 2 bcs tr wr *sdrg* plcd t e *s* . *w* . *E* ntrncs f *gnk* sns *lpmt* 2 fr wt prps wr *sdrg* plcd n tse svrl stns . 4 o *es* tt nn psd r rpsd *tb* sch *sa* wr dly qlfd grbl o whh cstm i ws csd o mt wh tse svl bst]avz[rctns n rdr tt i mt b dly xmd bfr i cd b md a n . 5 wy wr u csd o *lnk no ur dkn* lft *en* nd nt *on* ur rt r bth wn i rcd e *tho* r *obn* f *na Pe* 6 bcs e lflt s sd o b e wkst *ds* f a mns *ydb* t ws thfr o sgnf tt t ws e wkst *trp* f *ysm* tt i ws tn ntrg pn bng tt f n *P*. *e 7* wy wr u csd o ly ur *dkn* rt *dnh* nd nt ur lft r bth pn e h b *rqs* nd *sspmc* wn i rcd e *tho* r obn f *na Pe* 8 bcs e rt *dnh* ws sd by r ncnt brn o b e st f fdlt ty hd a *ytd* wm ty wr]emc[shpd y e nm f *sdif* wo s smts rp]ovez[rstd y e rt *sdnh* jnd tghr nd t thrs y e hmn *srgf* hldg ch thr y e rt *dnh* e rt *dnh* thrfr w mk *esu* f *no* ts gt nd smn csn o tstf n e stnst mnr e sncrt f r ntns n e bsn w wr tn nggd 9 . wy wr u prsd wh a *bml nks* r wt *rhtl nrp* nd wy s tt sd o b *na* mbm f ncnc 2 bcs e *bml* et (es mnr) 3 wy wr u rqsd o dpt smg f a mtle *dnk* n e g 4. t ws o rmd *em* tt *ym* tn xtrml *roop* nd pnyls stn sd e a strkg *nsl* o *em* sd i vr ftr mt a frnd *tb* mr spcl a *yhtrw* br n e lks tn i sd cnsdr t *ym* *ytd* o cntrbt lbrly o hs rlf *os* fr *sa* i cd d t wht njry o *flsm*. 5 wy wr u plcd n e *En* crnr f e g *sa* e yngst *Pe* 6 bcs n l prtv *ysm* e ꞉ast *nts* f vry bldg s sly plcd n e *En* crnr t ws thr fr ncsry tt i sd b plcd n tt stn bng e yngst *Pe* o b nr e *wRt rm* tr o rcv tse ꞉ast nstr]avce[ctns *no* whh i sd bld *ym* ftr mrl nd *cnsm* dfc ths ndh e ꞉end sc꞉

꞉Id SC. PE's L.

1 . u hv stsfd *em* *sa* o e mnr nd md f ur ntn nt ts dgr nd e rsns wy u wr csd o sbmt o e svl sng]vac[lrts md *esu* f *no* tt csn *tb* u hv nt *ty* nfmd *em* wt mks a g r y wt a g s gvnd . n e ꞉ast plc i wsh o no wt mks a g . 2 a crtn nmbr f ns dly ssmbd wh e h b rqs *sspme* nd a wrnt r crtr mprng tm o wrk . 3 whr dd r ncnt bn sly ssmbl 4 *no* a hi *il* r n a lo vl 5 wy *no* a hi *il* r n a lo vl 6 e btr o bsv e prch f cns nd evs *srprd* scng r dcng 1 . wt fm s a g 2 *gnlb* 3 hw ng 4 fm e o w . 5 hw brd 6 fm btn e n nd s . 7 hw hi 8 fm e rth o e vns 9 hw dp 2 fm e sfc f e rth o e cnr 3 wy s a g sd o b *os* ng *os* brd *os* hi nd *os* dp 4 t s o dnt e nvrsty f *ysm* nd tt a ns chty sd b qly xtnsv 5 vry gt wt spts ts vst brc 6 ꞉i gt prs 7 wt r ty cld 8 *mdsw htgnrts* nd *ytb* 9 wy s t ncsy thr sd b *mdsw htgnrts* nd *ytb* o spt a g 4 bcs t s nesy thr sd be *mdsw* o cntrv *htgnrts* o *spt* nd *ytb* o drn l gt nd mprt ndr]vec[tkgs 3 y wm r ty rprsnd 4 y e *wRt rm* s nd jns 5 wy r ty *sd* *o* rprsnt e prs f *mdsw htgnrts* nd *ytb* 6 e *wRt rm* rprsnts e pr f *mdsw* t bng

spsd tt h hs *mdsw* o rl nd gvn s g . e sn rp]rsnts e pr f *htgnrts* t bng s *ytd* o *yap* e *tfrc* tr ws f ny tr b du nd *es* tt nn *og* wy dssfd hrmy bng e *htgnrts* nd sprt f l scts *tb* mr spcly ts f rs e jn rprs]maz[nts e pr f *ytb* t bng s *ytd* o cl e *tfrc* fm *rbl* o *tnmhsfr* t e hr f hi! ae whh s e *ytb* nd *yrlg* f e *yad 7* wt s e cvrng f a g 8 a cldd *ypne* r *yrts* vn whr 1 *dg* ns hp t lst o rrv 9 y wt mns 4 y e hlp f a *rddl* 3 wt s tt *rddl* cld 2 e thlg]oz[cl *rddl* whh *bocj* n hs vsn sw scngn fm rth o vn 1 hw *ynm* prncpl *sdnr* hs ts *rddl* 4 !i 5 wt r ty cld 6 *htf eph* nd cty 3 wy *os* 4 bcs t s ncsy w sd hv *htf* n § *eph* n *ytltrmm* nd cty o l mkd 5 whh f tse !i r c gtst 6 e !ithd cty 7 wy *os* 8 bes r *htf yam* b lst n st r *eph* n frtn tb cty xnds bynd e *vrg* thrh e bndls *smler* f trny 9 wh r e rnmnts f a g . 8 e *ciasm tnmvp* e ndn]rqm[td *lsst* nd *gnzlb rts 7* wt r ty 6 e *ciasm tnmvp* s a rprs]pqm[nttn f e *dnrg* flr f *gnk* sns *lpmt* e ndntd *lsst* s tt butfl *dtlsst rdb* r *gntrks* tt srrndd t wh e *gnzlb rts* n e cntr whh s cmmm]ozp[rtv f tt butfl *rts* whh prd o gid e ws mn f e E o e plc f r *srvs* ntvy 5 hw d u mrlz tm 4 e *ciasm tnmvp* s mbmtcl f hmn lf whh s *drqhc* et (es Mnr) 3 hw mny *sxl* hv u n *na Pes* g 1 !i hw r ty plcd 2 e w nd s 3 hv u nn n e *htrn* 4 nn 5 wy nt 6 bcs *gnk* sns *lpmt* ws plcd *os* fr *htrn* f e cptc tt e *nus* nr *nm* t thr *ndrm* hgt cd drt *on* rys nt e *htrn trp* f t nd *sa ysm* !ast rs n e *tse* nd sprd o e *tsw os* w *yllcnsm* trm e *htrn* a plc f drkn . 7 wt s e frntr f a g 8 e h b *rqs* nd *sspmc* 9 o wm d ty blng 4 e h b o § e *rqs* o *e rm* nd e *sspmc* o e *tfrc 7* wy r ty ts dcd . 8 e h b w dct o § t bng e nslbl gft f § o mn nd *no* t w blgt a *wn* dmtd br e *rqs* o e *rm* t bng e prpr *cnsm mlbm* f hs ffc nd s cntnly o *dnmr* hm f e *ytd eh swo* o e g vr whh *eh* s pntd o prsd nd e *sspmc* ó e *tfrc* fr y a du ttnta o ts *esu* w r tht o rglt r tlsrs nd *pk* r psns wn du *sdnb* 9 hw mny jls hv u n *na* *Pes* g 2 ŕy ŕi *lbvm* nd ŕi *lbvmm* 3 wt r e ŕi *lbvm* jls 4 e *rqs* ll nd *bmlp* 3 wt d . ty mrly *hct* 4 e *rqs* mrlte ll qlt nd e *bmlp* rctd f lf 5 wt r e i *lbvmm* jls 6 e rf alr e prft alr nd e *drblssrt* 7 wt r ty 8: e rf alr s a *nts* tkn fm e qry n ts rd nd ntrl stt . e prft alr s a *nts* md *ydr* y e *sdnh* f e *nmkrw* o b djtd y e *gnkrw slt* f a *tfrcwlf* nd e *drblssrt* s fr e *mr* o *wrd* s *sngsd* pn 9 hw d u mrlz tm 8 y e *rf* alr et (*cs* mnr) 1 hw s a g std 2 du e nd w 3 wy *os* 4 fr svl rsns ŕast bcs e *nus* e *ytb* nd *yrlg* f e *yad* rs n e *tse* nd sts n e *tsw* 5 ŕend rsn 6 bcs l rts nd scncs *sa* wl *sa ysm* ŕast rs n e *tse* nd sprd o e *tsw* 7 ŕithd rsn 8 bcs l chs nd chls r r ogt o b *os* std 9 wy r l chs nd chls *os* std 2 bcs tt ws e stn f *gnk* sns *lpmt* 3 nd wy ws *gnk* sns *lpmt os* std 4 bcs ftr *ssom* hd bn ns tr]qua[mntl n cndtg e *ndlhc* f *lrsi* thrh e *es dr* wn prsd y . *horhp* nd hs hst *eh* tr y dvn cmnd rctd a *lcnrbt* whh *eh* plcd du *tse* nd *tsw* o prptt e mmry f tt mrls *tse dnw* y whh tr mty *cnrvld* ws wrt ts *lcnrbt* ws *na* xt mdl f *gnk* sns *lpmt* nd fr whh rsn ts nd vry rgh nd wl gvnd g s r ogt o b *os* std 5 o wm wr gs dcd n ncnt tms 6 o *gnk* sn 7 wy o *gnk* sn 8 bcs *eh* ws r ŕast mst xclt grd *rm* 8 o wm r gs dcd n mdrn tms 4 o st jn e *tstpb* nd st jn e *tslgnv* 1 wy o tse ŕe 2 bcs ty wr mnt xian ptrns f *ysm* nd snc tr tm thr s rprsntd n vry rgr nd wl gvnd g a crtn *tnp* wn a crcl (*es* Mnr) 3 wt r e tnts f ur prfsn *sa* a n 4 bry lv *flr* nd *htrt* 5 i wl tk u o xpln e tnt f bry lv 6 y e xrcs f bry lv et (*es* Mnr) 7 i wl tk u o xpln e tnt f *flr* 8 o *vlr* e dstrsd et (*es* Mnr) 9 i wl tk u s xpln e tnt f *htrt* 8 *htrt* s a dvn trbt et (*es* Mnr) 7 u nfmd *em* tt i sd no u o b a n y a crtn sn *nkt* wrd nd e prft *stnp* f ur ntnc e frmr u hv xplnd o *em tb* nt e ltr e *pnts* i wsh o no wt ty r nd hw *ynm*

10 ⁝ED SC. EP'S L.

thr r . 6 thr r ⁝o e gtrl e pctrl e mnl nd e pdl 5 wh d ty frthr lld o 4 o e ⁝ o *lndrc strv* whh r tmprnc *dtrf cndrp* nd *ctsj* 3 i wl tk u o xpln e *lndrc utrv* f tmprnc 4 cndt rss wh e du *drg* f *na Pe* nd sys tmprnc s tt du rstrnt et (*es* Mnr) wh ts ddn " nd whh wd *yltnqsnc* sbjt hm o e ⁝ast *ytnp* f hs obn tt f hvg s ‖ *tc ssrc* et whh llds o e gtrl 5 i wl tk u o xpln e *lndrc utrv* f *dtrf* 6 *dtrf* s tt nbl nd stdy prps f e *dnm* (*es* Mnr) wh ts ddn nd whh ws mbmtclg rprs]ovrc[ntd *no* hs ⁝*ast* dmsn nt e g y bng rcd *no* a *prhs* nst]abac[rmt prcng hs *dkn* lft *tsrb* wh llds o e pctrl . 7 i wl tk u o xpln e *lndrc utrv* f *cndrp* 8 *cndrp* tchs *su* o rglt r lvs nd ctns (*es* Mnr) wh ts ddn vr brng n *dnm* tt mmrbl prd wn hs lft *enk* ws br bnt hs rt frmg a *rqs* hs *ydb* rct hs lt *dnh* sprg e h b *rqs* nd *sspmc* hs *dkn* rt *dn* cvrng e sm whh llds o e mnl . 9 i wl tk u o xpln e *lndrc utrv* f *ctsj* . 4 *ctsj* s tt stndrd r bndr f rt et (*es* Mnr) wh ts ddn vr rmmbrg e tm wn *eh* ws plcd n e *htrn tse* crnr f e g *sa* e *tsgny Pe* hs ft frmg a *rqs* hs *ydb* rct t e rt *dnh* f e *wRm* wo ws tn plsd o *yas* tt *eh* thr std *sa* a *tsj* nd prt n nd gv t o hm strny n *grhc* vr o *klw* nd *tca sa* sch whh llds o e pdl . 3 wh wt dd *Pes* srv tr *srm* n ncnt tms nd wt ogt ty o n mdrn . 2 wh frdm frvnc nd zl . 1 y wt r ty rp]ova[sntd 6 y *klhc locrhc* nd *ylc* . 7 wy d *klhc locrhc* nd *ylc* rprs]pav[nt frdm frvm nd zl 8 bcs thr s nog mr *erf* thn *klhc* fr *no* e sltst *hct t* wl lv a trc *dnhb* thr s nog mr frvnt thn *locrhc* whh wn wl ltd wl cs e mst bdrt *sltm* o *dley* nd thr s nog mr zls tkn *ylc* r r *rhtm* rth whh s cnst]ovu[nty mpld fr mns *esu* nd t e sm tm rmng *su* tt *sa* fm t w cm *os* nt t w mst l rtrn ths ndh e *Pes L* .

⁝Ast SC n e *stfrc wllf* L.

1 br wl ŭ b ff r fm 2 i wl b fm 3 fm wt 4 fm e dgr f *na Pe* o tt f a *tfrc wllf* 5 tn u r a *tfrc wllf* i prsm . 6 i *ma yrt em* 7 hw wl u b *drt* 8 y e *rqs* 9 wy y e *rqs* 2 bcs tt s ⁝a f e wrkg *slt* f *ym* prfsn 3 wt s a *rqs* 4 *na lgna* f ⁝ zo dgrs r e ⁝oth *trp* f a crcl 5 wt ndcd u o bcm a *tfrc wllf* 6 n rdr tt i mt btn ws e btr o sprt *flsym* nd sst a *ythrw* ds]pnze[trsd *tfrc wllf* 1 . whr ws u md a *tfrc wllf* 4 n e *ydb* f a *tsj* nd lfl g *f stfrc wllf* dly ssm]pnq[bd nd *ylgl* cnstd 3 whr ws y prpd o b md a *tfrc wllf* 2 n a *moor* djct o e g . 5 hw wr u prpd . 6 y bng dvsd f l *sbrnm* nd *sltm* nhr *dkn* nr clhd bt nr † ‡ wh a ¶ ⁝ece rnd *ym dkn* rt *mr* 7 wy hd u a ‡ ⁝ ece rnd wr *dk*n rt *mr* 8 t ws o dnt *sa* a *tfrc wlllf* tt i ws ndr a dbl ti o e *ytnrtrf*. 9 whr wr u tn cndd 8 o e dr f e g y e *dnh* f a br whr i ws csd o gv ⁝i dstnt *skn* 7 o wt d ths ⁝i dstnt *shcnk* lld 6 o e jls f a *tfrc wllf* 5 wt r ty 4 e lsng *re* e nstrv *gnt* nd fhfl *trbs* 3 i wl thk u o xpn tm 2 e lsng *re* rcvs e snd fm e nstrv *gnt* nd e scrd *srtsym* f *erf ysm* r sfy gd n e rpstry f a fhfl *tsrb* 1 . wt ws sd o u fin wn 2 wo cms thr rpd 3 ur nsr 4 a br wo hs *ytsj* nd lfly srd hs tm *sa na Pe* nd nw sks fr *rhtrf xl* n *ysm* y bng psd o e dgr f a *tfrc wllf* 5 wt mr wr u skd 6 f i cm f *ym* wn *erf* wl nd crd f i ws dly nd trly prpd *yhtrw* nd wl *dflq* f i hd md e ncsy prfcnc n e prcdg dgr nd prpry *dchcv* fr l whh bng nsrd n e vtrff i ws skd y wt *rhtrf* rt r bnft i xpcd o gn dmsn . 7 ur nsr 8 y e bnft f a ps . 9 dd u gv tt ps . 2 i dd nt *tb ym* cndr gv t fr *em* . 2 pls o gv t o ur lt *dnh* br (ty rs nd gv t (!) t s rt i grt u br ? 3 wt flwd 4 i ws rqsd o wt a tm wh

ptnc ntl e *wRt rm* cd b nf [grm[rmd f *ym* rq]pct[st nd his nsr rtd 7 wt ws hs nsr wn rtd 8 lt *mh* ntr 5 hw dd u ntr 6 n e *lgna* f e *rqs* prsnd o *ym dkn* rt *tsrb* whh ws o *hct em* tt e *rqs* f *htrt* nd *utrv* sd b e rl nd gid f l *ym* trns]paz[cns thrh lf. 9 whr wr u tn cn]qmt[dctd . 8 !ece rnd e g o e jn n e s . whr e sm qs]pvt[tns wr skd nd e l k nsrs rtd *sa* t e dr 7 hw dd e jn n e s dsps f u 6 *eh* rdrd *em* o ps *no* o e sn n e W; whr e sm qs]avcc[tns wr skd nd e lk nsrs]pmq[rtd *sa* bfr 5 hw dd e sn n e W dsps f u 4 *eh* rdrd *em* o ps *no* o e *wRt rm* n e E whr e sm qs tns wr skd nd e lk nsrs rtd *sa* bfr . 3 hw dd e *wRt rm* n e E dsps f u 2 *eh* rdrd cm o b rcndd o e sn n e W. we tht em o dvnc y !e prt rgr *spts ym* ft frg e rt *lgna* f *na* blng rqs *ym ydb* rct twds e E . 1 wt dd e *wRt rm* tn d wh u 2 *eh* md *em* a *tfrc wllp* 3 hw 4 n du *mrf* 5 hw s tt du *mrf* 6 y *glnk no ym* rt *en ym* lt frmg a *rqs* ym *ydb* rct *ym* rt *dnh* cvg e h b *rqs* nd *sspmc* nd *ym* lt sprtd *no* e *rqs* n whh du *rmf* i rcd e *tho* r obn f a *tfrc wllf* . (*rm* gvs !i *skcnk* l rs) i wl tk u o rpt tt *tho* 8 i L M . f *ym* wn et (ntrdc e nm f e dgr nd s e sm *sa* e *tho* f *na Pe*) i *rmrhtrf* prs nd *rws* i wl nsr l lfl sns nd *snkt* tt *yam* b-snt r gvn nt *em* fm a *urt* nd lfl *tfrc wllf* r fm e *ydb* f a *tsj* nd lfl g f sch f wn e !ast *lgna* r *rqs* f *ym krw* (*eton* t e bldg f *gnk* sns *lpmt* e *stfrc wllf* hd crtn *slgna* r *srqs* mrkd *to* fr tm o *krw* n nd ty wr ndr *on* obn o ttnd ny sn r *nkt* gvn tm *dnyb* tt *lgna* r *rqs*) tt i wl *dia* nd sst l *yhtrw* ds]muz[trsd *stfrc wllf os* fr *sa* i cn d t wht njr o *flsym* l ts i d mt sly nd sncry prs nd *rws* wh a *mrf* nd *txf* et (*sa* n e *Pes tho* s fr *sa* e *ytnp*) thn tt f hvg *ym* lft *tsrb tc* pn *ym trh dklp* fm tnc nd tt gvn *sa* a *yrp* o e *stsb* f e flds nd *slwf* f e *ria os* lp *em* § et 1 . ftr revg e *tho* r *obn* f a *tfrc wllf* wt wr u tn skd 2 wt i mt dsrd 3 nr nsr 4 mr *xl* 5 dd u rcv t 6 i dd 7 hw 8 y rdr f e *wRt rm* wh e stnc f e bn . 9 *no* bng brt o *xl* wt dd u tn dscr mr thn u hd dn bfr 4 :a *tnf* f e *ssfmc* br e thr bng hdn whh ws o sgnf *sa* a *tfrc wllf* tt i hd rcd *xl sa ty tb* prtly 3 ftr tse tgs wr xpnd o u wt dd u *txn* bsv 2 e *wRt rm* ppchg *em* fm e E ndr e du *drg* nd sn f a *tfrc wllf* wo prsd *em* s rt *dnh* n *nkt* f a cntnc f s bry lv nd frdsp nd wh t e ps *nkt* f a ps *frg* nd *drw* f a *tfrc wllf* bd *em* rs *og* nd slt e j nd sns s sch 5 ftr sltg e j nd sns *sa* a *tfrc wllf* wt dd u *txn* bsv 6 e *wRt rm* n e E wo rdrd *em* o b rcndd o e sn n e W. wo tht *em* o wr *ym nrf sa* a *tfrc wllf*. 7 hw sd a *tfrc wllf* wr s *nrf* 8 wh e *ft* trnd *nwd* 6 tir bng tht hw o wr ur *nrf sa* a *tfrc wllf* hw wr u tn dspd f 2 i ws rdrd o b rcndd o e plc fm wnc i cm tr o b nvsd f wt i hd bn dvsd f nd n du tm rtd o e g fr *rhtrf nfmn*—ths ndh e :ast sc f e *stfrc wllf* L.

:End SC f *stfrc wllf* L.

1 hw *ynm sdnk* f *ysm* r tr 2 :e prtv nd spcltv 3 wt s mnt y prtv *ysm* 4 y prtv *ysm ew* lld et (*es* Mnr) 5 wt s mnt y spcltv *ysm* 6 y spcltv *ysm ew* lrn o sbd e psns et (*es* Mnr) 7 hv u vr wrt. 8 i hv n spcltv *ysm nly tb* r ncnt bn wrt n prtv *sa* wl *sa* spcltv. 9 whr dd r ncnt bn sly *krw* 2 t e bldg f *gnk* sns *lfmt* nd thr stly dfcs 3 hw mny *yds* ne *kew* dd ty *krw* 4 :y 5 dd ty nt *krw* n e :wth 6 ty dd nt 7 wy nt 8 bcs n :y *syd* § crtd e vns nd e rth nd rstd *no* e :wth e :wth *yd* thrfr r ncnt bn cnscrd *sa* a *yd* f st fm tr lbrs thry njng frnt pprys cn f]prm[tmp]ovrc[ltng e glrs *skrw* f crn nd f drng tr gt crtr. 1 dd ty rcv ny ws 2 ty dd 3 wt. 4 *nrc niw* nd ol 5 whr dd ty rcv tm 6 n e mdl chmr f *gnk* sns *lfmt* 7 hw gnd u ur *yw* thhr. 8 thrh a *hcrf* 9 n psng thrh ts *hcrf* dd u bsv ny tg *yhtrw* f ur ttn 4 i dd :e gt *srlf* :a *no* e rt nd e thr *no* e *lft* 5 wt s e :a *no* e rt

14 !END SC N E STFRC WLLF L.

cld 6 ¿ 7 wt s e !a *no* e lft cld 8 * 9 wt ds e !a *no* e rt dnt 1 *htgnrts* 3 wt ds e !a *no* e lt dnt 4 o stbsh 5 wt d ty *htb* tghr lld o 6 o a crtn xt n *rtfrcs* n *htgnrts* wl i stblsh ts *ym* hse frvr 7 wt wr tse *srlp* 3 ty wr mltn r cst *ssrb* 9 whr wr ty cst 2 n e clyy grnd btn *htccs* nd *nuhtrz* whr 1 e *ylh* vssls f e *lpmt* wr cst 3 y wm wr ty cst 4 y *mrih ffba* e *swdw nos* f e trb f *ilhthfn* 5 wr tse *srlp* hlw r sld 6 ty wr hlw 7 fr wt prps 8 *sa* a sf rpstr fr e rcrds n e rcvs f e g gnst nndtns nd cnfl]ovrt[grtns 9 hw hi wr tse *srlp* 4 !iu cbts ch 3 wr ty drnd wh ny tg 2 ty wr wh !e *srtiphc* !a *no* e *pt* f ch f !u cbts mkg n e whl !ox cbts hi 5 wr tse *srtiphc* drnd wh ny tg 6 ty wr wh *ylll krw* nt *krw* nd pmgrnts. 7 wt d ty dnt 8 pc nty nd *ytnlp* 9 wy *os* 8 bcs e *ylll* fm ts pry nd e rmt stn n whh t sly grws dnts pc e nt *krw* fm e ntmt cnctn f ts svl *strp* dnts nty nd e pmgrnt fm e xbrnc f ts sds dnts *ytnlp* 7. wr tse *srtiphc* drnd wh *ny* tg *rhtrf* 6 ty wr wh !e blls r pmls !a *no* e *pt* f ch rprsng e glbs 5 wt r e glbs 4 !e rtfcl sphrcl *sidb no* e cnvx srfc f whh r rprsntd e cntrs ss nd vrs *strp* f e rth e plntry rvlt]ovez[ns fc f e vns nd thr mprt prtclrs. 3 hw wr ty dstngshd 2 e sphr wh e *strp* f e rth dlntd *no* ts srfc s cld e trrsl glb nd tt wh e cnstltns nd thr vny *sidb* s cld e clstt glb. 1 n gng ur *yw* o e mdl chmr dd u bsv ny tg *rhtrf yhtrw f* ui ntc 2 i dd a flgt f *gdnw srts* cnssg f !i !u nd !w *spts* 3 o wt ds e nmr !i lld 4 o e !i prncl ffcrs f e g *wRt rm* s n d jns 5 o wt d ty *rhtrf* lld 6 o r !i ncnt gnd *srm* sn *gnk* f srl *mrih gnk* f *yrt* nd *mrih ffba* 7 o wt ds e nmr !u lld 8 o e !u rdrs n *rtcthcr* whh r e *ncst crd cni nhtnrc* nd cmpst 9 o wt d ty *rhtrf* lld 2 o e !w snss f hmn *rtn* whh r hrg sng flg smlg nd *gst*. 3 whh f tse r e mst ssntl o *su sa* ns 4 e !i !ast hrg sng nd flg 5 wy *os* 6 bcs y hrg *ew* hr e *drw* y sng *ew es* e sn nd y flg *ew* fl e *prg* wrb !a br *yam* no nhr n e *krd sa* wl *sa* n e *xl* 7 o wt ds e nmr !w lld. 8 o e !w lbl rts nd scncs whh r *rmrg* *cthr cgl cthtr ymg csm ymnrts* 9 whr wr u tn cndd 4 o e twrd dr f e mdl chmr f *gnk* sns *lpmt* whh i fnd *ddrg* y e j gnd n wo dmnd f *em* e ps nd *nkt* f a ps f a *tfrc wllf* 1 dd u gv tt ps 2 i dd 3 pls o gv t o ur lft *dnh* br (ty rs nd gv t ;) e *drw* s rt pls o ps) wt ds ts *drw* dnt 4 *ytnlp* (n *swerbh*) 5 hw s t rprs]pmet[ntd. 6 y a fld f *nrc* grg nr a wtrfl 7 fm wnc dd ts *drw* rgnt 8 t ws n cnsqnc f a qrl btn *ahtpj gdj* f ssl nd e *stmrhpe* (*sgdj* 'aeth *rtphc*) e *stmrhpe* hd lng bn a trblnt nd rbls ppl wm *ahtpj* hd ndvrd o sbd y lnt msrs *tb* whtt fft ty bng hiy ncnsd t nt bng cld n o shr e rch spls f e mmntsh *rw drhtg* tgr a mty *ymr ahtpj* ls *drhtg* tgr e mn f *dalig* gv tm bttl nd pt tm o flgt nd n rdr o mk s vctr mr cmplt *eh* plcd *sdrg* t e svl pssgs f *ndrj* nd cmmdd tm f ny sd cm tt *yw yas* nt tm *yas* nw ; *tb* ty bng f a dfrnt trb cd nt frm o prnc e *drw* rt nd sd sb ; whh trfg dft prvd tm o b nms nd cst tm tr lvs nd thr fl t tt tm 'ox nd 'e thsd snc wh ; hs bn stbshd *sa* e ps *drw* o b gvn bfr *ew* cn gn dmsn nt ny rglr nd wl gvd g t *tfrc wllf* 7 whr ws u tn cndd 8 o e nnr dr f e mdl chmr f *gnk* sns *lpmt* whh i fnd *ddrg* y e s gnd n wo dmnd f *em* e *prg* nd *drw* f a *tfrc wllf* 9 dd u gv t 2 i dd 3 pls o gv t o ur lft *dnh* br (ty rs nd gv t wht ny dvsn) t s rt pls o|ntr 3 *no* ntrg e mdl chmr f *gnk* sns *lpmt* wt wr e 'ast tgs prsnd o u 4 e *gkrw slt* f a *tfrc wllf* 5 wt r ty 6 e *bmlp rqs* nd ll 7 wh d ty mrly *hct* 8 e *bmlp* s n nstrmt et (*es* Mnr) 9 wt ws ur ttntn *rhtrf* drd o 2 o e *rttl* G whh s e ntl f *yrtmg* r e 'uth scnc *no* whh *ysm* s prncpy fndd 3 wt s mnt y *yrtmg* 4 y *yrtmg* et (*es* Mnr) 5 o wt ds e *rttl* G *rhtrf* lld (gvs 'i *skcnk* l rs) 6 o e scrd nm f *ytd* o wm l sd wh rvrnc *wb* (hr e whl g *wb*) fm e *tsgny* Pe. n e *En* crnr f e g o e *wRt rm* n e *rhc* ths ndh c *stfrc wllf* L.

Crmy *f gslc* ts dgr s e sm as e *Pes* xpt e nm f e dgr 'e *skcnk*. *stfrc wllf* g s lwys clsd *eid enis* t s lwys cnsdd *sa* a spcl g.

!Ast SC f *rm* ns L.

1 wl u b ff r fm 2 fm 3 fm wt 4 fm e dgr f a *tfrc wllf* o tt f a *rm* n 5tn u r a *rm* n i prsm (br sn r u a *rm* n) 6 i *ma* 7wt ndcd u o bcm a *rm* n 8 n rdr tt i mt btn mr ws e btr o spt *flsym* nd o sst l *yhtrw* dstrd *rm* ns tr *sdw* nd rfns 9 whr ws u md a *rm* n 2 n e *ydb* f a *tsj* nd lfl g f *rm* ns dly ssmbd nd lgly cnstd] *etn* tse qsns nd nsrs n [r ncssy qsns nd nsrs btn e *rm* nd sn n cmmncg e png f a *rms* g n png e *rm* tn sks hw mny cmps'sch a g nsr s !i !u !w r mr 3 whr wr u prpd o b md a *rm* n 4 n a *moor* jcnt o e g 5 hw wr u prpd 6 y bng dvsd f l *slrnm* nd *sltm* nhr *dkn* nr clhd bt nor † ‡ wh a ¶ !i tms rnd *ym dkn ydb* 7 wy hd u a ¶ !i tms rnd ur *ydb* 8 t ws o sgnf tt *sa* i dvncd n *ysm ym* obn bcm mr nd mr bndg *no em* 9 whr wr u tn cndd 8 o e dr f e g y e *dnh* f a br whr i ws csd o gv !i dstnt *skcnk* 7 o wt d tse !i dstnt *skcnk* lld 6 o e jls f a *rm* n 5 wt r ty 4 frnd]ovr[sp mrlt nd bry lv 3 wt ws sd o u fm wn2wo cms thr !ece rpd 1 ur nsr 4 a br wo hs *ytsj* nd lfly srvd s tm *sa an Pe* bn psd o e dgr f a *tfrc wllf* nd nw sks fr *rhtrf xl* n *ysm* y bng rsd o e sblm dgr f a *rm* n 5 wt mr wr u skd 6 f i cm f *ym* wn *erf* wl nd crd f i ws dly nd trly prprd *yhtrw* nd wl *dflq* f i hd md e ncsy prfcnc n e prcdg dgr nd prpry *dhcva* fr l whh bng nsrd n e *vtrff* i ws skd y wt *rhtrf* rt r bnft i xpcd o gn dmsn 7 ur nsr 8 y e bnft f a ps 9 dd u gv tt ps 4 i dd nt *tb ym* cndr gv t fr *em* 5 pls o gv t o ur lft *dnh* br 6 ty rs nd gv t !) [s rt i *trg* u br ! 3 wo ws ! 2 *eh* ws *na* ngns *nmkrw* n vrs *sltm* nd br o *lbuj* e nvntr f *csm* r e !yth scnc 1 wt flwd 2 i ws rqsd o wt a tm wh ptnc ntl e *wRt rm* cd b nfrmd f *ym* rq]paz[st nd s nsr rtd 3 wt ws s nsr wn

rtd 4 lt *mh* ntr nd b rcvd n du *mrf* 5 hw wr u rcd 6 *no* e *stnp* f e *ssfime* xtndd o *ym dkn stsrb* whh ws o sgnf tt *sa* e vtl prncpl f lf *yl* vn e *tsrb os* wr e mst vlbl tnts f *ysm* cntnd wn e *stnp* f e *ssfimc* whh r frndsp mrlt nd bry lv 9 whr wr u tn cndd 8 :i tms rnd e g o e jn n e s whr e sm qstns wr skd nd e lk nsrs rtd *sa* t e dr 7 hw dd e jn n e s dsps f u 6 *ch* drcd *em* o ps *no* o e sn n e W whr e s m qs] ovec [tns wr skd nd e lk nsrs rtd *sa* bfr 5 hw dd e sn n e W dsps f u 4 *eh* drcd *em* o ps *on* o e *wRt rm* n e E whr et 3 wt dd e *wRt rm* tn dmnd f u 2 fm wnc i cm. 1 ur nsr 8 fm e *tsw* 9 wt mr dd *eh* dmnd 6 whthr i ws trvlg 3 ur nsr 1 twds e *tse* 1 wt mr dd *eh* dmnd 4 wt i ws n prst f 5 ur nsr 6 tt whh ws *tsl* whh y *ym* wn nd vrs nd s sstnc i hpd o btn 7 wt mr dd *eh* dmnd 8 wt i lldd o 1 ur nsr 2 o e *strcs* f a *rm* n 3 hw dd e *wRt rm* tn dsps f u 4 *eh* rdrd *em* o b rcnd o e sn n e W wo tht *em* o dvnc y :i prt rglr *spts ym* ft frmg a *rqs ym ydb* rct twds e E 9 wt dd e *wRt rm* tn d wh u 8 *ch* md *em* a *rm* n. 7 hw 6 n du *mrf* 5 hw s tt du *mrf* 4 y *glnk no ym dkn sen ym ydb* rct *ym sdnh* cvg e h b *rqs nd ssfimc* n whh du *mrf* i rcd e *tho* r obn f a *rm* n (3 *rm* gvs :i *skcnk* 1 rs i wl tk u o rpt tt *tho* r obn) e *rm slnk* nd tks ff s ht ppst o e cndt) (n gvg e obn e ks hld e rds vr e hds f e cndt) 2 i M E f et 1 *rhtrf* prs nd *rws* tt i wl nsr 1 lfl sns nd smns tt *yam* b gvn r snt nt *em* fm a *tsj* nd lfl *rm* n r fm e *ydb* f a *tsj* nd ifl g f sch f wn e *htgnl* f *ym* ¶ tt i wl *dia* nd sst l *yhtrw* drtsd *rm* ns tr *sdw* nd rfns *os* fr *sa* i cn d t wht njr o *flsym* r *ylmf* tt i wl kp a brs *strcs sa ym* wn wn gvn o *em* n *grhc sa* sch mrdr nd *nsrt* xpd nd tt lft t *ym* wn dscrtn tt i wl bd y nd spt e by *swl* f e g f whh i *yam* bcm a mmbr e cnstn f e gnd g ndr whh e sm s hldn nd e gnl rgltns f *ysm* i *rmrhtrf* prs nd *rws* tt i wl nt b t e mkg f a *nmw* a n a yng mn

2*

llf em ts *tf* 9 wm dd u rpr] pqt [sn t 4 r gnd *rm mrih ffba* wo ws *nls* wn e *lpmt* ws nr ts cmpltn 1 ws s *htd* ndr *ega na* ld mn n s dtg *na tshta* a mdmn r a fl nog tm o b sch. tt i wl nt rng a br nr dprv *mh* f s gd nm nr sffr t o b dn y thrs f wn *ym* pwr o *tnvtrp* t *tb* wl pprz *mh* f 1 pphg *rgnd os* fr *as* t sl cm o *ym* nldg tt i wl nt vlt e *yttshc* f a brs wf dgr sstr r *rhtm* nog tm o b sch tt i wl nt gv e *rm* ns *drw* xpt *no* e !u *stnp* f *phs*wl*lf* nd nt tn bv *ym htrb* nls bslt ncst sl rqr t 1 ts i d mst sly nd sncy et bndg *flsm* ndr *on* ls *ytnp* tn tt f hvg *ym ydb* swd nt *ym slwb* tkn!fm tnce nd *dnrb* o *shs* nd tse *shs* sctrd o e !o wnds t vn *ym ydb* qrtd nd plcd *no* e !o crdl *stnp* f e *srvnu os* tt tr b *on* mr rmmbrc hd f *em gnm* mn r ns frvr *os* lp *em* § nd kp *em tsfdts* n ts *ym rm* ns *tho* r obn 1 ftr rcvg e *tho* r obn f a *rm* n wt wr u tn skd - 2 wt i mst dsrd 3 ur nsr 4 mr *xl* 5 dd u rcv t 6 i dd 7 hw 8 y rdr f e *wRt rm* wh e sstnc f e brn 9 ftr bng brt o *xl* wt dd u tn dscvr mr tn u hd dn bfr 2 *htb stnp* f e *sspmc* br whh ws o sgnf tt i nvr sd ls st f e mrl pplcn f tt sfl mplmt fr y a du ttntn o ts *esu ew* r tht o rglt r dsrs nd kp r psns wn du *sdnb* wh 1 *dnknm tb* mr spcly a br. 3 ftr tse tgs wr xpnd o u wt dd u *txn* bsv 4 e *wRt rm* ppchg *em* fm e E ndr e du *drg* nd sn f a *rm* n wo prsd *em* wh s rt *dnh* n *nkt* f a cntnc f s bry lv nd frdsp nd wh t e ps nd e *nkt* f a ps f a *rm* n bd *em* rs *og* nd slt e j nd sns *sa* sch 5 ftr sltg e j nd sns *sa* a *rm* n wt dd u *txn* bsv 6 e *wRtrm* n e E wo rdrd *em* o b rcndd o e sn n e W wo tht *em* o wr *ym nrp sa* a *rm* n 7 hw sd a *rm n* wr s *nrp* 8 wh e lft crnr tkd *pu* 9 ftr bng tht o wr ur *nrp sa* a *rm* n hw wr u tn dspd f 2 i ws rdrd o b rcndd o e plc fm wnc i cm tr o b nvsd f wt i hd bn dvsd nd n du tm rtd o e g fr *rhtrf* nfmn [*etn* bfr e cndt gs ot e *rm* gv *mh* e flg *grhc* — *rm* br A fbfr *ew* cn prcd ny *rhtrf* w u n ts slmn crmy t wl b ncssy r u o trvl n rdr o cnvnc e brn f ur *ytldf* nd frtd n e crs fur trvls u *yam tm* wh *sniffr* wo wl ndvr o xrt fm u e *strcs* f a *rm* n sm wl *og os* fr br A *sa* vn o *ntrht* o tk ur lf *tb* u mst b prpd vn o *yal nwd* ur lf *rhtr* tn o rvl ny f e *strcs* f *erf ysm* tt hv bn cmmntd o u trfr *no* ur frmn *ytldf* nd frtd rst r fr fvrs] cndct e cndt o e prprtv *moor* ths ndh e !ast sc f e *rm* ns L.

!End SC f *rm* L.

I u hv stsfd *em sa* o e mnr nd md f ur ntn nt ts dgr *tb* u hv nt *ty* nfmd *em* wt a *rm* ns g rprsnts nr hv u xpd o *em* e rgn r *lcrtsh trp* f ts dgr n e !ast plc i *hsw* o no wt a *rm* ns g rp] paz [rsn]ovez [ts 2 e *mtcns murctns* r *ylh* f *sylh* f *gnk* sns *lpmt.* 3 ftr bng nvsd f wt u hd bn dvsd nd *no* rtrng o e g whr wr u !ast cndd 4 o e *En* crnr f e g whr i ws csd o *lnk* nd hr e *rm* ns *ryrp* rpd (*etn* a *nhsc* s plcd *no* e *rlf* btn e *rtla* nd e *rms nrht* n e *En ds* f e g — e sk rcvs e cndt t e dr dvncg trds ts *nhsc* syng " t ws e *yld* csm f r gnd *rm mrih ffba* t e hr f hi !ae" et *es* !end sc f e *krw* n ts dgr) (*etn* gn whl e cndt s nvsg *flsmh* wh s *ghtlc* e *rm* ppnts e *snss* wo r sttnd *S W E* lkws !i *stfrc wllf* rprsg e !ae ls e wyfrg mn wh a *niac* nd pk *no* s bk *rm* gvs !i *sknck* l rs) 3 i wl tk u o rpt tt *ryrp* 4 " tho o § nost r *gstnwd*" et (*es* mr) 5 ftr hrg e *rm* ns *pyrp* rpd wt fld 6 i tn rs nd ws cndd o e S dr whr i ws cdsd y a *trfc wllf* wo dmnd f *em* t !i svl tms e *strcs* f a *rm* n r *eh* wd tk *ym* lf *tb no ym* !id rfsl *eh* strk *em no* e || wh e !eo *hnc* gg 5 whr wr u tn cndd 6 o e W dr whr i ws ccsd y a *tfrc wllf* wo n lk mnr dmnd f *em* t !i svl tms e *strcs* f a *rm* n r *eh* wd tk *ym* lf *tb no* ym !id rfsl *eh* strk *em no ym* rt *tsrb* wh a *rys* 7 whr wr u tn cndd 8 o e E dr whr i ws ccsd y a *tfrc wllf* wo n lk mnr dmnd f *em* t !i svl tms e *strcs* f a *rm* n r *eh* wd tk *ym* lf *tb no ym* !id rfsl *eh tms em no* e hd wh e cmn *lvg* r st!g *lm* whh *dttdmrfi* 2 t ws 8 y wm 6 y !au *stfrc wllf* wo sng e *lfimt* nr ts cmpltn wr frfl ty sd nt b bl o btn *rm* ns ws wn trvlg nt frn cntrs ntrd nt a hrd cnspry o xrt fm r gnd *rm mrih ffba* e *strcs* f a *rm* n r o tk s lf *tb* !ae f tm frg e vl cnsqcs wr strk wh hrr t e trct f e *mrc* nd rcnd *tb* e thr !i wo wr *aluj oluj mluj* bng mr rdnd n *ynlv* wr dtrmd o *tfi* tr mrdrs *snsd* nt xcn nd crdgy plcd *svlsmt* t e S- W nd E ntncs f e *lfimt* 6 t wt tm dd ts ppn 4 t e hr f hi !ae wn e *tfrc* wr cld fm *rbl* o *tnmhsfr* 7 hw cm *eh* ln t ts tm 8 t ws e *yld* csm f r gnd *rm mrih ffba* t e hr f hi !ae wn e *tfrc* wr cld fm *rbl* o *tnmhsfr* o *og* nt e *lfimt* o vw e *krw* o *es* f tr cd b ny mpvt md thr fr ts tlt r nmt nd ls o *wrd snsd no* s *lsrt drb* fr e *tfrc* o prs tr *srbl* ftr whh *eh* ntrd e *mtcncs murtcns* r *ylh* f *sylh* tr o ffr *fiu* s drtn nd *sryrfi* o e *urt* nd lvg § fr e sns f e pl 3 wt fld 4 ftr prfmg ts ps crmy *eh* tn rs nd tmpd o *og ut* f e *S* dr f e *lfimt* whh *eh dnf ddrg* y *aluj* wo dmnd f *mh* t !i svl tms e *strcs* f a *rm* n r *eh* wd tk s lf *tb no* s !id rfsl *eh* strk *mh ssrc* e || wh e !eo *hcn* gg 1 wt fld 2 *eh* tn tmpd o mk s *fics ut* f e W dr f e *lfimt* whh *eh dnf ddrg* y *oluj* wo dmnd f *mh* t !i svl tms e *strcs* f a *rm* n r *eh* wd tk s lf *tb no* s !id rfsl *eh* strk *mh* no s rt *tsrb* wh a *rqs* whh csd *mh* o *rgts* nd *ler* 3 wt fld 4 *eh* tn ndvrd o mk s *fics ut* f e E dr whh *eh dnf ddrg* y *mluj* wo n lk mnr dmnd f *mh* t !i svl tms e strcs f a *rm* n r *eh* wd tk s lf *tb no* s !id rfsl *eh tms mh no* hd wh a cmn *lvg* r sttg *lm* whh *llf mh* lfls t s *tf* 5 wt dd ty tn d wh e *ydb* 6 ty brd t n e *hsbr* f e *lfimt* t lo !ae r !ae t *tgn* wn ty grd o *tm* o cnst wt *rhtrf* o d wh t 7 dd ty *tm* grby o pntmt 8 ty dd 9 wt dd ty tn d wh e *ydb* 2 ty crd t a *ylrtsw* crs fm e *lfimt* nd brd t t e *wrb* f a il cld *tnm hrm* nd t e hd f e *vrg dtnlfisnrt* a *grfis* f *assc os* tt f csn sd rqr ty *svlsmt* mt no whr o *dnf* t tn fr *rf* f dtcn ty ndvrd o mk tr pcs *ut* f e *mdgnk* 3 wt fld

4 cnfsn n e *lpmt* 5 wt csnd ts cnfsn 6 y r gnd *rm mrih ffba* bng msg 7 hw *gnl* hd *eh* bn msg 8 snc e hr f hi !ae f *ydrtsy* 9 hw dd ty no *mh* o b msg 8 y tr bng *on snsd nwrd no* s *lsrt drb* fr e *tfrc* o prs tr *srbl* 7 wt dd *gnk* sn tn rdr 6 *eh* rdrd e s gnd n o cs e nnr prt] vza [mts f e *lpmt* o b *dhcres* nd ls e *llr* f e *nmkrw* o b cld 6 ws ts dn grb o s rdr 4 t ws 3 wt ws e s gnd ns *trpr* 2 tt e nnr prt]az[mts f e *lpmt* hd bn *dhcres* wht fct nd ls e *llr* f e *nmkrw* hh bn cld nd tr prd o b !i *stfrc wllf* msg wo wr *aluj oluj mluj* nd fm e smlrt f tr nms ty prd o b brn nd mn f *ryt* 1 wt dd *gnk* sn tn nfrm e s gnd n 2 tt tr hd prd bfr *mh* !ae *stfrc wllf dhtlc* n wht *snrp* nd wht *svlg* n *nkt* f tr ncnc nd mplrg s *ndrp* nd nfrmd *mh* tt ty !ae nd !i thrs sng e *lpmt rn* ts cmpltn wr frfl ty sd nt b bl o btn *rm* ns ws wn trvlg nt frn cntrs ntrd nt a hrd cnspry o xrt fm r gnd *rm mrih ffba* e *strcs* f a *rm* n r o tk s lf *tb* ty !ae frg e vl cnsqcs wr strk wh *rrh* t e trct f e *mrc* nd rcnd *tb* ty wr frfl tt e thr !i hd *tp* tr mrdrs *snsd* nt xcn 3 wt dd *gnk* sn tn rdr 4 *eh* rdrd e s gnd n o cs tse !ae *stfrc wllf* o b snt *ut* !i *tsc* !i *tsw* !i *htrn* nd !i *hts* n *hcres* f r gnd *rm mrih* nd e *srtrsd* fm e *lpmt* 5 wr ty snt *ut* grby o s rdr 6 ty wr 7 wt ws e s gnd ns *trpr no* tr rtrn 8 tt !i f *mt* trvlg *no* e cst f *pj tm* a *wyfrg* mn f wm ty nqrd f *eh* hd *nes* ny *nmkrw* fm e *lpmt* ps tt *yw eh* nfmd *mt* tt *eh* hd *nes* !i nqrg fr a psg o *aphte tb* nt bng bl o btn !a ty hd rtrd bk nt e cntr 9 wt dd *gnk* sn tn nfm e s gnd n 8 tt t ws f e hst mptnc tt r gnd *rm mrih ffba* sd b *dnf eh rfrht* rdrd e s gnd n o cs tse !ae *stfrc wllf* o b snt *ut* gn n e sm drcns nd wh ts njctn tt f ty dd nt scd n *gdnf* e *ydb* f r gnd *rm mrih ffba* r e *srtrsd* fm e *lpmt* ty *svlsmt* sd b dmd e mrdrs nd sfr crdgy 7 wr ty snt grby o s rdr 6 ty wr 5 wt ws e s gnd ns *trpr no* tr rtrn 4 tt !i f *mt* trvlg a *ylrtsw* crs fn e *lpmt* hd csn o scnd a il

cld *tnm hrm* t e *wrb* f whh ‘a f *mt* bng mr wry tn e rst st *nwd* o *hsrfr flsmh* nd *no* rsg *eh* cdnty tk hld f a *grps* f *assc* whh cmg *pu* sly e *dnrg* bng rcnty rmvd hd e prnc f a *vrg* whh xctd s sspn *no* whh *eh dlh* s brn nd whl cntm] svq[png *no* e *tps* ty hrd xclmtns fm e jcnt *stflc* ccsng nd xcsng ch thr wt wr tsc xclmtns 2 e ‘ast xcld " o tt i hd *ym* || ct " et tt prd o b e *ecv* f *aluj* e ‘end xcld *oluj* e ‘id xcld i *ma* wrs thn u *htb* t ws i tt dprvd *mh* f lf "O tt i hd *ym ydb*" et er i hd bn e mns f e *htd* f *os* gd nd gt a mn *sa* r *gnd rm mrih no* whh ty mmdty *dhsr* n pn *mt dzs mt* nd *dnb mt* nd crd *mt pu* o e *ytc* 1 wt dd *gnk* sn tn rdr 2 *eh* rdrd e s gnd n o cs *mt* o b snt *pu* bfr *mh* 3 wr ty snt *pu* grby o s rdr 4 ty wr 5 wt dd *gnk* sn tn rdr 6 *eh* rdrd e s gnd n o cs *mt* o b tkn wht e *stg* f e *ytc* nd thr svly xcd grby o e *sntcrpm* fm tr wn *shtm* 1 ws ts dn grbl o s rdr 2 t ws 3 wt dd *gnk* sn tn rdr 4 *eh* rdrd e s gnd n o cs tse ‘i *stfrc wllf* o b snt *tu* o e plc whr e wry br st *nwd* o rst nd *hsrfr flsmh* n *hcres* f e *ydb* f r gnd *rm mrih ffba* nd f *dnf* o *hcres* fr e *strcs* f a *rm* n nd *es* f ty cd b *dnf* n r bt e *ydb* r a *yk* o *mt* 7 wr ty snt *tu* grby o s rdr 8 ty wr 9 wt ws e s gnd ns *trpr no* thr rtrn 8 tt ty hd *dnf* e *ydb* 7 whr 6 t a *ylrtsw* crs fm e *lpmt* t e *wrb* f a il cld *tnm hrm* tt ty hd md *hcres* fr e *strcs* f a *rm* n *tb* ty wr nt o b *dnf no* r bt e *ydb* nr a *yk* o *mt* 5 wt dd *gnk* sn tn nfrm e s gnd n 4 tt e *rm* ns *drw* ws *tsl* 3 wt dd *gnk* sn tn rdr 2 *eh* rdrd e s gnd n o tk stbl sstnc nd *og tu* wh *mh* o ndvr o rs e *ydb* f r gnd *rm mrih ffba* fr a mr *tncd* ntrmt 1 dd ty *og tu* grby o s rdr 2 ty dd 3 hw dd *gnk* sn rdr e *ydb* o b rsd 4 y e *prg* f *na Pe* 5 wt ws e s gnd ws *trpr* 6 tt *eh* cd nt fr e *hslf* ws ptrd nd slpd 7 hw dd *eh* tn rdr e *ydb rsd* 8 y e *prg* f a *tfrc wllf* whh *eh* nfrmd *mh* ws e sm 9 hw dd *eh* tn rdr e *ydb* rsd 8 y e *gnrts* prg r *wp snl* nd *no* e ‘u *stnp* f *phswllf* nd e ꜝast *drw* tt sd b spn ftr e *ydb* ws ths rsd sd b a *tttss* fr e *rm* ns *drw* ntl ftr gs sd *dnf* e rt 7 wt ws e ꜝast *drw* spn ftr e *ydb* ws ths rsd 6 (5 wt r e ꜝu *stnp* f *phswllf* 4 *tf* o *tf en* o *en tsrb* o *tsrb dnh* o bk *khc* o *khc* wh *htm* o *re* 3 wt do ty dnt 2 *tf* o *tf* dnts tt *ew* sd nvr hstt o *og* a *tf tu* f r *yw* o sst a br *en* o *en* dnts tt *ew* sd rmbr a br n r dvns *tsrb* o *tsrb* tt *ew* sd kp r brs *tsrcs sa* r wn wn gvn o *su sa* sch mrdr nd *nsrt* xpd nd tt lft t r wn dscrtn *dnh* o bk dnts tt *ew* sd ndvr o sprt a br wn flg *khc* o *khc* wh *htm* o *re* e *yw* n whh e *rm* ns *drw* s gvn 1 wt s e ntrcty clus o ur obn *sa* a *rm* n 4 tt i wl lws *liah* frvr cncl nd nvr rvl et (*es* obn) 3 hw mny *stnp* hv u n ur obn *sa* a *rm* n 2 ꜝv ꜝo pstv nd ꜝo ngv 5 wt s e ꜝast pstv *tnp* 6 tt i wl nsr 1 lfl sns nd smns et (*es* obn) 7 wt s e ꜝend pstv *tnp* 8 tt i wl *dia* nd sst et (*es* obn) 9 wt s e ꜝid pstv *tnp* 8 tt i wl kp a brs *strcs* et (*es* obn) 7 wt s e ꜝoth pstv *tnp* 6 tt i wl bd y nd sprt et (*es obn*) 3 wt s e ꜝast ngv *tnp* 4 tt i wl nt b t e mkg et (*es* obn) 3 wt s e ꜝend ngv *tnp* 2 tt i wl nt rng a br et (*es* obn) 3 wt s e ꜝoth ngv *tnp* 4 tt i wl nt gv e *rm* ns *drw* et (*es* obn) 5 wt s e *ytnp* f ur obn *sa* a *rm* *n* 6 tt i wd *rhtr* hv *ym ydb* swd et (*es* obn) 7 wt r e *gnkrw slt* f a *rm* n 8 l e mplmts f *ysm* ndcrmtly *tb* mr spcl' e trl 9 i wl thk u o xpn e trl 2 e trl s *na* nstr]vamn mnt et (*es* Mnr) ths ndh e *rm* ns L. (*etn* ftr prsng e *gnkrw slt* o e cndt e *rm* rds e *grhc* nd sys ts *grhc* br A t ws *ym ytd sa* prsg ffcr f ts g o cmmnct o u nt dtg *tb* u wl *lt* e xclt *stpcrp* trn cntd hv tr du wt wh u n l ur trsctns thr lf e *rm* tn *swb* o e cndt nd sys br sk u wl pls o *hsnrf* br A wh a cnvt *ts* n e g *sa* a *yhtrw rm* n l st *sp* ꜝa mnt.

Crmy f png *Pes* g.

RM brn pls o clh *rm sog pu* o e E nd sys br sn u wl pls o prch e E nd rcv ur jls *rm* sys wh plsr i prs nt u wh e jls f ur ffc *rm* tn cls br jn n rdr tn T. S nd ks (1 slt fr !a mnt) *rm* sts *nwd* gvs !a *kcnk* nd sys pls o cm o rdr (1 rs) brn *ew* r bt png a g f *Pes* n whh i wl thk u fr ur sstnc nd ttntn *rm* br sn u wl pls o stsf *flsry* tt 1 prst r ns sn rss nd sys i *ma* stsf d *wRt* tt 1 prst r ns *rm* u wl pls o cl e brn o rdr *sa Pes* rsrvg *flsry* fr e lst . sn brn pls o cm o rdr *sa Pes* (gv du *sdrg sa Pes*) sn sts *nwd rm* gvs !a *kcnk* nd sys (jk rss) br jk e !ast cr f a n jk o *es* e g dly ttd *wRt rm* u wl pls o prfm tt *trp* f ur *ytd* nd nfrm e *rlyt* tt *ew* r bt png a g 1 *Pes* tt *eh* ss e dr s *dlt* crdgy jk *sog* o e dr gv !i dstct *skcnk* nd sys br *rlyt ew* r bt png a g f *Pes* u wl pls o *es* e dr s *dlt* crdgy *rlyt* nsrs *os* mte t b jk rtrns o s plc nd sys *ew* r *dlt wRt rm* hw r *ew dlt* br jk y a n wht e dr rmd wh a prpr mplmt f s ffc *rm* e *srlyt* plc jk t e dr wh a *nwrd* srd n s *dnh rm* s *ytd* tr jk o bsv e ᵕ pch f cwns nd *svsrprd* scndg r dcndg nd *es* tt nn ps tt rps wht prmsn fm e *wRt rm rm gvs* !e *skcnk* (ffcrs rs) nd sys br sn fm whc cm u *sa na Pe* sn fm e g f h st 'jn t *mlsrj rm* wt cm u hr o d sn o lrn o sbd *ym* psns nd mpv *flsym* n *ysm rm* tn u r a n i prsm sn i *ma os* !kn nd cptd mng brs nd *swllf rm* whr wr u md a n br sn u e *ydb* f a *tsj* nd lfl g f ns dly ssmbd nd lgly cnstd *rm* hw mny cmps sch a g sn !i !u !w r mr *rm* wn e g cnsts f !w wo cmps t sn *wRt rm* s nd jn T nd S s nd jks *rm* e jks plc n c g sn t e sns rt *rm* ur *ytd* tr br jk jk o cry msgs fm e sn n e W o e *wRt rm* n e E r lswr bt e g *sa eh yam* drct ls o *es* e g dly *dlt rm* e sks plc n e g jk t e *wRt rm* rt *rm* ur *ytd* thr br sk sk o cry rdrs fm e *wRt rm* n e E o e sn n e W r lswr bt e g *sa eh yam* drct ls o ntrdc l vstg brn *rm* Ss plc n e g sk t e *wRt rm* lft *rm* ur *ytd* tr br S S o bsv e wl nd plsr f e *wRt rm* o rcrd e rglr prcdgs f e g o rcv l mns nd py *mt* vr nt e *sdnh* f e T *rm* e Ts plc n e g S t e *wRt rms* rt *rm* ur *ytd* tr br T T o rcv l mns fm e *sdnh* f e S o kp a *tsj* nd rglr cct f e sm nd py *mt tu* t e wl nd plsr f e *wRt rm* wh e cnsnt f e brn *rm* e jns sttn n e g T n e S *wRt rm* ur yd n e S br jn jn *sa* e *nus* s n e S t ts mrdn ht whh s e *ytb* nd glry f e *yd os* stnds e jn n e s o cl e *tfrc* fm lbr o *tnmhsfr* nd fm *tnmhsfr* o lbr t e wl nd plsr f e *wRt rm rm* e sns sttn n e g jn n e W *wRt rm* ur *ytd* n e W br sn sn *sa* e *nus* sts n e W o cls e *yd os* stnds e sn n e W o sst e *wR*t *rm* n clsg e g o *yp* e *tfrc* tr ws f ny tr b du nd *es* tt nn *og wy* dsstsfd *ynmrh* bng e *htgnrts* nd sprt f l scts *tb* mr spcly ts f *rs rm rms* sttn n e g sn n e E *wRt rm* s *ytd* tr *sn sa* e *nus* rss n e E o pn nd drn e *yd os* stnds e *wRt rm* n e E o pn s g n du tm st e *tfrc* t *krw* nd gv *mt* prpr nstrc]ovrz[tns *rm* gvs :i *skcnk* nd rss wh e g nd sys br sn u wl pls o tk ntc t s *ym* drctn tt a g f *Pes* b nw pnd nd stnd pn fr e spc f :a hr fr e dsph f bsn u wl pls o rprt e sm o e jn n e S tt e brn *yam* hv du ntc trf nd gvn *svlsmht* crdgy. sn br jn u wl pls o tk ntc t s e *wRt rm* wl nd plsr tt a g f *Pes* b nw pnd nd stnd pnd fr e spc f :a hr fr e dsph f bsn u wl pls o rprt e sm o e brn tt ty *yam* hv du ntc trf nd gvn *sevlsmht* crdgy jn brn u hv hrd e wl nd plsr f e *wRt rm* u wl pls o tk du ntc trf nd lt t b crdgy *os* dn *rm rhtgt* brn (l gv e du *drg* nd sn f *Pe*) *rm* gvs :a *kcnk* (nsrd y s nd jn) nd sys :aiid slm wh s ht ff tn sys i dclr e g f *Pes* dly pnd fr e dsph f bsn (l st *nwd* slnt fr :a mnt) *rm* br S u wl pls o rd e prcdgs f e lst g (*eh* rss nd rds) *rm* brn f e prcdgs f e lst g *mt* ur prbtn u wl pls o sgnf t y e sl sn f *na Pe* (ty gv t) *rm* ty r prvd br S u wl pls o rcrd tt e prcdgs f e lst g wr rd nd prvd *rm* br sn hv u ny prtcr bsn n e W bfr e g f *Pes* sn i no f ntg n e W. *wRt rm* hv u ny tg in e S br jn jn i no f ntg n e S. *wRt rm* wt s ur plsr brn Br i wl prps *wRt* tt *ew* cmnc e Ls n ts dgr *rm* gvs !a *kcnk* br pls o cm o rdr (l slnt !a mnt.)

Crmy f clsg e *Pes* g.

Rm hv u ny *rhtrf* bsn n e W bfr ts g f *Pes* br sn sn i no f ntg *rhtrf* n e W *wRt rm* ny tg *rhtrf* n e S br jn jn i no f ntg *rhtrf* n e S *wRt rm* hs ny br ny tg o ffr fr e gd f *ysm tb* mr spcly fr ts g f nt *ew* wl prcd o cls (slnc !a mnt) *rm* gvs !a *kcnk* jk rss *rm* br jk e lst *sa* wl *sa* e *!ast* cr f a n jk o *es* e g dly *dlt wRt rm* u wl pls o prfm tt *trp* f ur *ytd* nd *nfm* e *rlyt ew* r bt o cls ts g f *Pes* nd tt *eh* ss e dr *dlt* crdgy jk *sog* o e dr (*sa* n png) f e g nd gvs e lrm nd rtrns o s plc nd sys *ew* r *dlt wRt rm* hw r *ew dlt* br jk y a n wht e dr rmd wh e prpr mpl]pzq[mnt f s ffc *rm* e *srlyt* plc jk t e dr wh a *nwrd* srd n s *dnh rm* s *ytd* tr jk o obsv e ppch f cns nd *svsrprd* scndg r dscndg nd *es* tt nn ps rps wht prmsn fm e *wRt rm rm* gvs !e dstct *skcnk* (e ffcrs rs) nd sys br sn t e png f ts g u nfrmd *em* tt u ws a n md n e *ydb* t a *tsj* nd lfl g f ns dly ssmbd nd lgly cnstd hw mny cmps sch a g sn !i !u !w r mr *rm* wn a g cnssts f !w wo cmps t sn *wRt rm* s nd jns T nd S s nd jks *rm* e jks plc n e g sn t e *sns* rt *rm* ur *ytd* tr br jk jk o cry mssgs fm e sn n e W et (*etn* hr e ffcrs l tl tr rspctv *sytd* e sm *sa* n png *pu* o e *rm*) *rm* gvs !i *skcnk* l rs wh e *rm* nd sys br jn pls o tk ntc t s *ym* drctn tt ts g f *Pes* b nw clsd nd stnd clsd tl r *txn* rglr mtg nls snr cld *no* sm spcl mrgncy f whh du ntc wl b gvn u wl pls o rprt e sm o e sn n e W tt e brn *yam* hv du ntc trf nd gvrn *svlsmht* crdgy jn br sn u wl pls o tk ntc t s e *wRt rms* wl nd plsr tt ts g f *Pes* b nw clsd nd stnd clsd *sa* bv sn brn u hv hrd e wl nd plsr f e *wRt rm* u wl pls o tk du ntc trf nd lt t b crdgy *os* dn *rm rhtgt* brn (l gv du *drg* nd sn f *Pe*) ftr whh *rm* gvs !a *kcnk* nsrd y e j nd sns *eh* tn tks ff s ht nd sys br jn hw sd ns mt jn *no* e ll *wRt rm* hw sd ty *trp* br sn sn *no* e *rys wRt rm* tks ff s ht nd sys *os yam ew* vr mt nd *trp ym* brn i dclr ts g f *Pes* dly clsd nd *yam* e blsg f § rst pn *su* nd l rglr gd ns brn l rspns *os* mte t b *rm* tks ff s jl nd sys e brn wl pls o dpst tr jls n e E.

Crmy f png a g f *stfrc wllf*

RM br sn u wl pls o *stsf flsry* tt l prst r *stfrc wllf* sn rss nd lks *dnr* e g nd sys i *ma* stsfd *wRt* tt l prst r *stfrc wllf rm* pls o cl e brn o rdr *sa stfrc wllf* rsrg *flsry* fr e lst sn u wl pls o cm o rdr *sa stfrc wllf* (*etn* ty *tp* e rt *dnh no* e lft *tsrb* nd e sn sts *nwd*) *rm* (gvs !a *kcnk* jk rss) br jk e !ast cr f a *tfrc wllf* jk o *es* e g *s* dly *dlt* (*etn* e jk hvg tld s *ytd*) e *rm* gvs !e *skcnk* nd ffcrs rs *rm* br sn r u a *tfrc wllf* sn i *ma yrt em rm* hw wl u b *drt* sn y e *rqs rm* wy y e *rqs* sn bcs tt s !a f e *gnkrw* tls f *ym* prfsn *rm* wt s a *rqs* sn *na* ngl f !za dgrs r e !oth *trp* f a *lcrc rm* wt ndcd u o bcm a *tfrc wllf* sn n rdr tt i mgt btn ws e btr o sprt *flsym* nd sst a *yhtrw* dstrsd *tfrc wllf rm* whr wr u md a *tfre wllf* sn n e *ydb* f o tsj nd lfl g f *stfrc wllf* dly ssmbd nd lglly cnstd *rm* hw mny, cmps seh a g sn !i !u !w r mr *rm* wn a g cnsts f !u wo cmps t sn *wRt rm* s nd jns s and jks *rm* e jks plc n e g sn t e sns rt *rm* ur *ytd* tr br jk jk o cry mssgs fm e sn n e W et (e ffcrs tll tr rspctv *sytd pu* o e *rm sa* n predg dgr *rm* (gvs !i skcnk nd l rs) nd *ch* sys br sn u wl pls o tk ntc t s *ym* drctn tt ts g f *stfrc wllf* be nw pnd nd stnd pn fr e spc f !a hr fr e dsph f bsn u wl pls o rprt e sm o e jn n e S tt e brn *yam* hv du ntc trf nd gvrn *svflsmht* crdgy sn br jn u wl pls o tk ntc t s e *wRt rms* wl nd plsr tt a g f *stfrc wllf* b pnd n ts plc fr e spc et *sa* bv jn brn u hv hrd e wl nd plsr f e *wRt rm* u wl pls o tk du ntc thrf nd gvrn *svlsry* crdgy *rm rhtgt* brn (l gv du *drg* nd sn f *tfrc wllf*) gvs !e skcnk i dclr ts g f *stfrc wllf* dly pn fr e dsph f bsn *rm* ny tg n e W. br sn sn ntg n e W *wRt rm* ny tg n e S br jn jn ntg n e S *wRt rm* wt s ur plsr brn—br i prps tt *ew* rcv e Ls n ts dgr. (*etn* e Crmy f clsg a *stfrc wllf* g s e sm *sa* e *Pcs* xpt e nm f e dgr !e *skcnk* et)

Crmy f png a g f *rm* ns.

Rm br sn u wl pls o stsf *flrsy* tt l prsnt r *rm* ns sn xmns nd rprts i *ma* stsfd *wRt* tt l prsnt r *rm* ns *rm* br sn pls o cl e brn o rdr *sa rm* ns rsrvg *fislry* fr e lst (*etn* wn e *rm* gvs !e *skcnk* n png *ch* sks e sn *sa* n e brkts f e !ast scn f e Ls ch ffcr tls s *ytd sa* n e predg dgrs *pu* o e *rm rm* (gvs !i *skcnk* l rs) br sn hv u vr trvld sn i hv *wRt rm* whthr sn fm W o E nd fm E o W gn *rm* wt wr u n prst f sn tt whh ws *tsl rm* wt d u lld o br sn sn o e *strcs* f a *rm* n *rm* d u pss *mt* sn i d nt *wRt tb* hv a *tttss rm* br sn u wl pls o tk

CRMY N CLSG RM NS G

ntc t *s ym* drctn tt e *tttss* f a *rm* ns *drw* b snt *pu* nt e E ttndd wh ts du *sdrg* nd sns *rm* sys brn u wl pls o *mrf* (e sk *smrf* !a ln *no* e rt f e *rm* e jk *smrf* e lft ln lvg *na* vnu e brn fcng e cntr e sk *sog* o e W o e hd f s ln e jk o e W o e hd f s c sn dscnds fm s sttn pst e sk e sk trng o e rt ths sn nd sk tn cmnc fm e du *drg* nd sn f *na Pe pu* o e gnd sn f a *rm* n tn *no* e !u *stnp* e sk gvs e sn e *rms drw* e sk tn trns o e !ast br *no* s ln and e sm crmy s prsd thr e ln *pu* o e *rm* e ppr br gvg e lst *drw* e jk prcds wh e sn n e sm mnr *sa* e sn hd dn nd prss wh s ln e s nd jks ftr hvg rcd e *drw* rspctly *wlf pu* tr rspctv lns wh tr rds o *es* tt ch br gvs e *drw* nd sns crcty n e lft ln ws a vcnc fr e jn o *pts* n nd fl e *cps* n e ln wn e *drw* hs rrvd o s vcnc gvs e *drw* nd *sog* bk o s sttn e *rm* dscnds fm s *nrht* nd gvs e *drw* o e lst br *no* ch ln rt nd lft tn rtrng o s *nrht* e brn rmn stndg *rm* sys br sn e *tttss* f a *rm* ns *drw* hs cm *pu* nt e E crcty u wl pls o tk ntc t s *ym* drctn tt a g f *rm* ns b nw pnd nd stnd pn et *sa* n thr dgrs sn sys *sa* n thr dgrs xpt e nm f e dgr jn sys *sa* n thr dgrs *rm* sys *rhtgt* brn nd gvs l'e sns *pu* o e *rm* n gvs !i dstnct *skcnk* nsrd y e s nd jns nd dclrs ts *rms* g o b dly pnd fr e dsph f bsn (l st) e *rm* nw cnslts e ffcrs nd brn *sa* n frmr dgrs.

Crmy n clsg *rm* ns g.

Rm br sn hv u ny *rhtrf* bsn n e W bfr ts g f *rm* ns sn i no f ntg *rhtrf* n e W *wRt rm* hv u ny rhtrf bsn n e S br jn jn i no f ntg rhtrf n e s *wRt rm* wt s ur plsr brn f tr s *on rhtrf* bsn bfr e g f *rm* ns *ew* wlprcd o cls t (ps !a mnt) *rm* gvs !a *kcnk* jk rss br jk e lst *sa*

CRMY N CLSG RM NS G.

wl *sa* e !ast cr f a *rm* n jk o *es* e g dly *dlt wRt rm* u wl pls o prfm tt *trp* f ur *ytd* nd nfrm e *rlyt* tt *ew* r bt o cls ts g f *rm* ns nd tt *eh* ss e dr dlt crdgy jk *sog* o e dr gvs !i dstt *skcnk* nsrd y e *rlyt* pns e dr nd sys br *rlyt* *ew* r bt clsg ts g f *rm* ns u wl pls o *es* e dr *dlt* crdgy *rlyt* *sths* e dr nd rtrns o s plc nd sys *ew* r *dlt wRt rm* hw r *ew dlt* br jk y a *rm* n wht e dr rmd wh e prpr mplmt f s ffc *rm* e *srlyt* plc jk t e dr wh a *nwrd* srd n s *dnh rm* s *ytd* tr jk o bsv e ppch f cns nd *srprdsv* scndg r dscndg. nd o *es* tt nn ps r rps wht prmsn fm e *wRt rm rm* (gvs !e *skcnk* ffcrs rs) br sn t e png f ts g u nfmd *em* tt u ws a *rm* n md n e *ydb* f a *tsj* nd lfl g f *rm* ns dly ssmbd nd lgly cnstd hw mny cmps sch a g sn !i !u !u r mr *rm* wn a g cnsts f !i wo cmps t sn e *wRt rm* s nd jns *rm* e *rms* sttn n e g sn n e E *wRt rm* s *ytd* tr sn *sa* e *nus* rss n e E o pn nd drn e yd et (*rm* gvs !i *skcnk* 1 rs) *rm* lfts s ht nd *swb* o e sn) br sn hv u vr trvld sn i hv *wRt rm* whthr sn fm W o E nd fm E o W gn *rm* wt wr u n prst f sn tt whh ws *tsl rm* wt d u lld o sn e *strcs* f a *rm* n *rm* d u pss *mt* br sn sn i d nt *wRt tb* i hd a *tttss* whh i snt *pu* nt e E. *rm* br sn u wl pls o tk ntc t s *ym* drctn tt e *tttss* f a *rm* ns *drw* b rtrnd nt e W tr o b dpstd ntl *rhtrf* cld fr ttndd wh ts du *sdrg* thr e ks *yln* (*etn* e s nd jks *og* bfr e *nrht* n e E e *rm* dscnds nd stnds btwn *mt* frntg e sk ty *og* thr e du *sdrg* nd sns fm *Pe pu* o *rm* n e sk tn gvs e *rms drw no* e !u stnp f *phswllf* o e *rm* ftr whh sk *swb* o *rm* nd *sog* o e W nd *sog* thr e sm crmy wh e sn nd e sn gvs e *drw* o e sk drng ts tm e jk s cmnctg e sns nd *rms drw* o e *wRt rm* jk *swb* nd *sog* o e W o sn nd *sog* thr e sm crmns wh e sn rcvg e *drw* fm e sn 1 tk tr sttns sn sys e *tttss* f a *rm* ns *drw* hs bn rtrnd nt e W crcty *wRt* tr o b dpsd ntl *rhtrf* cld fr grby o ur rdrs *rm* (*swb* o e jn nd sys) br jn pls o tk ntc t s *ym* drctn tt ts g f *rm* ns b nw clsd nd stnd clsd tl r *txn* rglr

XMNN F A RSTG BR N E SRLYT MOOR. 31

cmmntn nls snr cld *no* sm spcl mrgncy f whh du nct wl b gvn u wl pls o rprt e sm o e sn n e W tt e brn *yam* hv dn ntc trf nd gvrn *svlsmht* crdgy jn (*swb* o e sn nd sys) br sn u wl pls o tk ntc t s e *wRt rms* wl nd plsr *sa* bv et sn brn u hv hrd e wl nd plsr f e *wRt rm* u wl pls o tk du ntc trf nd lt t b crdgy *os* dn *rm rhtgt* brn (gvs l e sns fm *Pe* o *rm* n) gvs !i sprt *skcnk* nsrd y e j nd sns tks ff s ht nd sys brn i dclr ts g f *rm* ns dly clsd.

Xmnn f a vstg br n e *srlyt moor*:

Cmt pntd y e *wRt rm* f !i f whh *on* !a wrs a jl ty ssmbl n e *srlyt moor* e *rlyt* hs rprtd br A fm g t P et *rm* r tr ny brn n e g wo cn *hcva* fr br A. brs B. C nd H u r pntd a cmt o *og tu* nd o xmn br A (ty tk a b wh *mt*) *rlyt* ntrdcs *mt* o br A. Cmt br A *ew* r ppy o *es* u *ew* ndstnd u *hsw* o tk a *ts* wh *su* A i d srs f t s grbl cmt t s r sl cstm n ts g sr o dmnstr e *srlyt tho* r bn hv u ny bjctn sr o tk sch *na tho* A i hv nt cmt prsnt e h b pls o rpt ur nm nd sy ftr *em* i A f *ym* wn *erf* wl nd ccrd n e prsnc f *ythgml* § nd tse *nmltng* d hry nd hrn mst slmny nd sncry *rws* tt i hv bn rglry nttd *na Pe* psd o e dgr f a *tfrc wllf* nd rsd o e sblm dgr f a *rm* n n a tr nd lfl g f *erf* nd ccptd ns nd nvr hv bn st sd r xpld trfm crdng o e bst f *ym gdlwn os* hlp *em* § nd kp *me tsfdts* n ts *ym srlyt* tho r bn cmt hv u ny tg wry u cn stsf *su* tt u r a n A i hv sr sns *snkt* nd *sdrw* cmt gv *su* sm sns gvs e du *drg* nd sn f *Pe* et et e cmt rtrn nd rprt *wRt ew* r stsfd tt br A fm e g t P s a brt *rm* n.

Crmy f clg o *tnmhsfr.*

Rm gvs ;e *skcnk* br T e jns sttn n e g T n e S *wRt rm* ur *ytd* n e S br jn jn *sa* e *nus* et *rm* br jn wt s *kclc* jn hi ;ae *wRt rm* gvs ;i skcnk br sn u wl pls o tk ntc t s *ym* drctn tt e *tfrc* b nw cld fm lbr o *tnmhsfr* fr a *trhs* spc f tm u wl pls o rprt et; sn br jn u wl pls o tk ntc t s e *wRt rms* wl nd plsr jn brn u hv hrd e wl nd plsr et *rm rhigt* brn gv sns ;i *skcnk* i dclr e *tfrc* dly cld o *tnmhsfr* br jn e *tfrc* snw ndr ur drctn u wl pls o *es* ty r dly *dhsfr* o cl o lbr *rm* gvs ;a *kcnk* brn pls o cm o rdr l st slnt gvs ;e *skcnk* e ffcrs rs br T e jns sttn n e g T n e S *wRt rm* ur *ytd* n e s br jn jn sa e *nus* et *rm* br jn wt s e *kclc* jn ;a hr pst mrdn *wRt rm* t s tm e *tfrc* r cld o lbr gvs ;i *skcnk* l rs br sn u wl pls o tk ntc t s *ym* drctn tt e *tfrc* b nw cld fm *tnmhsfr* o lbr u wl pls o rprt et sn br jn u wl pls o tk ntc t s e *wRt rms* wl nd plsr tt e *tfrc* b cld fm *tnmhsfr* o lbr u wl pls o rprt e sm o e brn et jn brn u hv hrd e wl nd plsr et *rm rhtgt* brn gv sns gv *skcnk* i dclr e *tfrc* dly cld o lbr fr e dsph f bsn.

krW n *Pe.*

Nte wn e cndt s prprd nd brt o e dr e cmt gv ;a *kcnk sa* a prvt sgnl tt ty r nw t e dr *rm* gvs ;a *kcnk* nd sys sk nd u sl rcv ;a *kcnk* sk nd u sl *dnf* ;a *kcnk kcnk* nd t sl b pnd nt u e cmt tn gv e rglr lrm ;i *skcnk rm* sys br jk pls o ttnd l lrm jk *sog* o e dr nsrs e lrm pns e dr nd sys wo cms tr et *sa* n ;ast sc f L jk rtrns o s plc *rm* br jk wt csns e lrm jk a *roop dnlb* cndt et e sm *sa* t e dr ftr e qsns nd nsrs r thr btn e *rm* nd jk *rm* gvs ſi *skcnk* (l rs) nd sys brn u hv hrd e ccsn f e lrm t e dr n e crmns nw bt o b prfmd i wl thk·u fr ur sstnc nd ţtntn br sk u wl rcv e cndt *no* e *tnp* f a *prhs* nstr]ovac[mnt prstd o s *dnk* lft *tsrb* nd nfm hm *sa* t s *na* nstr]prz[mnt f trtr et (*es* ſend sc f L) ftr s crmy e sk tks e cndt ndr e rm nd ppchs twds e E syg *on* prsn sd vr ntr pn ny gt r mprt ndrtkg wht ſast nvkg e blsg f *yted* hr a *nhsc* s plcd btn e *rtla* nd e nrht ty *lnk* *rm* sys lt *su yrp fshcv* thn *dia* et (*es* Mnr) ftr *ryrp* e *rm* dscnds fm e *nrht stp* s rt *dnh no* e cndts hd nd sys n whm d u *tp* ur trst nsr n § *rm* ur trst bng n § rs *wllf* ur *rdl* nd fr *on* dngr sk rss *sog dnr* e g wnc o e jn n e S whr *eh* mks a rglr lrm jn wo cms tr sk a *roop* *dnlb* cndt et *sa* t e dr *es* ſast sc f L. sk tn pss *no* o e sn n e W whr e sm crmy s pi fmd *sa* bfr nd fm tnc o e *wRt rm* (*es* ſast sc) wn *eh* s rdrd o b rcndtd o e sn wo css *mh* o dvnc y ſa prt rglr *pts* s *tf* frmg e rt *lgn* f *na* blng *rqs* s ydb rct twds e E tn *slnk* t e *rtla rm slnk* ppst e cndt tks ffs ht nd rpts e obn drng ts crmy e brn *mrf* a crcl *dnr* e *rtla* l stndg slnt e s nd jks hld e rds vr e cnds hd n e *mrf* f *na hcr* ftr e obn *rm* rss nd sys br A. wt d u mst dsr nsr *xl rm* tn rpts e ſi ſast vrss f e ſast *rtphc* f *ssng* nd sys n mbl mttn f ts *tsgua* cmnd i *ys* lt ts r br *es* e *xl* y whh *rms krw rhtgt* brn ſa clp f e *sdnh* s gvn *rm* sys br A *no* bng brt o *xl* e ſast tgs tt r prstnd o ur vw r e ſi gt *sxl* n *ysm* sstd y e lp f ſi lsr hr *eh* xpns e *sxl sa* n e ſast sc f L hr e *krw* flws *sa* n L ſast sc vzt e *drw* nd *prg* f *Pe rm* pphg fm e E ſe nd tm—prsntg *bml nks* et *sa* n ſast sc f L o e cnclsn e cndt s nw rdrd *tu* o b nvsd et nd rtrng o e *en* crnr f e g *es* L ſast sc *sa* a *tsj* nd prt n et e *rm* tn prsnts e *gkrw slt* nd xpns tr sss nd tn rds e *grhc*.

Crmy nd *krw* n *stfrc wllf* g

Cndt s dvsd f l *slrnm* nd *sltm* nhr *dkn* nr *dhtlc* bt nr † ‡ wh a ¶ !ece *dnr* e *dkn* rt rm nd ths prpd s cndtd o e dr f e g nd gvs !i dstnt *skcnk rm* sys br jk u wl pls o ttnd e lrm jk *sog* o e dr nsrs e lrm pns *e* dr nd sys wo cms tr rptd hr e sm qstns nd nsrs *sa* bfr *es* !ast sc n L jk rtrns o s plc *rm* wt ccsns e lrm t e dr jk br A wo hs *yltsj* nd lfly srvd s tm *sa na Pe* et e sm qstns nd nsrs *sa* t e dr *rm* gvs !i *skcnk* l rs brn u hv hrd et i wl tk *sa* n Pes *krw* br sk (wo dvncs bfr e *nhrt*) ftr rmndg e cndt f e mnr n whh *eh* ws rcd n e prcdg dgr u wl rcv *mh no* e *lgna* f e *rqs* (prsng t o *mh*) nd nfrm *mh* tt e *rqs* f *htrt* nd vrt sd b e rl nd gid f l s trnsctns thr lf lt *mh* ntr sk tn *sog* o e dr nd sys lt *mh* ntr ftr whh *eh* sys br A wn u wr rcd nt a g f *Pes* u ntrd *no* e *tnſ* f a *ſrhs* nstr]mvg[mnt prsntd o ur *dkn* lft *tsrb* u nw ntr ts g f *stfrc wllf no* e *lgna* f e rqs et *sa* bv u wl flw ur ldr eh *sog* !ece *dnr* e g o jn n e S whr e sm et *sa* t e dr nd drcts *mh* o ps *no* o e sn n e W nd tn o e *wRt rm* n e E *sa* bfr tn rcndtd o e sn n e W.wo tht *em* o dvnc y !e prt et *sa* n !ast sc f L t e !ast *ſts* cndt slts e *wRt rm*, wh e du *drg* nd sn f *na Pe rm* tn dscnds o e *rlta* nd sys br A bfr *ew* cn prcd ny *rhtrf* wh u n ts slmn crmy t wl b ncsy fr u o tk e *tho* r obn wrb u wl *dnb flsry* o kp nvlbly e *strcs* f ts dgr e *rm* tn rdrs e sn o cs e cndt o *lnk* n s *dkn* rt *en* hs lft frmg a *rqs* et *sa* n L *rm slnk* ppst brn *mrf* a *lcrc dnr* e *rlta* e ks plcng tr rds n e *mrf* f *na hcr rm* gvs e obn ftr whh rm rss nd sys br A wt d u mstdsr nsr mr *xl rm* brn i wl thk u o sst *em* n brng ts r br o *es* mr *xl* n *ysm rhtgt* brn gvs !i clps f *sdnh* br A *no* bng brt o *xl* n ts dgr wt u nw dscvr mr thn u hv dn bfr s !a *tnſ* f e *ssfmc* br e thr bng hdn whh ws o sgnf *sa* a *tfrc wllf* tt u hd rcd *xl sa* yt *tb* prtly *rm* tn sys br B i nw pph u fm e E ndr e du *drg* nd sn f a *tfrc wllf* tn gvs *mh* e *frg* nd *drw* f a *tfrc wllf* e *krw* flws *sa* n L !ast sec

---

e !end sc

Wn e cndt s drssd e cmt pph e dr nd gv a rglr lrm *rm* sys br jk pls o ttnd e lrm jk *sog* o e dr rtrns nd sys *wRt rm* e cndt s rdy o b dmtd *rm* br sk u wl pls o rcv e cndt sk *sog* o e dr nd sys lt *mh* ntr tks *mh* y e *dnh* nd sys t ws *na* ncnt cstm fr l rglr *yhtrw stfrc wllf* o b rcd nd rcrdd n e mdl *rbmhc* f *gnk sns lfmt* n gng tr *yw* hhr ty hd o ps thr a *hcrf* t e ntrnc f whh wr !e gt *srlf* !a *no* e rt nd e thr *no* e lft e !e *no* e rt clld ¿ nd e !a *no* e lft * hr e !e *srlf* r *dklhc tu no* e flr tghr wh e flgt f *gdnw srts nwrd* n sch a mnr *sa* o brng e !w *sfts* ppst e jn *es* L !end ftr e xplntn f e *srlf* nd *srts* e sk nd cndt rrv t e jn nd gv a rglr lrm e jn rss nd sys wo cms tr sk nsrs br A wo hs *yltsj* nd lfly et *sa* t e dr *no* e !ast ntrnc e sm qstns nd nsrs jn dmnds e ps *drw* f a *tfrc wllf* t s gvn *eh* sys t s rt fm wnc dd ts *drw* rgnt sk t ws n cnsqnc f a qrl btn *ahtfj gdj* f srl nd e *stmrhfe sgdj* !ae *rtfhc* e *stmrfhe* et *es* !end sc f L ftr whh e jn sys t s wl t s *ym* drctn tt u ps *no* o e nnr dr f e *lfmt* whh u wl *dnf ddrg* y e s gnd n wo wl dmnd f u e *frg* nd *drw* f a *trfc wllf* ty ps *no* o e sn mk a rglr dmnd *eh* rss nd sys wo cms tr wo cms tr sk nsrs br A wo wshs o b rcd nd rcrdd n e mdl *rbmhc* f e *lfmt sa* a *yhtrw tfrc wllf* sn pls o gv *em* e *frg* nd *drw* f a *tfrc wllf* cndt gvs t sn e *drw* s rt pls o ntr ty ps *no* twrds e E. ps e *rtla rm* rss nd sys u r nw rcd nd rcrdd n e mdl *rbmhc* f *gnk* sns *lfmt sa* a *yhtrw tfrc wllf* i wl nw wh plsr prsnt u e *gkrw* tls f a *tfrc wllf* whh r e *bmlft rqs* nd ll e *rm* nw xpns *mt* (*es* mnr) ftr ts e *rm* sys i wl nw drct ur ttntn o e *rttl* G (*gtnft* o e *tftrc*) *rm* sys ts *rttl* G br A s e ntl f *yrtmg* r e ꞉uth scnc *no* whh *ysm* s prncply fndd y ‘*yrtmg* et (es mnr) ts *rttl* G *rhtrf* llds o e *drcs* nm f *yted* (*rm* gvs ꞉i skcnk l rs nd *wb* t e *drcs* nm f *yted*) o wm l sd *sa* n ꞉end sc f L nd e cnclsn *rm* tn rds e *grhc* ftr whh *eh* sys ts *grhc* br A t s *ym ytd* o cmnct o u nt dtng tt u wl lt e xclnt prcpts trn cntnd hv tr du wght pn u n l ur trnsctns thr lf. ths ndh e *krw* n *stfrc wllf* g.

---

krW n e *rm* ns dgr.

E cndt s prprd y bng dvsd et *sa* n e thr dgrs wh a ¶ ꞉i tms *dnr* s *dkn ydb* e cmt ;n mk e lrm t e dr *sa* n e prcdg dgrs *rm* br jk *es* wt csns e lrm t e dr jk ttnds e lrm nd nqrs wo cms tr wo cms tr cmt br A wo hs *yltsj* nd lfly srvd s tm *sa na Pe* bn psd o e dgr f a *tfrc w'lf* nd nw sks fr *rhtrf xl* n *ysm* y bng rsd o e sblm dgr f a *rm n* ftr e sl qstns nd nsrs e jk rtrns o s plc *rm* br jk wt csns e lrm t e dr jk nsrs *sa* t e dr *rm* gvs ꞉i *skcnk* l rs brn u hv hrd e csn f e lrm t e dr n e crmys nw bt o b prfmd i wl thk u fr ur sstnc nd ttntn br sk (*eh* dvncs bfr e *nrht*) ftr rmndg e cndt f e mnr n whh *eh* ws rcd nt e prcdg dgrs u wl rcv hm *no* e *stnft* f ts *ftrhs* nstrmnt xtndd o s *dkn stsrb* whh sgnf tt *sa* e vtl prncpl f lf ls wn e *tsrb os* r e mst vlbl *strcs* f *ysm* cntnd wn e *stnft* f e *ssftmc* wh r frndsp mrlt nd bry lv lt *mh* ntr jk *sog* o e dr nd sys lt *mh* ntr nd dds br A wn u wr rcd nt e g f *Pes* u ntrd n e *tnft* f a *ftths* nstr]avec[mnt f trtr o ur *hslf* whh u wr nfrmd e rclctn trf mt b o u sd u vr prsm o rvl e *strcs* f *erf ysm* nlfly wn u ntrd a g f *stfrc wllf* u wr rcd *no* e *lgna* f e *rqs* nd nfrmd tt e *rq*s f *htrt* nd vrtu sd b e rl nd gid f l ur trnsctns thr lf u nw ntr ts g f *rm* ns *no* e'*tnp* f e *ssfmc* xtndd et *sa* bv u wl flw ur ldr *sog* 'i tms *dnr* e g jn *skcnk* 'ace *sa eh* pss e 'ast tm nsrd y e sn nd *wRt rm* 'end *dnr* o jn, sn nd *wRt rm skcnk* 'ece nd e 'i *dnr* 'i tms ch drng ts crmy e *rm* rds rmmbr ty crtr et *lkze* 'ae *rtphc* (*es* mnr) ftr e 'id *dnr* mks *na* lrm t e jn n e S hr e sm qstns nd nsrs *sa* t e dr *eh* pss o e sn e sm—tnc o e *wRt rm* e sm qstns nd nsrs ftr *whh* e *rm* sys fm wnc cm u nsr fm e W rm whthr r u trvlg nsr o e E *rm* wt r u n prst f nsr tt whh ws *tsl* whh b *ym* wn ndvrs wh ur sstnc i hp o btn *rm* t s wl e *rm* tn rdrs *mh* o b cndtd o e sn n e W wo tchs *mh* o dvnc y 'i prt rglr *sfits* s *tf gmrf* a *rqs* nd s *ydb* rct o e E sltg e *rm no* e 'ast nd 'end dgrs e *rm* dscnds nd gvs e obn n du *mrf es* L *rm* tn rss nd sys br A wt d u mst dsr nsr mr *xl rm* sys brn i wl thk u o sst *em* n brng ts r br o *xl* l gv 'i ms 'i *rm* sys br *no* bng brt o *xl* n ts dgr wt u nw dscvr mr thn u hd dn bfr s *thb stnp* f e *ssfmc* br whh sgnfs tt u nvr sd ls st f e mrl pplctn f tt sfl mplmnt fr y a du ttntn o ts *esu ew* r tht o rglt r dsrs nd kp r psns wn du *sdnb* wh l *dnknm tb* mr spcly a br *rm* tn gvs *mh* e du *sdrg sns prg* nd ps *drw* nd rdrs *mh* o *og* nd slt e j nd sn e cndt tn pprhs e E nd rcvs e flwg *grhc* br A bfr *ew* cn prcd ny *rhtrf* wh u n ts slmn crmy t wl b ncsy fr u o trvl et *es* e cnclsn f e 'ast sc of e L n ts dgr. cndct e cndt o e prprn *moor*.

⁏End SC

Whl e cndt s *tu* e *rm* ppnts e ⁏i snss ⁏i *stfrc wllf* rprsng e ⁏ae nd e *wy.frg* mn ty tk tr rspctv sttns wn e cndt s *dhtlc eh* cms n *ddlfdnlb* ftr a rglr lrm *rm* rdrs e sk o rcv *mh* nd cndct *mh* twrds e *cn* crnr f e g syg t ws e *yld* cstm f r gnd *rm* et *es* ⁏end sc f L *nwd* o pl wn *eh* rrvs t e *nhsc eh slnk* e *rm*.. gvs ⁏i *skcnk* nd sys lt *su yrfi* " Thu o §" et (*es* Mnr) sk tn rss *sog no* twrds e S syg " ftr prfmg ts ps *ytd eh* tn rs nd ttmpd o *og tu* t e S dr hr e cndt s *dzs* y *aluj* wo sys wo cms hr sk ur gnd *rm mrih ffba aluj* e vry mn i hv bn wtg fr gv *em* e *strcs* f a *rm* n sk ts s nt a prpr tm o dmnd tse *strcs tw* wh ptnc nd n du tm u sl rcv tm *sa ylısj* nd lfly *sa* i hv dn *aluj klt* nt f tm plc r ptnc *tb* nstnty gv *em* e *strcs* f e *rm* n r i wl tk ur lf. jk ts s nt a prpr tm r plc *aluj klt* nt f tm nr plc i *ys* nd tn strks *mh ssrc* e || sk tn *sog no* o e W whr *eh* ndvrd o mk s *fics tu* t e W dr hr *eh* ws ttkd y *oluj* hr e sm qstns nd nsrs r gvn *sa* bfr *oluj* strks *mh* wh e *rqs* sk tn *sog* o e E *tg* whr *eh* is *dzs* y *mluj* nd e sm qstns nd nsrs r gvn wh ts ddn e sk sys e *lfimt* s *wn* nr ts cmpltn nd l tse wo r *dnf yhtrw* sl rcv tm *sa yltsj* nd lfly *sa* i hv dn *mluj* wt stl prst tn *eid* hr e *krw* flws lk e Ls ftr e *stfrc wllf* cry e *ydb ff* nd mk tr *fics* cnfsn nss *snss og* nt e *ws* crnr f e g *rm* gvs ⁏a *kcnk* nd sys br sn wt csns l s cnfn sn sys *sa* n L n e ⁏end cnfsn ftr rdrs r gvn o cl e *llr* f e *nmkrw* e ⁏i *stfrc wllf og fiu* o e *rm* nd cnfs tr *tlig krw* e sm *sa* n L vry tm e *stfrc wllf* r snt *tu* nd rtrn thr s cnfsn *rm* gvs ⁏a *kcnk* nd cls *no* e sn wo nsrs *sa* n L wn e *ydb* s rsd t s dn n e *wn* crnr f e g e brn *mrf* a *lcrc dnr* e cndt nd e sn rss *mh* no e ⁏u *stnfi* f *fihswllf* nd gvs *mh* e *drw* e brn nd ffcrs l rtrn o tr plcs nd st *nwd* e sk cndcts e cndt o e *nrht* wn e *wR: rm* rss nd rds o *mh* e flwng *yrtsh.*

DRCS *yrtsh* nfrms *su* tt t ws dtrmd n e cncls f nfnt *mdsw* tt a *lpmt* sd b *ddnf* n jrs]apz[lm whh sd b rctd o § nd ddctd o s h nm, e hi nr nd *dhsgntnsd* prvlg f prfmg ts *drcs* srvc ws dnd o dvd *gnk* f srl bcs *sa* e *srtprcs* nfrm *su* "eh was a mn f *dlb*" nd drng lmst e whl prd f s rgn *eh* ws gtd nd dstrtd y e tmlts cnfsn f *rw ew* lrn ls fm e sm src tt e § f srl prmsd dvd tt "*tu* f s lns *eh* wd rs *pu* a *des* o srv *mh*" ts dvn nd vr mmrbl prms ws ftrwds fflld n e *nsrp* f sn nd n e splnd n nxmpld crr f s prsprt ftr dvd was *drhtg* o e lnd f s *srhtf* nd e lst nrs pd o s mmr sn scndd e *nrht* nd wldd e *rtpcs* f srl pc rgnd wn s *srdrb* nd l e *nrdlhc* f srl lkd frwd wh pclr stsfctn fr e dspy f tt *mdsw* whh ws dstnd o *zma* nd *hsnts* e *dlrw* n e !end *htnm* f e !oth *ry* f s rgn sn cmncd e bldg f e *lpmt* whh grbl o dvn cmnd ws o b rctd o § nd ddctd o s h nm e crs *phsnmkrw* f whh ws clcltd o xct e *rdnw* nd *tnmhsnst* f l sccdg gs *shpsj* nfms *su* tt fr e spc f !w *sry* drng whh prd e *lpmt* ws rctd t dd nt rn xpt n e *tgn* ssn whn e *tfrc* wr cld fm lbr o *tnmhsfr os* tt e *krw* ws nt e lst mpdd n ts prgrs a strkg prf f e cr nd prtctn f dvn *cndvrp.* bt ts prd sn rcd a cngrtlty *rttl* fm s prtclr *dnrf mrih gnk* f *ryt* n whh *eh* ffrd *mh* vry sstnc n s *rwp* nd mnfsd a *gnrts* dspstn o prtcpt t lst n sm fbl dgr n tse hi nrs whh smd o clstr *dnra* e *nrht* f sn e bldg f e lpmt ths prgrsg wh e sstnc f *mrih gnk* f *ryt* nd ndr e mdt nspctn nd drctn f *mrih ffba* e *sdw ns* e *lpmt* ws wl ni cmptd wn svrl f e *tfrc* fr e prps f btng grtr wgs n frn *sdnl* bcm

e *snss* f e gnd *rm* *mrih* nd ths fr a *trhs* prd e cmpltn f
e *lpmt* ws mpdd u br A hv ts vng rprs]cvt[ntd r gnd.
rm mrih ffba e *fhc tcthcr* n e bldg f *gnk* sns *lpmt*, *sa* hs
bn *tsj* rmrkd *eh* ws sssntd nr e cmpltn f ts sprb dfc nd
s *htd* ws sldm qlld nd probly nvr xcld a cnspry ws
dmrf gnst s lf y !au *stfrc wllf* wo sng e *krw* nry *dhslpmc*,
wr frfl ty sd nt b bl o btn *rm* ns wgs wn trvlg nt frn
cnts ntrd nt a hrd cnspry o xrt fm r gnd *rm mrih*
ffba e *strcs* f a *rm* n r o tk s lf. *tb* !ae f *mt* drdg e vl
cnsqcs wr strk wh hrr t e trct f e *mrc* nd rcnd e thr !i
wo wr *aluj oluj* nd *mluj* bng mr hrdnd n *ynlv* wr dtrmd
o *tp* tr mrdrs *snsd* nt xcn nd crdgy plcd *svlsmt* t e *s.*
w. nd *e.* ntncs f e *lpmt* t e hr f hi !ae wn e *tfrc* wr cld
fm lbr o *tnmhsfr* t ws e *yld* cstm f r *gnd* rm *mrih ffba* t
ts hr o *og* nt e *lpmt* o vw e *krw* nd *es* f tr cd b ny mpvt
md thr fr ts tlt r nmnt nd ls o *wrd snsd no* s *lsrt drb* fr
e *tfrs* o prs tr lbrs ftr whh *eh* ntrd e *mtcns mnrtcns* r
ylh f *sylh* tr o ffr *pu* s drns nd *sryrp* o e *urt* nd lvg § fr
e sns f e pl ftr prfmg ts ps *ytd eh* rs nd tmpd o *og tu* t
e S dr whh *eh dnf ddrg* y *aluj* wo dmndd f *mh* t !i svl
tms n a brbrs mnr e *strcs* f a *rm* n r *eh* wd tk s lf ftr sm
ltrctn *eh* md s *pcs* nd ndvrd o ps *tu* t e W dr whh *eh*
dnf ddrg y *oluj* wo n lk mnr dmndd f *mh* t !i svl tms e
strcs f a *rm* n hr a scffl nsud *eh* tn ndvrd o mk s *pcs tu*
f e E dr whh *eh dnf ddrg* y *mluj* wo n lk mnr dmndd f
mh t !i svl tms e *strcs* f a *rm* n *tb no* s !ithd rfsl *eh tms*
mh no e hd wh a cmn *lvg* r *lm* sttg whh *llf mh* lfls t s *tf*
ty tn brd e *ydb* n e *hsbr* f e *lpmt* tl lo !ae r !ae t *tgn* wn
ty grd o *tm* nd cnst wt *rhtrf* o d wh t ty *tm* grby o
pntmt nd grd o cry e *ydb* a *ylrtsw* crs fm e *lpmt* nd brd
t t e *wrb* f a il cld *tnm hrm* n a *vrg* !y *tf gnl* nd !y *tf*
dp t e hd f e *vrg* ty *dtnlpsnrt* a *grps* f *assc* tt f csn rqrd
ty mt no whr o *dnf* t nd tn fr *rf* f dtcn ndvrd o mk tr

pics tu f e *mdgnk*, e *txn yd gnk* sn hrd f e cnfsn rprd o e *lpmt* nd nqd e cs e s gnd n nfrmd *mh* tt r gnd *rm mrih ffba* ws msg tt *eh* hd nt bn sn snc e hr f hi 'ae f *ydrtsy gnk* sn rdrd e s gnd n o cs e nnr prtmts f e *lpmt* o b *dhcres* nd ls a *llr* f e *nmkrw* o b cld whh bng dn e s gnd n nfrmd *mh* tt e nnr prtmts f e *lpmt* hd bn *dhcres* wht fct nd ls a *llr* f e *nmkrw* hd bn cld nd thr prd o b 'i *stfrc wllf* msg wo wr *aluj oluj mluj* and fm e smlrt f tr nms, ty prd o be brn nd mn f *ryt*, *gnk* sn nfrmd e s gnd n tt thr hd prd bfr *mh* 'ae *stfrc wllf*, *dhtlc* n *thw snrp* nd *thw svlg* n *nkt* f tr ncnc nd mplrg s *ndrp* nd nfrmd *mh*, tt ty 'ae wh 'i thrs hd ntrd nt a hrd cnspry o xrt fm r gnd *rm mrih ffba* e strcs f a *rm*, n r o tk s lf *tb* ty hd rcnd. *gnk* sn tn rdrd e s gnd n o cs e 'ae *stfrc wllf* o b snt *tu* 'i E. 'iW 'i N nd 'i S n *hcres* fr r gnd *rm mrih*, nd ls fr e *srtrsd* fm e *lpmt* ty wr snt *tu* crdgy nd 'i f *mt* trvlg *no* c cst f *pj* mt a *wyfrg* mn f wm ty nqd f *eh* hd *ns* ny *nmkrw* fm e *lpmt*, *eh* nfrmd *mt* tt *eh* hd *ns* 'i nqrg fr a psg o *aphtc*, *tb* nt bng bl o btn 'a ty hd rtrnd bk nt e cnty e *stfrc wllf* rtrnd o e *ytc* nd *dtrpr gnk* sn brsvd t ws f e hst mptnc tt r gnd *rm mrih* sd b *dnf* rdrd e *stfrc wllf* o b snt *tu* gn n e sm drctns ty wr crdgy snt *tu* nd trvld fr 'au *syd* wn 'i f *mt* scndg a il cld *tnm hrm* 'a f *mt* bng wry nd lmst xhsted st *nwd* o rst nd *hsrfr flsmh* n rsg *eh* cdnty cgt hld f a *grps* f *assc* whh cmng *pu* sly, e *dnrg* hvg bn rcnty rmvd hd e prnc f a *vrg* whh xctd s sspn *no* whh *eh dliah* s *nrhtrb* nd whl cntmpng *no* e *tps* ty hrd xclmtns fm e jcnt *sffle* ccsng nd xcsng ch thr whh prd o b e *scv* f e 'i *snss* r *srtrsd* fm e *lpmt* hr br A s e rgn f e 'i pnlts *aluj* xclmd "O tt i hd my || ct *ssrc*" et er i hd bn ccsry o e *htd* f r gnd *rm mrih*, *oluj* xclmd "O tt i hd hd *ym* lft *tsrb*" ct er et *mluj* xclmd i *ma* wrs thn u *htb* t ws i tt dprvd *mh*

42

f lf "o tt i hd *ym ydb* swd" et *no* whh ty mmdtly *dhsr* pſ
mt dnb mt nd crd *mt pu* o e *ytc gnk* sn rdrd *mt* o b snt
pu bfr *mh* whh ws crdgy dn nd thr cnfsd tr *tlig eh* tn
rdrd *mt* o b tkn wht e *stg* f e *ytc* nd thr svly xctd grby
o e *sntcrpm*, fm tr wn *shtm* ts ws dn ndr e drctn f e
s gnd n *gnk* sn tn rdrd *mh* o snd *tu* e ſi *stfrc wllf* o e
plc whr e wry br st *nwd* o rst nd *hsrfr flsmh* n *hcres* f
e *ydb* f r gnd *rm mrih* nd f *dnf* o *hcres* fr e *strcs* f a *rm*
n nd *es* f ty cn b *dnf no* r bt e *ydb* r a *yk* o *mt* ty wnt *tu*
md *hcres* nd rtrnd nd rprtd tt ty hd *dnf* e *ydb* n a
ylrtsw crs fm e *lpmt* t e *wrb* f a il cld *tnm hrm* n a *vrg*
ſy *tf gnl* nd ſy tf dp dg du *w*. nd *c* tt ty hd md *hcres* fr
e *strcs* f a *rm* n *tb* ty wr nt o b *dnf* n r bt e *ydb* nr a *yk*
o *mt gnk* sn tn xclmd e *rm* ns *drw* s *tsl eh* tn rqstd e s
gnd n o tk stbl sstnc nd *og tu* wh *mh* nd ndvr o rs e
ydb f r gnd *rm mrih* fr a mr dcnt ntrmt ty wnt *tu* n
prcsn nd *no* rvng t e *vrg gnk* sn lmntd e ft f s *yhtrw*
nd prtcr *dnrf* nd xclmd *sla rp mrih* nd *tpw* btry ftr sm
sp eh rdrd e s gnd n o ndvr o rs e *ydb* f r gnd *rm mrih*
y e *prg* f *na Pe eh* trd nd cd nt e *hslf* bng ptrd nd
slpd *eh* tn ndvrd o rs t y e *prg* f a *tfrc wllf* whh gv *yw*
n e sm mnr *gnk* sn tn rdrd e s gnd n o ndvr o rs e *ydb*
y e *gnrts prg* r *wpsnl* nd *no* e ſu *stnp* f *phswllf* nd e
ſast *drw* tt sd b spn ftr e *ydb* ws ths rsd sd b a *tttss* fr
e *rm* ns *drw* ntl ltr gs sd *dnf* e rt *eh* crdgy rsd e *ydb no*
e ſu *stnp* f *phswllf* nd e ſast *drw* tt ws spn ws y e s
gnd n wo xlmd (ts bng e ſast *drw* s cnsqty e *tttss* f a
rm n ts *drw*, s nhr *kreg wrbh* nr *hslgne*, ts s e rgn f ts
drw nd e *gnrts prg* wn e *stfrc wllf* wr snt *tu* o e *vrg*
no sng e *ydb* ty nvlntrly *dnf* tr *dnh* n ts pstn o kp ff e
fflv whh rs fm e *sprc* tt hd bn brd lrdy ſau *syd* nd s ths
cld e *du drg no* lkg nt e *vrg* nd *gdnf* e *ydb* n sch a hrd
nd mngd cndtn ty xclmd rsng tr rms o ∽ r § whh s cld

e gnd sn f a *rm* n wnvr u *es* ts sn t s ur *ytd* o rpr o tt sstnc r wn u hr tse *sdrw* xclmd n e *tgn* wn e sn cnt b sn u wl rpr o s rlf e !u *stnps* f *pihswllf* r *tf* o *tf en* o *en tsrb* o *tsrb dnh* o bk *khc* o *khc* wh *htm* o *re tf* o *tf* dnts *ew* sd nvr hstt o *og* a *tf tu* f r *yw* o sst a br *en* o *en* dnts tt *ew* sd rmbr a br n r dvns *tsrb* o *tsrb* tt *ew* sd kp a brs *strcs sa* r wn wn gvn o *su* n *grhc sa* sch mrdr nd *nsrt* xpd *drth* o bk tt *ew* sd ndvr o sprt a br wn flg *khc* o *khc* wh *htm* o *re* s e mnr n whh e *rms drw* s gvn u wl pls o gv *em* tt *drw sa* u rcd t fm e sn (ty gv t) e *rm* tn rtrns o s plc nd sys br A i wd nfrm u tt r gnd *rm mrih ffba* ws brd t !i svl tms !ast n e *hsbr* f e *lpmt* !end t e *wrb* f e il cld *tnm hrm* !ithd ndr e *mtcns mnrtcns* r *ylh* f *sylh gnk* sn rdrd a *lbrm* mnmt o b rctd o e mmr f *os* mbl nd *dhsgntsd* a *rtcrhc no* t ws a *ngrv* wpg bfr hr a *kb* pn n hr lft *dnh na nru* n hr rt *dnh* a *grps* f *assc dnhb* hr std tm wh s *sdnh* nfldd n e *stlgnr* f hr *rh* e *ngrv* wpg dnts e *lpmt dhsnfn* e *kb* pn dnts tt e lf nd *htd* f r gnd *rm mrih* r *no* prptl rcrd e *nru* dnts tt s shs wr sfl dpsd e *grps* f *assc* e tmy dscvy f s *vrg* tm *dnhb* hr wh s *sdnh* nfldd n e *stlgnr* f hr *rh* dnts tt lth r gnd *rm* ws dd nd e *lpmt dhsnfn* yt tm ptnc nd prsvrnc *hslpmc* l tgs e !zth nd lst *sslc* f mbms r e *lvg* e *dps* e *nffc* nd e *grps* f assc e *lvg* wh whh r gnd *rm mrih* ws *nls* e *dps* whh dg s *vrg* nd e *nffc* tt rcd s rmns tse o a *gnknht dnm* cs srs rfctns *tb* wn *ew* lk *drwrf* o e *grps* f *assc* whh blmd t e hd f s *vrg* t rmnds *su* f tt btr nd mrtl *trp* whh wl srvv e *vrg* t bng e nsprtn f tt sprm ntllgnc wm *ew* l *rda* nd bng e nrst rsmblnc o tt gt *ytid* tt prvds l ntr nd nfms *su* tt *ew* sl nvr nvr nvr *id yrtsh dhsnf rm* tn prcds ths i nw prsnt u wh e *gkrw slt* f a *rm* n whh r l e mplmts f *ysm* ndscrnmnty *tb* mr spcly e trl *eh* tn rds e *grhc* ftr whh *eh* sys ts *grhc* br **A** t

44

ws *ym ytd* o cmnct o u, nt dtg, *tb* u wl lt e xclnt prcts trn cntnd hv tr du wgt pn u n l ur tnsctns, thr lf, *rm* sys br. sk u wl pls o *hsnrf* br A wh a cnvnt *ts* n e g *sa* a *yhtrw* rm n (*etn* fr *rhtrf* nstctn e cndt s rfrd o e h b *suhpsj sdnpllv ttcs lnnP nsrdna* nd mny thr *srhta no ysm* fm wm *eh* wl rcv *hcm* nstctn

THE MASONIC TABLET

CHAPTER RITUAL

(Kingston, New York, 1822)
Facsimile

TP OS TCL.

E r u q tp o *P* z hv t. hnr ,t eb *A* hw rsjvd u .t y:
hnr *D* bi e bng dli lcjtd v nstjld .t prjsd vr q rgli cnjstd
m f frr v acjtd gs *I* bi wm wr u nsjtld *B* bi mi prjdcj-
ssr n ffc *A* wt wr t. prvs crmns .t ur nsjtln C z ws
cnjdcjtd .t t. ltr whr z ws esd .t nl v rcv .t th qt bo f ys
dgr *E* z wl thk u .t rpt yt th qt bo *F* z A B f mi wn frr
wl v ccrjd n t. prjsnc f A.D v ys WR m f tp os rctd
.t hm v ddjctd .t h IS d hzy v hzn mst slmi v snli pvs
n dtn .t mi frmr bos yt z wl lys hl frvr cnjcl v nvr rvl
ys dgr f q tp c wh z zm nw bt .t rcv .t ni n t. wrjld
xcjpt zt eb .t q tr v lwl F tp O qt ne lcjtd .t fll t. chr f
q Os m qt n .t bdi f q jst v lwl m f tp Os qr nto hm qt
ym ntl bi stjrt trl dxmn qt t. lwl nfjmtn f q F z shjl
hv fnd hm qt ym .t eb qs jsti v lwli ntld .t t. sm qs z
zm misf z frjthrr pvs yt z wl nsr ll lwl sgs v smns yt
my eb gvn qt snt nto zs fm q tr v lwl F tp o qt fm t. bdi
f q jst v lwl m f sch zf wtjhn t. lnjth f mi ct yt z wl ad
v sst ll wri dsjtrsd tp Os yr wds v rpjhns n prjfrnc .t
ni thr prjns sic rf qs z cn d zt wtjht njri .t msf v fmjli yt
z wl rl v gvjrn t. m vr wh z zm pptjtd .t prsd grbli .t
t. nct csjtms usjgs v lwjs f t. Jn yt z wl bde bi v spjpt t.
bi lws f t. m t. cnsjtn f t. gd m ndr wh t. sm zs hljdn
v t. gnl rgljns f gy z frjthrr pvs yt z wl nt rl v gojrn t.
m vr wh z zm ppjtd .t prjsd n zn rbjtri mnr yt z wl nt
prjsd vr ys qt ni thr m wtjht gvjg q Tcl qt pt f q Tcl
qt zf wtjhn mi pwjr csng t. sm .t eb dn yt z wl nt wrjg
ys m qt sfjfr zt .t eb dn bi thrs zf n mi pwjr .t prjvt zt
tb wl pprs ym f ll ppjhg dnjr sic fr qs zt shjl cm .t mi
knjlg ll ys z d mst slmi v snli pvs wtjht ni qvjctn mnjtl
rsjvtn qt sfvsn f mnjd n zs wtjvr bnjdg msf ndr on lss
pty thn qt f hvjg mi † clv sic yt z shjl on mr eb bl .t
prjnc twd f q th o sic hljp mi D v kp me stjdfjst n
ys mi th qt bo f q th o *I* ftr rcjvg t. th qt bo f q tp O
wt dd u yn bsjrv *K* t. W R O ppjhg mi fm t. E ndr t.
dgd v sg f q tp o ho pystd zs hs rt hd n tkn f hs cnjtnc f
Fri lv v frjndh v ytb zt t. gp v wd f q th o v bd zs og v
sljt t. S W Ss qs sch *E* hw wr u yn dsjpsd f *F* z ws
ken bi t. rt hnd bi t. o f crmjns v cndjctd bfr t. thjrn
whr z ws cs d .t gv mi sstt .t crtn nct chjrgs qs cnjtnd

[2]

n t. bk f Cnjstjns *A* wt fld *B* z ws yn ken bi t. rt h n d bi mi prdjcsr n ffc v cnjdtjd n .t t. chr f Sln whr z h d t. hnjr f rcjvg q gic slt fm t. m mi prdcsr xcjlmg Fn bhd ur O *O* wt r t. dus f q tp o *C* .t rl v gvjrn hs m grbli .t t. nct csjtms usgs v lws f t. Jn *I* wt s t. frthr du f q tp o *D* zt s t. frthr du f q Pt qt tp o t. prjsd ta ll fstjvls Injstjllns v ddjctns f ms ta t. lying f crnr stjns f ll chs ehjpls v thr stli dfcs *A* wt frjthr dusr rqrd f q Pt qt tp o *B* zt s t. du f q Pt qt tp o .t rpr .t t. hsz f mrng ta t. dcs f q wri F ere .t cnjslt yth hs frjnds tk chjrg f t. fnrl smn t. m frm q prjcssn v ttnd t. slm crmns ta t. grv *E* hv u ni sgs n ys dgr *F* zz hv *I* pls .t g-v zs t. prim (zh rs v gvs zt dgd,) *A* wt s qt cld *B* t. dgd f q tp O *I* .t wt ds yt lld *H* .t t. pty f mi bo yt z wljd rthr hv mi † clv-thn rvl t. scts f ys dgr nlfli *O* pls .t gv zs t. nxj t sg (t. nxjt F rs v g vs zt crssjg ll ptys) *E* wt S qt cld *D* t. gd sg f q tp o *A* .t wt ds qt sg lld *B* .t t. ptys f mi frmr bos *O* pls .t gv yr lft hnd F t. gp v wd f q tp o (yy rs v gv zt) *C* zt srt z grt u F G (G s hrd) *E* .t wt ds yt wd lld *T* .t t. ttl f q tp o *I* wt s t. ttll f q tp O *C* WR (O rs v tks t. F bi t. rt hnd v ss z grt u WR F A) (yus ndjth t. tp Os Tel)

Crmni f png q tp os m

Tp Os my eb mad n q mk os m. qt rthr.t. mk m s nt zlsd tb t. tp os s pnd pun zi t. W R yn tks ff hs Jl v ss F W S z hv mprt bsnss .t ttnd .t v z mut og zf t. Fn wl xcs zs t. WS ss WR zf u lve uz ere wl eb on ne .t prsd vr t. m WR ss z cn nt try mi bsnss s rgt WS ss zf u wl hv t. bonss t. prsd ntl zz cn lct q o WR u wl oblg uz WR ss zf u wl eb xpdts z wl zh rtns v ss Fn u wl pls .t brng n ur vts fr q o (t. vts r bfr prpd fr t Cdt) zh s dli lctd no bng nfmd zh s mh srpsd t. WS yn rcvs zhim v ntdcs hm qt t. o f crmns ds zt bi t. rdr f t. WS v cndts hm .t t. ltr whr zh rcvs t. bo zh s yn nstd n dfrm zh s yn cndctd .t t. chr .t Fn r yn rdrd bi t. o f crmns .t frm q prcssn v slt t. nov O ys bng dn sn.e ft t. Fn mk q dstbc sme f t. Fn sa WR z wsh u wld cl t. Fn .t rdr zh ncs to qt ter tms v ss gnm cm .t rdr yy d nt ttnd zh s rqstd agn .t cl .t rdr tb bng cnfsd ds nt gv hs rdr crrctli sme f t. Fn nfm hm .t gv tb ne nc zh ds sic v ll s rdr (tb ne Cdt cn eb bgt n ta q tm ftr ll r rcyd t. chg s gvn)

[3]

t. m my cls n dfrm qs n t. mk os dgr (t. Jls n q tp os m my eb t. sm qs n t. mk os dgr)

E M Os Tcl

E r u q E M o *C* z hv bn rcd v ckjnljgd qs sch *A* whr wr u rcd *B* n q rgli cnjstd m f EM Os *I* hw gnd u dm-jsn *B* bi sx dst ncs TA t. dr *I* wt ws sd .t u fm wijhn *D* ho cms ere *O* ur nsr *P* Fs A. B v C (qs my eb) ho hv jstli v lwli srjvd qr tms qs Eps bn psjd .t t. dgr f Fts rsd t. t. s blm dgr f o gs bn vnjcd t t. dgr f. mk o bn dli lcjtd v nsjtld tp o v nw wsjh fr frjthr prjmtn bi ebng rcd v ckjnljgd qs EM Os *A* wt mr wr u skd *B* zf z cm f mi wn frr wl v ccjrd zf z ws wri v wil qljfd dli v trli prpd zf z hd md t. ncsri prfci n t. prcdjng dgjrs v pr-pli vhd fr ll wh ebng nsd n t. fftv z ws skd bi wt frthr rt qt bnjft z xpjtd .t gn dmsn *E* ur nsr *F* bi t. bnjft f q ps *A* dd u gv zt *C* z dd nt tb mi cnjdcjtr gv zt fr zs *O* pls t. gv zt .t ur lft hnd F (yy rs v gv zt) *N* zt s rt z grt u F G .*I* .t wt ds qt wd lld *B* .t t. ttl f q tp o t. xr z yn stnd *O* dd ys gn u dmns *L* zt dd *E* hw wr u yn ds psp f *C* z ws cnjdcjtd sx tms rd t. m .t t. ltr whr z ws csd .t nl v rcv t. th qt bo f q E M O .*U* z wl thk u .t rpt qt th *S* z A B f mi wn frr wl v ccjrd n t. prjsnc f A D v ys m of E M Os rctd .t hm v ddjctd .t h IS d hzy v hrn n dtn .t mi frmr bos mst slmi v snli pvs yt z wl lys hl frvr cnjcl v nvr rvl ys dgr f E M O wh z zm nw bt .t rcv .t ni f zn nfrr dgr qt .t ni n t. wrjld xcpt zt shjl eb .t q tr v lwl E M O qt n t. bdi f q jst v lwl m f E M Os qr nto hm qt ym ntl bi stct trl dxmn qt t. lwl nfjmtn f q E M O z shjl hv fnjd hm qt ym .t eb qs jsti v lwli ntld .t t. sm qs z zm msf z frjthr pvs qt z wl nsr ll lwl sgs v smjns yt my eb gvn qt snjt nto zs fm a tr v lwl E M O qt fm t. bdi f q jst v lwl m f. sch zf wt bn t. lnjth f mi ct yt z wl ad v sst ll wri dstsd E M Os yr wds v rpjhns n prfrnc .t ni thr prns os rt qs z cn d zt wtht njri .t msf qt fmjli yt z wl bde bi v sppt ll t lws rls v rgjlns f q E M Os M t. Conjstn lws v dits f t. gd R f t. stt ndr wh t. sm s hldn v t. gnl gd R f t US yt z wl dspns lt v knjlg t q E M M O os rf qs z cn d zt ccr-dg .t t. bst f mi blts z frjthrr pvs qt z wl nt cndt n q mnr drgtri .t t. xr z nw stn qt .t t. nm bi wh z zm bt .t eb cld wh s qt f g E M O ll ys z do mst slmi v snjli pvs

[4]

yth q fyrm v fxt rsljtn .t kp t. sm wtht ni qvjctn mnti
isvtn qt sct vsn f mnd n zs wtvr bndg msf ndr on lss
pty thn .yt f hvg mi || trn et v mi bv t. rth os hlp me et
E ftr rcjvg t. th qt bo f q E M O wt dd u yn bsrv *F* t.
W R O ppjhg zs fm t. E ndr t. dgd v sg f q E M O ho
prstd zs hs rt hnd n tkn f q cntnc f hs Fri lv v frnjdh v
yth zt t. gp v wd f q E M o *A* hv u ni sgs n ys dgr *B*
zz hv *I* pls .t gv zs t. prim *C* (zh gvs t. dgd) *O* wt s qt
cld *P* t. dgd f q E M O *E* .t wt ds qt lld *F* .t t. pty f mi
bo qt z wljd rtlir hv mi || et thn r vl t. scjts f ys dgr nfli
U pls .t gv zs t. nxjt sg *C* (zh rs v gvs zt) *I* wt s yt
cld *B* t. gd sg f q E M O qt sg f dmjrtn *A* .t wt ds yt lld
I .t t. gd sg v xcjlmn qs gvn bi t. E M Os ven t. Kis
ws pljcd n t. Y C f Gr Slns tpl *E* pls .t gv ur lft hnd Fr
t. gp v wd f q E M O *C* (yy rs v gv zt) zt s rt z grt u F
R *A* .t wt ds yt wd lld *P* .t t. ttl f q E M O t. xr z nw
hv t. hnr .t stn *E* hv u ni thr sgs *B* zz hv *I* pls .t gv zs
t. nxjt *C* (yy rs v gv zt gp cvrg ll gps) *A* wt s yt cld
C t. gd tkn f q E M O *I* .t wt ds zt lld *D* .t ll t. gps f
mi frjmr dgjrs qt t. gp f ll gps. (yus ndjth t. E M Os
Tcl)

Crmni f png q E M Os M

T. ffcrs t. sm qs n t mk v tp os dgrs v t. Js t. sm t. o
f crmns my cmnc n t mk os dgr v cntn tro t. tp o v E M
Os dgrs t. W R ss F WS pls .t stsfi ursf qt ll prst r E
M Os WS z zm stsfd WR yt ll prst r E M Os W R
pls .t cl t. Fn .t rdr qs E M Os rsvg ur sf fr .t lst W
S Fn pls t. cm t rdr qs EM Os (yy cm .t rdr yth t. dgd
f q E M) t W S sts dwn W R gvs ter ncs O S qt J D
rs WR ss F OS r zz tld OS z wl og r vid WR (zh ogs
.t t. dr v gvs bis ter v s nsd bi t. Tli zh rtns .t hs plc v
ss) zz r tld WR. WR ss hw OS ss bi q E M O wtht t.
dr rmd yth t. prpr mplts f hs ffc (t. sm qsns v nsrs flw
yth t. ffcrs qs n t. thr dgrs.) WR gvs bis ter (ll rs) v zh
ss F O f crmus u wl pls t. frm t Fn n rdr fr png q E M
Os M O f crmns ss Fn u wl pls .t frm n du rdr rd t. ltr
(t. Fn frm rd t. ltr nlg no t. rt kn t lft frmg q sqr rt
rms vr t. lft lveg zn png ta t. E W v No fr t ffers) O f
crmns ss t. Fn r nw n du rdr fr png q E M os M WR
ss F SW Ss wl u hv t bonss .t sst zs n png q M f E M
Os (t. WR O S W Ss dsend .t t. ltr n yr svrl plcs v t.

WR O leg t. vig quotr Ps statg ftr legg t. ffcrs nl yth yr Fn lchg rms ll gv bis ter n slnc or blce.bis ter yn ll rs WR O S WSs og .t qr rspt stss WR leg t. cent v vig cnd Ps) WR yn ss F WS pls .t tk ntc zt s mi drctn qt q M f EM Os eb nw pnd v stnd pn fr t. dsph f bsnss ntl clsd agn bi mi rdr u wl pls .t rpt t. Sm .t t. SS n t. No yt t. Fn my hv dntc trf v gvrn ymsfs ccdli WS ss F SS u hv herd t. drctn f t WR O u wl pls .t rprt t. sm .t t. Fn yt yy my hv duntc trf v gvrn ymsfs ccdli t. SS s Fn u hv herd t. drctn f t WR O u wl pls .t tk duntc trf v tel zt eb ccdli os dn WR ss tgr Fn (v gvs ll t sgs fm t Ep pu t. E M Os dgr yn gvs bis ter ncs nt nsd bi t. SWS v dcls t. M t eb dli pnd)

Wk n t. E M Os dgr

Rcv qs mni Cdts ta nce qs u pls t. of crmns v'O J og ort t. O f crmns rtns v ss WR t. Cdts r rdi (t. O J mks t. lrm ta t. dr) W R ss F OS pls .t ttnd t. lrm OS ogs .t t. dr gvs bis ter ncs zh s nsd bi t. O J zh pns t. dr v ss ho cmns ere zh s nsd qs n Tcl bi O J. Fs A B v C ho hv bn rgli Et v t. ps wd s gvn OS rtns .t hs plc WR ss wt ocns t. lrm ta t. dr F OS OS nsrs Fs AB v C ho hv bn rgli Et qs ta t. dr v gvs t. ps wd WR gvs ter nes ll rs v zh ss F O O u wl pls .t rcv t. Cdts v cndt ym sx tms rd t. M .t WR leg cnd of Chr sz cap qt vig quotr Ps t. Cdts stp n t. W v fce t. E v gv t. WR O q nov sg vri rd bgng yth t. Ep pu .t t. sx rd ven yy stp t. WRO dscnds .t t. ltr v gvs t. bo ftr t. bo t. WR O prsts ym yth t. ps wd prim t. tp Os wd yn t. E M Os wd yy rs v zh rdrs ym .t slt t. S W S qs E M Os WR O tks hs plc (ere s nw q cnfsn) WR gvs ter ncs v rs yth t. M v nqrs wt ocns ll ys cnfsn WS ss t. crftm r ta q stant yt q Ki stn s wntg bfr yy cn fnsh yr wk qt non f ym hd rcvd rdrs .t mk zt yt t. wkm hd nog frthr .t d wtht ur rdrs WR ss sch q stn hvs bn md v fnshd on bdt grbl .t t. rgnl dsn f t. tpl u wl thfr tk ntc qt zt s mi rdr yt nqri eb md f t. ovs zf ni stn f yt shp (pntg .t t. mk n t. C) hvs bn prstd fr nspn WS rdrs t. O f crmns .t nqr t. O f crmns ogs pu .t ym ho r nu ssmbd yy nfm hm ere ws q stn prpd tb zt nt hvg t. mk f ni f t. crft tm v yy nt knwg zts us agrd .t hev zt vr mng t. ibh WR ss zts mi rdr yt strt sych eb md fr zt n v bt t. tpl mng t.

A 2

rth yy il lk bt fr zt v t. Cdt fnds zt q prcssn s yn frmd bi t. o f crmns yy ps rd t. m ter tms cant ll hl .t t mane cntdd bi t, o f crmns t. Cdt crris t. stn t terd tm yy hlt ta t. C t. crmns nw bgn yy stp cant t. Cdt yn plcs t. Kistn n t. C yy ll step bck v gv t. gd sg r wd t. WR nw ds-scnds yth t. SW Ss v xplns .t ym t. orgn f t. sg (yy rtn agn t. o f crmns rdrs t. prcssn frmd agn yy og rd t. m ter tms mr v fnsh t. cant t. prim f t. lst ter rds t. Fn tk ff yr prns v plc ym pun t. ltr cnd tm rd yr Jls (E M Os M s clsd ftr t. mnr f png t. Of crmns frms t. Fn rd t. ltr nlg no t lft kn t. rt frm q sqr v lft rms vr t. rt yn cls. n dfrm)

Y C Tcl scj prim lsn prim *E* r u q Y C g *F* z zm yt z zm *I* hw shjl z kw u .t eb q Y C g *G* bi ter tms ter v ndjr q lvg C *A* whr wr u md q Y C g *H* n q rgli cnjst-jd R f Y C gs *O* hw mni mck q rgli cnjstjd R *N* nn rgli Y C gs cnjstg f t. AS Gr v V NT YCN SP v t. ter Os f t. wz *U* wm d t ter prim rpjst *B* yos ter nct Fn ho cmj psjd t. gd Cl ta Jlm v hljd yr mtjgs n t. tc *I* wm d t. ter ltjtr rpst *M* Gah Shoj v Urez yy wr t. ter wris ho prim bgt .t lt t. prnl scts f ys dgjr ftr yy hd bn brd n dkn fm t. ch f or gd O Ah .t t. rctn f t. cnd tpl ta Jlm v qs q rwd fr yr mrs wr vncd .t eb t. ter Os f t. wz *E* hw mni wz wr ere *A* quot *A* wt wr yr cljrs *L* lb ppl scljt v wht *I* wt ds t. clr f lb dnt *P* zt s zn blm f frjndjh v qs sch s xric f q O g *O* wt ds t. ppl dnt *R* zt ebng cmjpsd f lb v rd s thir plcd bwjtn t. prim v terd wz f yos clrs .t dnt t. ntmt cnxn yt sbts bwjtn ys sblm dgjr v nct crft gy *U* wt ds t. sclt dnt *P* yt frvy v zl wh ogt .t ctute ll Y C gs s t. prnl xric f ys dgr *E* wt ds t. wht dnt *R* yt prty f ntntn v rctd f cndt wh ogt .t gvrn ll yos ho sk .t gn dmsn n .t t. sc sctr qt h f hcs *A* whr wr yos wz plzd *F* ta t. otc f t. tc *E* whi ere *C* .t srv qs q cvrg fr t. tc v q sts fr t. g ds. *I* whi wr gds plsd ere *B* .t tk spcl cre yt non psd xcpt sch qs wr dli qlfd qs non wr ald t. prsnc f t AS Gr v V tb t. dscdjnts f t. drod trbs f Is *E* hw dd t. chdi mck y sfs kwn .t t. gds *F* bi t. sm wds v sgs qs wr gvn .t Sm ven zh ws cmjdd .t ld t. chdi ort f t. terr f Yge v ort f t. hsz f bnjdg (yus ndjth t. prim sc)

Sc cnd

I whr wr u prpd fr ur xljtn .t ys dgjr *G* n q plc

[7]

rpstg t. otc ft. tc *E* hw wr u prpd *H* bi ebng dvjstd fmi ortr ppl mi rms v brjsts br hdwk slphd yth q ct sep tms rd mi bdi compjnd bi to wri Fn yth lke qljfns yth msf n wh stnn zz wr cndjctd .t t. dr f t. m bi t hd f q Cn whr zz wr csd .t gv sep dst ncs *Y* .t wt d yos sep dst ncs lld *L* .t t. sep dgr f gy no wh zz wr yn bt .t ntr. *O* wt ws sd .t u frn wtjhn *N* ur nsr *B* tres wri Fn ho hv jsti v lwli srvd yr tms qs Eps bn psd .t t. dgr f Fts rs d .t t. sblm dgr f o gs bn vncd .t t. dgr f mk o bn dli lcjfd v nsjtld tp Os bn rcjvd v ckjnlgd qs EM Os v nw wsjh fr frthr prjmn bi ebng xltd t t. sblm dgr f Y C gs *E* wt mr wr u skd *G* zf zz cme f or wn frr wl v ccrd zf zz wr wri v wil qljfd dli v trli prpd zf zz hd md t. ncsri prfci n t. prcdjng dgrs v prpli vhd fr ll wh ebng nsjrd n t. ffiv zz wr skd bi wt frthr rt qt bnjft zz xpjtd .t gn dmjsn *A* ur nsr *C* bi t. bnft f q ps. *I* dd u gv yt ps *D* zz dd nt tb or cnjdcjtr gve zt fr uz *O* pls .t gv zt t. ur lft hd Cn (yy rs v gv zt) *C* zt s rt z grt u F R *E* t. wt ds yt ps lld *F* .t t. ttl f q E M O t. xr zz yn stnd *I* wt fld *H* zz wr rqsjtd .t vat q tm yth ptnc ntl t N T cud eb njmd f or rqst v hs nsr rtnd *E* wt ws hs nsr vev rtnd *H* tel ym ntr v eb rcvjd n du frm *A* hw wr u rcvjd *B* ndr q lvg C *E* whi ndr q lvg C *D*. -t mps pun or mnds yt t. prnl scts £ ys dgr shd nvr eb cmnctd xcpt ndr t. lvg C.

(yus ndj th t. prim lsn f t. cnd sc)

Cnd lsn

(prim Rd) *E* hw wr u yn dsjpsd f *B* zz wr cnjdctd nce rd t. otc f-t. tc ven zz wr csd .t nl v nvk t. blsg of D̃ *I* z wl thk u .t rpt yt pr *C* (yy rs v zh. rpts) "Sup Arch" (vid Nom) (Cnd Rd) *A* ftr prjfmg ys pus du hw wr u yn dsjpsd f *B* zz wr cnjdcjtd agn rd t. otc f t. tc whr zz wr mt bi t. NT ho dmjnd f uz ho zz wr v wt wr or ntjnts *E* ur nsr *D* zz r tres wri Fn ho hv jsti v lwli srjvd or tms qs Eps bn psd .t t. dgr f Fts rsd .t t. sbjlm dgr f o gs vnjcd .t t. dgr f mk o bn dli lctd v nsjtd tp Os bn rcjvd v ckjnlgd qs E M Os v nw wsh fr frthr pymn bi ebng xltd .t t. sblm dgr f Y C Os *O* wt ws yn sd .t u *P* zz wr nfjmd yt n prsng or ntjntns zz shjld eb ndr t. ncsti f psg yos dsgrb v rggd ptjhs wh ll rgli Y C Os hd trvd bfr uz tb bfr zz prjcdd frtnr zt wld eb ncsri fr uz .t nl n dfrm v rcv t. th qt bo f ys dgr *F*

[8]

(gvs sep dst ncs ll rs) z wl thk u .t rpt yt th *F* z A B f mi wn frr wl v ccrd n t. prsjnc f A D v ys E M R f Y C gs rctd .t hm v ddctd .t h 1S d hzy v hzn n dtn t mi frmr bos mst slmi v snli pvs yt z'wl lys hl frvr cncl v nvr rvl ni f t. sct rts pts qt pirs f t mstrs f frr gy pptng .t ys dgr f q Y C g .t ni prsn ndr t. cnpi f hev xcpt zt shl eb .t q tr v lwl Y C g qt wtjhn t. bdi f a jst v rgli cnstd R f sch qr nto hm qt ym ntl bl st ct trl dxmn qt t. lwltnfmtn f q Cn Y C g z shl hv fnd hm qt ym .t eb qs jsti v lwli ntld .t t. sm qs z zm msf z frthr pvs yt z wl nsr ll lwl sgs v smns yt my eb gvn qt snt nto zs frm q tr v rgli Y C g qt fm q rgli cnstd R f sch zf wthn t. lnjth f mi ct yt z wl ad v fst ll wri dsjtsd Y C gs yr wds v rphjns n prfjrnc .t ni thr prns os rf qs z cn d zt, wtht njri t msf v fmjli yt z wl bde bi v sppt ll t. lws rls v rglns f t. R f wh z my bcm q mbr t. cnsjtn lws v dcts f t. gd R f t. Stt ndr wh t. sm s hljdn v t. gnl gd R f t. US yt z wl kp q Cn Y C gs scts qs mi wn ven gvn .t zs n chrg qs sch mzjdr v trsn xcjptjd v yt lft ta mi wn dscrjn yt z wl sps t. cse f q Cn Y C g rt qt wrg os rf qs .t dlvr hm ort f mmdt dnr z frthr pvs yt z wl nt drw t. bld f q Cn Y C g n ngr knjwg hm .t eb sch yt z wl nt eb ta t. png f q R nls ere r nn rgli Y C gs pt ncljdg t. Tli qr wl z eb ta t. xltn f mr qt lss thn ter ta ne v t. sm tm Yt z wl nt xpln t. Ki qt xrs f ys dgr .t ni prsn xcjpt zt eb .t q rgli Y C g yt z wl nt gv t. gd Y C gs wd xcjpt n .t prjsnc f ter rgli Y C gs zz prim grng bi ter tms ter v ndr q lvg G ll ys z d mst slmi v snli pvs yth q fyrm v fxt rsjltn .t prfm t. sm wtjht ni qvj ctn mnjtl rsvtn qt sct vsn f mjnd n zs wtvr bnjdg msf ndr on lss pty thn yt f hvg t et — os hlp zs Et (terd Rd) *I* ftr rcvjg t. th qt bo f q Y C g hw wr u yn dsjpsd f *F* zz wr cnjdctjdrd. t. otc f t. tc whr ws xhjhtd t uz q smj-bl f q brngb *E* whi ws q smjbl f q brngb xhjbtd .t u ta ur xltn *D* .t mps pun or mnds yt t wds v sgs flwg wr f q dvn Jn v qs sch scdli rcvd bi t. chdi v bi ym trnsjtd t. yr pstri qs mks bi wh yy myt mck ymsfs kwn v eb dstj-ghd bi ch thr frva ftr *A* wt fld *B* q rpstn f t. dstrn f Gr Slns tpl *E* bi wm ws zt dsjtyd *C* bi Benzr Gr f Bya ho n t. und an f t. rgn f Dezk Gr f Dujh bsgd t. civ dstdd t. tpl tokny ll t. h skus trf yth t. to brsn pirs v t. rmjnt f t. pop yt scpd t. swd crrd zh wy cpv .t Bya whr yy rmnd svts .t hm v hs scjsssjrs ntl t. rgn f Ryc Gr f Rep *I* f wt drtn ws yr cpvi B. sepi ann *O* bi wm wr yy lbrtd *P* bi Ryc Gr f Rep ho n t. und an f hs rgn ssud hs prcjimn ssg yus ssh Ryc Gr f Rep (Rze cnd vid Nom) *U* wm dd u yn rpst *T* ter chdi rtng fm t. Byan cpvi *Y* n ys stnn wt nsr dd u mck .t t. ffrs f Ryc qs cntnd n hs prcjlmn *C* ebng bdtfl qs .t t. rcptn zz shjld mtt yth fm or Fn zz sd ven zz shl cm nto or Fn v shl sa nto ym t. DD f or patrs hv snt uz nto u v yy shl sa nto uz wt s hs nm wt shl zz sa nto ym *E* ur nsr *D* z zm yt z zm v yus shl u sa nto t. chdi z zm hvh snt uz nto u (yus ndh t. cnd lsn f t. cnd sc) (quotr Rd) *A*. dd u prsu ur jrn *C* zz dd tro hrd v rggd pths *A* wt dd yos hrd v rgg d pths rpst *B* t. jrng f t. chdi n t. wljdns E dd u mtt yth ni bstrjcns *D* zz dd yth svrl *I* whr dd u mtt yth t. prim *G* ta t. prim wz f t. tc whr no mckg t rgli dmd zz herd t. o trf xclm ho das pph ys prim wz f or scd tc zh sppsg zn nmi .t cb ner lrmd hs Cns ho ven ssmjbd dmnd ho cms ere *I* ur nsr *K* ter vri sjrs ho hv cm pu .t hlp ad v sst n rbjldg t. hsz f t. Dl wtht hp f fe qt rwd *E* wt wr u yn skd *D* fm vnc zz cme *O* wt wr u yn nfmd *R* yt bi zn rdr f l. gd Cl yn sttg ta Jlm md u cnqs f dflts yt hd rsn mng t. wkmn bi t. ntdcn f stgrs non wr ad .t hlp vd v fst n ys os nbl v glrs zn ndtkg tb t. dscdnts f t. duod trbs f Js zt ws thfr nesri yt zz shld eb mr prtclr n trcng or gnlgi v dmnd f uz ho zz wr *A* ur nsr *C* zz r f ur Fn v knrd chn f t. cpvi ho hv bn rgli nctd qs Eps bn psd .t t. dgr f Fts rsd .t t. sblm dgr f o gs vncd .t t. dgr f mk Os rcvd v cknj lgd qs E M Os ta t. cmpln f t. tpl wr ta t. dstrn trf bi Benzr Gr f Bya ho n t. und an f t. rgn f Degk Gr f Dujh bsgd t. civ dstyd t. tpl tok wy ll t. h skus trf yth t. to brsn plrs v t. rmnt f t. pop yt scpd t. swd crrd zh wy cpv .t Bya whr yy rmnd svts .t hm v hs scssjrs ntl t. rgn f Ryc Gr f Rep bi hos rdrs zz r nw lbrtd v hv cm pu .t hlp ad v sst n ys os nbl v glrs zn ndtkg *I* wt mr wr u skd *H* bi wt frthr rt qt bnft zz xptd .t gn dmsn *A* nr nsr *C* bi t. bnft f q ps *E* wt ws yt ps *D* z zm yt z zm z zm hvh snt uz nto u *I* dd ys gn u dmsn *H* zt dd *A* wt ws yn sd .t u *L* bon mn v tr zz mut hv bn qt yus rf cud nt hv cm frthr zz cud nt eg wtht hs wd sg v wd f xhtn *E* wt ws hs wd *B* z zm yt z zm z zm hvh snt uz nto u Mesh Mah y Paj *O* wt ws hs sg *P* zt ws n mtn f yt qs

[10]

gvn .t Som ven zh ws cmdd .t cst hs rdd pun t. terr r zt bcm q srpt v no tkg zt pu zt bcm q rdd n hs hnd qs bfr *I* wt ws hs wd f xhtn *H* z t ws xplni f yt sg v s cntnd n t. bk f Som Ex quotr cap prim .t dec vrs (yus ndjth t. terd lsn f t. cnd sc) (quotr lsn f t. cnd sc qunq Rd) *O* whr dd u mtt ytn t. nxt bstrcn *P* ta t. cnd wz f t. tc whr no mkg q rgli dmd zz herd t. o trf xclm ho das pph ys cnd wz f or scd tc ho cms erc *E* ur nsr *D* ter vri sjrs ho hv cm pu .t hlp ad v sst n rbljdg t hsz f t. Dl wtht hp f fe qt rwd *A* wt ws yn sd .t u *B* zz wr skd bi wt frthr rt qt bnft zz xptd .t gn dmsn *E* ur nsr *F* bi t. bnft f q wd sg v wd f xhtn qs gvn uz bi t. O f t. prim wz *I* dd ys gn u dmsn *C* zt dd *O* wt ws yn sd .t u *P* bon mn v tr zz mut hv bn qt yus rf cud nt hv cm frthr zz cud nt og wtht hs wd sg v wd f xhtn *A* wt ws hs wd *B* z zm yt z zm z zm hvh snt uz nto u Mesh Mah v Paj Mesh Paj v Adam *E* wt ws hs sg *D* zt ws n mtn f yt qs gvn .t Som ven zh ws cmdd .t pet hs hnd nto hs bsm v zt bcm lprs qs snw v pctg hs hnd nto hs bsm agn zt bcm qs hs thr fls *E* wt ws hs wd f exhtn *D* zt ws xplni f yt sg v s cntjnd n t. bk f Som Ex quotr cap fm t. prim .t t. dec vrs (vid Nom) (yus ndjth t quotr lsn f t. cnd sc) (qunq lsn f sc cnd) (sx Rd) *E* whr dd u mtt yth t. nxt bstrcn *B* ta t. terd wz f t. tc whr no mkg t. rgli dmd zz herd t. O trf xclm ho das pph ys terd wz f or scd tc ho cms ere *A* ur nsr *C* ter vri sjrs ho hv cm pu .t hlp ad v sst n rbljdg t. hsz f t. Dl wtht hp f fe qt rwd *A* wt ws yn sd .t u *B* zz wr skd bi wt frthr rt qt bnft zz xptd .t gn dmn *I* ur nsr *G* bi t bnft f t. wds sgs v wds f xhtn qs gvn uz bi t. O's f t. prim v cnd wz *O* dd yes gn u dmsn *D* yy dd *I* wt ws yn sd .t u *F* bon mn v tr zz mut hv bn qt yus rf cud nt hv cm frthr zz cud nt og wtht hs sg wd f xhtn v sgt *E* wt ws hs sg *B* zt ws n mtn f yt qs gvn .t Som ven zh ws cmdd .t tk t. aq f t flu v prr zt pun t. dri terr v t. aq wh zh tok fm t. flu bcme qs bld pun t. dri terr *I* wt ws hs wd f xhtn *K* zt ws xplni f yt sg v s cntnd n t. bk f Som Ex quotr cap prim .t dec vrs (sep Rd) *O* whr dd u mlt yth t. nxt bstrcn *B* ta t quotr wz f t. tc whr no mkg t. rgli dmd zz herd t. Y C N xclm ho das pph ys quotr wz f or scd tc whr nscs urt des v nox pun t. h ltr ho cms ere *O* ur nsr *P* ter vri sjrs ho hv cm pu .t hlp ad v sst n rbljdg t. hsz f

[11]

t Dl wtht hp f fe qt rwd *E* wt wr u yn skd *D* fm vne zz cme *A* ur nsr *C* fm Bya *I* vt wr u yn nfmd *F* yt bi zn rdr f t. gd Cl yn sttg ta Jlm md n cnqc f dflts yt hd rsn mng t. wkmn bi t. ntdcn f stgrs non wr ald .t hlp ad v sst n ys os nbl v glrs zn ndtkg tb t dscdnts f t. duod trbs f Is zt ws thfr ncsri yt zz shld eb mr prtjclr n trcng or gnlgi v dmnd f uz ho zz wr *A* ur nsc *B* zz r f ur Fn v knrd chn f t. cpvi ho hv bn rgli nctd qs Eps bn psd .t t. dgr f Fts rsd .t t. sblm dgr f O gs vncd .t t. dgr f mk O rcvd v cknjlgd qs E M Os ta t- cmpln f t tpl wr ta t. dstrn trf bi Benzr Gr f Bya ho n t. und an f t. rgn f Dezk Gr f Dujh bsgd t. civ dstrjd t. tpl tok wy ll t. h skus trf yth t, to brsn plrs v t. rmnt f t. pop yt scpd t. swd crrd zh wy cpv t. Bya whr yy rmnd svts .t hm v hs scssjrs ntl t. rgn f Ryc Gr f Rep bi hos rdrs zz r nw lbrtd v hv cm pu .t hlp ad v sst n ys os nbl v g-lrs zn ndtkg *E* wt mr wr u skd *H* bi wt frthr rt qt bnft zz xptd t. gn dmn *A* ur nsr *C* bi t. bnft f t. wds sgs v wds f xhtn qs gvn uz bi t. Os f t, prim cnd v terd wz v t. sgt *E* dd yes gn u dmsn *C* yy dd *I* bi wm wr u rcvd *D* bi t Y C N ho cndctd uz .t t. prsnc f t. A S Gr v V ho wr yn sttg n gd Cl bi wm zz wr xmnd qs zt rsptd or slk n t. prcdg dgrs wh nttg yr pprbn zz wr skd wt pt f t. bldg zz wr wing .t ndtk *I* ur nsr *K* yt zz wr nclnd .t ndtk ni pt evn t. mst srvl n prmng os nbl v glrs zn ndtkg *E* wt fld *F* zz wr prstd yth t. wkg tls v nfmd yt fm t spms zz hd gvn f or slk n t. prcdg dgrs on bdt cud eb ntnd f or blty .t prfm ni pt evn t. mst dflt tb qs zt ws ncsri yt t. rbh shld eb rmvd fm t. Estmst pt f t. rnsns n rdr .t ly t. fndn f t. cnd tpl zz wr drctd .t cmnc or pprns ere v zt ws gvn uz strcy n chrg .t bsrv v prsv vri thg f vlu qs on bdt mni mdls f xclnc li brd ere wh zf brt .t lt wld eb f sstl srvc .t t. frty *O* wt fld *P* zz rprd .t t. plc qs drctd v wrt quot des wtht dscvg ni thg f mprtc xcpt psg svrl plrs n t. dfnt rdrs f rchtr t. qung des zz cm .t wt zz ta prim spsd .t eb zn mptrb sax tb ne f mi Cns strkg zt yth q crw zz bsrvd zt rtnd q hlw snd ta wh zz rdbld or sdyt v ftr rmvg mr f t. rbh zz fnd zt rsmld t apex f zn C no t. vrtx f wh ws q stn f sngl frm v no zt crtn mstris xrs wh fm t. lnth f tm zt hd bn brd wr nw nrly ffcd *E* wt fld *F* zz yth sme dflty rsd zt v nox drwg no zz rprd yth zt .t t. prsnc f t- AS Gr v V ho wr yn sttg n gd Cl fr zts xmn *A* wt ws yr pnn f ys stn *B* yt zt ws t. K i S f q mk o g v frm t. plc n wh zt ws fnd wld on bdt ld .t frthr dscvrs f mprtc .t t. crft no wh zz wr skd zf zz wr wlng .t pntrt ys C n qust f frthr trsrs *E* ur nsr *F* yt on bdt t. tsk wld cb ttndd yth dflty v dnr vet zz wr wlng .t ndtk zt evn ta t. hzd f or lvs *I* wt fld *K* zz rprd .t t. plc v ftr rmvg svrl ft. stns n rdr .t wdn t. pptr ne f t. Cns fstnd q ct sep tms rd mi bdi v zt ws agrd yt zf z shld fnd t. plc ffsnv ethr .t hlth qt sght z shld shk zt no t. rt qs q sgl fr scndg v zf z shld wsh .t dscnd stl frthr z shld shk zt no t. lft n ys mnr z dscndd *E* wt fld *F* ftr sme srch z fnd n t. rcss f t. C ter Jls t. plc nw bcmg ffsnv n cnsqc f t. myst aer yt hd lng bn cnfnd ere z gve t. sgl v scndd *O* wt fld *P* zz rprd yth ym .t t. prsnc f t. AS Gr v V ho wr yn sttg n gd Cl fr yr xmn *A* wt ws yr pnn f ys trsr *B* yt yy wr t. Jls f or ter nct gd Os Sln Gr f Is Rih Gr f Ty v Ah v fm t. plc n wh yy wr fnd on bdt wld ld .t stl frthr dscvrs f mprtc .t t. crft no wh zz wr skd zf zz wr wlng .t pntrt ys C n qust f frthr trsrs yth zn srnc yt or mrts shld nt og nrwd *E* wt fld *F* zz rprd .t t. plc v z dscndd qs bfr t. sol ws nw ta zts merid hit wh drid zts rflgt rys n .t t. nmst rcsss f t. C wh nbld mi .t dscvr n t. Estmst pt ere f q pdsl f snglr frm vrld yth gld v no zts sds v apex wr crtn mstris xrs *I* wt fld *H* vlg msf f ys trsr z gve t. sgl fr scndg t. vrtcl rys f t. sol nw drtg ful n mi fce z nvlty fnd mi hnd n ys pstn .t gd mi oc fm t. ntse lt v het *I* wt fld *H* zz rprd yth zt .t t. prsnc f t. AS Gr v V ho wr yn sttg n gd Cl fr zts xmn *A* wt ws yr pnn f ys trsr *B* yt zt ws t. ac f t. tsty tb nt knwg t. xrs no zts sds v apex rdrd zt .t eb pnd *U* wt wr zts cnts z q pat a rdd v q bk f . lw n wh wr dpstd q ki .t yos xrs v n wh zt ws wrtn z zm yt z zm v D spke nto som et *I* wt ws yr pnn f t. cnts *H* yt t. pat ws t. pat f mna wh Som bi dvn cmd lyd pu n t. ac f t. cvnt qs q meml f t. mrcls mnr bi wh t. chdi wr spld yth yt artl hle trvlg tro t. wldns v t. rdd ws t. rdd f Aa wh bdd v blmsd v bgt frth frux n q des v wh ws lkws lyd pu n t. sde f t. ac f t. cvnt qs q meml f t. pptnt f t. Lvts .t t. Psth *E* hw wr yos xrs xplnd *D* yos no zts sds cmpsd t. nms f or ter nct gd Os v yos no zts apex yt mag v scrd nm wh z zm nt autrsd .t gv tb n t. mnr z rcvd zt *I* hw wr ur mrts rcvdd *X* t. AS Gr v V dscndd fm yr thrn v nvstd uz yth t. prnl scts f ys dgr *E* hw wr yos scts. cmncd *D* t. gd Y C wd n t prsnc f ter Y C gs zz prim. grng bi ter tms ter v ndr q lvg C v yt mag v scrd nm n q rvnti mnr

Ffcrs n q Y C R yth yr Jls v clthg Frntr. v Tls.

AS Gr V NT YCN SP ter Os f t. wz v Tli AS wrs q vht rbe v rrd vlvt mtre yth q trng n frnt q brstp f dud brlit stns f vrus clrs rpstg t. dud trbs f Js spnd fm t. cerv bi crms vlvt q Os Jl v crris q mlt Gr wrs q ppl crwn v ibe carris q scptr v wrs t. W Ss Jl V wrs q vht trbn qt bntt q sclt rbe v crris q rll f chrt zh wrs t. SSs Jl NT wrs t. OOs Jl wh s q ylw mlt v crris q swd YCN wrs t. OSs Jl q ylw mlt v swd SP wrs t. OJs Jl q ylw mlt v crris q rdd t. Os f t. wz crri swds v t. O f t. sclt hvs q sgt spnd fm q bttn Tli wrs to crs swds v crris q swd Frntr s t. ac f t. cvnt bng q bx f ylw clr nm no t. apex s G n gic xrs v no t. sds Sh Gr f Js Rih Gr f Ty v Ah n gic xrs cntng q pat f mna n q parv bx q parv rdd v t. bk f t. lw n t. bk s q Ki no chrt flld v n t. bx r O gs Jls ter sqrs yth lb rbns Tls r q crw spd v pex

Crmni f png q Y C R

AS gvs ter ncs N T rs AS r ll pt Y C Os Cn NT zz r EM AS r ll t. avns t t. tpl gdd v scr NT z wl mit v vld EM NT rdrs t. SP .t d zt SP ogs .t t. dr v gvs bis ter v ne Tli nsrs SP yn sstts .t t. NT yt zt s gdd t. NT ss t. avns .t t. tpl r scr EM AS gvs bis ter ncs Y C N rs v ss Cns zt s or EM ASs wl v plsr yt u frm n rdr fr png q Y C R yy ll ssmbl rd t ltr nl no t. rt kn lchg hnds rt vr lft n flshp E lft pn fr t. AS Gr v V t Y C N ss r nw n rdr fr png EM AS Gr v V rs AS leg cnd Thes terd cap fm sx .t decsep vrs t. gd Cl yn dscnd .t t. ltr jn hnds blce ter tms n sinc ll rs fm trngs v pn q Y C R AS Gr v V yn rtn .t yr plcs v t. Cns .t yr plcs AS ss E Cn Gr pls .t tk ntc zt s mi drctu yt ys Y C R eb nw pnd v stnd pn ntl clsd agn bi mi rdr u wl pls t. rprt t. sm .t E Cn V yt t Cns my hv dntc trf v gvrn ymsfs ccdli t. Gr ss zt s t. drctn f t. EM AS yt q Y C R eb nw pnd v stnd pn ntl clsd agn bi hs rdr u wl pls .t

B

rprt t. sme .t t. Cns yt yy my hv dntc trf v gvrn ymsfs ccdli t. V ss Cns u hv hrd t. drctn f t. EM AS u wl tk dntc trf v tel zt eb ccdli os dn AS ss tgr Cns ll t. sgs r gvn fm t. Ep .t t. YC t. AS yn gvs bis ter v ne ncs v ss z dcl ys YCR .t eb dli pn fr t. dsph f bsnss Cn Sec pls .t leg t. prcdgs f t. lst R Sec leg AS yn cls fr q vt ppvd bi t. Ep sg

Crmni f clsg q Y C R

AS s ere ni frthr bsnss E Cn Gr bfr ys Cl Gr z kw f nog frthr EM AS d u kw f ni thg frthr E Cn V V z kw f nog frthr EM AS gvs ter ncs Cn N T r ll t. avns .t t. tpl gdd q scr N T z wl mit v vid E M SP ogs gvs bis ter v nc ta t. dr Tli nsrs N T rtns v ss zz r scr EM t. AS gvs bis ter v nc Y C N rs v ss Cns zt zs or EM ASs wl v plsr yt u frm n rdr fr clsg yy frm rd t. ltr qs bfr nl no t. lft kn lchg hnds lft vr t. rt Y C N stat ta t. pes f t. ltr frntg t. Cl v ss EM zz r nw n rdr fr clsg AS ss E Cns Gr v V wl u sst zs n clsg ys Y C R Cl dscnd v nl yn rpt t. flg pr bi t. wsd f t. Sup AS my zz eb Et (vid Noni) ftr ys pr yy lck hnds blc ter tms ter ll rs frm tngs ftr wh ll frnt t. ltr v t. AS ss E Cn Gr u wl pls .t tk ntc zt s mi wl v plsr yt ys R f Y C gs eb nw clsd v stat clsd ntl cnvnd agn bi mi rdr u wl pls .t rprt t. sm .t t. V yt t Cns My hv dntc trf v gvrn ymsfs ccdli t. Gr ss E Cn V u wl pls .t tk ntc zt s t. drctn f or EM AS yt ys Y C R cb nw clsd v stat clsd ntl cnvnd agn bi hs rdr u wl pls .t rprt t. sm t t Cns yt yy my hv dntc trf v gvrn ymsfs ccdli t. V ss Cns u hv herd t. drctn f t. EM AS u wl pls .t tk dntc trf v tel zt eb ccdli os dn AS. ss tgr Cns gvs ll t. sgs fm t. Ep pu v fm t. Y C dgrdwn gvs bis ter v ne v ss E Cn V hw shld zz mtt V ss no t. lvl AS ss hw shld zz pt E Cn Gr t. Gr ss no t. sqr AS ss os my zz mtt v pt Cns z dcl ys R. dli clsd.

Wk n t. Y C dgr

Ftr t. R s dli pnd t. Cdts ebng prpd qs n tcl yy mk q rglr dmd bi bis ter v ne NT rdrs .t Y C N .t ttnd t. lrm Y C N ogs v nsrs t. lrm v dmds ho cms ere t. SP cndts t. Cdts v ss ter wri Fn ho hv jsti v lwli srvd yr tms qs Ep Et (qs n t Tcl) v nw-wsjh fr frthr prjmn bi ebng xltd .t t. sblm dgr f Y C gs ftr gvg t. ps wd yy r dmtd yy r yn

[15]

cntdd bi t. SP tro q lvg C t. Fn frm lchg hnds dng ys rd t. SP rpts t. flg n Ish cap quot cnd decsx vrs ftr psg rd t. prim tm yy r stpd n t. W bi t. SP v csd .t nl v rcv t. bnft f q pr qs fls Sup acht f nvsl nat Et (vid Nom) (cnd Rd) yy r cntdd t. cnd tm rd .t t. sm plc ndr t. C t. Cdts nw mtt t. NT ho dmds f ym ho yy r fm vnc yy cme v wt r yr ntntns t. SP nsrs yy r ter wri Fn ho hv bn rgli nctd Et (as ta dr) bi ebng xltd .t t. sblm dgr f Y C gs NT ss zt s wil n prsng ur ntntns u wl eb ndr t. ncsti f psg tro yos dsgrb rggd pths wh ll Y C gs hv trvd tb bfr u prcd ni frthr zt wl eb ncsri fr u .t nl v rcv t. th qt bo f ys dgr Cdts rcv zt fm t. NT (terd Rd) t. Cdts rs v og rd t. terd tm qs yy r trvlg t. SP rpts t. flg n Ex terd cap fm t. prim .t t. sep vrs t. Cdts rrv ta t. bn ta t. wds Som Som v r nbld ven Som hyd hs fce yy r bldd agn zf ere s tm leg cnd Chrtrigsx cap fm und .t t. vig vrs nw t. dstrn f t. tpl cmncs clshg f swds ner t. Cdts mkg mag tmlt Et ftr wh yy r tkn cpv v crrid n.t zn thr rm t. flg s legt bi t. SP his yy r n cpvi t. Cdts ebng stl blndd r s ccnt guadra prim cnd v terd qt ethr f ym ftr ys s legt t. NT ogs .t t. dr pns zt v leg t. flg n t. hrng f t. Cdts Ez cap prim fm prim .t terd vrs. ftr zh hvs fnshd rdng SP ss z wl og pu v trns .t t. Cdts v ss wl u yy nsr etiam SP ss .t t. NT hw shl zz eb bl .t ps t. gds NT ss bi yes wds u shl eb bl .t ps z zm yt z zm z zm hvh snt uz nto u (quotr Rd) t. SP cndts ym rd t. quotr tm qs bfr vr rggd pths yy r yn cndd .t t. prim wz whr yy gv sx dst ncs bis ter t. O f t. wz xclms ho cms ere ho das pph ys prim wz f or scd tc (sme lrm) t. Cdts r nw nbld tb vid nog tb t. lb wz t. gds ll ssmbl n t. prim wz v nqr t. cse t. O f t. wz rfms ym yt z ws ndctv f t. pph f nmis t. wz s yn drwn v t. ter Os prst yr swds .t t. brsts f t. Cdts yth q stmp ho cms ere SPss ter vri sjrs ho hv em pu .t hlp ad v sst n rbldg t. hsz f t. Dl wtht hp f fe qt rwd O f t wz ss fm vnc cme u SP fm Bya O f t. wz ss bi zn rer f t. gd Cl nw sttg ta Jlm nd n cnqc f dflts yt hd rsn mng t. wkmn bi t. ntdcn f stgrs non wr ald .t hlp ad v sst n ys os nbl v glrs zn ndtkg tb t. dscdjnts f t. duod trbs f Is z s thfr ncsri yt u shld eb mr ptclr n trcng yr gnlgi zz thfr wsh .t kw ho u r SP ss zz r f ur Fn v knrd chn f t. cpvi ho hv bn rglii nctd qs Eps bn psd .t t. dgr f Fts rs d .t t. sblm dgr f O gs vncd .t

t. dgr f mk O bn rcvd v cknjlgd qs EM Os ta t. cmpla f t. tpl wr ta t. dstrn trf bi Ber zer Gr f Bya ho n t. und an f t. rgn f Dezh Gr f Dujh bsgd t. civ dstyd t tpl tok wy ll t. h skus trf vth t. to brsn plrs v t. mnnt f t pop yt scpd t. swd crrd zh wy cpv .t Bya whr yy rmnd svts .t hm v hs scssjrs ntl t. rgn f Ryc Gr f Rep bi hos rdrs zz r nw lbrtd v hv cm pu .t hlp ad v sst n ys os nbl v glrs zn ndtkg O f t. wz ss bi wt fthr rt qt bdft d u xpt .t gn dmsn SPss bi t. bnft f q ps O f t wz ss pls t gv zs yt ps SP z zm yt z zm z zm hvh snt uz nto u O f t wz ss bon mn v tr u mst hv bn qt yus rf cnd nt hv cm fthr u cn nt og wtbt mi wd sq v wd f xhtn mi wd s ys z zm yt z zm z zm hvh snt ur nto u Mesh Mah v Paj mi sg s n mtn f yt gvn .t Som ven zh ws cmdd .t cst hs rdd pun t. terr v zt bcm q srpt v no tkg zt pu agn zt bcm q rdd qs bfr t. wd f xhtn s xplni f ys sg v s cntnd n t. bk f Som Ex quotr cap fm prim .t t. dec vrs (qunq Rd) t Cdts r agn cntdd rd t. R v rrv ta t. ppl whr yy mk q dmd qs ta t. prim wz bi bis ter ncs O f t. wz ho das pph ys cnd wz f or scd tc ho cms ere SP ter vri sjrs ho hv cm pu .t hlp ad v sst n rbljdg t. hsz f t. Dl wtht hp f fe qt rwd O f t. wz bi wt frthr rt qt bnft d u xpt .t gn dmsn SP bi t. bnft f t. wd sg v wd f xhtn gvn uz bi t. O f t. prim wz O f t. wz pls .t gv ym .t zs SP gvs ym ll qs zh rcvd ym O f t. wz bon mn Et mi wd s ys z zm yt z zm zm hvh snt uz nto u Mesh Mah v Paj Mefh Paj v Adam mi sg s n mtn f yt gvn .t Som ven zh ws cmdd .t pet hs hnd n .t hs bsm v zt bcm lprs qs snw v petg zt n .t hs bsm agn zt bcm qs t. thr fls mi wd f xhin s xplri f ys sg v s cntjnd n t. bk f Som Ex quotr cap fm t. prim .t t. dec vrs (sx Rd) t. Cdts rrv ta t. sclt qt terd wz whr yy mk q rglr dmd bi bis ter ncs O f t. wz ho das pph ys terd wz f or sed tc ho cms ere SP ter vri sjrs Et O f t. wz bi wt frthr rt Et SP bi t. bnft f t. wds sgs v wds f xhtn qs gvn uz bi t. Os f t. wz pls .t gv ym .t zs SP gvs ym ll O f t. wz bon mn v tr Et fthr u cn nt og wtht mi sg wd f xhtn v sgt mi sg s n mtn f yt qs gvn .t Som ven zh ws cmdd .t tk t. aq f t. flu v prr zt pun t. dri terr v t. aq yt zh tok fm t. flu bcmc qs bld pun t. dri terr mi wd f xhtn s xplni f ys sg v s cnjtnd n t. bk f Som Ex quotr cap fm t. prim .t t. dec vrs ys s t. sgt (sep Rd) drng ys rd f t. Cdts t. flg s lcgt bi t. AS Hag cnd cap fm t. prim .t t. vig terd v nds yth qs q sgt fr a hv chsn te ta t. sm m t. Cdts r rrv ta t. whr wz qt quotr wz SP mks t. lrn qs bfr ni bis ter Y C N ho das pph ys quotr wz f or scd tc whr nscs urt des v nox pun t. h ltr SP ter wri sjrs Et Y C N ho r u v fm vne cm u SP fm Bya Y C N bi zn rdr f t. gd Cl nw sttg ta Jlm Et (qs ta t. prim wz) SP zz r f ur Fn v kmd chn f t. cpr Et (qs ta t. prim wz) Y C N bi wt frthr rt qt bnft Et SP bi t. bnft f t. wds v sgs qs gvn uz bi t. Os f t. prim cnd v terd wz v.t. sgt Y C N pls .t gv z t. ps SP z zm yt z zm Et Et Et Y C N. wt sgs hv u SP ta t prim wz zz vid t rdd Et ta t. cnd t. lprs hnd Et ta t. terd wz t. aq prrd pun t dri terr Et v hre s t. sgt f Urez bi yes sgs v wds zz hv psd tro t. wz Y C N z zm stsfd bon mn v tr n mut hv bn qt yus rf cud nt hv cm z wl nw yth plsr ntdc u bfr t. gd Cl n t. te (zh yn cndts ym bfr t. gd Cl v ss EM AS Gr v V z hv t plsr f ntrdcg ter wri Fn ho wr cpvs n Bya yy hv prvd ymsfs .t eb rglr dscnj-dts f t. duod trbs f Is v hv stsfd zs qs .t t. lgl mnt n wh yy hv gnd dmsn n .t t h tc bi gvg zs t. rglr sgs wds v tkns v hre EM s t. sgt f or wri Cn Urez AS is v rcvs zt ys s t. sgt f or wri Cn Ur z z kw zt wii (.t t. Cdts) hv u wrt n t. svrl dgrs n t. tpl v bn vncd lgli v rgli SP zz hv EM AS pls t gv zs t sgsn t prcdjng dgrs ((yy gv ym) AS ta t cmct f ur jrr cd u mtt yth ni dflys n gng ur wa thrwd SP zz dd EM AS whr cd u rcv t. prim ps wd SP fm t. N F AS wt ws yt ps wd SP z zm yt z zm z zm bvh snt uz nto AS hv u xmnd ym tro t. wz Cn Y C N Y CN z hv EM AS Fn bon mn v tr u mut hv bn qt yus f cnd nt hv cm zz r plsd y h u v u il mrt cr pp-rbtn wt pt f t bldg r u wlg .t ndik SP zz r wlg t ndik ni pt EM evn t mst srvl n t. prmn f os ubl v glis zn nd-tkg AS yn psts ym yth q crwb a spd v a pcx v ss fm t spms u hv xbhtd n t. prcdg dgrs on bdt cn eb ntnd n or wr jds f ur bty .t prfm ni pt evn t. mst dflt tb zt s ncsri t rmv t. rbh fm t Estmst pt f t rnsns f t. tpl u wl thfr cmnc ur pprns ere v zz gv zt .t u strcy n chrg .t bsrv v prsv vri thg f vnu wh my eb fnd qs on bdt mni mcls f xclnc li hrd ere wh zt gt .t lt wl prv f sstl srvc .t t. crft (Cdts bw v eg ort AS legr Zeb quotr cap fm sx .t dec vrs Cdts rtn v sa SP zz wrt quotr des ta t. Estmst pt f t. rnsns wtbt mkg ni dscvrs f mprtc xcpt psg bi t. rnsss f svrl plrs n t. dfnt rdrs f rchtr tb .t des ebng t. qunq des stl prsng or lbrs zz cm .t wt zz ta prim spsd zn tnptrb sax tb ne f mi Cns strkg zt yth q crw zz bsrvd zt rtnd q hlw snd ta wh zz rdbld or sdyt v ftr rmvg mr f t. rbh zz fnd zt rsmbl t. apex f zn C no t. vrtx f wh ws q stn f sngl frm wh yth sme dflty zz rsd v fnd pun zt crtn xrs wh bi lnth f tm r nw nrly ffcd nox drwg no zz cncld .t rpa yth zt bfr ur EM Cl (gvs t. stn .t t. AS ho rcvs zt) AS ys ws on bdt zn elgt pec f wk n zts des (shs zt .t t. Gr v V) wt r ur pnns E Cns Gr v V yy sa zt s or pnn yt ys mut hv bn t. KiS f q mk O g AS zt mut eb os zt s vlbl (zh yn pss zt vr hs oc v ddcts zt) hns .t t. Dl (AS yn gvs zt .t t. Gr ho ds t. sm v yn .t t. V) AS ys stn fm t. ple n wh zt ws fnd wl on bdt ld .t stl frthr dscvrs r u wlg no t. cras .t pntrt ys C n qust f frthr trsrs SP zt s prbl t. tsk wl eb ttndd yth dflty v dnr vet zz r wlg EM evn ta t. hzd f or lvs .t prmt os nbl v glrs zn ndtkg AS u wl rpr .t t. sm plc v wk dlgtli v ctsli (Cdts bw v og ort agn rtn) SP EM no rprng .t t. plc grbli .t ur rdr zz rmvd svrl f t. stns .t wdn t. pptr mi Cns fstnd q ct sep tms rd mi bdi .t sst mi n dscndg t. C v zt ws agrd zf z shld fnd t. plc ffsnv ethr .t hlth qt sght z shld shk zt no t. rt sde qs q tkn fr scndg v shld z wsh t dscnd stl frthr z shld shk zt no t. lft n ys mnr z dscndd v fter sme srch fnd yos ter Jls tid tgr t. plc yn bcmg ffenv bi rsn f t. myst aer wh hd fr q lng tm bn cnfnd ere z gve t. sgl v scndd zz hv nw rprd yth ym bfr ys EM Cl fr ur xmn (zh gvs ym .t t AS) AS xmns ym v ss yes wr t. Jls l or nct gd Os Sh Gr f Is Rih Gr f Ty v Ah yy r prcs v vlbl rlcs (yy ddct ym) AS r u wlg agn .t pntr ys C n qust f frthr trsrs u my eb ssrd ur mrts shl nt og nrwd SP hwr dfct v dnros t. tsk EM zz r wlg .t hzd or lvs n prnng os nbl v glrs zn ndtkg AS u wl yn rpr .t t. sm plc agn v eb prtclr n ur rschs (yy bw v og ort agn rtn yth t. ac) SP EM zz rprd t t. C agn grbli .t ur rdrs v ftr rmvg svrl mr f t. stns z agn dscndd qs bfr t. sol hd nw rsn .t zts merid hit v drtd hs rflgt rys n .t t. nmst rcss f t. C os yt z ws nbld .t dssvr n t Estmst pt trf q pdst f snglr frm vld yth pre gld no t. sds v apex f wh r crtn mstrls xars vlg msf f ys trsr z gve t. sgl v scndg t. vrtcl sol drtg zts rys ful n mi fce z nvlty fnd mi hnd n ys pstn .t dfnd mi oc fm zts ntsc lt v het zz hv nw rprd yth ys vlbl crsty bfr t. prsnc f ys EM gd Cl fr ur nsptn (zn gvs t. ac .t t. AS AS ys s sme thg mst prcs v vlbl Gr zt s ndd wt xrs r yos no t. sds v apex V zt wl pn wl zt nt AS ys mut eb t. ac f t. tsty tel uz ndvr .t pn zt (zh pns zt) AS hre s q rdd Gr hre s q bx V hre s q bk lkws (za pns t. bk) wt s ys zt mut eb q Ki .t yos wds no zs sds v apex AS tel zs vid zt (zh pns t. bk v leg Ino prim cap fm prim .t qunq vrs v Deut trig prim cap fm vig quotr .t vigsx vrs v Ex vig qunq cap vig prim vr v Ex dec sx cap fm trig cnd .t trig quotr vrs v Num dec sep cap v dec vr v Heb nn cap fm cnd .t qunq vrs v Ex cap cnd v terd vrs (t. AS yn lys dwn t. bk v pns t. gldn pat f mna yy ll tst f zt t. AS Gr v V cnslt tgr) AS ss Cns zt s t. pnn f ys EM Cl yt ys s t. ac f t. cvnt yt ys s t. pat f mna wh Som bi dvn cmd lyd pu n t. sd f t. ac f t. cvnt qs q meml f t. mrcls mnr n wh t. chdi wr spld yth yt artl n t. wldns yt t. rdd ws t. rd f Aa wh bdd blmsd v bgt frth frux n q des v wh ws sla lyd pu n t. ac t. cvnt qs q meml f t. pptnt f t Lvts .t t. Psth yos xrs no t. sds f t. ac r t nms f t. ter nct gd Os v ys s t. bk f t. lw wrtn bi Som ys s t. Ki .t t. xrs no t. apex f ys ac s yt mag v scrd nm wh z zm nt autrsd .t gv tb n t. mnr n wh z shl cmnct zt .t n mi wri Cns qs q rwd fr ur fdlty v frtd (t. AS plcs t. cnts n t. ac agn cls zt v ss) ys ac s q scd v vlbl Meml f t. bonss f D zz wl thfr ddct zt .t hm n dfrm (yy ll ddct zt) t. Cdts nw stnd bfr t thrn t. AS Gr v V ds-cnd v cmnct t. gd sct wd f q Y C g—t, AS Y C N v ne Cdt t. Gr NT v ne Cdt t. V SP v ne Cdt ftr wh t. AS cmncts t. sgs v leg t. chrg f t. scd wd t. prim slb s Heb t. cnd s Samr v t. terd s Cal v ch slb sgfs t, scd wd n t. rspt lngg v yus cms ter tms ter t. Samr lngg s t. gic lngg qt t. Ki lngg f Y C gs.

THE MASONIC TABLET

CRAFT CIPHER KEY

(Kingston, New York, 1822)
Facsimile

1.

A. klamighyte
ac bckrads
acted ocaceptder
A D plamighytgodd
ad bediant
Adam odaainramp
aer coriash
Af betsewen
Agn haniags
agrd jadeergo
Ah lihramaffibt
ald plalowder
an chraeyst
ann bosraeyck
apex dapoted
aq pawterk
artl pratielck
A S jhgihtseirps
assis inepynk
autrsd luathordezid
avns hvaaseung
Bck bokcaben
benzr abenudahcnezrazk
bcm hebemock
bcs jebesuack
bdd adubdeds
bdi jaedibg
bdi nobdys
bd dedibel
bdt cetbuodom
bdtf jtbuodlufs
bfr heberoft
bgn jebnigs
bgng jebnig,
bgt cathguoben
bh bohsuber
bhd jebdloht
bi blybon
bis bleciwted
bk cakooben
bl haelbs
blce plablancer
bld cadoolbug
bldg adliub,
blgs jebsgnold
blm jmemlabs
blmsd osolbsomdez
blndd ednilbder
blsg iselbgnist
blts halibiseits
blty halibiyth
bn boneebeg
bndg adnib,
bnft onebetifk
bntt knobneth
bo eboliag'
bon cadooged
bonss idoogssent
bos eboliagtionss
br brerabet
brd pubridet
brllt illirbitnas
brng bognirbal
brngb onrubinghsube
brsn garbsent
brst batsaerben
brstp itsaerbetalpt
bsgd gebsiegden
bsm kobsomg
bsnss nubsissent
bst betsebld
bsrv iboevrest
bsrvd uboserdeyt
bt hatuobe
bti muaebtys
btn ubotaing
bttn otubtonk
bv haevobs
bw cawobed
bx doxobsh
Bya obabynolt
C bahcrald
Cal glahcdenat
cant bognis,
cap opahctern
ccrd jcadrock
ccdli ocacorgnidlyt
cct icatnuocs
cdt anacdietadg
cent inuhderds

chdi olihcdrenfoisralet
cerv bekcensh
ch behcaelp
chn hlihcnerds
chpd jpihcdept
chpls jpahcsleph
chr gnorhciscled
chr biriahcon
chrg duegrahces
chrt japrept
chs thcruhcest
chsn hohcnest
civ oticyn
Cl jnuoclick
cl cullache
cld placledg
clr slocourn
clsd ssolcedt
clshg phsalc,
clthg shtolc,
clv brevaelced
cm bremocer
cmd imocdnamn
cme dremacht
cmncs amocmenseck
cmnct omocmencetnemp
cmnctd omocmuincadeth
cmpln omocple'
cmpsd amocpodest
Cn amocpannoik
cn conacmy
cncl jnoclaeck
cndctd hnoctcuddeg
cndctr hnoctcudrog
cncld jnoclaecdek
cnfnd inoc .ifdeg
cnfsd hnocufdest
cnfsn hnocufnoisd
cnpi onacoypt
cnsqc enocsececneuqr
cnslt hnoctlush
cnstd anocstiutteds
cnd hcesdnot
cnts jnocstnets
ctnnc hnocnitucenak
cntn anoctineug
cntnd hnocniatdel
cnvnd jnocnevden
cnxn hnoccen'
covnt avocetnand
cpi epocyt
cpv jpacevits
cpvi hpacvitiyth
cras notmorwork
cre breracsk
crft detfarcom
crftm jstfarcnemp
crfli jeraclufyls
crmni areceomnyt
crms amircsont
crmsts griccumnatscest
crnr procnerp
crrctli jroctceryld
crrd gracriden
crri gracrym
crrg gracry,
crs cossorcsk
crstp tucrisoiyth
crtn jrecniath
crw coworcst
crwb aworcbarn
crwn bonworcgt
csd osuacedg
cse dresuacop
csng ysuac,
cst cetsacom
cstms hsucsmoth
ct macblewoth
ctsli huacsuoityld
ctute ocatuetan
cud bedluocel
cvrg avocer,
D cadoged
d d idroldogs
d blodge
das coseradst
dcl jederalck
dezh odezeikahs
dcs hedesaeck
dcts hestcids

dd dedidum
ddct hedidacdetl
ddctns jdediac'
dec boneted
des cryadge
decsep avesenneets
decsx hxisneeth
deut juedretnooymp
dfcs odeiifcesm
dflt efidfitluck
dflty afidfiluctyp
dfm heudmorft
dfnt ifidreftnep
dfnd jeddneff
dgd heuddrags
dgr jedcergt
dh bohtaedst
dkn ikradssent
dlgtli gliditneglys
dlty pifdeliyth
dmd heddnamp
dmnd jednamdedt
dmrtn odamiar'
dmsn odamisnoist
dmtd idatimdeth
dn crenoded
dnr knadgerm
dnros hnadregsuop
dnt pednoten
dntc jeudonecith
dpstd hedsoptideg
dr caroodge
drctn hidcer'
drctd jidcerdets
drgtri hedgoraotyrn
dri clyrded
drtd strradeds
drtg strad,
drtn hudar'
drw cowardly
drwn bonwardom
drwg award,
ds boseodeg
dscdnts jsednecstnak
dscnd iseddnect
dscng iseddnec,
dsendts iseddnecstnag
dscrsn hsiderc'
dscv jsidvocres
dsgrl hsidaeergaelbs
dsph jsidhctapk
dspd isidsopdel
dsn hedngist
dst isidtcnith
dstrn isedcurt'
dstghd isidnithsiugder
dstb jsidbruth
dstbc jsidbrutecnal
dstsd hsidssertden
dstyd isedyortdel
dtn adadi'
dvn jidenivg
dvstd hidsevdeth
du judyth
dud brevlewten
dujh hujhads
duod crevlewter
dus judseith
dwgs hegdeesiwn
dwn bonwodel
dxmn jeudxemaian'
dy peditys
E betsaern
eb bleber
ebng bleb,
elgt pleetnags
Em itsomxelectnell
Ep ineretdepanerpecitt
ere brerehtam
estmst itsaeretsomp
et adnasohtrofs
etiam coseyth
ethr hierehtl
ev blevelk
evn henevr
ex oxeosuds
ez ozerah
F ghtorberp
f coform
fce blecafed

4

fc cleefed
ff boffosk
ffc hfoecifg
ffcd jfeafdeck
ffcrs ufofisreck
ffrs jfosreft
ffsnv afofenevist
fftv jfarifamevitg
fld jlofwoldep
fll bellifen
flld glofdedt
fls duhselfed
flshp hlefwolpihst
flu avirerg
flw jlofwolt
fm bomorfst
fmli smafiyls
fn phterbrent
fnd codnuofer
fndn onuofda'
fnrl pufnelarm
fnsh jnifhsit
fr carofel
frgg perofog,
fri jhtorbreyld
frm comrofsk
frmd jrofdemn
frmr profremt
frnd cadneirfog
frndh idneirfpihst
frnt batnorfed
frntg atnorf,
frntr prufnieruth
frr bleerfog
frtd hrofiteduts
frth cyhtrofer
frthr jrufrehts
frthrr jrufrehteromp
frty harfretinyts
frvr proferevt
frvy jrefnevych
frux datiurfom
fs rhtorbersk
fstnd isafnetdel
fstvls isefits lavk
ftr afaterb
fts jlefwolstfarck
ful dellufs
fxd ixifdel
fyrm bamrifch
g hamnost
gah igahagil
gd cednargel
gdd idraugeds
gic jamnoscit
gld cadloger
gldn jlogneds
glrs holgirsuom
gnd iniagdel
gug iniag,
gngli inegelaoygs
gnl pnegelart
gnm inegeltnemp
gn deniagst
gp bepirght
gr begnikal
grb haeergaelbs
grbli jaeergaylbs
grng haeerg,
grt dateergen
grv dlevargst
gs hamsnost
gt bletager
gv blevigon
gve crevaged
gvrn ivognrel
gy hamnosyrs
h johyld
hcs johseilt
hd cadahst
heb iehswerbg
herd cidraehls
het ceteaheg
hdwk idoohkniwdeg
hev ivaehneg
hev brevaehng
hit cuthgiehet
hh johylfoohseilk
hl caliahed
hld codlohts

5

hldn jlohneds
hle clelihweg
hlp capleher
hlt catlahst
hlth cohtlaehol
hlw jlohwolt
hm demihst
hnd cadnahgs
hnr jnohrmog
hnri incneaeyrs
hns jcnhilssent
ho blohwot
hos clesohwen
hp drepohal
hpnd ipahnepder
hrd cadrahek
hre drerehst
hrng beraeh,
hs cisihel
hsz blesuohlm
hv chevahel
hvg avah,
hvh bihtahnt
hyd cedihel
hyv dlevohas
hzd izahdrazk
hzn jerehnot
hzy herehybs
js isileark
ish hiiashap
jd inujroiaednock
jdgg bogduj,
jl iwejled
jlm hejurasmelt
jn jniitsut'
jn deniojad
jno bdnhojol
jrn iruojyent
js itniasnhojl
jst bitsujen
jstli itsujylt
ken hatneks
ki bryekom
kis hyekenotsp
kn boleenker

knlg ilwonkegdel
knrd inikderdt
knwg swonk,
kp copeeked
kw cowonkel
lb cleulben
lbl pilaelbs
lbrs halobirsoun
lbrtd ibileardets
lch dehcoler
lchg phcol,
lct jetcelp
lctd jetcelden
ld codealsh
leg bisdaerso
legg odaer,
lft detfells
lgl jellags
lgli hellagyls
li cleilgs
lk dekoolon
lke clekills
lkws jekilesiwn
ll ballars
lld ilaedulf
lng dognolld
lngg inalegaugs
lnth dahtgnelks
lob ibognols
lprs ipelsuorg
lrm hamrald
lsn iselnost
lss bessellt
lst cetsalps
lt dethgillo
ltr ilarats
lttr italrets
lv brevolst
lve vlevaelgs
lvl avelels
lvs desevilsa
lvts helsetive
lw bowalsk
lwl iwallufs
lwli iwallufyls

6

ly clyalsk
lyng gyal,
lys ilasyaws
m bregdolch
mag cataergat
mah damahst
mal cedabel
mane knrom,
mbr imemrebs
mck dlekamns
md bledamel
mdls domleds
meml memoirlap
mesh dimehseg
mih dehcumns
mi blymed
mit cadnesth
mk bekramst
mlt ilamteli
mmdt imiemidetal
mn cenemps
mna inamand
mnd dednimer
mng hagnomp
mni jamyns
mnr inamrens
mntl inemlats
mpld imeyolpdeg
mplts imielpstnemt
mprtc imitropcenap
mps imisserps
mpsd imisopdel
mpstr imisoprets
mptrb iminepeartelbd
mr bleromel
mrcls himcarusols
mrng onrom,
mrt jremtil
msf jymflesh
mst ditsomed
mstrs isymetseirg
mstris isymetirsuom
mt detemer
mtgs iteemsgnis
mth bihtuomed
mtn pimiat'
mtre himrets
mtrls hametirslat
mtt diteemen
mut betsumst
my bryamer
myst betsiomel
myt bethgimon
n denigs
nat haneruts
nbl honelby
nbld ineadelbs
nbld inudnilbdel
nc dekconkel
nce doecnols
ncldg inidulc,
nclnd ininilcdeg
ncsri hensecasyrg
ncsti jensecisyts
nct inatneics
nctd jiniaitdets
ndd pnideeds
nditv inicidaevitt
ndr inureds
nds besdnelt
ndth inehteds
ndtk inuredekats
ndvr ineveadruon
ne blenong
ner coracnds
nfli inuwallufylt
nfm jnimroft
nfmn inirofam
nfrr iniefirrop
nft inutiff
ngv inevarg,
ni jayns
njri iniujyrs
nl bileenker
nls inussell
nm blemanel
nmi kneeymt
nmr imunrebs
nmst initsomp
nn dreninst

7

No byhtuosel
no blonge
nog thton,
nom gnomirots
non blenoner
nov cawengs
nox bethginer
nqr ineeriuqe
nqri ineiuqyrs
nrly jraenylt
nrwd inuerdrawdel
nscs iniesneck
nsd inarewsdeg
nspn iniceps'
nsptn iniceps'
nsptd initcepsdeth
nstd inillatsdel
nstln inilatsal'
NT ipacniatfochttsohs
nt detoned
ntc honecits
ntdc iniortecuds
ntdcn iniortcud'
ntl inullitt
ntld ineitdelts
ntmt iniitetamp
ntnd ineretniatdel
ntntn ininet'
nto inuots
ntr inerets
ntse iniesnets
num imunsrebs
nvk iniekovs
nvlty inilovnuatiryls
nvr ivenred
nvsl guiarevlast
nvstd inisevdets
nw bowongs
nwlg inulliw,
nxt cetxenst
O isamrets
oblg poegilbt
oc beseyest
octgi ihgieytuohtdnast
ocns icoacsnoisg
og blogst
ogs biseoged
ogt dithguord
OJ inujroiorevreest
on blonel
or diruors
orgn ironags
ort cituold
ortr ituored
OS inesroiorevesres
Os isamsreth
otc ituoretruock
otwd ituodraws
ous chraest
ovs joreveessret
p imorpesig
Paj hajtehpt
parv dillamson
pat botopst
patrs hafsrehts
pex ikcepexal
pdsl jepsedlats
pec breceiper
pes catoofel
pet cotupon
petg cotup,
pits cistniopeg
plc blecalpod
plm comlapeg
pln donalpor
plrs jlipsrals
pls drsaelped
plsr isaelperud
pn honeps
pnd honepdel
pnd bednuopet
pnn jonipnoil
pntg betniop,
pntrt onepeetarth
pop hoepelps
pph ipahcaorps
ppl iparapleg
ppl irupelps
pplg ipaylp,
pprbn ipaorpab'

8

pprns ipoearsnoith
pprs ipaesirpt
pptd ipatnoipdel
pptng iparepniat,
pptnt ipatnoiptnemp
pprtt hatraptnemp
pptr ipareperuts
ppvd ipavorpdel
pr hyarprel
prcdd jorpdeecdel
prcdg jerpdeec,
prcdng jorpdeec,
prb iborpaelbs
prclms horpsmialck
prclmn icropalam'
prcs jerpsuoick
prcss horpsecnoist
prdcsr idrepesecrosh
pre bleruped
prfci horpifneicyck
prfm irepmroft
prfrnc jrepmrofcenad
prim betsrifel
prmn jorpom'
prmng horpomt,
prmt jorpetomp
prnc horpecnuont
prnl inirpicelph
prns hasnorps
prpd jerprapdeg
prpl iporpreyls
prpr iporpreg
prpri herprapaotyrg
prr coruopal
prsd jerpedish
prsnc iserpecnes
prsng irupus,
prstd jerptnesdeg
prst herptnest
prsu irupeust
prsv herpevrest
prtclr irapciturald
prty hupiryth
prv brevorped
prvs jerpivsuot
prvt herptneve
ps dissaped
psd isapdest
psn jrepnosk
psth itseirpdoohs
pstn hopis'
ptnc hapecneits
pstri isopretiyts
pt iserptnet
pt butraphs
pth cihtapks
pts distrapel
pty ineplayts
pu dipulp
pun ipunol
pus jipsuol
pvs imorpesidnaraewst
pur iwoprel
pyg blyap,
q chart
qlfd ilauqiifdeg
qlfns ilauqiifac'
qr chronol
qri jrauqyrs
qrs hienreths
qs bosame
qt borows
quadra jrofyts
qung dyhtfifst
quot beruofks
quotcnd irofytcesdnol
quotr chhtruofks
qusns ciseuq'
qust detseuqed
qvctn jeviuqiac'
r blerant
R ipabcrett
rbe cleborst
rbh iburhsibs
rbldg herdluib,
rbns ibirsdnabs
rbtri jraibartyrs
rcht jraihctcets
rchtr jraihcceteruts
rcptn herpec'

'9

rcss ' herssecs
rctd jetcerdeg
rctd iceriteduts
rctn jerca'
rcv jerevieck
rd badnuorlm
rdd cedorsk
rdbld jerbuoddeld
rdi idaerys
rdnd ironiaddel
rdng didaer,
rdr jroreds
Rep jrepaist
rf corafer
rflgt herluftnegs
rggd igurdegs
rgli igerurald
rglns igerual'
rgn bongierst
rgnl hoirniglam
rgt jrutnegs
Rih hihmars
rjt iertccjs
rl blelursh
rlcs jlerscit
rll collorsh
rm demoorsk
rmd imradel
rmnd herniamdel
rmnt imertnant
rms bosmrank
rmv herevomp
rnsns hursnip
rpr herriaph
rprng herriap,
rprt jertrops
rpst ipererrtness
rpt hertaeps
rqst herseuqdets
rrd biderps
rrvd jrairdevs
rs hirsest
rschs herhcraessel
rsd isiardel
rstln iseroul'
rsmld hermesdelbs
rsn jasirnel
rsn haernost
rspt isercepevits
rsvtn iserreav'
rsvg hervres,
rt bithgirds
rthd ithgirdnahs
rth cohtraels
rthr ihtarren
rtn jernruth
rts bistrant
rvl herlaevs
rvntl iverenerlaits
rwdd herdrawdeg
Ryc hycsurs
rys bisyargs
rze izears
s desint
sa blyaser
sami hasamirnats
sax dekcorns
sblm ibusemile
sbts ibusstsist
sc boces'
scd hasderck
scdli jasdercyls
sch bihcusts
scndd isadnecdel
scpd iseacdeph
scptr ipecsrots
scr heseruck
sclt iracstels
scrd hasderck
scrch cohcraesth
scsctr icnasmutcnasotmurt
scssrs icussecsrost
sct hesteres
sd codiaske
sde bledisth
sds desedisth
sdyt isaisudiyth
sec iceseratyrs
sep jesnevs
sepi jesnevytl

10

sf beflesed
sffr ifusrefs
sg dengisel
sgf igisinsiefs
sgh bethgiser
sgl igislans
shl bellahset
shld dedluohstt
Shoj ihsojuat
shp clepahsth
shs deswohset
sic blo:om
sjrs josnruojsrel
sk dekeesth
skd iksadel
skus isevslest
sla jlaost
slb ilysalelbs
slk billiksed
slm hosnmels
slmi josnmelylt
Sln ilosonomk
sln binialsth
slnc hisecnels
slphd ipilsdobst
slt hasetulb
sm blemasel
smbl imyslobs
sme blemoser
smlr omisirals
smn imusnoms
smt bletomsen
snd cednuosel
sngli inisugrals
snli iniserecyls
snr inoosred
snt detnesth
snw dewonser
sol denuser
Som homsest
SP inirpicelposnuojred
spcl hepslaick
spd cledapsem
spk blekopsel
spld ipusilpdeg
spms hepsmicsnet
spnd isusdnepdeg
sps iseesuops
spsd ipussopdeg
sppsg ipussop,
sppt ipustrops
sqr blerauqset
srnc isarusecnat
srpd irusirpdest
srpt irestneps
srv blevrests
srve iresecive
srvl ireselive
SS inujroirawneds
ss bisyasth
ssg blyas,
ssh dcht:asth
ssmbl isameselbs
ssrd isarusdel
sst isatsist
sstl iseneslaits
sstt isatnest
ssud isiusdel
stat desdnatsel
stdfst idet:tsafs
stant dednatsed
statg dednats,
stgrs inartssregs
stli hetatsyls
stl billitsts
stmp bipmatsks
stn chenotsks
stn isusniats
stnd isusniatdel
stnd bednatseg
stnn itisua'
stp bopotsom
strcy itcirtsyls
strkg bokirts,
strt betcirtseg
sts blats'
sts dististh
stsfd itassiifdel
stsfi itassiyfs
stt bletatsed

11

sttg bettis,
sup husemerps
svrl iveselars
svts iresstnavs
swd dedraowsel
sx bexisth
sxh blhtxiseg
SWSS inesroidnanujroira wsneds
t. clehter
.t clotts
ta betate
tb catubel
tc ibatreanelck
tcl iceleruts
te dleehths
tel datelor
ter bleerhter
terd cedrihter
terr cadnuorgas
terr bednaled
tgr hothtegred
th clhtaogs
thes isehtasolinsnal
thfr herehterofs
thg bignightel
thk bcknahths
thn denahten
thr ihtorel
thrn bienorhtel
thrwd ihtihtredraws
tid hitdel
tk blekatel
tkg bekat,
tkn hotneks
tld jitdelt
tli jytrell
tls dislootes
tm blemitel
tmlt juttlums
to blowted
tok bokootel
tp betsaper
tpl imetelps
tpO itsapsamrets
trbleurtel
trbn irutnabs
trbs disebirteg
trf herehterofs
tri blyrted
tri iratyrs
trigsx jrihtytxist
trl hirtlan
trli hurtyls
trng hirtnaelgs
trns cisnruths
trnttd isnarttimdets
tro bihguorhted
trsn heartnost
trsr isaerterut
trvd ivartledelt
trvlg jartlev,
tsfy isetityfs
tsk dcksateg
tsmi isetitomynt
tst bletsater
ttl hitelts
ttnd itadnets
Ty dleryteg
u cluoyel
und hevelhtneg
ur beruoyer
urez hezburalebs
urt betnrubeg
us blesuel
US huindetsetatsk
usgs huassegs
uz bisusk
v bidnant
vat cetiawer
ven bonehwel
vet dateyis
vhd jaheuovdel
vid bleeseg
vig inewtyts
vigterd inewtytdrihts
vlbl ilavuaelbs
vlg haliav,
vlte hivoetals
vlu ilaveur

12

vlvt jlevtevs
vnc blecnehwel
vncd idanavdeck
vnct idaecnavtnemp
vr porevs
vri iveeyrs
vri jaewyrs
vrld horevdials
vrs irevsest
vrtcl jrevitlack
vrtx prevtext
vrus havirsuot
vsn heavnoist
vt bletovet
W betsewer
wa blyawel
wd bidrowel
wdn idiwnel
wds idiwswog
wh cehcihwel
whi blyhweg
whr blerehwel
wht cletihweg
wil cellewed
wk bikrower
wkm dikrownemp
wl dilliwel
wld bedluoweg
wle blelohwen
wm domohwer
wn conword
wldns iliwredssent
wp jrowpihslufs
wr blereweg
WR ithgirrowpihslufs
wrg bignorwel
wri hrowyhte
wrld bidlrowel
wrs bisraewed
wrt bithguorweg
wrtg chirw,
WS inesroirawneds
ws bisawel
wsd isiwmods
wsh crhsiwer

wt catahweg
wthn ihtiwnit
wtht ihtiwtuol
wtvr itahwveret
wy hayaws
wz bisliavst
xbhtd ixebihtidel
xclm ixemialck
xclnc ixelececnell
xcpt ixetpeck
xcs ixeesuck
xhtn ixerohat'
xltd ixeladets
xltn ixelaat'
xmn ixemaian'
xpdts ixeepidsuoith
xpl ixenialph
xplnd ixenialpdeg
xplni ixenalpaotyrs
xptd ixetcepdeg
xr jrahccareth
xric jrahccaretsicith
y hyorlas
YC hyorlahcral
YCN hyorlahcrapacniath
yes blesehtfs
yge jetpyge
ylw ileywoll
ym bomehtel
ymsfs imehtsevlest
yn dinehtel
yng dignuoyes
yos blesohtel
yr deriehtag
ys disihtel
yt betahtor
yth dehtiwal
yus bosuhtan
yy blyehter
z blith—zch ichazairhad
zf cafing—zh blehol
zl calaezst—zm damask
zn donald—zrt bitrals
zs clemet—zs cotiag
zts bistils—zz blewer

THE MASONIC TABLET

CHAPTEER CIPHER KEY

(Kingston, New York, 1822)
Facsimile

(1)

: ast	seafirstuce
: a	tonez
: ae	attwelveam
alr	rmdashleripe
ahtfj	mandajepthanoves
: aeth	ovimtwelfthpine
aluj	eveijabulumsevn
asse	overcassianove
aphte	mandaethiopianacet
: aiid	coma133desut
br	aebrotherse
b	abeu
bn	sebeenus
bry	asebrotherlyamc
bng	manbeingust
bt	acbarefootum
bcm	macbecameust
bes	ovebecausenat
brt	tmabroughtamt
bfr	acebeforecus
brn	cesbornave
bnfts	avecubenefitsumsac
brs	obebrotherseve
bd	acbideen
blng	mistoblongaves
b	abiblem
btnd	mustobtainedaces
bndg	remnbindingrace
brn	sucbrethrenaws
bnds	aoetboundsucan
bng	gadburningrac
bml	raplambuct
bg	rubadgeur
bldg	namebuildingnone
bsn	acebusinessuch
bdnt	rastobedientubes
bt	seabouter
bts	zembeautiesant
blf	wambeliefsna
bstrctns	wampumotobstructio-nsamenessu
bth	combothrus
bld	numbuildeeu
btr	sumbetterice
bsv	omiobservenat
brd	sevbroadman
btn	wanbetweenruc
brc	antfabricist

bmlp	acreplumbastic
brng	nesibearingcame
br	ecbareum
bnt	elabentume
bndr	muchboundaryfrom
bdrt	ecelobdurateasks
btn	canobtainmus
bttl	mintbattleusma
bl	crablent
brd	venburiedces
bk	esbackus
bd	crabideus
bocj	mundjacobandi
bynd	cratbeyondantz
bndls	extreboundlessaltim
butfl	avecebeautifulastic
blng	vermbelongasto
brkts	vermibracketsolsti
blsg	crimblessingmast
brng	comabringaust
brbrs	crmebarbarousmaze
brsvd	accusobservedtalla
blmd	cusebloomedasts
bttr	trubetterick
cptd	eccaacceptedanta
crd	dreaccordant
ct	tuacton
cms	satcomeseta
cd	dacouldin
cvg	naccoveringsus
chr	amrcharacterswa
cm	eccameso
crtn	mastcertaintitu
ct	tacutum
cncl	mastconcealaste
cld	evrcalledunt
cn	nacanda
clhd	maseclothedusty
cndd	dicoconductedetal
cndt	maracandidatesome
cncnc	episeconciencetamec
cnr	reccentremin
csd	daccausedum
ctns	mauactionsettl
cnfrd	danteconferredustys
csm	miscustomsim
crnr	nobacornerusty
cmn	miscommonuts

(2)

ccsm	adepoccasionests
cry	dincarrymad
crd	avecarriedmaz
cnvd	naseconveyedancu
cmpd	darscompleteduman
cnfrmt	sumastconformityastras
cncrng	destasconcerningustoma
chngg	brantchangingrance
cnfm	ruseconfirmance
crmns	caperceremoniesetsum
cnfd	destconfideuses
cfi	reeachas
cntrbt	oaresacontributeoarcs
crtr	estacharterucas
cns	asacowansant
chty	yamacharityosto
cl	accallus
cldd	redacloudedasas
ciasm	maustmosaicustin
cmmmrtv	ractastcommemorativepastins
cptc	astuecliptieranc
cntnly	drasticontinuallyestuma
chs	samchurchesuas
chls	drischapelswama
cndtg	semasconductingramas
cmnd	dustacommandarst
cnrvld	episondeliverancemastin
crcl	dintcirclestum
cndrp	zumtaprudenceaston
ctsj	vampjusticenati
cnstnty	vrmocasconstantlyustomas
cndr	dragconductoristi
cntnc	vastacontinuancesumos
crtd	dumacreatedanas
cnscrd	vintagconsecratedumasti
cntmpltng	esucansatcontemplatingestumasva
crn	evacrcationas

crtr	novecreatorumat
chmr	addachamberusen
cst	doncastrac
cbts	eccacubitsoman
cnvx	dramconvexuston
cntrs	epinscountriesamats
cnstltns	dampysisconstellationsumsastit
clstl	yempicelestialistan
cnssg	etanacconsistingratel
crd	evadoricast
cmpst	natascompositevance
cthr	dantrethoricosmo
cgl	easlogicate
cthtr	samasearithmeticatatan
csm	nicmusicsnn
cnsqnc	ristecconsequenceamanta
cmplt	uacetcompleteyasec
crmy	nisecerenonyasec
cmmncg	dristacommencingnayats
cnstn	ecansconstitutionastem
cmpltn	dasantcompletionosenti
crdl	evaccardinalsuma
cnvnc	epantconvinceutean
crs	esacourseant
cmmndt	doscotcommunicatediveste
ccsd	evacaccostedrims
cnspry	pimentconspiracyapimac
cnsqcs	ancantconsequencesignesas
cnfsn	detsoconfusionaveco
cst	emacoastant
ccsng	secusaccusingesmin
cr	recaresu
crdgy	manisaccordinglysactan
cnstd	evecuconstitutedansec
cnsts	draceconsistsumace
cnsnt	secusconsentimyas
clsg	masaclosingnaws

(8)

cmnc	distcommencesums
crcty	rmantcorrectlyastum
cnslts	evampaconsultsacetsa
cmnctg	rampascommunicat-ingestinc
cmt	dustcommitteever
cmns	edaceceremoniesalast
clps	destclapsoces
cntnd	veriscontainedestum
cnclsn	vertzaconclusionam-azta
cnfs	evasconfessumac
cncls	esactcouncilsestum
crs	salcuriousols
clcltd	zampascalculatedent-zas
cndvrfi	eustacprovidenceasta-cu
cngrtlty	naseumascongratulat-orymeasanta
clstr	astonclusteronanc
ccsry	enltaaccessaryamast
cnsqty	yastamconsequentlye-stump
cndtn	esanconditionalsac
cnfrd	estacconferredioces
d	adot
dnd	casdeniedest
dd	rididis
dsps	castdisposest
dvsd	eccadivesteduces
dr	redoorus
dstnt	astocdistinctustom
dnlb	sucablindasta
dsrs	ecusdesirousonta
drkn	novedarknessunte
ddctd	remnadedicetedressu
dn	nadonest
dly	yaldulyast
dflq	sectqualifiederon
dgr	resdegreetan
dchcv	smandavouchedranse
djct	mustadjacentismu
dmssn	secusadmissionatsec
dia	rasaidasa
dmng	secuadmittingasta
dnf	racfindus
dnh	sechandums

dkn	sumnakedist
dnfi	saropendeuc
drw	slawordals
drd	secordereduca
dvnc	magaadvanceusta
du	saduece
dcd	sucdedicateduso
dsrd	rustdesiredumas
dpt	sacdepositace
dstt	romadestitutepaus
dvsd	secudivestedusto
dfnsv	redicdefensivestuco
dns	radsoundama
dwh	sechewedumo
drqs	avacsquaredamac
dkrm	remamarkeddasta
dpd	resadoptedent
dr	esreadas
dsfr	sacarefusedascom
dsrvg	rantadiscoveringumat
dsk	recaskeduma
dnr	randangerest
dfc	dasedeficeuma
dp	dedeepun
dnt	ramdenoteute
drn	naradornuma
dssfd	dintasatisfiedinast
dg	gagoodric
dtllst	ristatessellatedatema
dryhc	crostchequeredrasma
drt	tardartams
dct	casdedeicateasa
dmtd	senaadmittedanes
dnmr	remaremindanac
drblssrt	samacanatressselboar-dumascont
djtd	secaadjustedrast
dvn	nasdivineust
dnw	sumwindasa
dstrsd	dusomadistressedast-ana
dtrf	slamfortiudentas
drg	graguardams
ddn	nasadditionast
dmn	rommindum
dley	sracyieldraca
drt	trutriedumo
dbl	laddoublemas

(4)

dklp	rosapluckedorsa
dscr	somadiscoveromas
drnd	dasadornedanas
dstngshd	damacostdistinguishedanaagnes
ddrg	ragaguardedroma
dmnd	drusdemandedruso
drhtg	gnosogatheredogoso
datig	desingileadomona
dft	tradefectast
dfrnt	mosandifferentomase
dvsn	nostdivisionamin
drcd	nasadirectedaman
dscrtn	romansdiscretionumbrac
dtg	gatdotagegos
dgr	namdaughterose
dvncg	rostaadvancingumasa
dttdmrp	esancampremeditatedonasent
dtrmd	numasdeterminedrancas
dten	dumadetectionasan
dhcres	rantassearchedornda
dhtlc	danaccloathedranci
dmd	naddeemedrom
dnrg	rosugrounderis
dprvd	dentedeprivedesoma
dtg	gatdoubtinguma
dlt	domtiledans
drctn	mosesdirectionovals
dsph	humadispatcharms
dclr	rudadeclaretoma
dnr	romaroundums
drng	sonaduringenta
drssd	enasedressedumasa
drcs	romasacredreas
dsrs	remadesiresananc
ddlfdnlb	secundamblindfolded
dtrmd	nastadeterminedasuas
dhsgntnsd	dragosontdistinguishedumostanta
dspy	yadadisplayamaz
dsnd	rosetdestinedastru
dmrf	ecusformedrast
dhslpmc	reccomaaccomplishedanaceos
drdg	sunadreadingmova

drns	remaadorationsoces
dcnt	nosadecentumas
dnhb	brombehindrast
dhsnfn	rastanunfinishedestan
dscvy	solandiscoveryamats
dps	solspadecor
dg	redugas
drwrf	masnaforwardamsan
ega	acaagesto
erf	panfreezasta
em	moment
eton	nosanotemuma
2 endy	cramsecondlyamza
e	athen
2 e	itwos
ey	yayens
es	nuseeru
eh	rahear
esu	usausecum
fm	mafromas
fndly	yadkifriendlyasamas
frnd	drasfriendamas
fnd	doefounduma
fr	roforum
flwd	risefollowedsecu
flw	racfollowama
fr	refearom
gv	rogivees
grt	tomgreetum
gng	nagainingost
gt	tagreatog
gn	nigainos
gd	dogoodam
h	sholyt
hr	wherece
hw	awhower
hvg	gruhavingust
hs	sahasto
hv	vohavest
jrsalm	osecajerusalemanast
jn	adjuniorwardenus
lrn	naolearnust
lft	traleftuns
lfl	limlawfulsom
ldr	droleaderest
lk	kilikest
mks	seemakesund
md	drmadest

(5)

mr	ramorest
mn	nomanca
nvr	runneveroma
nm	nonamest
nt	trnotos
nthr	romaneitheronsa
nr	ranoris
obn	nabobligationes
psns	romapassionsecta
prsm	morapresumestort
prft	torsperfrctumon
pls	esapleaseest
prncs	solvapronounceacred
prpd	dmaspreparedumos
prsn	nosaprisonites
prpy	quamproperlyston
ps	ropassum
qstns	nomiquestionsanta
rt	torightbe
rss	resrisesess
rthr	nomaratheresto
rvl	revrevealorst
rcv	morreceivemon
rstnc	tonasresistanceumoso
rsns	solareasonsumas
rmd	eraremindona
rcnmdn	sextanrecommenda-tionistama
rcd	dronreçeiveduca
rčln	morarecollectionumo
roop	pronpoorasa
rts	storightstom
rctd	romaerectedumos
rhtrf	risunfurtheromast
rprt	torareportomum
rcmnd	sultrecommendedale-to
rqsd	domerequestedthat
rcvg	monareceivingasto
rs	erisent
rtd	droreturnedamo
stjn	somisaintjohnsona
sbdu	duossubduecest
shl	losshallum
sc	cosectionro
sn	nosignes
strcs	esorasecretsomoni
sys	romsaysona
sch	hicsuchoma

stn	nossituationros
sk	roaskum
sgt	tossoughtesa
sd	doshouldest
s	msouths
sn	raseniorwardenar
tn	nothenas
tkn	romtakenove
trd	rostriedust
tt	mothated
thn	nosthanast
tr	rothereum
thr	romthoughtest
trtr	romtortureman
thrf	fromthereofasty
tuo	roaoutams
trp	propartest
trly	yolstrulyerst
thn	nosthineems
trst	etomtrustansa
u	nyous
urslf	romasyourselfistn
whce	eastwhenceusto
wh	trwhates
wlng	dosewillingomas
wd	dawouldbe
wrb	bomwherebyast
wl	Jowellas
wn	nowhence
whr	roswheresto
wr	aswereas
whh	hoswhichema
ws	sowashe
wm	mowhomen
wy	yowhyst
wtt	trowithoutthe
wo	oswhoma
wn	noownem
wt	sowaiter
wnce	ercawonceomes
w	twesta
xpcd	domaexceptedu
ynm	rosmanyest
yhtrw	rosanworthysec
y	obys
ydb	rombodyama
ytd	domdutyosa
ysm	rocmasonryest

THE APPENDICES

The appendices reprint in facsimile—for the first time—two important contemporary exposures which should be compared with the *Masonic Tablet*. They offer us our earliest corroborating witness of Parker's work, and are the second earliest descriptions we have of both Craft and York Rite American Masonic ritual.

APPENDIX 1

[William Morgan] *Illustrations of Masonry, by one of the fraternity, who has devoted thirty years to the subject* (Batavia, Printed for the author [by David. C. Miller], 1826)

Although the "Morgan exposure" has remained in print since 1826, the original edition has never been reproduced in facsimile. Parker's *Masonic Tablet* was printed at a time when there were two Grand Lodges operating in New York, commonly known and the "City" and "Country" Grand Lodges. Although no ritual uniformity was enforced, Parker's ritual represents a sample from the former, while William Morgan's infamous exposure offers a sample of the latter. In this regard it is convenient to have both for the sake of comparison.

William Morgan was born in Culpepper County, Virginia, on August 7, 1774. Often referred to as "Captain Morgan," he may have fought under General Andrew Jackson at the Battle of New Orleans in 1815.[1] In 1819 he married Lucinda Pendelton, and in 1821 they moved to Upper Canada where he worked as a brewer. After a fire destroyed his business he was reduced to poverty, whence he commenced work as a stonemason. He thus worked in the environs of Rochester and Batavia, New York. While in the area he began attending local Masonic lodges, and he may have claimed to have been made a Mason in Canada, where

1. William S. Simons claimed that during the Battle of New Orleans (Jan. 8, 1815) he fought by the side of "Capt. William Morgan." *Anti-Masonic Christian Herald* vol. 1 (Boston, Thursday, Feb. 26, 1829) 7:26. In another publication, it was asserted that Morgan's military commission as a "Capt. in a Militia Regiment, at the battle of New Orleans" was stolen by Masons and never returned. See Edward Giddins, *The Pennsylvania anti-Masonic Almanac, for the Year of our Lord 1830* (Lancaster: Published at the Office of the Anti-Masonic Herald, [1830]), 43.

the ceremonies and initiation rituals differed. Indeed, no evidence of his initiation or "regularity" (Masonic legitimacy) has been discovered. It is possible that he had studied an exposé, such as the oft-reprinted *Jachin and Boaz*, and he may thus have been admitted into the lodge after passing a "Tiler's examination" (a test of the signs, tokens, and passwords).

Morgan as an Itinerant Lecturer

Morgan, who was able to memorize the rituals, gained a reputation as a "bright Mason," and apparently acted as an itinerant lecturer in the Craft Degrees. Itinerant or traveling lecturers (called "degree peddlers" by their detractors) helped support themselves by selling or conferring Masonic degrees. Although they contributed both to the spread of Freemasonry and to the uniformity of the rituals, they were sometimes viewed with suspicion. Today, most American Masons look upon Thomas Smith Webb, Jeremy L. Cross, Benjamin Gleason, John Barney, and John Snow as great promoters of the Fraternity, but their contemporaries sometimes held different opinions. Today, Jeremy L. Cross is remembered, and even revered, as the author of *The True Masonic Chart, or Hieroglyphic Monitor* (1819),[2] the first Masonic monitor to include illustrations. During his lifetime, however (and in spite of the official positions he held), some high-degree Masons were suspicious and wary of him. For example, Dr. Moses Holbrook, Grand Commander of the Scottish Rite's Southern Supreme Council wrote, "Jeremy L. Cross & all the whole traveling Caravan of wandering Lecturers, never extended the nor propagated any knowled[g]e of the *science* of Freemasonry, though they may have made their fortunes by their labors & publications."[3] Holbrook's criticisms were not reserved for "rivals." He also noted that Comte Alexandre Francois de Grasse-Tilly, founder of the Scottish Rite in France, Italy, Spain, and Belgium, reputedly made his living "by making Masons clandestinely."[4] If de Grasse-Tilly's culpability is debatable, there are straightforward examples of opportunists, such as Dr. James H. C. Miller, a struggling physician who sought Masonic charity while peddling his chivalric "Order of the Holy Cross." Miller's

2. Jeremy L. Cross, *The True Masonic Chart, or Hieroglyphic Monitor; containing all the Emblems Explained in the Degrees of Entered Apprentice, Fellow-Craft, Master Mason, Mark Master, Past Master, Most Excellent Master, Royal Arch, Royal Master, and Select Master* (New Haven, [CT]: Flagg & Gray, Printers, 1819).

3. Moses Holbrook, Charleston, S.C., Aug. 21, 1830, to J. J. Gourgas, New York, N.Y. Original in the archives of the Supreme Council, 33°, NMJ, copy in the Archives of the Supreme Council, 33°, S.J.

4. Moses Holbrook, Charleston, S.C., May 12, 1828, to J. J. Gourgas, New York, N.Y. Original in the archives of the Supreme Council, 33°, NMJ, copy in the Archives of the Supreme Council, 33°, S.J.

system was eventually condemned, and eventually disappeared from the Masonic scene (although its rituals, which were exposed and scavenged by other systems, including the prestigious Red Cross of Constantine).[5]

In spite of concerns, many Masons were sympathetic to the itinerant lecturers, and some local lodges were all too happy to employ an "expert," as Robert Morris explained in *William Morgan; or Political Anti-Masonry* (1883):

> [William Morgan] became a regular visitor and soon picked up a superficial acquaintance with the ceremonies of the Order. Traveling from place to place, in his vocation as journeyman bricklayer, he timed his stay at each place to cover the regular and called meetings of the Lodges, which were then almost as numerous in western New York as now, and he made it a point to attend them. The Lodges were full of work at every meeting, candidates were initiated, passed and raised, and the Lodges soon found use for a Brother whose voice was loud and sonorous, who displayed an easy manner as one who had mixed much with mankind, who could sit up all night if need be, to finish the whole work at hand, and who at the festive board could sing his song with the best, offer his toast, and also, drink his glass with the merriest....
>
> These peculiar gifts of William Morgan, his physical endurance, strong voice, dramatic style and social disposition, caused him, after a while, to be in demand. Lodges, learning that he had a job of bricklaying in the vicinity, would invite him to assist them in their labors. He learned to handle the Senior Deacon's rod expertly. The lengthy utterances of the Fellowcraft Degree which few learn, he memorized and delivered with emphasis and effect. In return for this his Brethren paid his hotel bills and often contributed sums for the support of his family. In one instance where he remained several days, and gave the Lodge more than ordinary assistance, an appropriation of ten dollars was made him.[6]

The Exposé

No one knows for certain the cause of Morgan's disaffection. Reduced to desperate circumstances he may have succumbed to the "gnaw of poverty," which has tempted even good men to commit dishonorable acts; or perhaps he was angered that his personal intemperate habits ("he was a hard drinker"[7]) caused the lodge

5. Arturo de Hoyos, "The Posthumous Success of James H. C. Miller, Degree Peddler," in *Heredom* 8 (1999–2000), 169–217.

6. Rob Morris, *William Morgan; or Political Anti-Masonry, its Rise, Growth and Decadence* (New York: Robert Macoy, Masonic Publisher, 1883), 82–84. The cover title of this work is *William Morgan. What the Freemasons Say.*

7. Stone, *Letters on Masonry and Anti-Masonry*, 124, 127, 128, 133.

door to close to his face. Richard Carlile, an English freethinker and champion for a free press, contended that his own exposé of Freemasonry (first published in 1825 while a prisoner in Dorchester jail), induced Morgan to write his own.[8] An oft-repeated story asserts that because Morgan's Masonic regularity could not be ascertained, his signature on the records of his Royal Arch Chapter (dated May 31, 1825) was besmeared with ink.[9] This smear presumably stained his reputation as well and embittered him to the Fraternity. However, Stone's aforementioned *Letters on Masonry and Anti-Masonry* states that Morgan may have been working on his book several months earlier: "Morgan had commenced writing something upon the subject of Freemasonry, for what purpose it is not known, as early as the winter or spring of 1825."[10] In selecting his title Morgan mimicked one of the most renowned Masonic works, William Preston's *Illustrations of Masonry* (London: 1772),[11] a guidebook used by English-speaking Freemasons on both sides of the Atlantic. Most historians accept that Morgan and his intended publisher, David Cade Miller (a 1°, Entered Apprentice Mason who never advanced), encountered a series of obstacles and misfortunes connected with their venture. Among these were intimidation, an attempt to burn down the printing house, an offer to buy the manuscripts, and the theft of said manuscripts. The abduction and alleged murder of Morgan (probably drowned in the Niagara), in September 1826, was but the final *coup* in an ill-conceived—and unsuccessful—attempt to halt publication. The resulting fury delivered such a blow to the Fraternity that it only began to recover about 1842, although the aftershock of the Morgan Affair still agitates anti-Masons today. Considering the similarities between Daniel Parker's and William Morgan's offenses we may well ask, *what was their material difference*? And why would Morgan's intended work have outraged the Fraternity any more than Parker's? The difference, I suggest, was motive. Because Parker valued his membership in the Fraternity he enciphered the *Masonic Tablet* which he intended as nothing more than an *aide-mémoire* for his Brethren. *William Morgan, on the other hand, was most likely a "cowan."* He had never been initiated into Masonry, and his entire Masonic experience was built upon deception. This

8. [Richard Carlile,] *The Republican* vol. 12 (London, 1825); Richard Carlile, *Manual of Freemasonry*, 91.

9. The facsimile of Morgan's signature, reproduced as figure 3, appears in Morris, *William Morgan*, 70–71.

10. Stone, *Letters on Masonry and Anti-Masonry*, 129.

11. All nine editions of this work are available on Andrew Prescott's CD-ROM, *Preston's Illustrations of Masonry* (Academy Electronic Publications Ltd., 2001).

stood in stark contrast with the principles of Masonry, which Morgan himself repeated: "Truth is a divine attribute, and the foundation of every virtue. To be good and true are the first lessons we are taught in Masonry" (see facsimile, pp. 34–35). Embittered toward the Craft and influenced by mercenary motives, he intended his own work as a purely commercial venture. He boasted that he would not only expose the Craft rituals, *but the hitherto unpublished American Royal Arch Chapter Degrees in plain English*. Early American Masons would have viewed Morgan's treachery much more gravely than Parker's indiscretion. Rob Morris explained:

> When, therefore, it was announced that William Morgan was about to expose the mysteries of Masonry to the profane world, a general feeling of wrath animated the Craft. Ashamed of the patronage they had extended to him, wounded in pocket and reputation for cherishing so base a man, ridiculed by wives and daughters for their associations with so unworthy a character, the indignation of the Brethren was sufficiently hot to call out threats and violent speeches from the more imprudent, and inward searchings of heart from all.
>
> But how much worse the matter when it was discovered (about March, 1826) that Morgan had never been made a Mason. They had cherished an imposter in their bosoms. The man to whom they had communicated their Masonic esotery was under no obligations binding him to keep it secret ... for he was neither a non-affiliating Mason nor a seceding Mason—*he was not a Mason at all.*[12]

Appendix 2

A Revelation of Free Masonry, as Published to the World by a Convention of Seceding Masons, held at Le Roy, Genesee County, N.Y. on the 4th and 5th of July 1828: Containing a True and Genuine Development of The Mode of Initiation, and also of the Several Degrees: To Wit: in the Chapter, Mark Master, Past Master, Most Excellent Master, and Royal Arch. In the Encampment, Knight of the Red Cross, Knight Templar, Knight of the Christian Mark, and Guards of the Conclave, and Knights of the Holy Sepulcher. In the Ancient Council of the Trinity, Denominated the Holy and Thrice Illustrious Order of the Cross, The Illustrious, Most Illustrious, and Thrice Illustrious Degrees. Published by the Lewiston Committee **(Rochester, N.Y.: Printed by Weed & Heron, 1828).**

12. Morris, *William Morgan; or Political Anti-Masonry*, 166–67.

William Morgan's exposure was originally intended to cover both Craft and Capitular Masonry. The unpublished rituals of the Mark Master, Past Master, and Most Excellent Master were obtained in a manuscript supplied by Mrs. Morgan, following her husband's disappearance, and first published in this work. Morgan had also written out the Royal Arch Degree, but that manuscript was taken, and never returned. The text of the Royal Arch ritual, as printed in this work, is said to have been obtained from a companion who resided near Jeremy L. Cross, until the text could be transcribed. The Encampment degrees were transcribed directly from an official ritual manuscript, as was the so-called "Ancient Council of the Trinity" (for information on this body see my article "The Posthumous Success of *James H. C. Miller, Degree Peddler*," in *Heredom* 8 (1999–2000): 169–217). The bulk of the *Revelation of Free Masonry* would later be collated and reprinted, with improvements, in David Bernard, *Light on Masonry* (Utica: William Williams, 1829).

APPENDIX 1

William Morgan's *Illustrations of Masonry, by One of the Fraternity* (Batavia, New York, 1826) Facsimile

ILLUSTRATIONS

OF

MASONRY,

BY

ONE OF THE FRATERNITY,

WHO HAS DEVOTED THIRTY YEARS TO THE SUBJECT.

"God said let there be Light,
And there was Light."

Batavia:

PRINTED FOR THE AUTHOR.

1826.

Northern District of New-York, to wit:

L S BE IT REMEMBERED, That on the fourteenth day of August, in the fifty-first year of the Independence of the United States of America, A. D. 1826, William Morgan, of the said district, hath deposited in this office the title of a book, the right whereof he claims as author, in the words following, to wit:

"Illustrations of Masonry, by one of the fraternity, who has devoted thirty years to the subject. 'God said, let there be light, and there was light.'"

In conformity to the act of Congress of the United States, entitled "an act for the encouragement of learning, by securing the copies of maps, charts, and books, to the authors and proprietors of such copies, during the times therein mentioned:" and also to the act, entitled "an act supplementary to the act entitled 'an act for the encouragement of learning, by securing the copies of maps, charts, and books, to the authors and proprietors of such copies during the times therein mentioned,' and extending the benefits thereof to the arts of designing, engraving, and etching historical and other prints."

R. R. LANSING.
Clerk of the Northern Dist. of N. York.

INTRODUCTION.

In the absence of the author, or rather compiler of the following work, who was kidnapped, and carried away from the village of Batavia, on the 11th day of September, 1826, by a number of Freemasons, it devolves upon the publisher to attempt to set forth some of the leading views that governed those who embarked in the undertaking.

To contend with prejudice, and to struggle against customs and opinions, which superstition, time, and ignorance have hallowed, requires time, patience, and magnanimity. When we begin to pull down the strong holds of error, the batteries we level against them, though strong and powerful and victorious at last, are at first received with violence; and when in our conquering career we meet with scoffs and revilings from the besieged partisans of untenable positions, it the more forcibly impresses us we are but men; and that in every work of reformation and renovation we must encounter various difficulties. For a full confirmation of our statement we might refer to the history of the world. It is not our intention however, to give a full detail of the *whims* and *caprices* of man—to bring forth the historic records of other years as proofs of the windings and shiftings of the various characters who have "Strutted their brief hour on life's stage," in order to convince, that customs, associations, and institutions are like the lives of

A 2

the authors and abettors, fleeting and fragile. Many of them rise up as bubbles on the ocean, and die away. Circumstances give them existence, and when these causes cease to exist, they go into the same gulph of oblivion as countless exploded opinions and tenets have gone before them. The mind that formed and planned them goes on in its dazzling flight, bounding over barrier after barrier, till it has arrived at the ultimate goal of consummation.

The daily occurrences before us bring forth the full conviction, that the emanation from the God of light is gradually ascending to regions of greater intellectual brilliancy.

When we view man, in the infancy of society, as in the childhood of his existence, he is weak, powerless, and defenceless; but in his manhood and riper years, he has grown to his full stature, and stands forth in commanding attitude, the favored and acknowledged lord of the world. For his comfort and well being, as a member of society, rules and regulations are necessary. In the various stages of his progress, these systematic improvements undergo various changes, according to circumstances and situations.—What is proper and necessary in one grade of society, is wholly useless, and may be alarming in another. Opinions and usages, that go down in tradition, and interfere not with our improvements in social concerns, adhere to us more closely, and become entwined in all our feelings. It is to this we owe our bigotted attachment to antiquity—it is this that demands from us a superstitious reverence for the opinions and practices of men of former times, and closes the ear against truth, and blinds the eyes to the glare of new light and new accessions of knowledge; through which medium only can they break in upon the mind.

We have within ourselves the knowledge, and every where around us the proofs that we are beings destined not to *stand* still. In our present state of advancement, we look with pity on the small progress of our Fathers in arts and sciences, and social institutions; and when compared with our elevated rank, we have just cause of pride and of grateful feelings.—They did well for the times in which they lived, but to the ultimatum of perfectability we are nearer—and in the monuments we have before us of the skill and genius of our times and age, we have only fulfilled those destinies for which we were created; and we object to every obstacle that opposes or attempts to oppose the will of Heaven.

In the present enlightened state, to which society has advanced we contend that the opinions and tenets, and pretended secrecies of "olden times," handed down to us, should be fully, fairly and freely canvassed; that from the mist and darkness which have hung over them, they should come out before the open light of day, and be subjected to the rigid test of candid investigation. These preliminary remarks lead us to the main object of our introduction.

We come to lay before the world the claims of an institution which has been sanctioned by ages, venerated for wisdom, and exalted for "light;" but, an institution whose benefits have always been overrated, and whose continuance is not, in the slightest degree, necessary. We meet it with its high requirements, its "time-honoured customs," its swelling titles, and shall show it in its nakedness and simplicity. Strip it of its "borrowed trappings," and it is a *mere nothing*—a toy not now worthy the notice of a child to sport with. We look back to it as, at one period, a "cement of society, and bond of union."—We view it as, at one time, a venerable fort,—but now in ruins—which contained within its walls many things that dignified and adorned human nature. We give it due credit for the services it has done; but at present, when light has gone abroad into the uttermost recesses and corners of the world—when information is scattered wide around us, and knowledge is not closeted in cloisters and cells, but "stalks abroad with her beams of light, and her honors and rewards," we may now, when our minority has expired, act up to our character, and look no longer to Masonry as our guide and conductor: it has nothing in it now valuable that is not known to every enquiring mind: it contains, wrapped up in its supposed mysteries, no useful truth, no necesssary knowledge, that has not gone forth to the world through other channels and by other means. If we would have a knowledge of sacred history—of the religion and practices of the Jews, and the terms and technicalities of the Mosaic institution, we can have recourse to the Bible. If we wish further communications from Heaven, we have open to our view the pages of the New Testament. If we would "climb the high ascent of human science, and trace the mighty progress of human genius in every gigantic effort of mind in logic, geometry, mathematics, chemistry, and every other branch of knowledge," we ridicule the idea that Masonry, in her retirements, contains the arts and sciences. The sturdiest Mason in the whole fraternity is not bold enough to uphold or maintain the opinion, for one moment, in sober reality. The origin of the institution is easily traced to the rude ages of the world, —to a body of mechanics, or a corporation of operative workmen, who formed signs and regulations, the more easily to carry on their work, and to protect their order. [The very obligations solemly tendered to every member, carry the strongest internal evidence of the semi-barbarity that prevailed at the time of the institution of the order.] In the course of time, as society increased, and knowledge became more general, it spread, and embracing in its grasp other objects than at first, it enrolled in its ranks men of the first respectability in wealth, talents, and worth. But that there is any thing intrinsically valuable in the signs, symbols, or works of Masonry, no man of sense will contend. That there is any hidden secret which operates as a talismanic charm on its possessors, every man of intelligence, Mason or no Mason, must candidly acknowledge. It is worse than idleness for the defenders of the order, at the present day, to entrench themselves behind their outward show—the semblance before the world—and to say *they are in possession of superior knowledge.*

We pretend not to act under a cover. We shall "tell the truth, the whole truth, and nothing but the truth." Masonry, it is true, has long been eulogised in songs—it has formed the burthen of the poet's theme, and been the subject of the orator's best performances. Fancy has been almost exhausted in bringing out "new flowers to deck the fairy queen;" but when we come behind the scenes, what is the picture we behold! Are we to rest satisfied with the *ipse dixit* of others, or to examine the truth for ourselves? The touchstone is before our readers in the present publication.

Masonry is, of itself, naked and worthless. It consists of gleanings from the Holy Scriptures, and from the arts and sciences which have shone in the world. Linking itself with philosophy and science and religion, on this it rests all its claims to veneration and respect. Take away this borrowed aid, and it falls into ruins.

Much weight is still attached to the argument, that as a tie uniting men—that, as a significant speech, symbolical speaking every language, and at the same time embodying in its constitution every thing that is valuable, it should command respect. We meet this argument with facts that cannot be controverted. We put it on a basis that will fling into the back-ground every quibble and artifice on the subject; and, in the language of a polemic writer, we challenge opposition to our position :—

"The religion inculcated by the Son of Man does all this; and in no possible situation can man be placed, that the benign influence of Christianity does not completely supersede the use of a mere human institution. Place a brother in a desert, unfriended and unknown,—leave him in a wilderness where human footsteps never printed the ground, the Divine Benefactor is at his side, and watches over him with parental guidance. Let him be driven on a barbarous coast in the midst of savage men, and there it is that the breathings of the divine influence spreads around him its shield: bring him into civilized society—in the busy walks of men, and are we to be told that as members of community, sojourners on earth, and candidates for heaven, we must be taught our duty at a Mason's Lodge? Wherever Masonry exercises its influence with success, there Christianity can have, or should have a more powerful effect. Whenever Masonry claims "kindred with the skies," and exalts herself above every living sublunary thing, then, with an unhallowed step, it obtrudes on the sacred borders of religion, and decks itself in borrowed garments."

Entrenched within these strong walls—decked with all the glitter of high sounding professions, claiming what do not belong to it,—dazzles "but to bewilder and destroy." In its train, in these United States, is enrolled many periodical works devoted to Masonry; and under the guise of patronizing mechanics—the arts and sciences—lend their aid to carry on the imposing delusion. They take up the specious title of throwing a little illumination on this benighted country, from their secret depositories. Arrogating to itself what should deck others' brows—assuming to be the patron, the life and soul of all that is great and valuable—it deceives many of its votaries, and from its *gaudy* premises the most untenable and onerous conclusions are drawn.

Are we astonished at the wild and heedless manner in which many of the votaries of Masonry rush into every excess—putting at defiance the laws of our civil institutions, which suffer no one to be put in jeopardy but by due forms, and disregarding the command of the Most High, which says, "Thou shalt not kill?"—we can readily trace the cause to the impressions and practices obtained from its false tenets and deceptive arrogance. Masonry is to the modern world, what the whore of Babylon was to the ancient; and is the beast with seven heads and ten horns, ready to tear out our bowels, and *scatter them to the four winds of heaven.*

Masonry gives rogues and evil minded characters an opportunity of visiting upon their devoted victim, all the ills attending combined power, when exerted to accomplish destruction. It works unseen, at all silent hours, and secret times and places; and like *death*, when summoning his diseases, pounces upon its devoted subject, and lays him prostrate in the dust. Like the great enemy of man, it has shown its cloven foot, and put the public upon its guard against its secret machinations.

This part of the subject requires no farther discussion, either by way of ridicule or downright sincerity, but the remark, which cannot be too often reiterated, that the world, in its present advanced state, requires no such order for our social intercourse; and when the masonic mania prevails as it now does in this country, we are exalting a mere human ordinance, with its useless trumpery and laughable accompaniments for the sublime and unadorned lessons of Heaven.

To some men it is galling and mortifying in the extreme to give up their darling systems. With the increase of years their fondnesss becomes so great that they cling to them with wild and bewildered attachment.—But we would ask them where now are the Knights of Malta and Jerusalem, and the objects that called forth their perils and journeyings? Where are the crusades, and excursions on which our Grand Commanders, Generalissimos and Sir Knights are to be engaged..............In no other excursions than Cervantes describes of his redoubtable Hero, *Don Quixotte.* The days and occasions that called forth these deeds of chivalry and valor have passed like those before the flood; and the *mock* dignitaries and *Puppet-show* actions of Masons in their imitation call forth pity and indignation. When we now see the gaudy show in a lodge room, and a train of nominal officers with their distinctions and badges, it may give us some faint idea of scenes that are past, and may gratify an idle curiosity, but produce no substantial good under heaven. When monasteries and cloisters, and Inquisitor's cells and prisons have been broke up before the sweeping march of the moral mind, why this unnecessary mummery should be so much countenanced in this country, above all other countries in the world, is a matter of astonishment.

The day we trust will never arrive here, when ranks in Masonry will be stepping stones to places of dignity and power—when this institution will be a machine to press down the free born spirit of men. We have now no tyrant to rule over us—no kingly potentate to move over our heads the rod of authority; but high in our elevation, and invincible in our strong holds, we put at defiance secret cabals and associations. The public opinion is like a mighty river, and gigantic in its course, it will sweep every interposing obstacle before it.

In the work which we submit to the public, we have given false coloring to nothing: nor in these remarks have we set down aught in malice. In the firm discharge of our undertaking we have been stern and unbending as the rugged mountain oak: and persecutions, pains, and perils have not deterred us from our purpose. We have triumphed over tumlt, and clamor, and evil speaking.

When our book goes out to the world, it will meet with attacks of a violent nature from one source, and men of mock titles and order will endeavor to heap upon it every calumny. Men more tenacious of absolute forms and practice than they are attentive to truth and honor, will deny our expositions, and call us Liars and Impostors.

Such is the treatment, however ungenerous and unjust, which we expect to meet, and for which we are prepared. Truth we know is majestic and will finally prevail The little petty effusions of malice that will be thrown out, will die with their authors, whom this work will survive.

We now aver in defiance of whatever may be said to the contrary—no matter by whom, how exalted his rank —that this Book is what it pretends to be—that it is a Master Key to the secrets of Masonry; that in the pages before him, the man of candor and inquiry can judge for himself, and then a proper judgment will be formed ot our intention.

ILLUSTRATIONS
OF
MASONRY, &c.

A DESCRIPTION of the ceremonies used in opening a Lodge of Entered Apprentice Masons; which is the same in all the upper degrees, with the exception of the difference in the signs, due-guards, grips, pass-grips, words and their several names; all of which will be given and explained in their proper places as the work progresses.

One rap calls the Lodge to order—one calls up the Junior and Senior Deacons—two raps call up all the subordinate officers, and three, all the members of the lodge.

The Master having called the Lodge to order, and the officers all seated, the Master says to the Junior Warden, 'Brother Junior, are they all Entered Apprentice Masons in the South?' *Ans.* 'They are, Worshipful.' Master to the Senior Warden, 'Brother Senior, are they all Entered Apprentice Masons in the West? *Ans.* 'They are, Worshipful.' The Master then says, 'They are, in the East,' at the same time he gives a rap with the common gavel or mallet, which calls up both Deacons. Master to Junior Deacon, 'Brother Junior, the first care of a Mason?' *Ans.* 'To see the Lodge tyled, Worshipful.' Master to Junior Deacon, 'Attend to that part of your duty, and inform the Tyler that we are about to open a lodge of Entered Apprentice Masons, and direct him to tyle accordingly.' The Tyler then steps to the door and gives three raps, which are answered by three from without; the Junior Deacon then gives one, which is also answered by the Tyler with one; the door is then partly opened, and the Junior Deacon delivers his message, and resumes his situation, and says, 'the door is tyled, Worshipful.' (at the same time giving the due-guard, which is never omitted when the Master is ad-

B

dressed.) The Master to the Junior Deacon, 'By whom?' *Ans.* 'By a Master Mason without the door, armed with the proper implement of his office.' Master to Junior Deacon, 'His duty there?' *Ans.* 'To keep off all cowans and eaves-droppers, see that none pass or repass without permission from the Master.' [Some say, without permission from the chair.] Master to Junior Deacon, 'Brother Junior, your place in the lodge?' *Ans.* At the right hand of the Senior Warden in the West.' Master to Junior Deacon, 'Your business there, Brother Junior?' *Ans.* 'To wait on the Worshipful Master and Wardens, act as their proxy in the active duties of the Lodge and take charge of the door.' Master to Junior Deacon, 'The Senior Deacon's place in the Lodge?' *Ans.* 'At the right hand of the Worshipful Master in the East' [The Master, while asking the last question, gives two raps, which calls up all the subordinate officers.] Master to Senior Deacon, 'Your duty there, Brother Senior?' *Ans.* 'To wait on the Worshipful Master and Wardens, act as their proxy in the active duties of the Lodge, attend to the preparation and introduction of candidates, and welcome and clothe all visiting Brethren, [i. e. furnish them with an apron.] Master to Senior Deacon, 'The Secretary's place in the Lodge, Brother Senior?' *Ans.* 'At the left hnnd of the Worshipful Master in the East.' Master to Secretary, 'Your duty there, Brother Secretary?' *Ans.* 'The better to observe the Worshipful Master's will and pleasure, record the proceedings of the Lodge; transmit a copy of the same to the Grand Lodge, if required; receive all monies and money bills from the hands of the Brethren, pay them over to the Treasurer, and take his receipt for the same.' The Master to the Secretary, 'The Treasurer's place in the Lodge?' *Ans.* 'At the right hand of the Worshipful Master.' Master to Treasurer, 'Your duty there, Brother Treasurer?' *Ans.* 'Duly to observe the Worshipful Master's will and pleasure; receive all monies and money bills from the hands of the Secretary; keep a just and true account of the same; pay them out by order of the Worshipful master and consent of the Brethren.' The Master to the Treasurer, 'The Junior Warden's place in the lodge, Brother Treasurer?' *Ans.* 'In the South, Worshipful.' Master to Junior Warden, 'Your business there, Brother Junior? *Ans.* 'As the sun in the South at high meridian is the beauty and glory of the day, so stands the Junior Warden in the South, the better to observe the time, call the crafts from labour to refreshment, superintend them during the hours thereof, see that none convert the hours of refreshment into that of intemperance or excess; and call them on again in due season, that the Worshipful Master may have honour, and they pleasure and profit thereby.' Master to the Junior Warden, 'The Senior Warden's place in the Lodge?' *Ans.* 'In the West, Worshipful?' Master to Senior Warden, 'Your duty there, Brother Senior?' *Ans.* 'As the sun sets in the West to close the day, so stands the Senior Warden in the West to assist the Worshipful Master in opening his Lodge, take care of the jewels and implements, see that none be lost, pay the craft their wages, if any be due, and see that none go away dissatisfied.' Master to the Senior Warden, 'The Master's place in the Lodge?' *Ans.* 'In the East, Worshipful.' Master to the Senior Warden, 'His duty there?' *Ans.* 'As the sun rises in the East to open and adorn the day, so presides the Worshipful Master in the East to open and adorn his lodge, set his crafts to work with good and wholesome laws, or cause the same to be done.' The Master now gives three raps, when all the brethren rise, and the Master, taking off his hat, proceeds as follows: 'In like manner so do I, strictly forbidding all profane language, private committees, or any other disorderly conduct whereby the peace and harmony of this Lodge may be interrupted while engaged in its lawful pursuits, under no less penalty than the bye-laws, or such penalty as a majority of the brethren present may see fit to inflict. Brethren, attend to giving the signs.' [Here lodges differ very much. In some, they declare the Lodge opened as follows, before they give the signs:] The Master (all the Brethren imitating him) extends his left arm from his body so as to form an angle of about forty-five degrees, and holds his right hand transversely across his left, the palms thereof about one inch apart. This is called the first sign of a Mason—is the sign of distress in this degree, and alludes to the position a candidate's hands are placed in when he takes the obligation of an Entered Apprentice Mason. The Master then draws his right hand across his throat, the hand open, with the thumb next to the throat, and drops it down by his side.

This is called the due-guard of an Entered Apprentice Mason, (many call it the sign) and alludes to the penalty of the obligation. (See obligation.) The Master then declares the Lodge opened, in the following manner: 'I now declare this Lodge of Entered Apprentice Masons duly opened for the despatch of business.' The Senior Warden declares it to the Junior Warden, and he to the Brethren. 'Come, Brethren, let us pray.' One of the following prayers is used:

Most holy and glorious God! the great Architect of the Universe; the giver of all good gifts and graces; Thou hast promised that "Where two or three are gathered together in thy name, thou wilt be in the midst of them, and bless them." In thy name we assemble, most humbly beseeching thee to bless us in all our undertakings; that we may know and serve thee aright, and that all our actions may tend to thy glory and our advancement in knowledge and virtue. And we beseech thee, O Lord God, to bless our present assembling; and to illuminate our minds through the influence of the Son of Righteousness, that we may walk in the light of thy countenance; and when the trials of our probationary state are over, be admitted into the Temple not made with hands, eternal in the heavens. Amen. So mote it be.

Another prayer as often used at opening as closing.

Behold how good and how pleasant it is for brethren to dwell together in unity; it is like the precious ointment upon the head, that ran down upon the beard, even Aaron's beard, that went down to the skirts of his garment: as the dew of Hermon, and as the dew that descended upon the mountains of Zion, for there the Lord commanded the blessing, even life for evermore. Amen. So mote it be.

The lodge being now open and ready to proceed to business, the Master directs the Secretary to read the minutes of the last meeting which naturally brings to view the business of the present.

If there are any candidates to be brought forward, that will be the first business attended to. I will therefore proceed with a description of the ceremonies used in the admission and initiation of a candidate into the first degree of Masonry.

A person wishing to become a Mason must get some one who is a Mason to present his petition to a lodge, when, if there are no serious objections, it will be entered on the minutes, and a committee of two or three appointed to enquire into his character, and report to the next regular communication. The following is the form of a petition used by a candidate; but a worthy candidate will not be rejected for the want of formality in his petition.

To the Worshipful Master Wardens and Brethren of Lodge No. —, of Free and Accepted Masons.

The Subscriber, residing in ———, of lawful age, and by occupation a ———, begs leave to state that, unbiassed by friends, and uninfluenced by mercenary motives, he freely and voluntarily offers himself a candidate for the mysteries of Masonry, and that he is prompt to solicit this privilege by a favourable opinion conceived of the institution, a desire of knowledge and a sincere wish of being serviceable to his fellow-creatures. Should his petition be granted, he will cheerfully conform to all the ancient established usages and customs of the fraternity.

(Signed) A. B.

At the next regular communication, (if no very serious objection appears against the candidate) the ballot-boxes will be passed; one black ball will reject a candidate. The boxes may be passed three times. The Deacons are the proper persons to pass them; one of the boxes has black and white beans, or balls in it, the other empty; the one with the balls in it goes before, and furnishes each member with a black and white ball; the empty box follows and receives them. There are two holes in the top of this box with a small tube, (generally) in each, one of which is black, and the other white, with a partition in the box. The members put both their balls into this box as their feelings dictate; when the balls are received, the box is presented to the Master, Senior and Junior Wardens, who pronounce clear or not clear, as the case may be. The ballot proving clear, the Candidate (if present) is conducted into a small preparation room adjoining the Lodge, when he is asked the following questions, and gives the following answers. Senior Deacon to Candidate, 'Do you sincerely declare, upon

B2

your honor before these gentlemen, that unbiased by friends, uninfluenced by unworthy motives, you freely and voluntarily offer yourself a Candidate for the mysteries of masonry?' *Ans.* 'I do.' Senior Deacon to Candidate, 'Do you sincerely declare upon your honour before these gentlemen, that you are prompt to solicit the principles of masonry, by a favorable opinion conceived of the institution, a desire of knowledge, and a sincere wish of being serviceable to your fellow creatures?' *Ans.* 'I do.' Senior Deacon to Candidate, 'Do you sincerely declare upon your honour before these gentlemen, that you will cheerfully conform to all the ancient established usages and customs of the fraternity?' *Ans.* 'I do.' After the above questions are proposed and answered, and the result reported to the Master, he says 'Brethren at the request of Mr. A. B. he has been proposed and accepted in regular form. I therefore recommend him as a proper Candidate for the mysteries of masonry, and worthy to partake of the privileges of the fraternity; and in consequence of a declaration of his intentions, voluntarily made, I believe he will cheerfully conform to the rules of the order.' The candidate during the time is divested of all his apparel (shirt excepted) and furnished with a pair of drawers kept in the lodge for the use of Candidates, the Candidate is then blindfolded, his left foot bare, his right in a slipper, his left breast and arm naked, and a rope called a Cable-Tow round his neck and left arm, (the rope is not put round the arm in all lodges) in which posture the Candidate is conducted to the door where he is caused to give, or the conductor gives three distinct knocks, which are answered by three from within, the conductor gives one more, which is also answered by one from within. The door is then partly opened and the Junior Deacon generally asks, 'who comes there? who comes there? who comes there?' The conductor, alias the Senior Deacon answers, 'A poor blind Candidate who has long been desirous of having and receiving a part of the rights and benefits of this worshipful lodge dedicated (some say erected) to God and held forth to the holy order of St. John, as all true fellows and brothers have done, who have gone this way before him.' The Junior Deacon then asks, 'Is it of his own free will and accord he makes this request? is he duly and truly prepared? worthy and well qualified? and properly avouched for?' All of which being answered in the affirmative, the Junior Deacon to Senior Deacon; 'By what further rights does he expect to obtain this benefit?' *Ans.* 'By being a man, free born, of lawful age, and under the tongue of good report.' The Junior Deacon then says, 'since this is the case you will wait 'till the worshipful Master in the East is made acquainted with his request, and his answer returned;' the Junior Deacon repairs to the Master, when the same questions are asked and answers returned as at the door; after which, the Master says, 'since he comes endowed with all these necessary qualifications, let him enter this worshipful lodge in the name of the Lord and take heed on what he enters.' The Candidate then enters, the Junior Deacon at the same time pressing his naked left breast with the point of the compass, and asks the Candidate, 'Did you feel any thing?' *Ans.* 'I Did.' Junior Deacon to Candidate, 'what was it?' *Ans.* 'A torture.' The Junior Deacon then says, 'as this is a torture to your flesh, so may it ever be to your mind and conscience if ever you should attempt to reveal the secrets of masonry unlawfully. The Candidate is then conducted to the centre of the lodge, where he and the Senior Deacon kneels, and the Deacon says the following prayer:

"Vouchsafe thine aid, Almighty Father of the universe, to this our present convention; and grant that this candidate for masonry may dedicate and devote his life to thy service, and become a true and faithful brother among us! Endue him with a competency of thy divine wisdom, that by the secrets of our art, he may be the better enabled to display the beauties of holiness, to the honour of thy holy name." So mote it be——Amen!

The Master then asks the candidate, 'In whom do you put your trust?' *Ans.* 'In God.' The Master then takes him by the right hand and says, 'Since in God you put your trust, arise, follow your leader and fear no danger.' The Senior Deacon then conducts the candidate three times regularly round the lodge, and halts at the Junior Warden in the South, where the same questions are asked and answers returned as at the door.

As the candidate and conductor are passing round the room the Master reads the following passage of Scripture, and takes the same time to read it that they do to go round the lodge three times.

"Behold how good and how pleasant it is for brethren to dwell together in unity! It is like the precious ointment upon the head, that ran down upon the beard, even Aaron's beard, that went down to the skirts of his garment: as the dew of Hermon, and as the dew that descended upon the mountains of Zion; for there the Lord commanded the blessing, even life for ever more."

The candidate is then conducted to the Senior Warden in the West, where the same questions are asked and answers returned as before, from thence he is conducted to the worshipful Master in the East, where the same questions are asked and answers returned as before. The Master likewise demands of him, from whence he came and whither he is travelling. The candidate answers, 'from the West and travelling to the East.' Master inquires; 'Why do you leave the West and travel to the East?' Ans. 'In search of light.' Master then says, 'Since the candidate is travelling in search of light, you will please conduct him back to the West from whence he came, and put him in the care of the Senior Warden, who will teach him how to approach the East, the place of light, by advancing upon one upright regular step, to the first step, his feet forming the right angle of an oblong square, his body erect at the altar before the Master, and place him in a proper position to take upon him the solemn oath or obligation of an entered Apprentice Mason.' The Senior Warden receives the candidate, and instructs him as directed. He first steps off with the left foot and brings up the heel of the right into the hollow thereof, the heel of the right foot against the ancle of the left, will of course form the right angle of an oblong square; the candidate then kneels on his left knee, and places his right foot so as to form a square with the left, he turns his foot round until the ancle bone is as much in front of him as the toes on the left foot; the candidate's left hand is then put under the Holy Bible, square and compass, and the right on them. This is the position in which a candidate is placed when he takes upon him the oath or obligation of an entered Apprentice Mason. As soon as the candidate is placed in this position, the worshipful Master approaches him, and says, 'Mr. A. B. you are now placed in a proper position to take upon you the solemn oath or obligation of an entered Apprentice Mason, which I assure you is neither to effect your religion nor politics, if you are willing to take it, repeat your name and say after me;' [and although many have refused to take any kind of an obligation, and begged for the privilege of retiring, yet none have ever made their escape; they have been either coerced, or persuaded to submit. There are housands who never return to the lodge after they are initiated];the following obligation is then administered.

"I, A. B. of my own free will and accord, in presence of Almighty God and this worshipful lodge of free and accepted masons, dedicated to God and held forth to the holy order of St. John, do hereby and hereon most solemnly and sincerely promise and swear that I will always hail, ever conceal and never reveal any part, or parts, art, or arts, point, or points of the secret arts and mysteries of ancient freemasonry, which I have received, am about to receive, or may hereafter be instructed in, to any person, or persons in the known world, except it be to a true and lawful brother mason, or within the body of a just and lawfully constituted lodge, of such; and not unto him, nor unto them who I shall hear so to be, but unto him and them only whom I shall find so to be after strict trial and due examination, or lawful information. Furthermore, do I promise and swear that I will not write, print, stamp, stain, hugh, cut, carve, indent, paint, or engrave it on any thing moveable or immoveable, under the whole canopy of Heaven, whereby, or whereon the least letter, figure, character, mark, stain, shadow, or resemblance of the same may become legible or intelligible to myself or any other person in the known world, whereby the secrets of masonry may be unlawfully obtained through my unworthiness. To all which I do most solemnly and sincerely promise and swear, without the least equivocation, mental reservation, or self evasion of mind in me whatever; binding myself under no less penalty, than to have my throat cut across, my tongue torn out by the roots, and my body buried in the rough sands of the sea at low water mark, where the tide ebbs and flows twice in twenty-four hours; so help me God, and keep me steadfast in the due performance of the same."

After the obligation the master addresses the candidate in the following manner: 'Brother to you the secrets of masonry are about to be unveiled, and a brighter sun never shone lustre on your eyes; while prostrate before this sacred altar, do you not shudder at every crime?

have you not confidence in every virtue? May these thoughts ever inspire you with the most noble sentiments; may you ever feel that elevation of soul, that shall scorn a dishonest act. Brother, what do you most desire?' Ans. 'light.' Master to brethren, 'Brethren, stretch forth your hands and assist in bringing this new made brother from darkness to light.' The members having formed a circle round the candidate, the Master says, 'And God said, let there be light, and there was light.' At the same time, all the brethren clap their hands, and stamp on the floor with their right foot as heavy as possible, the bandage dropping from the candidate's eyes at the same instant, which, after having been so long blind, and full of fearful apprehensions all the time, this great and sudden transition from perfect darkness to a light brighter (if possible) than the meridian sun in a mid-summer day, sometimes produces an alarming effect. I once knew a man to faint on being brought to light; and his recovery was quite doubtful for some time; however, he did come too, but he never returned to the lodge again. I have often conversed with him on the subject, he is yet living, and will give a certificate in support of the above statement at any time if requested.

After the candidate is brought to light, the Master addresses him as follows: 'Brother, on being brought to light, you first discover three great lights; in masonry by the assistance of three lesser, they are thus explained; the three great lights in masonry are the Holy Bible, Square and Compass. The Holy Bible is given to us as a rule and guide for our faith and practice; the Square, to square our actions, and the Compass to keep us in due bounds with all mankind but more especially with the brethren. The three lesser lights are three burning tapers, or candles placed on candlesticks, (some say or candles on pedestals) they represent the Sun, Moon and Master of the lodge and are thus explained. As the sun rules the day and the moon governs the night, so ought the worshipful Master with equal regularity to rule and govern his lodge, or cause the same to be done; you next discover me as Master of this lodge, approaching you from the East upon the first step of masonry, under the sign and due-guard of an entered Apprentice mason. (The sign and due-guard has been explained.) This is the manner of giving them, imitate me as near as you can, keeping your position. First, step off with your left foot and bring the heel of the right into the hollow thereof, so as to form a square.' (This is the first step in masonry.) The following is the sign of an Entered Apprentice mason, and is the sign of distress in this degree ; you are not to give it unless in distress. (It is given by holding your two hands transversely across each other, the right hand upwards and one inch from the left.) The following is the due-guard of an entered Apprentice Mason. (This is given by drawing your right hand across your throat, the thumb next to your throat, your arm as high as the elbow in a horizontal position.) 'Brother, I now present you my right hand in token of brotherly love and esteem, and with it the grip and name of the grip of an entered Apprentice mason.' The right hands are joined together as in shaking hands, and each sticks his thumb nail into the third joint or upper end of the fore finger ; the name of the grip is *Boaz*, and is to be given in the following manner and no other ; the Master first gives the grip and word, and divides it for the instruction of the candidate ; the questions are as follows : The Master and candidate holding each other by the grip as before described, the Master says, 'what is this.' Ans. 'A grip.' Q. 'a grip of what.' A. The grip of an entered Apprentice mason. Q. Has it a name ? A. It has. Q. Will you give it to me ? A. I did not so receive it, neither can I so impart it. Q. What will you do with it ? A. Letter it or halve it. Q. Halve it and begin. A. You begin. Q. Begin you. A. 'B-O.' Q. 'A-Z.' A. 'BOAZ.' Master says, 'Right ,brother *Boaz*, I greet you. It is the name of the left hand pillar of the porch of king Solomon's Temple—arise, brother Boaz, and salute the Junior and Senior Wardens as such, and convince them that you have been regularly initiated as an Entered Apprentice Mason, and have got the sign, grip, and word.' The Master returns to his seat while the Wardens are examining the candidate, and gets a lamb-skin or white apron, presents it to the candidate, and observes, 'Brother, I now present you with a lamb-skin or white apron : it is an emblem of innocence, and the badge of a Mason : it has been worn by kings, princes, and potentates of the earth who have never been ashamed to wear it : it is more honourable than the diadems of kings, or pearls of princesses, when worthily worn : it is more ancient than the Golden Fleece or Roman Eagle: more honourable than the Star and Garter, or any other order that can be conferred upon you at this, or any other time, except it be in the body of a just and lawfully constituted lodge; you will carry it to the Senior Warden in the West, who will teach you how to wear it as an Entered Apprentice Mason.' The Senior Warden ties the apron on and turns up the flap instead of letting it fall down in front of the top of the apron. This is the way Entered Apprentice Masons wear, or ought to wear their aprons until they are advanced. The candidate is now conducted to the Master in the East, who says, 'Brother, as you are dressed, it is necessary you should have tools to work with; I will now present you with the working tools of an Entered Apprentice Mason, which are the twenty-four inch guage and common gavel; they are thus explained:—The twenty-four inch guage is an instrument made use of by operative Masons to measure and lay out their work, but we as Free and Accepted Masons, make use of it for the more noble and glorious purpose of dividing our time. The twenty-four inches on the guage, are emblematical of the twenty-four houss in the day, which we are taught to divide into three equal parts, whereby we find eight hours for the service of God, and a worthy distressed brother; eight hours for our usual vocations, and eight for refreshment and sleep; the common gavel is an instrument made use of by operative Masons to break off the corners of rough stones; the better to fit them for the builders use, but we as Free and Accepted Masons use it for the more noble and glorious purpose of divesting our hearts and consciences of all the vices and superfluities of life, thereby fitting our minds as living and lively stones, for that spiritual building, that house not made with hands, eternal in the heavens; I also present you with a new name; it is CAUTION, it teaches you that as you are barely instructed in the rudiments of Masonry, that you should be cautious over all your words and actions, particularly when before the enemies of Masonry. I shall next present you with three precious jewels which are, a *listening ear*, a *silent tongue*, and a *faithful heart*. A listening ear teaches you to listen to the instructions of the Worshipful Master; but more especially that you should listen to the calls and cries of a worthy distressed brother. A silent tongue teaches you to be silent while in the lodge, that the peace and harmony thereof may not be disturbed, but more especially, that you should be silent before the enemies of Masonry, that the craft may not be brought into disrepute by your imprudence. A faithful heart teaches you to be faithful to the instructions of the Worshipful Master at all times, but more especially, that you should be faithful, and keep and conceal the secrets of Masonry, and those of a brother when given to you in charge as such, that they may remain as secure and inviolable in your breast as in his own, before communicated to you. I further present you with check words two; their names are *truth* and *union*, and are thus explained. Truth is a divine attribute, and the foundation of every virtue; to be good and true, is the first lesson we are taught in Masonry; on this theme we contemplate, and by its dictates endeavour to regulate our conduct; hence, while influenced by this principle hypocricy and deceit are unknown among us; sincerity and plain dealing distinguish us, and the heart and tongue join in promoting each other's welfare and rejoicing in each others prosperity.

Union, is that kind of friendship, which ought to appear conspicuous in every Mason's conduct. It is so closely allied to the divine attribute, truth, that he who enjoys the one, is seldom destitute of the other. Should interest, honour, prejudice, or human depravity, ever induce you to violate any part of the sacred trust we now repose in you, let these two important words, at the earliest insinuation, teach you to put on the check-line of truth, which will infallibly direct you to pursue that straight and narrow path which ends in the full enjoyment of the Grand Lodge above; where we shall all meet as Masons and members of the same family, in peace, harmony and love; where all discord on account of politicks, religion or private opinion shall be unknown, and banished from within our walls.

Brother it has been a custom from time immemorial to demand, or ask from a newly made brother something of a metalic kind, not so much on account of its intrinsic value, but that it may be deposited in the archives of the Lodge, as a memorial, that you was herein made a Mason; —a small trifle will be sufficient;—any thing of a metalic kind will do; if you have no money, any thing of a metalic nature will be sufficient; even a button will do.

C

(The candidate says he has nothing about him; it is known he has nothing.) 'Search yourself,' the Master replies. He is assisted in searching, nothing is found; 'perhaps you can borrow a trifle,' says the Master. (He tries to borrow, none will lend him—he proposes to go into the other room where his clothes are; he is not permitted.—If a stranger, he is very much embarrassed]; Master to candidate, 'Brother let this ever be a striking lesson to you, and teach you, if you should ever see a friend, but more especially a brother in a like pennyless situation, to contribute as liberally to his relief as his situation may require, and your abilities will admit without material injury to yurself or family.' Master to Senior Deacon, 'You will conduct the candidate back from whence he came, and invest him of what he has been divested, and let him return for further instruction.' The candidate is then conducted to the preparation room, and invested of what he had been divested, and returns to the North East corner of the Lodge, and is taught how to stand upright like a man; when and where the following charge is, or ought to be delivered to him; though it is omitted nine times out of ten, as are near one half of the ceremonies.

Master to the candidate, 'Brother as you are now initiated into the first principles of Masonry, I congratulate you on having been accepted into this ancient and honorable order; ancient, as having subsisted from time immemorial; and honourable, as tending in every particular, so to render all men who will become conformable to its principles. No institution was ever raised on a better principle, or more solid foundation, nor were ever more excellent rules and useful maxims laid down than are inculcated in the several Masonic lectures. The greatest and best of men in all ages have been encouragers and promoters of the art, and have never deemed it derogatory to their dignity, to level themselves with the fraternity—extend their privileges, and patronize their assemblies.'

'There are three great duties, which, as a Mason, you are charged to inculcate. To God, your neighbour, and yourself. To God, in never mentioning his name, but with that reverential awe that is due from a creature to his Creator; to implore his aid in all your laudable undertakings, and to esteem him as the chief Good.—To your neighbour, in acting upon the square, and doing unto him as you wish he should do unto you: and to yourself in avoiding all irregularity, or intemperance which may impair your faculties, or debase the dignity of your profession. A zealous attachment to these principles will ensure public and private esteem. In the state, you are to be a quiet and peaceable subject, true to your government and just to your country; you are not to countenance disloyalty, but faithfully submit to legal authority, and conform with cheerfulness to the government of the country in which you live. In your outward demeanor be particularly careful to avoid censure or reproach. Although your frequent appearance at our regular meetings is earnestly solicited, yet it is not meant that Masonry should interfere with your necessary vocations: for these are on no account to be neglected; neither are you to suffer your zeal for the institution to lead you into argument with those, who, through ignorance, may ridicule it. At your leisure hours, that you may improve in Masonic knowledge, you are to converse with well informed Brethren, who will be always as ready to give, as you will be to receive information. Finally, keep sacred and inviolable the mysteries of the order, as these are to distinguish you from the rest of the community, and mark your consequences among Masons. If, in the circle of your acquaintance, you find a person desirous of being initiated into Masonry, be particularly attentive not to recommend him, unless you are convinced he will conform to our rules; that the honour, glory, and reputation of the institution may be firmly established, and the world at large convinced of its good effects.'

The work of the evening being over, I will proceed to give a description of the manner of closing the Lodge. It is a very common practice in Lodges to close a Lodge of Entered Apprentices, and open a Lodge of Fellow Crafts, and close that, and open a Master Mason's Lodge, all in the same evening.

Some Brother generally makes a motion that the Lodge be closed; it being seconded and carried:—

The Master to the Junior Deacon—'Brother Junior,' (giving one rap which calls up both Deacons,) 'the first as well as the last care of a Mason?' *Ans.* 'To see the Lodge tyled, Worshipful.' Master to Junior Deacon, 'Attend to that part of your duty, and inform the Tyler that we are about to close the Lodge of Entered Apprentice Masons, and direct him to tyle accordingly.' The Junior Deacon steps to the door and gives three raps, which are answered by the Tyler with three more; the Junior Deacon then gives one, which is also answered by the Tyler by one. The Junior Deacon then opens the door, delivers his message, and resumes his place in the Lodge, and says, 'the door is tyled, Worshipful.' Master to Junior Deacon, 'By whom?' *Ans.* 'By a Master Mason without the door, armed with the proper implement of his office.' Master to Junior Deacon, 'His business there?' *Ans.* 'To keep off all cowans and eaves-droppers, and see that none pass or repass without permission from the chair.' Master to Junior Deacon, 'Your place in the Lodge, brother Junior?' *Ans.* 'At the right hand of the Senior Warden in the West.' Master to Junior Deacon, 'Your duty there?' *Ans.* 'To wait on the Worshipful Master and Wardens, act as their proxy in the active duties of the Lodge, and take charge of the door.' Master to the Junior Deacon, 'The Senior Deacon's place in the Lodge?' *Ans.* 'At the right hand of the Worshipful Master in the East.' Master to Senior Deacon, 'Your duty there, brother Senior?' *Ans.* 'To wait on the Worshipful Master and Wardens, act as their proxy in the active duties of the Lodge; attend to the preparation and introduction of candidates, receive and clothe all visiting brethren.' Master to the Senior Deacon, 'The Secretary's place in the Lodge?' *Ans.* 'At your left hand, Worshipful.' Master to Secretary, 'Your duty there, brother Secretary?' *Ans.* 'Duly to observe the Master's will and pleasure; record the proceedings of the Lodge; transmit a copy of the same to the Grand Lodge, if required; receive all monies and money bills from the hands of the brethren; pay them over to the Treasurer, and take his receipt for the same.' Master to the Secretary, 'The Treasurer's place in the Lodge?' *Ans.* 'At the right hand of the Worshipful Master.' Master to Treasurer, 'Your business there, brother Treasurer?' *Ans.* 'Duly to observe the Worshipful Master's will and pleasure; receive all monies and money bills from the hands of the Secretary; keep a just and accurate account of the same; pay them out by order of the Worshipful Master and consent of the Brethren.' Master to the Treasurer.' 'The Junior Warden's place in the Lodge?' *Ans.* 'In the South, Worshipful.' Master to the Junior Warden, 'Your business there, brother Junior?' *Ans.* 'As the sun in the South, at high meridian, is the beauty and glory of the day; so stands the Junior Warden in the South, at high twelve, the better to observe the time; call the crafts from labour to refreshment; superintend them during the hours thereof; see that none convert the purposes of refreshment into that of excess or intemperance; call them on again in due season, that the Worshipful Master may have honor, and they pleasure and profit thereby.' The Master to the Junior Warden, [I wish the reader to take particular notice, that in closing the Lodge, the Master asks the Junior Warden as follows: 'The Master's place in the Lodge?' and in opening he asks the Senior Warden the same question] 'The Master's place in the Lodge?' *Ans.* 'In the East, Worshipful.' Master to Junior Warden, 'His duty there?' *Ans.* 'As the sun rises in the East, to open and adorn the day, so presides the Worshipful Master in the East to open and adorn his Lodge; set his crafts to work with good and wholesome laws, or cause the same to be done.' Master to the Junior Warden, 'The Senior Warden's place in the Lodge?' *Ans.* 'In the West, Worshipful.' Master to Senior Warden, 'Your business there, brother Senior?' *Ans.* 'As the sun sets in the West to close the day, so stands the Senior Warden in the West to assist the Worshipful Master in opening and closing the Lodge; take care of the jewels and implements; see that none be lost; pay the crafts their wages, if any be due, and see that none go away dissatisfied.' The Master now gives three raps, when all the brethren rise, and the Master asks, 'Are you all satisfied? They answer in the affirmative, by giving the due-guard. Should the Master discover that any declined giving it, enquiry is immediately made, why it is so; and if any member is dissatisfied with any part of the proceedings, or with any brother, the subject is immediately investigajd. Maester to the Brethren, 'Attend to giving the signs; as I do, so do you; give them downwards.' (which is by giving the last in opening, first in closing. In closing, on this degree, you first draw your right hand across your throat, as herein before described, and then hold your two hands over each other as before described. This is the method pursued through all the degrees; and when opening on any of the upper degrees, all the signs,

C 2

of all the preceding degrees, are given before you give the signs of the degree on which you are opening.) This being done, the Master proceeds, 'I now declare this Lodge of Entered Apprentice Masons regularly closed in due and ancient form. Brother Junior Warden, please inform brother Senior Warden, and request him to inform the brethren that it is my will and pleasure that this Lodge of Entered Apprentice Masons be now closed, and stand closed until our next regular communication, unless a case or cases of emergency shall require earlier convention, of which every member shall be notified; during which time it is seriously hoped and expected that every Brother will demean himself as becomes a Free and Accepted Mason.' Junior Warden to Senior Warden, 'Brother Senior, it is the Worshipful Master's will and pleasure that this Lodge of Entered Apprentice Masons be closed, and stand closed until our next regular communication, unless a case or cases of emergency shall require earlier convention, of which every Brother shall be notified; during which time it is seriously hoped and expected that every Brother will demean himself as becomes a Free and Accepted Mason.' Senior Warden to the Brethren, 'Brethren, you have heard the Worshipful Master's will and pleasure, as communicated to me by Brother Junior; so let it be done.' Master to the Junior Warden, 'Brother Junior, how do Masons meet?' *Ans.* 'On the level.' Master to Senior Warden, 'How do Masons part?' *Ans.* 'On the square.' Master to the Junior and Senior Wardens, 'Since we meet on the level, Brother Junior, and part on the square, Brother Senior, so let us ever meet and part, in the name of the Lord.' Here follows a prayer sometimes used. Master to the Brethren, 'Brethren let us pray.

'Supreme Architect of the Universe! accept our humble praises for the many mercies and blessings which thy bounty has conferred upon us, and especially for this friendly and social intercourse. Pardon, we beseech thee, whatever thou hast seen amiss in us since we have been together; and continue to us thy presence, protection, and blessing. Make us sensible of the renewed obligations we are under to love thee supremely, and to be friendly to each other. May all our irregular passions be subdued, and may we daily increase in faith, hope and charity; but more especially in that charity which is the bond of peace, and perfection of every virtue. May we so practice thy precepts, that through the merits of the Redeemer, we may finally obtain thy promises, and find an acceptance through the Gates, and into the Temple and City of our God. So mote it be.——Amen.'

A Benediction, oftener used at closing than the preceding Prayer.

May the blessing of Heaven rest upon us and all regular Masons! may brotherly love prevail, and every moral and social virtue cement us. So mote it be.——Amen.

After the prayer the following charge ought to be delivered; but it is seldom attended to; in a majority of Lodges it is never attended to.

Master to Brethren, 'Brethren, we are now about to quit this sacred retreat of friendship and virtue, to mix again with the world. Amidst its concerns and employments forget not the duties which you have heard so frequently inculcated, and so forcibly recommended in this Lodge. Remember that around this altar, you have promised to befriend and relieve every Brother who shall need your assistance. You have promised in the most friendly manner to remind him of his errors and aid a reformation. These generous principles are to extend further: Every human being has a claim upon your kind offices. Do good unto all. Recommend it more "especially to the household of the faithful." Finally, Brethren, be ye all of one mind, live in peace, and may the God of love and peace, delight to dwell with and bless you.'

In some Lodges, after the charge is delivered, the Master says' 'Brethren, form on the square.' When all the Brethren, form a circle, and the Master, followed by every Brother (except in using the words) says, "And God said, let there be light and there was light." At the same moment that the last of these words drops from the Master's lips, every member stamps with his right foot on the floor, and at the same instant bring their hands together with equal force, and in such perfect unison with each other, that persons situated so as to hear it, would suppose it the precursor of some dreadful catastrophe. This is called '*the shock.*'

Having described all the ceremonies and forms appertaining to the opening of a Lodge of Entered Apprentice Masons; setting them to work; initiating a candidate, and closing the Lodge, I will now proceed to give the Lecture on this degree. It is divided into three sections. The lecture is nothing more or less than a capitulation of the preceding ceremonies and forms by way of question and answer, and fully explains the same. In fact, the ceremonies and forms (generally masonically called *the work*) and lectures are so much the same that he who possesses a knowledge of the lectures cannot be destitute of a knowledge of what the ceremonies and forms are. As the ceremonies used in opening and closing are the same in all the degrees, it is thought best to give the whole one insertion; it being the sincere wish of the writer, that every reader should perfectly understand all the formulas of the whole masonic fabric, as he then will thereby be able to form correct opinions of the propriety or impropriety, advantages or disadvantages of the same.

First Section of the Lecture on the First Degree of Masonry.

Q. From whence come you as an Entered Apprentice Mason?

A. From the holy Lodge of St. John, at Jerusalem.

Q. What recommendations do you bring?

A. Recommendations from the Worshipful Master, Wardens and Brethren of that Right Worshipful Lodge, whom greet you.

Q. What comest thou hither to do?

A. To learn to subdue my passions, and improve myself in the secret arts and mysteries of ancient Free Masonry.

Q. You are a Mason, then, I presume?

A. I am.

Q. How shall I know you to be a Mason?

A. By certain signs and a token. Q. What are signs?

A. All right angles, horizontals, and perpendiculars.

Q. What is a token?

A. A certain friendly and brotherly grip, whereby one Mason may know another in the dark as well as in the light.

Q. Where was you first proposed to be made a Mason?

A. In my heart. Q. Where secondly?

A. In a room adjacent to the body of a just and lawfully constituted Lodge of sucn.

Q. How was you prepared ?

A. By being divested of all metals, neither naked nor clothed, barefoot nor shod, hood-winked with a Cable-Tow* about my neck, in which situation I was conducted to the door of the Lodge.

Q. You being hood-winked how did you know it to be a door ?

A. By first meeting with resistance and afterwards gaining admission.

Q. How did you gain admission ?

A. By three distinct knocks from without, answered by the same from within.

Q. What was said to you from within ?

A. Who comes there, who comes there, who comes there.

Q. Your answer.

A. A Poor blind candidate who has long been desirous of having and receiving a part of the rights and benefits of this Worshipful Lodge, dedicated to God, and held forth to the holy order of St. John, as all true fellows and brothers have done, who have gone this way before me.

Q. What further was said to you from within ?

A. I was asked if it was of my own free will and accord I made this request, if I was duly and truly proposed, worthy and well qualified, all of which being answered in the affirmative, I was asked by what further rights I expected to obtain so great a favour or benefit.

Q. Your answer ?

A. By being a man, free born, of lawful age and well recommended.

Q. What was then said to you ?

A. I was bid to wait 'till the Worshipful Master in the East was made acquainted with my request and his answer returned.

Q. After his answer returned what followed ?

A. I was caused to enter the Lodge.

Q. How ?

A. On the point of some sharp instrument pressing my naked left breast in the name of the Lord.

*Three miles long.

Q. How was you then disposed of of?

A. I was conducted to the center of the Lodge and there caused to kneel for the benefit of a prayer. (See page 19.)

Q. After prayer what was said to you?

A. I was asked in whom I put my trust.

Q. Your answer? A. In God.

Q. What followed?

A. The Worshipful Master took me by the right hand and said, since in God you put your trust, arise follow your leader and fear no danger.

Q. How was you then disposed of?

A. I was conducted three times regularly round the Lodge and halted at the Junior Warden in the South, where the same questions were asked and answers returned as at the door.

Q. How did the Junior Warden dispose of you?

A. He ordered me to be conducted to the Senior Warden in the West, where the same questions were asked and answers returned as before.

Q. How did the Senior Warden dispose of you?

A. He ordered me to be conducted to the Worshipful Master in the East, where the same questions were asked and answers returned as before, who likewise demanded of me from whence I came and whither I was travelling.

Q. Your answer?

A. from the West and travelling to the East.

Q. Why do you leave the West and travel to the East?

A. In search of light.

Q. How did the Worshipful Master then dispose of you?

A. He ordered me to be conducted back to the West from whence I came, and put in care of the Senior Warden, who taught me how to approach the East, the place of light, by advancing upon one upright regular step to the first step, my feet forming the right angle of an oblong square, my body erect at the altar before the Worshipful Master.

Q. What did the the worshipful master do with you?

A. He made an Entered Apprentice Mason of me.

Q. How? A. In due form.

Q. What was that due form?

A. My left knee bare bent, my right forming a square,

my left hand supporting the Holy Bible, Square and Compass, and my right covering the same; in which position I took upon me the solemd oath or obligation of an Entered Apprentice Mason. [See page 21.]

Q. After you had taken your obligation what was said to you?

A. I was asked what I most desired.

Q. Your answer? A. Light.

Q. Was you immediately brought to light?

A. I was. Q. How? A. By the direction of the Master and assistance of the brethren.

Q. What did you first discover after being brought to light?

A. Three great Lights, in Masonry, by the assistance of three lesser.

Q. What were those three great Lights in Masonry?

A. The Holy Bible, Square, and Compass.

Q. How are they explained?

A. The Holy Bible is given to us as a guide for our faith and practice; the Square to square our actions; and the Compass to keep us in due bounds with all mankind, but more especially with the brethren.

Q. What were those three lesser lights?

A. Three burning tapers, or candles on candle-sticks.

Q. What do they represent?

A. The Sun, Moon, and Master of the Lodge.

Q. How are they explained?

A. As the Sun rules the day and the Moon governs the night, so ought the Worshipful Master to use his endeavors to rule and govern his Lodge with equal regularity, or cause the same to be done.

Q. What did you next discover?

A. The Worshipful Master approaching me from the East, under the sign and due-guard of an Entered Apprentice Mason, who presented me with his right hand in token of brotherly love and esteem, and proceeded to give me the grip and word of an Entered Apprentice Mason, and bid me arise and salute the Junior and Senior Wardens and convince them that I had been regularly initiated as an Entered Apprentice Mason, and was in possession of the sign, grip and word.

Q. What did you next discover?

A. The Worshipful Master a second time approaching me from the East, who presented me with a lamb-skin or white apron, which he said was an emblem of innocence, and the badge of a Mason; that it had been worn by kings, princes and potentates of the earth who had never been ashamed to wear it; that it was more honourable than the diadems of kings, or pearls of princesses when worthily worn, and more ancient than the Golden Fleece or Roman Eagle, more honourable than the star or garter, or any other order that could be conferred upon me at that time, or any time thereafter, except it be in the body of a just and lawfully constituted Lodge of Masons; and bid me carry it to the Senior Warden in the West, who taught me how to wear it as an Entered Apprentice Mason.

Q. What was you next presented with?

A. The working tools of an Entered Apprentice Mason?

Q. What were they?

A. The twenty-four inch guage and common gavel.

Q. How were they explained?

A. The twenty four inch guage is an instrument made use of by operative Masons to measure and lay out their work, but we as Free and Accepted Masons are taught to make use of it for the more noble and glorious purpose of dividing our time; the twenty-four inches on the guage are emblematical of the twenty-four hours in the day, which we are taught to divide into three equal parts, whereby we find eight hours for the service of God and a worthy distressed brother; eight hours for our usual vocation, and eight hours for refreshment and sleep. The common gavel is an instrument made use of by operative Masons to break off the corners of rough stones, the better to fit them for the builders use, but we as Free and Accepted Masons are taught to make use of it for the more noble and glorious purpose of divesting our hearts and consciences of all the vices and superfluities of life, thereby fitting our minds as lively and living stones for that spiritual building, that House not made with hands, eternal in the heavens.

Q. What was you next presented with?

A. A new name. Q. What was that? A. Caution.

Q. What does it teach?

A. It teaches me as I was barely instructed in the rudiments of Masonry, that I should be cautious over all my words and actions, especially when before its enemies

Q. What was you next presented with?

A. Three precious jewels.

Q. What were they?

A. A listening ear, a silent tongue and a faithful heart.

Q. What do they teach?

A. A listening ear teaches me to listen to the instructions of the Worshipful Master, but more especially that I should listen to the calls and cries of a worthy distressed brother. A silent tongue teaches me to be silent in the Lodge, that the peace and harmony thereof may not be disturbed; but more especially that I should be silent when before the enemies of Masonry. A faithful heart, that I should be faithful to the instructions of the Worshipful Master at all times, but more especially that I should be faithful, and keep and conceal the secrets of Masonry, and those of a brother, when delivered to me in charge as such, that they may remain as secure and inviolable in my breast, as in his own before communicated to me.

Q. What was you next presented with.

A. Check-words two. Q. What were they?

A. Truth and Union. Q. How explained?

A. Truth is a divine attribute, and the foundation of every virtue. To be good and true are the first lessons we are taught in Masonry. On this theme we contemplate, and by its dictates endeavour to regulate our conduct: hence, while influenced by this principle, hypocrisy and deceit are unknown amongst us; sincerity and plain dealing distinguishes us; and the heart and tongue join in promoting each others welfare, and rejoicing in each others prosperity.

Union is that kind of friendship that ought to appear conspicuous in the conduct of every Mason. It is so closely allied to the divine attribute truth, that he who enjoys the one, is seldom destitute of the other. Should interest, honor, prejudice, or human depravity ever influence you to violate any part of the sacred trust we now repose in you, let these two important words at the earliest insinuation, teach you to put on the checkline of truth, which will infallibly direct you to pursue that straight and narrow path, which ends in the full enjoyment of the Grand Lodge above, where we shall all meet as Masons and members of one family; where all discord on account of religion, politics, or private opin-

D

ion shall be unknown and banished from within our walls.

Q. What followed?

A. The Worshipful Master in the East made a demand of me of something of a metalic kind, which he said was not so much on account of its intrinsic value, as that it might be deposited in the archives of the Lodge, as a memorial that I had therein been made a Mason.

Q. How did the Worshipful Master then dispose of you?

A. He ordered me to be conducted out of the Lodge and invested of what I had been divested, and returned for further instructions.

Q. After you returned how was you disposed of?

A. I was conducted to the North East corner of the Lodge, and there caused to stand upright like a man, my feet forming a square, and received a solemn injunction, ever to walk and act uprightly before God and man, and in addition thereto received the following charge, (For this charge see page 31.)

SECOND SECTION.

Q. Why was you divested of all metals when you was made a Mason?

A. Because Masonry regards no man on account of his worldly wealth or honors; it is therefore the internal, and not the external qualifications that recommends a man to Masons.

Q. A second reason?

A. There was neither the sound of an axe, hammer, or any other metal tool heard at the building of King Solomon's Temple.

Q. How could so stupendous a fabrick be erected without the sound of axe, hammer, or any other metal tool?

A. All the stones were hewed, squared and numbered in the quarries where they were raised, all the timbers felled and prepared in the forests of Lebanon, and carried down to Joppa on floats, and taken from thence up to Jerusalem and set up with wooden malls, prepared for that purpose; which, when completed, every part thereof fitted with that exact nicety, that it had more the resemblance of the handy workmanship of the Supreme Architect of the Universe, than that of human hands.

Q. Why was you neither naked nor clothed?

A. As I was an object of distress at that time, it was to remind me, if ever I saw a friend, more especially a brother in a like distressed situation, that I should contribute as liberally to his relief as his situation required, and my abilities would admit, without material injury to myself or family.

Q. Why was you neither barefoot nor shod?

A. It was an ancient Israelitish custom, adopted among Masons; and we read in the book of Ruth concerning their mode and manner of changing and redeeming, "and to confirm all things, a brother plucked off his shoe and gave it to his neighbour, and that was testimony in Israel." This then, therefore we do in confirmation of a token, and as a pledge of our fidelity; thereby signifying that we will renounce our own wills in all things, and become obedient to the laws of our ancient institutions.

Q. Why was you hood-winked?

A. That my heart might conceive, before my eyes beheld the beauties of Masonry.

Q. A second reason?

A. As I was in darkness at that time, it was to remind me that I should keep the whole world so respecting Masonry.

Q. Why had you a Cable-Tow about your neck?

A. In case I had not submitted to the manner and mode of my initiation that I might have been led out of the Lodge without seeing the form and beauties thereof.

Q. Why did you give three distinct knocks at the door?

A. To alarm the Lodge, and let the Worshipful Master, Wardens and brethren know that a poor blind candidate prayed admission.

Q. What does those three distinct knocks allude to?

A. A certain passage in Scripture wherein it says, 'ask and it shall be given, seek and ye shall find, knock and it shall be opened unto you.'

Q. How did you apply this to your then case in Masonry?

A. I asked the recommendations of a friend to become a Mason, I sought admission through his recommendations, and knocked and the door of Masonry opened unto me.

Q. Why was you caused to enter on the point of some sharp instrument pressing your naked left breast in the name of the Lord?

A. As this was a torture to my flesh, so might the recollection of it ever be to my heart and conscience if ever I attempted to reveal the secrets of Masonry unlawfully.

Q. Why was you conducted to the centre of the Lodge, and there caused to kneel for the benefit of a prayer?

A. Before entering on this, or any other great and important undertaking, it is highly necessary to implore a blessing from Deity.

Q. Why was you asked in whom you put your trust?

A. Agreeable to the laws of our ancient institution, no Atheist could be made a Mason; it was therefore necessary that I should believe in Deity; otherwise, no oath or obligation could bind me

Q. Why did the Worshipful Master take you by the right hand, and bid you rise, follow your leader and fear no danger?

A. As I was in darkness at that time and could neither foresee nor avoid danger, it was to remind me that I was in the hands of an affectionate friend, in whose fidelity I might with safety confide.

Q Why was you conducted three times regularly round the Lodge?

A. That the Worshipful Master, Wardens, and brethren might see that I was duly and truly prepared.

Q. Why did you meet with those several obstructions on the way?

A. This and every other Lodge is, or ought to be a true representation of King Solomon's Temple, which, when completed, had guards stationed at the East, West and South gates.

Q. Why had they guards stationed at those several gates?

A. To prevent any one from passing or repassing that was not duly qualified.

Q. Why did you kneel on your left knee and not on your right, or both?

A. The left side has ever been considered the weakest part of the body, it was therefore to remind me that the part I was then taking upon me was the weakest part of Masonry, it being that only of an Entered Apprentice.

Q. Why was your right hand placed on the Holy Bible, Square and Compass, and not your left, or both?

A. The right hand has ever been considered the seat of fidelity, and our ancient brethren worshipped Deity under the name of Fides; which has sometimes been represented by two right hands joined together; at others, by two human figures holding each other by the right hand; the right hand, therefore, we use in this great and important undertaking, to signify in the strongest manner possible the sincerity of our intentions in the business we are engaged.

Q. Why did the Worshipful Master present you with a lamb-skin, or white apron?

A. The lamb-skin has, in all ages, been deemed an emblem of innocence; he, therefore, who wears the lamb-skin, as a badge of a Mason, is thereby continually reminded of that purity of life and rectitude of conduct which is so essentially necessary to our gaining admission into the Celestial Lodge above, where the Supreme Architect of the Universe presides.

Q. Why did the Master make a demand of you of something of a metalic nature?

A. As I was in a poor and pennyless situation at that time, it was to remind me if ever I saw a friend, but more especially a brother in the like poor and pennyless situation, that I should contribute as liberally to his relief as my abilities would admit and his situation required, without injuring myself or family.

Q. Why was you conducted to the north-east corner of the Lodge, and there caused to stand upright like a man, your feet forming a square, receiving at the same time a solemn charge ever to walk and act uprightly before God and man?

A. The first stone in every masonic edifice is, or ought to be placed at the north-east corner, that being the place where an Entered Apprentice Mason receives his first instructions to build his future masonic edifice upon.

THIRD SECTION.

Q. We have been saying a good deal about a Lodge, I want to know what constitutes a Lodge?

A. A certain number of Free and Accepted Masons duly assembled in a room, or place, with the Holy Bible, Square and Compass, and other masonic implements, with a Charter from the Grand Lodge empowering them to work.

D 2

Q. Where did our ancient brethren meet before lodges were erected?

A. On the highest hills, and in the lowest vales.

Q. Why on the highest hills and in the lowest vales?

A. The better to guard against cowans and enemies either ascending or descending, that the brethren might have timely notice of their approach to prevent being surprised.

Q. What is the form of your Lodge?

A. An oblong square.

Q. How, long? A. From East to West.

Q. How, wide? A. Between North and South.

Q. How, high? A. From the surface of the earth to the highest heavens.

Q. How, deep? A. From the surface to the centre.

Q. What supports your Lodge?

A. Three Large Columns or Pillars.

Q. What are their names?

A. Wisdom, Strength, and Beauty.

Q. Why so? A. It is necessary there should be Wisdom to contrive, Strength to support, and Beauty to adorn all great and important undertakings; but more especially this of ours.

Q. Has your lodge any covering?

A. It has; a clouded canopy, or starry decked heaven, where all good masons hope to arrive.

Q. How do they hope to arrive there?

A. By the assistance of Jacob's ladder.

Q. How many principal rounds has it got?

A. Three. Q. What are their names? A. Faith, Hope, and Charity.

Q. What do they teach? A. Faith in God, Hope in immortality, and Charity to all mankind.

Q. Has your lodge any furniture?

A. It has; the Holy Bible, Square, and Compass.

Q. To whom do they belong?

A. The Bible to God, the Square to the Master, and the Compass to the Craft.

Q. How explained? A. The Bible to God; it being the inestimable gift of God to man, for his instruction to guide him through the rugged paths of life; the Square to the Master, it being the proper emblem of his office; the Compass to the Craft—by a due attention to which, we are taught to limit our desires, curb our ambition, subdue our irregular appetites, and keep our passions and prejudices in due bounds with all mankind, but more especially with the brethren.

Q. Has your Lodge any ornaments?

A. It has; the mosaic, or chequered pavement; the indented tessel, that beautiful tesselated border which surrounds it, with the blazing star in the centre.

Q. What do they represent?

A. The Mosaic, or chequered pavement, represents this world, which, though chequered over with good and evil, yet brethren may walk together thereon and not stumble—the indented Tessel, with the blazing star in the centre, the manifold blessings and comforts with which we are surrounded in this life, but more especially those which we hope to enjoy hereafter—the Blazing Star, that prudence which ought to appear conspicuous in the conduct of every Mason; but more especially commemorative of the Star which appeared in the East, to guide the wise men to Bethlehem, to proclaim the birth and the presence of the Son of God.

Q. Has your Lodge any lights?

A. It has three. Q. How are they situated?

A. East, West, and South.

Q. Has it none in the North? A. It has not.

Q. Why so? A. Because this and every other lodge is, or ought to be a true representation of King Solomon's Temple, which was situated north of the ecliptic; the sun and moon therefore darting her rays from the south, no light was to be expected from the north; we, therefore, masonically, term the north a place of darkness.

Q. Has your Lodge any Jewels?

A. It has six; three moveable and three immoveable.

Q. What are the three moveable Jewels?

A. The Square, Level, and Plumb.

Q. What do they teach?

A. The Square, morality; the Level, equality; and the Plumb, rectitude of life and conduct.

Q. What are the three immoveable Jewels?

A. The rough Ashlar, the perfect Ashlar, and the Trestle-Board. Q. What are they?

A. The rough Ashlar is a stone in its rough and natural state; the perfect Ashlar is also a stone made ready by the working tools of the Fellow-Craft to be adjusted in the building; and the Trestle-board is for the master workman to draw his plans and designs upon.

Q. What do they represent?

A. The rough Ashlar represents man in his rude and imperfect state by nature; the perfect Ashlar also represents man in that state of perfection to which we all hope to arrive by means of a virtuous life and education, our own endeavors and the blessing of God. In erecting our temporal building we pursue the plans and designs laid down by the master workman on his Trestle-board; but in erecting our spiritual building we pursue the plans and designs laid down by the Supreme Geometrician of the Universe in the Book of Life, which we, masonically, term our spiritual trestle-board.

Q. Who did you serve? A. My Master.

Q. How long? A. Six days.

Q. What did you serve him with?

A. Freedom, fervency, and zeal.

Q. What do they represent?

A. Chalk, Charcoal, and Earth. Q. Why so.

A. There is nothing freer than Chalk, the slightest touch of which leaves a trace behind; nothing more fervent than heated Charcoal, it will melt the most obdurate metals; nothing more zealous than the Earth to bring forth.

Q. How is your lodge situated? A. Due east and west.

Q. Why so? A. Because the sun rises in the east and sets in the west.

Q. A second reason? A. The gospel was first preached in the east, and is spreading to the west.

Q. A third reason? A. The liberal arts and sciences began in the east and are extending to the west.

Q. A fourth reason? A. Because all Churches and Chapels are, or ought to be so situated.

Q. Why are all Churches and Chapels so situated?

A. Because King Solomon's Temple was so situated.

Q. Why was King Solomon's Temple so situated?

A. Because Moses, after conducting the children of Israel through the Red Sea by Divine command, erected a tabernacle to God, and placed it due east and west; which was to commemorate, to the latest posterity, that miraculous East wind that wrought their mighty deliverance; and this was an exact model of King Solomon's Temple. Since which time, every well regulated and governed Lodge is, or ought to be so situated.

Q. To whom did our ancient brethren dedicate their Lodges? A. To King Solomon.

Q. Why so? A. Because King Solomon was our most ancient Grand Master.

Q. To whom do modern masons dedicate their lodges?

A. To St. John the Baptist, & St. John the Evangelist.

Q. Why so? A. Because they were the two most ancient Christian patrons of Masonry; and since their time, in every well regulated and governed Lodge, there has been a certain point within a circle, which circle is bounded on the East and the West by two perpendicular parallel lines, representing the anniversary of St. John, the Baptist, and St. John, the Evangelist, who were two perfect parallels as well in Masonry as Christianity; on the vortex of which rests the book of the Holy Scriptures, supporting Jacob's Ladder which is said to reach to the watery clouds; and in passing round this circle we naturally touch on both these perpendicular parallel lines, as well as the Book of the Holy Scriptures, and while a Mason keeps himself thus circumscribed, he cannot materially err.' [Thus ends the first degree of Masonry, and the reader, who has read and paid attention to it, knows more of Masonry than any Entered Apprentice in christendom, and more of this degree than one-hundredth part of the Master Masons, or even Royal Arch Masons; for very few ever attempt to learn the Lectures, or even the Obligations: They merely receive the degrees, and there stop, with the exception of a few who are fascinated with the idea of holding an office: they sometimes endeavour to qualify themselves to discharge the duties which devolve on them in their respective offices. The offices of Secretary and Treasurer, are by some considered the most important in the Lodge, particularly where there is much business done.]

I will now introduce the reader to the second degree of Masonry. It is generally called passing, as will be seen in the lecture. I shall omit the ceremonies of opening and closing, as they are precisely the same as in the first degree, except two knocks are used in this degree, and the door is entered by the benefit of a password: it is *Shiboleth*. It will be explained in the lecture.

The candidate, as before, is taken into the preparation room and prepared in the manner following: All his clothing taken off, except his shirt; furnished with a pair of drawers; his right breast bare? his left foot in a slipper, the right bare; a cable-tow twice round his neck; semihood winked; in which situation he is conducted to the door of the Lodge, where he gives two knocks, when the Senior Warden rises, and says, 'Worshipful, while we are peaceable at work on the second degree of Masonry, under the influence of faith, hope, and charity, the door of our Lodge is alarmed.' Master to Junior Deacon, 'Bro-Junior, enquire the cause of that alarm.' [In many Lodges they come to the door, knock, are answered by the Junior Deacon, and come in without their being noticed by the Senior Warden or Master.] The Junior Deacon gives two raps on the inside of the door. The candidate gives one without; it is answered by the Junior Deacon with one, when the door is partly opened by the Junior Deacon, who inquires, 'who comes here? who comes here?' The Senior Deacon, who is or ought to be the conductor, answers, 'A worthy Brother who has been regularly initiated as an Entered Apprentice Mason, served a proper time as such, and now wishes for further light in Masonry by being passed to the degree of Fellow-Craft.' Junior Deacon to Senior Deacon, 'Is it of his own free will and accord he makes this request?' *Ans.* 'It is.' Junior Deacon to Senior Deacon, 'Is he duly and truly and well prepared?' *Ans.* 'He is.' Junior Deacon to Senior Deacon, 'Is he worthy and well qualified?' *Ans.* 'He is.' Junior Deacon to Senior Deacon, 'Has he made suitable proficiency in the preceding degree?' *Ans.* 'He has.' [Very few know any more than they did the night they were initiated; have not heard their obligation repeated, nor one section of the lecture, and in fact a very small proportion of Masons ever learn either.] Junior Deacon to Senior Deacon, 'By what further rights does he expect to obtain this benefit?' *Ans.* 'By the benefit of a pass-word.' Junior Deacon to Senior Deacon, '*Has he a pass-word?*' *Ans.* 'He has not, but I have it for him.' Junior Deacon to Senior Deacon, 'Give it to me?' The Senior Deacon whispers in the Junior Deacon's ear, *Shiboleth.* The Junior Deacon says, 'The pass is right; since this is the case, you will wait 'till the Worshipful Master in the East is made acquainted with his request, and his answer returned.' The Junior Deacon then repairs to the Master and gives two knocks, as at the door, which are answered by two by the Master. When the same questions are asked and answers returned as at the door, after which the Master says, 'Since he comes endued with all these necessary qualifications, let him enter this Worshipful Lodge in the name of the Lord, and take heed on what he enters.' As he enters, the angle of the square is pressed hard against his naked right breast, at which time the Junior Deacon says, 'Brother, when you entered this Lodge the first time, you entered on the point of the compass pressing your naked left breast, which was then explained to you. You now enter it on the angle of the square, pressing your naked right breast, which is to teach you to act upon the square with all mankind, but more especially with the brethren.' The candidate is then conducted twice regularly round the Lodge and halted at the Junior Warden in the South, where he gives two raps, and is answered by two, when the same questions are asked and answers returned as at the door; from thence he is conducted to the Senior Warden, where the same questions are asked and answers returned as before; he is then conducted to the Master in the East, where the same questions are asked and answers returned as before; the Master likewise demands of him, from whence he came, and whither he was travelling; he answers, 'From the West and travelling to the East.' The Master asks, 'why do you leave the West and travel to the East?' *Ans.* "In search of more light.' The Master then says to the candidate, 'Since this is the case, you will please conduct the candidate back to the West from whence he came, and put him in care of the Senior Warden, who will teach him how to approach the East, 'the place of light,' by advancing upon two upright regular steps to the second step, [his heel is in the hollow of the right foot on this degree,] his feet forming the right angle of an oblong square, and his body erect at the altar before the Worshipful Master, and place him in a proper position to take the solemn oath, or obligation of a Fellow Craft Mason.' The Master then leaves his seat and approaches the kneeling candidate, [the candidate kneels on the right knee, the left forming a square, his left arm as far as the elbow in a horizontal position, and the rest of the arm in a vertical position, so as to form a square, his arm supported by the square held under his elbow] and says, 'Brother you are now placed in a proper position to take on you the solemn oath, or obligation of a Fellow-Craft Mason, which I assure you as before, is neither to affect your religion nor politics; if you are willing to take it, repeat your name and say after me'—

'I A. B. of my own free will and accord, in the presence of Almighty God, and this Worshipful Lodge of Fellow-Craft Masons, dedicated to God, and held forth to the holy order of St. John, do hereby and hereon most solemnly and sincerely promise and swear, in addition to my former obligation, that I will not give the degree of a Fellow-Craft Mason to any one of an inferior degree, nor to any other being in the known world, except it be to a true and lawful brother, or brethren Fellow-Craft Masons, or within the body of a just and lawfully constituted lodge of such; and not unto him nor unto them whom I shall hear so to be, but unto him and them only whom I shall find so to be after strict trial and due examination, or lawful information. Furthermore do I promise and swear, that I will not wrong this Lodge, nor a brother of this degree to the value of two cents knowingly, myself, nor suffer it to be done by others if in my power to prevent it. Furthermore do I promise and swear, that I will support the Constitution of the Grand Lodge of the United States, and of the Grand Lodge of this State, under which this Lodge is held, and conform to all the bye-laws, rules and regulations of this or any other Lodge of which I may at any time hereafter become a member, as far as in my power. Furthermore do I promise and swear, that I will obey all regular signs and summons' given, handed, sent or thrown to me by the hand of a brother Fellow-Craft Mason, or from the body of a just and lawfully constituted Lodge of such, provided that it be within the length of my Cable-Tow, or square and angle of my work. Furthermore do I promise and swear, that I will be aiding and assisting all poor and pennyless brethren Fellow-Crafts, their widows and orphans wheresoever disposed round the globe, they applying to me as such, as far as in my power without injuring myself or family. To all which I do most solemnly and sincerely promise and swear, without the least hesitation, mental reservation, or self evasion of mind in me whatever, binding myself under no less penalty than to have my left breast torn open, and my heart and vitals taken from thence and thrown over my left shoulder and carried into the valley of Jehosaphat, there to become a prey to the wild beasts of the field, and vultures of the air, if ever I should prove wilfully guilty of violating any part of this my solemn oath or obligation of a Fellow Craft-Mason; so keep me God, and keep me stedfast in the due performance of the same. 'Detatch your hands and kiss the book which is the Holy Bible twice.' The bandage is now (by one of the brethren) dropt over the other eye, and the Master says, 'Brother, [at the same time laying his hand on the top of the candidate's head] what do you most desire?' the candidate answers after his prompter, 'more light.' The Master says, 'Brethren form on the square and assist in bringing our new made brother from darkness to light, 'And God said, let there be light, and there was light.' At this instant all the brethren clap their hands and stamp on the floor as in the preceding degree. The Master says to the candidate, 'Br. what do you discover different from before?' The Master says, after a short pause, 'You now discover one point of the compass elevated above the square, which denotes light in this degree; but as one is yet in obscurity, it is to remind you that you are yet one material point in the dark, respecting Masonry.' The Master steps off from the candidate three or four steps, and says, 'Brother, you now discover me as Master of this Lodge approaching you from the East, under the sign and due-guard of a Fellow-Craft Mason, do as I do as near as you can and keep your position.' The sign is given by drawing your right hand flat with the palm of it next to your breast, across your breast from the left to the right side with some quickness, and dropping it down by your side; the due-guard is given by raising the left arm until that part of it between the elbow and shoulder is perfectly horizontal, and raising the rest of the arm in a vertical position, so that that part of the arm below the elbow, and that part above it, forms a square. This is is called the due-guard of a Fellow-Craft Mason. The two given together, are called the sign and due-guard of a Fellow Craft Mason, and they are never given separately: they would not be recognized by a Mason if given separately. The Master by the time he gives his steps, sign, and due-guard, arrives at the candidate and says, 'Brother, I now present you with my right hand in token of brotherly love and confidence, and with it the pass grip and word of a Fellow-Craft Mason.' The pass, or more properly the pass-grip, is given by taking each other by the right hand as though going to shake hands, and each putting his thumb between the fore and second fingers where they join the hand, and pressing the thumb between the joints. This is the pass-grip of a Fellow-Craft Mason, the name of it is *Shiboleth*. Its origin will be explained in the lecture—the pass-grip some give without lettering or syllabling, and others give it in the same way they do the real grip; the real grip of a Fellow-Craft Mason is given by putting the thumb on the joint of the second finger where it joins the hand, and crooking your thumb so that each can stick the nail of his thumb into the joint of the other; this is the real grip of a Fellow-Craft

E

Mason; the name of it is *Jachin;* it is given in the following manner: If you wish to examine a person, after having taken each other by the grip, ask him 'what is this?' Ans. 'A grip.' Q. 'A grip of what?' Ans. 'The grip of a Fellow-Craft Mason.' Q. 'Has it a name?' Ans. 'It has.' Q. 'Will you give to me?' Ans. 'I did not so receive it, neither can I so impart it.' Q. 'What will you do with it?' Ans. 'I'll letter it or halve it.' Q, 'Halve it and you begin?' Ans. 'No, begin you.' Q. 'You begin?' Ans. 'J-A-' Q. C-H-I-N.' A. 'JACHIN.' Q. 'Right, brother *Jachin*. 'I greet you.'

As the signs, due-guards, grips, pass-grips, words, pass-words, and their several names, comprise pretty much all the secrets of Masonry, and *all* the information necessary to pass us as Masons, I intend to appropriate a few passages in the latter part of this work, to the exclusive purpose of explaining them; I shall not therefore, spend much time in examining them as I progress.—After the Master gives the candidate the pass-grip, and grip, and their names, he says, 'Brother, you will rise and salute the Junior and Senior Wardens as such, and convince them that you have been regularly passed to the degree of a Fellow-Craft Mason, and have got the sign and pass-grip, real grip, and their names.' [I do not here express it as expressed in Lodges generally; the Master generally says 'you will arise and salute the Wardens, &c. and convince them &c. that you have got the sign, pass-grip, and word.' It is obviously wrong, because the first thing he gives is the sign, then due-guard, then the pass-grip, real grip and their names.] While the Wardens are examining the candidate, the Master gets an apron and returns to the candidate and says 'Brother, I now have the honour of presenting you with a lamb-skin or white apron as before, which I hope you will continue to wear with honour to yourself and satisfaction to the brethren; you will please carry it to the Senior Warden in the West, who will teach you how to wear it as a Fellow-Craft Mason.' The Senior Warden ties on his apron and turns up one corner of the lower end of the apron and tucks it under the apron string. The Senior Deacon then conducts his pupil to the Master, who has by this time resumed his seat in the East, where he has or ought to have the floor carpet to assist him in his explanations. Master to the candidate, 'Brother, as you are dressed, it is necessary you should have tools to work with, I will therefore present you with the tools of a Fellow-Craft Mason. They are the plumb, square, and level. The plumb is an instrument made use of by operative Masons to raise perpendiculars; the square to square their work; and the level to lay horizontals; but we, as Free and Accepted Masons, are taught to use them for more noble and glorious purposes; the plumb teaches us to walk uprightly in our several stations before God and man, squaring our actions by the square of virtue, and remembering that we are travelling on the level of time to that undiscovered country from whose bourn no traveller has returned. I further present you with three precious jewels; their names are faith, hope, and charity; they teach us to have faith in God, hope in immortality, and charity to all mankind.' The Master to the Senior Deacon: 'You will now conduct the candidate out of the Lodge, and invest him with what he has been divested.' After he is clothed and the necessary arrangements made for his reception, such as placing the colums and floor carpet if they have any, and the candidate is re-conducted back to the Lodge, as he enters the door the Senior Deacon observes, 'we are now about to return to the middle chamber of King Solomon's Temple.' When within the door the Senior Deacon proceeds, 'Brother, we have worked in speculative Masonry, but our forefathers wrought both in speculative and operative Masonry, they worked at the building of King Solomon's Temple, and many other masonic edifices, they wrought six days, they did not work on the seventh, because in six days God created the heavens and earth and rested on the seventh day—the seventh therefore our ancient brethren consecrated as a day of rest, thereby enjoying more frequent opportunities to contemplate the glorious works of creation, and to adore their great creator.' Moving a step or two the Senior Deacon, proceeds, 'Brother, the first thing that attracts our attention, are two large columns, or pillars, one on the left hand and the other on the right; the name of the one on the left hand is Boaz, and denotes strength, the name of the one on the right hand is *Jachin*, and denotes establishment; they collectively allude to a passage in scripture, wherein God has declared in his word, 'In strength shall this House be established.' These columns are eighteen cubits high, twelve in circumference, and four in diameter; they are adorned with two large Chapiters, one on each, and these Chapiters are ornamented with net work, lilly work, and pomegrantes; they denote unity, peace and plenty. The net work, from its connection denotes union, the lilly work from its whiteness, purity and peace, and the pomegranates from the exuberance of its seed denotes plenty. They also have two large globes or balls, one on each; these globes or balls contain on their convex surfaces all the maps and charts of the celestial and terrestrial bodies, they are said to be thus extensive, to denote the universality of masonry, and that a Mason's charity ought to be equally extensive. Their composition is molten, or cast brass; they were cast on the banks of the river Jordan, on the clay-ground between Succoth and Zaradatha, where King Solomon ordered these and all other holy vessels to be cast; they were cast hollow; and were four inches or a hands breadth thick; they were cast hollow, the better to withstand inundations and conflagrations—were the archives of masonry; and contained the constitution, rolls, and records.' The Senior Deacon having explained the columns, he passes between them, advancing a step or two, observing as he advances, 'Brother, we will pursue our travels; the next thing that we come to, is a long winding stair case, with three, five, seven steps or more.' The three first allude to the three principal supports in masonry, viz: wisdom, strength, and beauty; the five steps allude to the five orders in architecture, and the five human senses; the five orders in architecture, are the Tuscan, Doric, Ionic, Corinthian, & Composite; the five human senses, are hearing, seeing, feeling, smelling and tasting; the three first of which, have ever been highly essential among Masons, hearing, to hear the word, seeing, to see the sign, and feeling, to feel the grip, whereby one Mason may know another in the dark as well as in the light. The seven steps allude to the seven sabbatical years, seven years of famine, seven years in building the Temple, seven golden candlesticks, seven wonders of the world; seven planets, but more especially the several liberal arts and sciences, which are grammar, rhetoric, logic, arithmetic, geometry, music, and astronomy; for this and many other reasons, the number seven has ever been held in high estimation among Masons.' Advancing a few steps, the Senior Deacon proceeds; 'Brother, the next thing we come to is the outer door of the middle chamber of King Solomon's Temple, which is partly open, but closely Tyled by the Junior Warden;' [It is the Junior Warden in the South who represents the Tyler at the outer door of the middle chamber of King Solomon's Temple,] who on the approach of the Senior Deacon and candidate enquires, 'who comes here, who comes here?' The Senior Deacon answers, 'A Fellow-Craft Mason.' Junior Warden to Senior Deacon, 'How do you expect to gain admission?' Ans. 'By a passs and token of a pass.' Junior Warden to Senior Deacon, 'Will you give them to me?' [The Senior Deacon or the candidate (prompted by him) gives them; this and many other tokens or grips are frequently given by strangers, when first introduced to each other; If given to a Mason he will immediately return it; they can be given in any company unobserved, even by Masons, when shaking hands. *A pass and token of a pass*; the pass is the word *Shiboleth*; the token, alias, the pass-grip is given as before described, by taking each other by the right hand as if shaking hands, and placing the thumb between the fore finger and second finger at the third joint, or where they join the hand, and pressing it hard enough to attract attention. In the lecture it is called a token but generally called the pass-grip; it is an undeniable fact that Masons express themselves so differently, when they mean the same thing, that they frequently wholly misunderstand each other.]

After the Junior Warden has received the pass *Shiboleth*, he enquires, 'What does it denote?' *Ans.* 'Plenty.' Jnnior Warden to Senior Deacon, 'Why so?' *Ans.* 'From an ear of corn being placed at the water-ford.' Junior Warden to Senior Deacon, 'Why was this pass instituted?' *Ans.* 'In consequence of a quarrel which had long existed between Jeptha, judge of Israel, and the Ephraimites, the latter of whom had long been a stubborn, rebellious people, whom Jeptha had endeavoured to subdue by lenient measures, but to no effect. The Ephraimites being highly incensed against Jeptha for not being called to fight and share in the rich spoils of the Amonitish war, assembled a mighty army and passed over the river Jordan to give Jeptha battle; but he being apprised of their approach, called together the men of Israel, and gave them battle, and put them to flight; and, to make his victory more complete, he ordered guards to be placed at the different passes on the banks of the river Jordan, and commanded, if the Ephraimites passed that way, that they should pronounce the word *Shiboleth*: but they, being of a different tribe,

E2

pronounced it Seboleth, which trifling defect proved them spies, and cost them their lives: and there fell that day, at the different passes on the banks of the river Jordan, forty and two thousand. This word was also used by our ancient brethren to distinguish a friend from a foe, and has since been adopted as a proper pass-word to be given before entering any well regulated and governed Lodge of Fellow-Craft Masons.' 'Since this is the case, you will pass on to the Senior Warden in the West, for further examination.' As they approach the Senior Warden in the West, the Senior Deacon says to the candidate, 'Brother, the next thing we come to is the inner door of the middle chamber of king Solomon's Temple, which we find partly open, but more closely tyled by the Senior Warden,' when the Senior Warden enquires, 'Who comes here? who comes here?' The Senior Deacon answers. 'A Fellow-Craft Mason.' Senior Warden to Senior Deacon, 'How do you expect to gain admission?' *Ans.* 'By the grip and word.' The Senior Warden to the Junior Deacon, 'Will yon give them to me?' They are then given as herein before described. The word is *Jachin.* After they are given, the Senior Warden says, 'They are right; you can pass on to the Worshipful Master in the East. As they approach the Master, he enquires, 'Who comes here? who comes here?' Junior Deacon answers, 'A Fellow-Craft Mason.' The Master then says to the candidate, 'Brother, you have been admitted into the middle chamber of king Solomon's Temple, for the sake of the letter G. It denotes Deity, before whom we all ought to bow with reverence, worship and adore. It also denotes Geometry, the fifth science, it being that on which this degree was principally founded. By Geometry we may curiously trace nature through her various windings to her most concealed recesses: By it, we may discover the power, the wisdom, and the goodness of the grand Artificer of the Universe, and view with delight the proportions which connect this vast Machine: By it, we may discover how the planets move in their different orbits, and demonstrate their various revolutions: By it, we account for the return of seasons, and the variety of scenes which each season displays to the discerning eye. Numberless worlds surround us, all formed by the same divine Architect, which roll through this vast expanse, and all conducted by the same unerring law of nature. A survey of nature, and the observations of her beautiful proportions, first determined man to imitate the divine plan, and study symmetry and order. The Architect began to design; and the plans which he laid down, being improved by experience and time, have produced works which are the admiration of every age. The lapse of time, the ruthless hand of ignorance, and the devastations of war have laid waste and destroyed many valuable monuments of antiquity, on which the utmost exertions of human genius have been employed. Even the Temple of Solomon, so spacious and magnificent, and constructed by so many celebrated artists, escaped not the unsparing ravages of barbarous force. The *attentive ear* receives the sound from the *instructive tongue;* and the mysteries of Freemasonry are safely lodged in the repository of *faithful breasts.* Tools and implements of architecture, and symbolic emblems, most expressive, are selected by the fraternity, to imprint on the mind wise and serious truths; and thus, through a succession of ages, are transmitted, unimpaired, the most excellent tenets of our institution.' Here ends the work part of the Fellow-Craft's degree. It will be observed that the candidate has received, in this place, the second section of the lecture on this degree. This course is not generally pursued, but it is much the most instructive method, and when it is omitted, I generally conclude that it is for want of a knowledge of the lecture. Monitorial writers [who are by no means coeval with Masonry] all write or copy very much after each other, and they have all inserted in their books all those clauses of the several lectures which are not considered by the wise ones as tending to develope the secrets of Masonry. In some instances they change the phraseology a little; in others, they are literal extracts from the lectures. This, it is said, is done to facilitate the progress of learners, or young Masons, when in fact it has the contrary effect. All lecture teachers, [and there are many travelling about the country with recommendations from some of their distinguished brethren] when they come to any of those clauses, will say to their pupils, 'I have not committed that, it is in the Monitor, you can learn it at your leisure.' This course of procedure subjects the learner to the necessity of making his own questions, and, of course, answering monitorially, whether the extracts from the lectures are literal or not. Again, there is not a *perfect* sameness in all the Monitors, or they could not all get copy-rights; hence the great diversity in the lectures as well as the work. The following charge is, or ought to be, delivered to the candidate after he has got through the ceremonies; but he is generally told, 'It is in the Monitor, and you can read it at your leisure.'

Brother, 'being advanced to the second degree of Masonry, we congratulate you on your preferment. The internal, and not the external, qualifications of a man, are what Masonry regards. As you increase in knowledge, you will improve in social intercourse.

'It is unnecessary to recapitulate the duties which, as a Mason, you are bound to discharge; or enlarge on the necessity of a strict adherence to them, as your own experience must have established their value.

'Our laws and regulations you are strenuously to support; and be always ready to assist in seeing them duly executed. You are not to palliate or aggravate the offences of your brethren; but in the decision of every trespass against our rules, you are to judge with candour, admonish with friendship, and reprehend with justice.

'The study of the liberal arts, that valuable branch of education, which tends so effectually to polish and adorn the mind, is earnestly recommended to your consideration; especially the science of geometry, which is established as the basis of our art. Geometry, or Masonry, originally synonimous terms, being of a divine moral nature, is enriched with the most useful knowledge: while it proves the wonderful properties of nature, it demonstrates the more important truths of morality.

'Your past behaviour and regular deportment have merited the honour which we have now conferred; and in your new character it is expected that you will conform to the principles of the order, by steadily persevering in the practice of every commendable virtue.

'Such is the nature of your engagements as a Fellow-Craft, and to these duties you are bound by the most sacred ties.

I will now proceed with the Lecture on this degree. It is divided into two sections.

SECTION FIRST.

Q. Are you a Fellow-Craft Mason?

A. I am—try me.

Q. By what will you be tried?

A. By the Square.

Q. Why by the Square?

A. Because it is an emblem of virtue.

Q. What is a Square?

A. An angle extending to ninety degrees, or the fourth part of a circle.

Q. Where was you prepared to be made a Fellow-Craft Mason?

A. In a room adjacent to the body of a just and lawfully constituted Lodge of such, duly assembled in a room or place, representing the middle chamber of king Solomon's Temple.

Q. How was you prepared?

A. By being divested of all metals; neither naked nor clothed; barefoot nor shod; hood-winked; with a cable-tow twice round my neck; in which situation I was conducted to the door of the Lodge, where I gave two distinct knocks.

Q. What did those two distinct knocks allude to?

A. The second degree in Masonry, it being that on which I was about to enter.

Q. What was said to you from within?

A. Who comes there? who comes there?

Q. Your answer?

A. A worthy Brother who has been regularly initiated as an Entered Apprentice Mason; served a proper time as such, and now wishes for further light in Masonry by being passsed to the degree of a Fellow-Craft.

Q. What was then said to you from within?

A. I was asked if it was of my own free will and accord I made this request; if I was duly and truly prepared; worthy and well qualified, and had made suitable proficiency in the preceding degree; all of which being answered in the affirmative, I was asked, by what further rights I expected to obtain so great a benefit.

Q. Your answer?

A. By the benefit of a pass word.

Q. What is that pass word? A *Shiboleth.*

Q. What further was said to you from within?

A. I was bid to wait till the Worshipful Master in the East was made acquainted with my request and his answer returned.

Q. After his answer was returned what followed?

A. I was caused to enter the Lodge.

Q. How did you enter?

A. On the angle of the square presented to my naked right breast in the name of the Lord.

Q. How was you then disposed of?

A. I was conducted twice regularly round the Lodge and halted at the Junior Warden in the South, where the same questions were asked and answers returned as at the door.

Q. How did the Junior Warden dispose of you?

A. He ordered me to be conducted to the Senior Warden in the West, where the same questions were asked and answers returned as before.

Q. How did the Senior Warden dispose of you?

A. He ordered me to be conducted to the Worshipful Master in the East, where the same questions were asked and answers returned as before, who likewise demanded of me from whence I came and whether I was travelling.

Q. Your answer?

A. From the West and travelling to the East.

Q. Why do you leave the West and travel to the East?

A. In search of more light.

Q. How did the Worshipful Master then dispose of you?

A. He ordered me to be conducted back to the West from whence I came, and put in care of the Senior Warden, who taught me how to approach the East, by advancing upon two upright regular steps to the second step, my feet forming the right angle of an oblong square, and my body erect at the altar before the Worshipful Master.

Q. What did the Worshipful Master do with you?

A. He made a Fellow Craft Mason of me.

Q. How? A. In due form.

Q. What was that due form?

A. My right knee bare bent, my left knee forming a square, my right hand on the Holy Bible, square and compass, my left arm forming an angle supported by the square, and my hand in a vertical position, in which pos-

fore I took upon me the solemn oath or obligation of a Fellow-Craft Mason. [See page 48 for obligation.

Q. After your oath or obligation what was said to you?

A. I was asked what I most desired.

Q. Your answer? A. More light.

Q. On being brought to light, what did you discover different from before it?

A. One point of the compass elevated above the square which denoted light in this degree, but as one point was yet in obscurity, it was to remind me that I was yet one material point in the dark respecting Masonry.

Q. What did you next discover?

A. The Worshipful Master approaching me from the East, under the sign and due-guard of a Fellow-Craft Mason, who presented me with his right hand in token of brotherly love and confidence, and proceeded to give me the pass-grip and word of a Fellow-Craft Mason, and bid me rise an salute the Junior and Senior Wardens, and convince them that I had been regularly passed to the degree of a Fellow-Craft, and had the sign, grip and word of a Fellow-Craft Mason.

Q. What did you next discover?

A. The Worshipful Master approaching me a second time from the East, who presented me with a lambskin or white apron, which he said he hoped I would continue to wear with honour to myself, and satisfaction and advantage to the brethren.

Q. What was you next presented with?

A. The working tools of a Fellow-Craft Mason,

Q. What are they?

A. The Plumb, Square, and Level.

Q. What do they teach? [I think this question ought to be, 'How explained?']

A. The Plumb is an instrument made use of by operative Masons to raise perpendiculars; the Square, to square their work; and the Level to lay horizontals; but we, as Free and Accepted Masons, are taught to make use of them for more noble and glorious purposes: The Plumb admonishes us to walk uprightly in our several stations before God and man, squaring our actions by the square of virtue, and remembering that we are all travelling upon the level of time to that undiscovered country from whose bourn no traveller returns.

Q. What was you next presented with?

A. Three precious jewels.

Q. What are they ? A. Faith, Hope, and Charity.

Q. What do they teach ?

A. Faith in God, hope in immortality, and charity to all mankind.

Q. How was you then disposed of ?

A. I was conducted out of the Lodge, and invested of what I had been divested.

SECTION SECOND.

Q. Have you ever worked as a Fellow-Craft Mason ?

A. I have, in speculative : but our forefathers wrought both in speculative and operative Masonry.

Q. Where did they work ?

A. At the building of king Solomon's Temple, and mamany other masonic edifices.

Q. How long did they work ? A. Six days.

Q. Did they not work on the seventh ?

A. They did not.

Q. Why so ?

A. Because, in six days God created the Heavens and the Earth, and rested on the seventh day ; the seventh day, therefore, our ancient brethren consecrated as a day of rest from their labours ; thereby enjoying more frequent opportunities to contemplate the glorious works of creation, and adore their great Creator !

Q. Did you ever return to the sanctum sanctorum, or holy of holies of King Solomon's Temple ?

A. I did. Q. By what way ?

A. Through a long porch or alley.

Q. Did any thing particular strike your attention on your return ?

A. There did, viz : two large columns, or pillars, one on the left hand and the other on the right.

Q. What was the name of the one on your left hand ?

A. *Boaz*, to denote strength.

Q. What was the name of the one on your right hand ?

A. *Jachin*, denoting establishment.

Q. What do they collectively allude to ?

A. A passage in Scripture wherein God has declared in his word, 'In strength shall this House be established.'

Q. What were their dimensions ?

A. Eighteen cubits in height, twelve in circumference, and four in diameter.

Q. Were they adorned with any thing?

A. They were with two large Chapiters, one on each.

Q. Were they ornamented with any thing?

A. They were with wreaths of net-work, lilly-work and pomegranates.

Q. What do they denote?

A Unity, peace and plenty. Q. Why so?

A. Net-work from its connection, denotes union, lilly-work, from its whiteness and purity, denotes peace, and pomegranates, from the the exuberance of its seed, denotes plenty.

Q. Were those columns adorned with any thing further?

A. They were, viz: Two large globes or balls, one on each.

Q. Did they contain any thing?

A. They did, viz: All the maps and charts of the celestial and terrestrial bodies.

Q. Why are they said to be so extensive?

A. To denote the universality of Masonry, and that a Mason's charity ought to be equally extensive.

Q. What was their composition?

A. Molten, or cast brass. Q. Who cast them?

A. Our Grand Master, Hiram Abiff.

Q. Where were they cast?

A. On the banks of the river Jordan, in the clay ground between Succoth and Zaradatha, where King Solomon ordered these and all other Holy vessels to be cast.

Q Were they cast sound or hollow? A. Hollow.

Q. What was their thickness?

A. Four inches or a hands breadth.

Q. Why were they cast hollow?

A. The better to withstand inundations and conflagrations; were the archives of masonry, and contained the constitution, rolls and records.

Q. What did you next come to?

A. A long winding stair case, with three, five, seven steps or more.

Q. What does the three steps allude to?

A. The three principal supports in masonry, viz: Wisdom, strength, and beauty.

Q. What does the five steps allude to?

A. The five orders in architecture, and the five human senses.

F

Q. What are the five orders in architecture?

A. The Tuscan, Doric, Ionic, Corinthian, and Composite.

Q. What are the five human senses?

A. Hearing, seeing, feeling, smelling, and tasting, the first three of which has ever been deemed highly essential among Masons; hearing, to hear the word, seeing, to see the sign, and feeling, to feel the grip, whereby one Mason may know another in the dark as well as the light.

Q. What does the seven steps allude to?

A. The seven sabbatical years, seven years of famine, seven years in building the Temple, seven golden candlesticks, seven wonders of the world, seven planets; but more especially the seven liberal arts and sciences, which are grammar, rhetoric, logic, arithmetic, geometry, music and astronomy. For these and many other reasons the number seven has ever been held in high estimation among Masons.

Q. What did you next come to?

A. The outer door of the middle chamber of King Solomon's Temple, which I found partly open, but closely tyled by the Junior Warden.

Q. How did you gain admission?

A. By a pass, and token of a pass.

Q. What was the name of the pass? A. *Shiboleth.*

Q. What does it denote? A. Plenty. Q. Why so.

A. From an ear of corn being placed at the water-ford.

Q. Why was this pass instituted?

A. In consequence of a quarrel which had long existed between Jeptha, judge of Israel, and the Ephraimites; the latter of whom had long been a stubborn, rebellious people, whom Jeptha had endeavoured to subdue by lenient measures; but to no effect. The Ephraimites being highly incensed against Jeptha for not being called to fight and share in the rich spoils of the Amonitish war, assembled a mighty army and passed over the river Jordan to give Jeptha battle; but he, being apprised of their approach, called together the men of Israel, and gave them battle, and put them to flight; and, to make his victory more complete, he ordered guards to be placed at the different passes on the banks of the river Jordan, and commanded, if the Ephraimites passed that way, that they should pronounce the word *Shiboleth.*

but they, being of a different tribe, pronounced it *Seboleth;* which trifling defect proved them spies, and cost them their lives; and there fell that day at the different passes on the banks of the river Jordan, forty and two thousand. This word was also used by our ancient brethren to distinguish a friend from a foe, and has since been adopted as a proper pass-word to be given before entering any well regulated and governed Lodge of Fellow-Craft Masons.

Q. What did you next come to?

A. The inner door of the middle chamber of king Solomon's Temple, which I found partly open, but closely tyled by the Senior Warden.

Q. How did you gain admission?

A. By the grip and word.

Q. How did the Senior Warden dispose of you?

A. He ordered me to be conducted to the Worshipful Master in the East, who informed me that I had been admitted into the middle chamber of king Solomon's Temple for the sake of the letter G.

Q. Does it denote any thing?'

A. It does: Deity, before whom we should all bow with reverence, worship and adore. It also denotes Geometry, the fifth science; it being that on which this degree was principally founded.

Thus ends the second degree of Masonry.

THE THIRD, OR MASTER MASON'S DEGREE.

The traditional account of the death, several burials, and resurrection of Hiram Abiff, the widow's son, [as hereafter narrated] admitted as facts, this degree is certainly very interesting. The Bible informs us, that there was a person of that name employed at the building of king Solomon's Temple; but neither the Bible, the writings of Josephus, nor any other writings, however ancient, of which I have any knowledge, furnish any information respecting his death. It certainly is very singular, that a man so celebrated as Hiram Abiff, was an arbiter between Solomon, king of Israel, and Hiram, king of Tyre, universally acknowledged as the third most distinguished man then living, and in many respects the greatest man in the world, should pass off the stage of action in the presence of King Solomon, three thousand three hundred grand overseers, and one hundred and fifty thousond workmen, with whom he had spent a number of years, and neither king Solomon, his bosom friend, nor any other among his numerons friends even recorded his death or any thing about him. I make these remarks now, hoping that they may induce some person who has time and capacity to investigate the subject, and promulgate the result of their investigations. I shall let the subject restwhere it is at present; it is not intended that it should form any part of this little volume. The principal object of this work is to lay before the world a true history of Freemasonry, without saying any thing for or against it.

A person who has received the two preceding degrees, and wishes to be raised to the sublime degree of a Master Mason, is [the Lodge being opened as in the preceding degrees] conducted from the preparation room to the door, [the manner of preparing him is particularly explained in the lecture] where he gives three distinct knocks, when the Senior Warden rises and says, 'Worshipful, while we are peaceably at work on the third degree of Masonry, under the influence of humanity, brotherly love, and affection, the door of our Lodge appears to be alarmed' The Master to the Junior Deacon, 'Brother Junior, enquire the cause of that alarm.' The Senior Deacon then steps to the door and answers the three knocks that had been given, by three more; [These knocks are much louder than those given on any occasion, other than that of the admission of candidates in the several degrees] one knock is then given without, and answered by one from within, when the door is partly opened, and the Junior Deacon asks, 'Who comes there? who comes there? who comes there?' The Sen'r Deacon answers 'A worthy brother who has been regularly initiated as an Entered Apprentice Mason, passed to the degree of a Fellow Craft, and now wishes for further light in masonry, by being raised to the sublime degree of a Master Mason.' Junior Deacon to Senior Deacon, 'Is it of his own free will and accord, he makes this request?' *Ans.* 'It is.' Junior Deacon to Senior Deacon, 'Is he duly and truly prepared?' *Ans.* 'He is. Junior Deacon to Senior Deacon, 'Is he worthy and well qualified?' *Ans.* 'He is.' Jun'r Deacon to Senior Deacon, 'Has he made suitable proficiency in the preceding degrees?'

Ans. 'He has.' Junior Deacon to Senior Deacon, 'By what further rights does he expect to obtain this benefit?' *Ans.* 'By the benefit of a pass-word.' Junior Deacon to Senior Deacon, '*Has he a pass-word?*' *Ans.* 'He has not, but I have got it for him.' The Junior Deacon to Senior Deacon, 'Will you give it to me?' The Senior Deacon then whispers in the ear of the Junior Deacon, '*Tubal Cain.*' Junior Deacon says, 'the pass is right.' Since this is the case, you will wait till the Worshipful Master be made acquainted with his request and his answer returned.' The Junior Deacon then repairs to the Master and gives three knocks as at the door; after answering which, the same questions are asked and answers returned as at the door, when the Master says, 'Since he comes endued with all these necessary qualifications, let him enter this Worshipful Lodge in the name of the Lord, and take heed on what he enters.' The Junior Deacon returns to the door and says, 'Let him enter this worshipful Lodge, in the name of the Lord, and take heed on what he enters.' In entering, both points of the compass are pressed against his naked right and left breasts, when the Junior Deacon stops the candidate and says, 'Brother, when you first entered this Lodge, you was received on the point of the compass pressing your naked left breast, which was then explained to you; when you entered it the second time you was received on the angle of the square, which was also explained to you; on entering it now you are received on the two extreme points of the compass pressing your naked right and left breasts, which are thus explained: As the most vital parts of man are contained between the two breasts, so are the most valuable tenets of Masonry contained between the two extreme points of the compass, which are virtue, morality, and brotherly love.' The Senior Deacon then conducts the candidate three times regularly round the Lodge. [I wish the reader to observe, that on this, as well as every other degree, that the Junior Warden is the first of the three principal officers that the candidate passes, travelling with the sun when he starts round the Lodge, and that as he passes the Junior Warden, Senior Warden, and Master, the first time going round, they each give one rap; the second time two raps; and the third time three raps each. The number of raps given on those occasions are the same as

F 2

A. At high twelve at noon, when the Crafts were from labour to refreshment.

Q. How come he to be one at that time?

A. Because it was the usual custom of our Grand Master Hiram Abiff, every day at high twelve, when the Crafts were from labour to refreshment, to enter into the sanctum sanctorum or holy of holies, and offer up his adoration to the ever living God, and draw out his plans and designs on his trestle-board for the Crafts to pursue their labour-

Q. At what time was he missing?

A. At low six in the morning, when King Solomon came up to the Temple as usual to view the work, and found the Crafts all in confusion, and on inquiring the cause, he was informed that their Grand Master Hiram Abiff was missing, and no plans or designs were laid down on the trestle-board for the Crafts to pursue their labour.

Q. What observations did King Solomon make at that time?

A. He observed, that our Grand Master Hiram Abiff had always been very punctual in attending, and feared that he was indisposed, and ordered search to be made in and about the Temple to see if he could be found.

Q. Search being madeand he not found, what further remarks did King Solomon make?

A. He observed, he feared some fatal accident had befallen our Grand Master Hiram Abiff: that morning, twelve Fellow-Crafts, clothed in white gloves and aprons in token of their inocence, had confessed that they twelve, with three others, had conspired to extort the Master Mason's word from their Grand Master Hiram Abiff or take his life; that they twelve had recanted but feared the other three had been base enough to carry their atrocious designs into exeution.

Q. What followed?

A. King Solomon ordered the roll of workmen to be called to see if there were any missing.

Q. The roll being called, were there any missing?

A. There were three, viz; Jubela, Jubelo and Jubelum.

Q. Were the ruffians ever found?

A. They were. Q. How?

A. By the wisdom of King Solomon, who ordered

twelve Fellow-Crafts to be selected from the band of the workmen, clothed in white gloves and aprons in token of their innocence, and sent three East, three West, three North, and three South in search of the ruffians, and if found to bring them forward.

Q. What success?

A. The three that travelled a westerly course from the Temple, coming near the coast of Joppa, were in formed by a way-fairing man,hat three men had been seen that way that morning, who from their appearance and dress were workmen from the Temple, inquirtng for a passage to Ethiopia but were unable to obtain one in consequence of an embargo which had recently been laid on all the shipping, and had turned back into the country.

Q. What followed?

A. King Solomon ordered them to go and search again, and search til they were found if possible, and if they were not found, that the twelve who had confessed should be considered as the reputed murderers, and suffer accordingly.

Q. What success?

A. One of the three that travelled a westely course from the temple, being more weary than the rest, sat down under the brow of a hill to rest and refresh himself, and in attempting to rise, caught hold of a sprig of cassia, which easily gave way, and excited his curiosity and made him suspicious of a deception, on which he hailed his companions, who immediately assembled, and on examination, found that the earth had recently been moved, and on moving the rubbish discovered the appearance of a grave; and while they were confabulating about what measures to take, they heard voices issuing from a cavern in the clefts of the rocks; on which they immediately repaired to the place, where they heard the voice of Jubela exclaim, 'O, that my throat had been cut across, my tongue torn out, and my body buried in the rough sands of the sea at low water mark, where the tide ebbs and flows twice in twenty-four hours, ere I had been accessary to the death of so good a man as our Grand Master Hiram Abiff?' On which they distinctly heard the voice of Jubelo exclaim, 'O, that my left breast had been torn open, and my heart and vitals taken from thence, thrown over my left shoulder, carried

such. Furthermore, do I promise and swear, that, I will not be at the initiating of an old man in dotage, a young man in non-age, an Atheist, irreligious libertine, idiot, mad man, hermaphrodite nor woman. Furthermore, do I promise and swear, that, I will not speak evil of a brother Master Mason, neither behind his back nor before his face, but will apprize him of all approaching danger, if in my power. Furthermore, do I promise and swear, that, I will not violate the chastity of a Master Mason's wife, mother, sister, or daughter, I knowing them to be such, nor suffer it to be done by othes, if in my power to prevent it. Furthermore, do I promise and swear, that, I will support the Constitution of the Grand Lodge of the state of ———, under which this Lodge is held, and conform to all the bye-laws, rules and regulations of this, or any other Lodge of which I may at any time hereafter become a member. Furthermore, do I promise and swear, that, I will obey all regular signs, summons' or tokens, given, handed, sent, or thrown to me from the hand of a brother Master Mason, or from the body of a just and lawfully constituted Lodge of such, provided it be within the length of my Cable-Tow. Furthermore, do I promise and swear, that, a Master Mason's secrets given to me in charge as such, and I knowing him to be such, shall remain as secure and inviolable in my breast, as in his own when communicated to me, murder and treason excepted; and they left to my own election. Furthermore, do I promise, and swear, that, I will go on a Master Mason's errand whenever required, even should I have to go barefoot, and barehead, if within the length of my Cable-Tow. Furthermore, do I promise and swear, that, I will always remember a brother Master Mason, when on my knees offering up my devotions to Almighty God. Furthermore, do I promise and swear, that I will be aiding and assisting all poor, indigent Master Mason's, their wives and orphans, wheresoever disposed round the globe; as far as in my power, without injuring myself or family materially. Furthermore, do I promise and swear; that if any part of this my solemn oath or obligation be omitted at this time, that I will hold myself amenable thereto whenever informed. To all which I do most solemnly, and sincerely promise and swear, with a fixed and steady purpose of mind in me to keep and perform the same, binding myself under no less penalty than to have my by body severed in two in the midst, and divided to the North and South, my bowels burnt to ashes in the centre, and the ashes scattered before the four winds of heaven, that there might not the least track or trace of remembrance remain among men or Masons of so vile and perjured a wretch as I should be, were I ever to prove wilfully guilty of violating any part of this my solemn oath or obligation of a Master Mason. So help me God, and keep me stedfast in the due performance of the same.' The Master then asks the candidate, 'What do you most desire?' The candidate answers after his prompter, 'More light.' The bandage, which was tied round his head in the preparation room, is, by one of the brethren who stands behind him for that purpose, loosened and put over both eyes, and he is immediately brought to light in the same manner as in the preceding degree, except three stamps on the floor, and three claps of the hands are given in this degree. On being brought to light, the Master says to the candidate, 'You first discover as before, three great lights in masonry by the assistance of three lesser, with this difference; both points of the compass, are elevated above the square, which denotes to you, that you are about to receive all the light that can be conferred on you in a Master's Lodge.' The Master steps back from the candidate and says, 'Brother, you now discover me as Master of this Lodge approaching you from the East, under the sign and due-guard of a Master Mason.' The sign is given by raising both hands and arms to the elbows perpendicularly, one on either side of the head, the elbows forming a square. The words accompanying this sign in case of distress, are 'O Lord, my God, is there no help for the widow's son.' As the last words drop from your lips, you let your hands fall in that manner, best calculated to indicate solemnity. King Solomon is said to have made this exclamation on the receipt of the information of the death of Hiram Abiff. Masons are all charged never to give the *words* except in the dark when the sign cannot be seen. Here Masons differ very much; some contend that Solomon gave this sign, and made this exclamation when informed of Hiram's death, and work accordingly in their Lodges. Others say the sign was given and the exclamation made at the grave when Solomon went there to raise Hiram, and of course they work accordingly; that is to say, the Master who governs a Lodge, holding the latter opinion, gives the sign &c. at the gave, when he goes to raise the body, and vice versa. The due-guard is given by putting the right hand to the left side of the bowels, the hand open with the thumb next to the belly, and drawing it across the belly, and let it fall; this is done tolerably quick. After the Master has given the sign and due-guard 'which does not take more than a minute, he says, 'Brother, I now present you with my right hand in token of brotherly love and affection, and with it the pass-grip and word.' The pass-grip is given by pressing the thumb between the joints of the second and third fingers where they join the hand, the word or name is *Tubal Cain.* It is the pass-word to the Master's degree. The Master after giving the candidate the pass-grip and word bids him rise and salute the Junior and Senior Wardens, and convince them that he is an obligated Master Mason, and is in possession of the pass-grip and word. While the Wardens are examining the candidate, the Master returns to the East and gets an apron, as he returns to the candidate, one of the Wardens [some times both] says to the Master, 'Worshipful, we are satisfied that Br. —— —— is an obligated Master Mason.' The Master then says to the candidate, 'Brother, I now have the honour to present you with a lamb skin or white apron as before which I hope you will continue to wear with credit to yourself, and satisfaction and advantage to the brethren you will please carry it to the Senior Warden in the West, who will teach you how to wear it as a Master Mason.

The Senior Warden ties on the apron, and lets the flap fall down before in its natural and common situation.

The Master returns to his seat and the candidate conducted to him. Master to candidate, 'Brother, I perceive you are dressed, it is of course necessary you should have tools to work with. I will now present you with the working tools of a Master Mason, and explain their uses to you. The working tools of a Master Mason are all the implements of masonry indiscriminately but more especially the trowel. The trowel is an instrument made use of by operative Masons, to spread the cement which unites a building into one common mass but we, as free and accepted Masons, are taught to make use of it for the more noble and glorious purpose, of spreading the cement of *brotherly love* and affection; that cement which unites us into one sacred band or society of friends and brothers among whom no contention should ever exist, but that noble contention, or rather emulation of who can best work or best agree. I also present you with three precious jewels; their names are *humanity*, *friendship*, and *brotherly love*.'

'Brother, you are not yet invested with all the secrets of this degree, nor do I know whether you ever will until I know how you withstand the amazing trials and dangers that await you.'

'You are now about to travel to give us a specimen of yor fortitude, perseverance and fidelity in the preservation of what you have already received.—Fare you well, and may the Lord be with you, and support you through all your trials and difficulties.' [In some Lodges they make him pray before he starts.] The candidate is then conducted out of the Lodge, clothed, and returns; as he enters the door, his conductor says to him, 'Brother, we are in a place representing the *sanctum sanctorum*, or *holy of holies* of King Solomons Temple. It was the custom of our Grand Master Hiram Abiff, every day at high twelve, when the Crafts were from labour to refreshment, to enter in to the *sanctum sanctorum*, and offer up his devotion to the ever living God. Let us in imatation of him kneel and pray.' They then kneel and the conductor says the following prayer. 'Thou, O God, knowest our down setting and upraising, and understandest our thoughts afar off, shield and defend us from the evil intentions of our enemies, and support us under the trials and afflictions we are destined to endure while travelling through this vale of tears. Man that is born of a woman, is of few days and full of trouble. He cometh forth as a flower, and is cut down; he fleeth also as a shadow, and continueth not. Seeing his days are determined, the number of his months are with thee, thou hast appointed his bounds that he cannot pass; turn from him that he may rest 'till he shall accomplish his day. For there is hope of a tree, if it be cut down, that it will sprout again, and that the tender branch thereof will not cease. But man dieth and wasteth away: yea, man giveth up the ghost, and where is he? As the waters fail from the sea, and the flood decayeth and drieth up, so man lieth down, and riseth not up till the heavens shall be no more. Yet, O Lord! have compassion on the children of thy creation; administer unto them comfort in time of trouble' and save them with an everlasting salvation.' Amen—so mote it be. They then rise, and the conductor says to the candidate, 'Brother, in further imitation of our Grand Master Hiram Abiff, let us retire at the South Gate.' They then advance to the Junior Warden [who represents *Jubela*, one of the ruffians] who exclaims, 'Who comes here?' [The room is dark, or the candidate hood-winked,] the conductor answers, 'Our Grand Master Hiram Abiff.' '*Our Grand Master Hiram Abiff*!' exclaims the ruffian, 'he is the very man I wanted to see. [Seizing the candidate by the throat at the same time, and jerking him about with violence] give me the Master Mason's word, or I'll take your life.' The conductor replies, 'I cannot give it now, but, if you will wait till the Grand Lodge assembles at Jerusalem, if you are found worthy, you shall then receive it, otherwise you cannot.' The ruffian then gives the candidate a blow with the twenty-four inch guage across the throat, on which he fled to the West gate, where he was accosted by the second ruffian, *Jubelo*, with more violence, and on his refusal to comply with his request, he gave him a severe blow with the square across his breast; on which he attempted to make his escape at the East gate, where he was accosted by the third ruffian *Jubelum*, with still more violence and on refusing to comply with his request, the ruffian gave him a violent blow with the common gavel on the fore-head which brought him to the floor; on which one of them exclaimed, 'What shall we do; we have killed our Grand Master Hiram Abiff? another answers, less carry him out at the East gate and bury him in the rubbish till low twelve, and then meet and carry him a Westerly course and bury him.' The candidate is then taken up in a blanket, on which he fell, and carried to the West end of the Lodge, and covered up and left, by this time the Master has resumed his seat, [king Solomon is supposed to arrive at the Temple at this juncture] and calls to order, and asks the Senior Warden the cause of all that confusion; the Senior Warden answers, 'Our Grand Master Hiram Abiff is missing, and there are no plans, or designs laid down on the Trestle-board, for the Crafts to pursue their labours.' The Master, alias king Solomon replies, 'Our Grand Master missing? our Grand Master has always been very punctual in his attendance? I fear he is indisposed; assemble the Crafts and search in and about the temple and see if he can be found.' They all shuffle about the floor a while, when the Master calls them to order and asks the Senior Warden 'what success,' he answers 'we cannot find our Grand Master, my lord.' The Master then orders the Secretary to call the roll of workmen, and see whether any of them are missing.' The Secretary calls the roll, and says, I have called the roll my lord, and find that there are three missing, viz: *Jubela, Jubelo*, and *Jubelum*.' His lordship then observed: 'This brings to my mind a circumstance that took place this morning; twelve Fellow-Crafts, clothed in white gloves and aprons, in token of their innocence, came to me and confessed that they twelve, with three others, had conspired to extort the Master Mason's word from their Grand Master Hiram Abiff; and in case of refusal to take his life—they twelve had recanted, but feared the other three had been base enough to carry their atrocious designs into execution. Solomon then ordered twelve Fellow-Crafts to be drawn from the bands of the workmen clothed in white gloves and aprons, in token of their innocence, and sent three east, three west, three north and three south, in search of the ruffians, and if found to bring them forward. Here the members all shuffle about the floor awhile and fall in with a reputed traveller, and inquire of him if he had seen any travelling men that way; he tells them that he had seen three that morning near the coast of Joppa, who from their dress and appearance were Jews, and were workmen from the temple, inquiring for a passage to Ethiopia, but were unable to obtain one in consequence of an embargo which had recently been laid on all the shipping, and had turned back into the country.

The Master now calls them to order again, and asks the Senior Warden, 'what success;' he answers by relating what had taken place; Solomon observes, 'I had this embargo, laid to prevent the ruffians from making their escape;' and adds, you will go and search again, and search till you find them if possible, and if they are not found the twelve who confessed, shall be considered as the reputed murderers and suffer accordingly.' The members all start again and shuffle about awhile, until one them as if by accident, finds the body of Hiram Abiff, alias the candidate, and hails his travelling companions who join him, and while they are humming out something over the candidate, the three reputed ruffians

G

who are seated in a private corner near the candidate, are heard to exclaim in the following manner; first *Jubela*, 'O that my throat had been cut across, my tongue torn out, and my body buried in the rough sands of the sea at low water mark, where the tide ebbs and flows twice in twenty-four hours, ere I had been accessary to the death of so good a man as our Grand Master Hiram Abiff.

The second, *Jubelo*, 'O that my left breast had been torn open, and my heart and vitals taken from thence and thrown over my left shoulder, carried into the valley of Jehosaphat, and there to become a prey to the wild beasts of the field and vultures of the air, ere I had conspired the death of so good a man as our Grand Master Hiram Abiff.

The third, *Jubelum*, 'O that my body had been severed in two in the midst, and divided to the North and the South, my bowels burnt to ashes in the centre, and the ashes scattered by the four winds of heaven, that there might not the least track or trace of remembrance remain among men, or Masons of so vile and perjured a wretch as I am—Ah, *Jubela* and *Jubelo*, it was I that struck him harder than you both; it was I that gave him the fatal blow; it was I that killed him outright.' The three Fellow-Crafts who had stood by the candidate all this time listening to the ruffians, whose voices they recognised, says one to the other, 'what shall we do, there are three of them, and only three of us;' 'it is,' said one, in reply, 'our cause is good, let us seize them;' on which they rush forward, seize and carry them to the Master, to whom they relate what had passed; the Master then addresses them in the following manner: [they in many Lodges kneel, or lie down in token of their guilt and penitence.] 'Well Jubela, what have you got to say for yourself, guilty or not guilty?' *Ans.* 'Guilty my Lord.' 'Jubelo, guilty or not guilty?' *Ans.* 'Guilty my Lord.' 'Jubelum, guilty or not guilty?' *Ans.* 'Guilty my Lord.' The Master to the three Fellow-Crafts who took them, 'Take them without the West gate of the temple and have them executed according to the several imprecations of their own mouths.' They are then hurried off to the West end of the room. Here this part of the farce ends. The Master then orders fifteen Fellow-Crafts to be selected from the bands of the workmen, and sent three East, three West, three North, three South and three in and about the temple in search of their Grand Master Hiram Abiff, [in some Lodges they only send twelve, when their own lectures say fifteen, were sent] and charges them if they find the body to examine carefully on and about it for the Master's word or a key to it. The three that travelled a westerly course, comes to the candidate and finger about him a little and are called to order by the Master, when they report that they had found the grave of their Grand Master Hiram Abiff, and on moving the earth till they come to the body they involuntarily found their hands raised in this position, [shewing it at the same time; it is the due-guard of this degree] to guard their nostrils against the offensive effluvia which arose from the grave, and that they had searched carefully on and about the body for the Master's word, but had not discovered any thing but a feint resemblance of the letter G on the left breast. The Master on the receipt of this information, (raising himself,) raises his hands three several times above his head [as herein before described] and exclaims, 'Nothing but a faint resemblance of the letter G! that is not the Master's word nor a key to it. I fear the Master's word is forever lost! Nothing but a feint resemblance of the letter G! that is not the Master's word nor a key to it. I fear the Master's word is forever lost!' [The third exclamation is different from the other two—attend to it, is has been described in page 69.] 'Nothing but a feint resemblance of the letter G! that is not the Master's word nor a key to it. 'O Lord my God, is there no help for the widows son!' The Master then orders the Junior Warden to summon a Lodge of Entered Apprentice Masons, and repair to the grave and try to raise the body of their Grand Master, by the Entered Apprentice's grip.' They go to the candidate and take hold of his fore finger and pull it, return and tell the Master that they could not raise him by the Entered Apprentice's grip, that the skin cleaved from the bone. A Lodge of Fellow-Crafts are then sent, who act as before, except they pull the candidate's second finger. The Master then directs the Senior Warden [generally] to summon a Lodge of Master Masons and says, 'I will go with them myself in person, and try to raise the body by the Master's grip, or lion's paw.' [Some say by the strong grip or lion's paw.] They then all assemble round the candidate, the Master having declared that the first word spoken after the body was raised, should be adopted as a substitute for the Master's word, for the government of Master Mason's Lodges in all future generations; he proceeds to raise the candidate, alias the representative of the dead body of Hiram Abiff. He [the candidate] is raised on what is called the five points of fellowship, which are foot to foot, knee to knee, breast to breast, hand to back, and mouth to ear. This is done by putting the inside of your right foot to the inside of the right foot of the person to whom you are going to give the word, the inside of your knee to his, laying your right breast against his, your left hands on the back of each other, and your mouths to each other's right ear, [in which position alone you are permitted to give the word] and whisper the word *Mah-hah-bone*. The Master's grip is given by taking hold of each other's right hand as though you were going to shake hands, and sticking the nails of each of your fingers into the joint of the other's wrist where it unites with the hand. In this position the candidate is raised, he keeping his whole body stiff as though dead. The Master in raising him is assisted by some of the brethren who take hold of the candidate by the arms and shoulders; as soon as he is raised to his feet they step back, and the Master whispers the word *Mah-hah-bone* in his ear and causes the candidate to repeat it, telling him at the same time that he must never give it in any manner other than that which he receives it.—He is also told that *Mah-hah-bone*, signifies marrow in the bone.—They then separate, and the Master makes the following explanation respecting the five points of fellowship.—Master to candidate, 'Brother, foot to foot, teaches you that you should, whenever asked, go on a brother's errand if within the length of your Cable-Tow, even if you should have to go barefoot and barehead. Knee to knee, that you should always remember a Master Mason in your devotion to Almighty God. Breast to breast, that you should keep the Master Mason's secrets, when given to you in charge as such, as secure and inviolable in your breast, as they were in his own before communicated to you. Hand to back, that you should support a Master Mason behind his back as well as before his face. Mouth to ear, that you should support his good name as well behind his back as before his face.' After the candidate is through with what is called the work part, the Master addresses him in the following manner: 'Brother, you may suppose from the manner you have been dealt with to night, that we have been fooling with you, or that we have treated you different from others, but I assure you that is not the case. You have this night represented one of the greatest men that ever lived, in the tragical catastrophe of his death, burial and resurrection; I mean Hiram Abiff the widow's son, who was slain by three ruffians at the building of king Solomon's Temple, and who, in his inflexibility, integrity and fortitude, never was surpassed by man. The history of that momentous event is thus related. Masonic tradition informs us that at the building of king Solomon's Temple, fifteen Fellow-Crafts discovering that the Temple was almost finished, and not having the *Master* Mason's word, became very impatientt and entered into a horrid conspiracy to extort the Master Mason's word from their Grand Master Hiram Abiff, the first time they met him alone, or take his life, that they might pass as Masters in other countries and receive wages as such, but before they could accomplish their designs, twelve of them recanted but the other three were base enough to carry their atrocious designs into execution. Their names were *Jubela Jubelo Jubelum.*'

'It was the custom of our Grand Master Hiram Abiff every day at high twelve, when the Crafts were from labour to refreshment, to enter into the *Sanctum Sanctorum* and offer up his devotions to the ever living God, and draw out his plans and designs on his trestle-board for the Crafts to pursue their labour. On a certain day, [not named in any of our traditional accounts] *Jubela*, *Jubelo* and *Jubelum* placed themselves at the South, West and East gates of the Temple, and Hiram having finished his devotions and labour, attempted (as was his usual custom) to retire at the South gate, where he was met by *Jubela*, who demanded of him the Master Mason's word,(some say the secrets of a Master Mason) and on his refusal to give it *Jubela* gave him a violent blow with the twenty four inch guage across the throat, on which Hiram fled to the West gate, where he was accosted in the same manner by *Jubelo*, but with more violance. Hiram told him that he could not give the word then be-

G 2

cause Solomon, King of Isreal, Hiram, King of Tyre, and himself had entered into a solemn league, that the word never should be given unless they three were present, but if he would wait with patience. till the Grand Lodge assembled at Jerusalem if he was then found worthy he should receive it, otherwise he could not; *Jubelo* replied in a very peremptory manner; 'If you do not give me the Master's word, I'll take your life; and on Hiram's refusing to give it, Jubelo gave him a severe blow with the square accross the left breast, on which he fled to the East gate, where he was accosted by *Jubelum* in the same manner, but with still more violence. Here Hiram reasoned as before; Jubelum told him that he had heard his cavilling with Jubela and Jubelo long enough, and that the Master's word had been promised to him from time to time for a long time, that he was still put off and the temple was almost finished and he was determined to have the word or take his life; 'I want it so that I may be able to get wages as a Master Mason in any country to which I may go for employ, after the Temple is finished, and that I may be able to support my wife and children.' Hiram persisting in his refusal; he give Hiram a violent blow with the gavel on the forehead which felled him to the floor and killed him—they took the body and carried it out of the West gate and buried it in the rubbish till low twelve at night, (which is twelve o'clock) when they three met agreeable to appointment, and carried the body a westerly course and buried it at the brow of a hill in a grave, dug due East and West six feet perpendicular, and made their escape. King Solomon coming up to the Temple at low six in the morning' [as was his usual custom] found the Crafts all in confusion; and on enquiring the cause, was informed that their Grand Master Hiram Abiff was missing, and there were no plans and designs laid down on the trestle-board for the Crafts to pursue their labour. Solomon ordered immediate search to be made in and about the Temple for him; no discovery being made, he then ordered the Secretary to call the roll of workmen to see if any were missing; it appearing that there were three viz: *Jubela*, *Jubelo*, and *Jubelum*; Solomon observed, 'This springs to my mind a circumstance that took place this morning. Twelve Fellow-Crafts came to me dressed in white gloves and aprons in token of their innocence, and confessed that they twelve with three others had conspired to extort the Master Mason's word from their Grand Master Hiram Abiff, and in case of his refusal to take his life; they twelve had recanted, but feared the other three had been base enough to carry their atrocious design into execution.' Solomon immediately ordered twelve Fellow-Crafts to be selected from the bands of the workmen, clothed in white gloves and aprons in token of their innocence, and sent three East, three West, three North and three South, in search of the ruffians, and if found to bring them up before him. The three that travelled a westerly course, coming near the coast of Joppa, fell in with a way-faring man who informed them that he had seen three men pass that way that morning, who, from their appearance and dress, were workmen from the Temple, inquiring for a passage to Ethiopa, but were unable to obtain one in consequence of an embargo which had recently been laid on all the shipping, and had turned back into the country. After making still further and more diligent search, and making no further discovery, they returned to the Temple and reported to Solomon the result of their pursuit and inquiries. On which Solomon directed them to go and search again, and search until they found their Grand Master Hiram Abiff, if possible, and if he was not found, the twelve who had confessed, should be considered as the murderers and suffer accordingly.

They returned again in pursuit of the ruffians, and one of the three that travelled a westerly course, being more weary than the rest, sat down at the brow of a hill to rest and refresh himself; and, in attempting to rise, caught hold of a sprig of cassia, which easily gave way, and excited his curiosity, and made him suspicious of a deception, on which he hailed his companions, who immediately assembled, and, on examination, found that the earth had been recently moved; and on moving the rubbish, discovered the appearance of a grave; and while they were confabulating about what measures to take, they heard voices issuing from a cavern in the clefts of the rocks, on which, they immediately repaired to the place, where they heard the voice of *Jubela* exclaim, 'O! that my throat had been cut across, my tongue torn out, and my body buried in the rough sands of the sea at low water mark; where the tide ebbs and flows twice in twenty-four hours, ere I had been accessary to the death of so good a man as our Grand Master Hiram Abiff,—on which, they distinctly heard the voice of *Jubelo* exclaim, 'O! that my left breast had been torn open, and my heart and vitals taken from thence and thrown over my left shoulder, to the valley of Jehoshaphat, there to become a prey to the wild beasts of the field and vultures of the air, ere I had conspired to take the life of so good a man as our Grand Master Hiram Abiff'—when they more distinctly heard the voice of *Jubelum* exclaim, 'O! that my body had been severed in two in the midst, and divided to the north and the south, my bowels burnt to ashes in the centre, and the ashes scattered by the four winds of heaven, that there might not remain the least track or trace of remembrance among men or Masons of so vile and perjured a wretch as I am, who wilfully took the life of so good a man as our Grand Master Hiram Abiff. Ah! *Jubela* and *Jubelo*, it was I that struck him harder than you both! it was I that gave him the fatal blow! it was I that killed him outright!' On which, they rushed forward, seized, bound, and carried them up before king Solomon, who, after hearing the testimony of the three Fellow-Crafts, and the three ruffians having plead guilty, ordered them to be taken out at the West gate of the Temple and executed agreeable to the several imprecations of their own mouths. King Solomon then ordered fifteen Fellow-Crafts to be selected from the bands of the workmen clothed with white gloves and aprons, in token of their innocence, and sent three East, three West, three North, three South, and three in and about the Temple, in search of the body of their Grand Master Hiram Abiff; and the three that travelled a westerly course found it under that sprig of Cassia where a worthy Brother sat down to rest and refresh himself; and on removing the earth till they came to the coffin, they involuntarily found thetr hands raised, as herein before described, to guard their nostrils against the offensive effluvia that arose from the grave. It is also said that the body had lain there fourteen days, some say fifteen. The body was raised in the manner herein before described, carried up to the Temple, and buried as explained in the closing clauses of the lecture. Not one third part of the preceding history of this degree is ever given to a candidate. A few general desultory unconnected remarks are made to him, and he is generally referred to the manner of raising, and the lecture, for information as to the particulars. Here follows a charge which ought to be, and sometimes is delivered to the candidate after hearing the history of the degree.

An Address to be delivered to the Candidate after the history has been given.

'Brother, your zeal for the institution of Masonry, the progress you have made in the mystery, and your conformity to our regulations, have pointed you out as a proper object of our favour and esteem.

'You are bound by duty, honour, and gratitude, to be faithful to your trust; to support the dignity of your character on every occasion; and to enforce, by precept and example, obedience to the tenets of the order.

'In the character of a Master Mason, you are authorized to correct the errors and irregularities of your uninformed brethren, and to guard them against a breach of fidelity.

'To preserve the reputation of the fraternity unsullied, must be your constant care; and for this purpose it is your province to recommend to your inferiors, obedience and submission; to your equals, courtesy and affability; to your superiors, kindness and condescension. Universal benevolence you are always to inculcate; and, by the regularity of your own behaviour, afford the best example for the conduct of others less informed. The ancient landmarks of the order, entrusted to your care, you are carefully to preserve; and never suffer them to be infringed, or countenance a deviation from the established usages and customs of the fraternity.

'Your virtue, honour, and reputation are concerned in supporting with dignity the character you now bear. Let no motive, therefore, make you swerve from your duty, violate your vows, or betray your trust; but be true and faithful, and imitate the example of that celebrated artist whom you this evening represent; thus you will render yourself deserving the honour which we have conferred, and merit the confidence that we have reposed.'

Here follows the lecture on this degree, which is divided into three sections.

SECTION FIRST.

Q. Are you a Master Mason?

A. I am—try me, prove me—disprove me, if you can.

Q. Where was you prepared to be made a Master Mason?

A. In a room adjacent to the body of a just and lawfully constituted Lodge of such, duly assembled u a room, representing the sanctum sanctorum, or holy of holies of king Solomon's Temple.

Q. How was you prepared?

A. By being divested of all metals; neither naked nor clothed; barefoot nor shod; with a cable-tow three times about my naked body; in which posture I was conducted to door of the Lodge, where I gave three distinct knocks.

Q. What did those three distinct knocks allude to?

A. To the third degree of Masonry; it being that on which I was about to enter.

Q. What was said to you from within?

A. Who comes there? who comes there? who comes there?

Q. Your answer?

A. A worthy Brother who has been regularly initiated as an Entered Apprentice Mason, passed to the degree of a Fellow-Craft, and now wishes for further light in Masonry by being raised to the sublime degree of a Master Mason.

Q. What further was said to you from within?

A. I was asked if it was of my own free will and accord I made that request; if I was duly and truly prepared; worthy and well qualified, and had made suitable proficiency in the preceding degrees; all of which being answered in the affirmative, I was asked by what further rights I expected to obtain that benefit.

Q. Your answer? A. By the benefit of a pass-word.

Q. What is that pass-word? A. *Tubal Cain.*

Q. What next was said to you?

A. I was bid to wait till the Worshipful Master in the East was made acquainted with my request, and his answer returned.

Q What followed after his answer was returned?

A. I was caused to enter the Lodge on the two extreme points of the compass, pressing my naked right and left breasts, in the name of the Lord.

Q. How was you then disposed of?

A. I was conducted three times regularly round the Lodge, and halted at the Junior Warden in the South, where the same questions were asked and answers returned as at the door.

Q. How did the Junior Warden dispose of you?

A. He ordered me to be conducted to the Senior Warden in the West, where the same questions were asked and answers returned as before.

Q. How did the Senior Warden dispose of you?

A. He ordered me to be conducted to the Worshipful Master in the East, where, by him, the same questions were asked and answers returned as before, who likewise demanded of me, from whence I came, and whether I was traveling.

Q. Your answer?

A. From the West and traveling to the East.

Q. Why do you leave the West and travel to the East.

A. In search of light.

Q. How did the Worshipful Master then dispose of you?

A. He ordered me to be conducted back to the West from whence I came, and put in care of the Senior Warden, who taught me how to approach the East, by advancing upon three upright regular steps to the third step, my feet forming a square, and my body erect at the altar before the Worshipful Master.

Q. What did the Worshipful Master do with you?

A. He made an obligated Master Mason of me.

Q. How? A. In due form.

Q. What was that due form?

A. Both my knees bare bent, they forming a square; both hands on the holy Bible, square and compass; in which posture I took upon me the solemn oath or obligation of a Master Mason.

Q. After your obligation, what was said to you?

A. What do you most desire?

Q. Your answer?

A. More light. [The bandage round the head is now dropped over the eyes.]

Q. Did you received light? A. I did.

Q. On being brought to light on this degree, what did you first discover?

A. Three great lights in Masonry, by the assistance

of three less, and both points of the compass elevat above the square, which denoted to me that I had rece ved or was about to receive all the light that could I conferred on me in a Master's Lodge.

Q. What did you next discover?

A. The Worshipful Master approaching me from th East under the sign and due-guard of a Master Maso who presented me with his right hand in token of broth erly love and confidence, and proceeded to give me th pass-grip and word of a Master Mason, [the word is th name of the pass-drip] and bid me rise and salute the Ju ior and Senior Wardens, and convince them that I was obligated Master Mason, and had the sign, pass-grip a word. [Tubal-Cain.]

Q. What did you next discover?

A. The Worshipful Master approaching me a secon time from the East, who presented me with a lamb.skil or white apron, which he said he hoped I would contin ue to wear with honour to myself, and satisfaction and ad vantage to the brethren.

Q. What was you next presented with?

A. The working tools of a Master Mason.

Q. What are they?

A. All the implements of masonry indiscriminately but more especially the trowel.

Q. How explained?

A. The trowel is an instrument made use of by ope rative Masons to spread the cement which unites a buil ding into one common mass, but we as free and Accep ted Masons are taught to make use of it for the more noble and glorious purpose, of spreading the cement o brotherly love and affection; that cement which unite us into one sacred band or society of brothers, amon whom no contention should ever exist, but that nobl emulation, of who can best work or best agree.

Q. What was you next presented with?

A. Three precious jewels.

Q. What are they?

A. Humanity, friendship and brotherly love.

Q. How was you then disposed of?

A I was conducted out of the Lodge and investe with what I had been divested, and returned again in du season.

SECTION SECOND.

Q. Did you ever return to the sanctum sanctorum or holy of holies of King Solomon's Temple?

A. I did.

Q. Was there any thing particular took place on your return?

A. There was, viz: I was accosted by three ruffians; who demanded of me the Master Mason's word.

Q. Did you give it to them?

A. I did not, but bid them wait with time and patience till the Grand Lodge assembled at Jerusalem; and then if they were found worthy, they should receive it; otherwise they could not.

Q. In what manner was you accosted?

A. In attempting to retire to the South gate, I was accosted by one of them, who demanded of me the Master Mason's word, and on my refusing to comply with his request, he gave me a blow with the twenty-four inch guage across my breast, on which I fled to the West gate where I was accosted by the second with more violence, and on my refusing to comply with his request, he gave me a severe blow with the square across my breast, on which I attempted to make my escape at the East gate, where I was accosted by the third with still more violence, and on my refusing to comply with his request, he gave me a violent blow with the common gavel on the forehead, and brougnt me to the floor.

Q. Whom did you represent at that time?

A. Our Grand Mater Hiram Abiff, who was slain at the building of King Solomon's Temple.

Q. Was his death premeditated?

A. It was by fifteen Fellow-Crafts, who conspired to extort from him the Master Mason's word; twelve of whom recanted, but the other three were base enough to carry their atrocious designs to execution.

Q. What did they do with the body?

A. They carried it out at the West gate of the Temple and buried it till low twelve at night, when they three met agreeable to appointment, and carried it a westerly course from the Temple, and buried it under the brow of a hill in a grave six feet due East and West, six feet perpendicular' and made their escape.

Q. What time was he slain?

A. At high twelve at noon, when the Crafts were from labour to refreshment.

Q. How come he to be one at that time ?

A. Because it was the usual custom of our Grand Master Hiram Abiff, every day at high twelve, when the Crafts were from labour to refreshment, to enter into the sanctum sanctorum or holy of holies, and offer up his adoration to the ever living God, and draw out his plans and designs on his trestle-board for the Crafts to pursue their labour-

Q. At what time was he missing ?

A. At low six in the morning, when King Solomon came up to the Temple as usual to view the work, and found the Crafts all in confusion, and on inquiring the cause, he was informed that their Grand Master Hiram Abiff was missing, and no plans or designs were laid down on the trestle-board for the Crafts to pursue their labour.

Q. What observations did King Solomon make at that time ?

A. He observed, that our Grand Master Hiram Abiff had always been very punctual in attending, and feared that he was indisposed, and ordered search to be made in and about the Temple to see if he could be found.

Q. Search being madeand he not found, what further remarks did King Solomon make ?

A. He observed, he feared some fatal accident had befallen our Grand Master Hiram Abiff: that morning, twelve Fellow-Crafts, clothed in white gloves and aprons in token of their inocence, had confessed that they twelve, with three others, had conspired to extort the Master Mason's word from their Grand Master Hiram Abiff or take his life ; that they twelve had recanted but feared the other three had been base enough to carry their atrocious designs into exeution.

Q. What followed ?

A. King Solomon ordered the roll of workmen to be called to see if there were any missing.

Q. The roll being called, were there any missing ?

A. There were three, viz; Jubela, Jubelo and Jubelum.

Q. Were the ruffians ever found ?

A. They were. Q. How ?

A. By the wisdom of King Solomon, who ordered

twelve Fellow-Crafts to be selected from the band of the workmen, clothed in white gloves and aprons in token of their innocence, and sent three East, three West, three North, and three South in search of the ruffians, and if found to bring them forward.

Q. What success ?

A. The three that travelled a westerly course from the Temple, coming near the coast of Joppa, were in formed by a way-fairing man,hat three men had been seen that way that morning, who from their appearance and dress were workmen from the Temple, inquirtng for a passage to Ethiopia but were unable to obtain one in consequence of an embargo which had recently been laid on all the shipping, and had turned back into the country.

Q. What followed ?

A. King Solomon ordered them to go and search again, and search til they were found if possible, and if they were not found, that the twelve who had confessed should be considered as the reputed murderers, and suffer accordingly.

Q. What success ?

A. One of the three that travelled a westely course from the temple, being more weary than the rest, sat down under the brow of a hill to rest and refresh himself, and in attempting to rise, caught hold of a sprig of cassia, which easily gave way, and excited his curiosity and made him suspicious of a deception, on which he hailed his companions, who immediately assembled, and on examination, found that the earth had recently been moved, and on moving the rubbish discovered the appearance of a grave ; and while they were confabulating about what measures to take, they heard voices issuing from a cavern in the clefts of the rocks ; on which they immediately repaired to the place, where they heard the voice of Jubela exclaim, 'O, that my throat had been cut across, my tongue torn out, and my body buried in the rough sands of the sea at low water mark, where the tide ebbs and flows twice in twenty-four hours, ere I had been accessary to the death of so good a man as our Grand Master Hiram Abiff?' On which they distinctly heard the voice of Jubelo exclaim, 'O, that my left breast had been torn open, and my heart and vitals taken from thence, thrown over my left shoulder, carried to the valley of Jehosaphat, there to become a prey to the wild beasts of the field and vultures of the air, ere I had conspired to take the life of so good a man as our Grand Master Hiram Abiff!' When they more distinctly heard the voice of Jubelum exclaim, 'O, that my body had been severed in two in the midst, and divided to the North and the South, and my bowels burnt to ashes in the centre, and the ashes scattered before (or by) the four winds of heaven, that there might not remain the least track or trace of remembrance among men or Masons of so vile and perjured a wretch as I am, who wilfully took the life of so good a man as our Grand Master Hiram Abiff! Ah, Jubela and Jubelo, it was I that struck him harder than you both, it was I that gave him the fatal blow, it was I that killed him outright.' On which they rushed forward, seized, bound and carried them up to the Temple of King Solomon.

Q. What did King Solomon do with them ?

A. He ordered them to be executed agreeable to the several imprecations of their own mouths.

Q. Was the body of our Grand Master Hiram Abiff ever found ?

A. It was. Q. How ?

A. By the Wisdom of King Solomon, who ordered fifteen (in some Lodges they say twelve) Fellow-Crafts to be selected from the bands of the workmen, and sent three East, three West, three North, three South and three in and about the Temple to search for the body.

Q. Where was it found ?

A. Under that sprig of cassia where a worthy brother sat down to rest and refresh himself.

Q. Was there any thing particular took place on the discovery of the body ?

A. There was, viz : on moving the earth till we came to the coffin, we involuntarily found our hands in this position, to guard our nostrils against the offensive effluvia which arose from the grave.

Q. How long had the body lain there ?

A. Fourteen days.

Q. What did they do with the body ?

A. Raised it in a Masonic form and carried it up to the Temple for more decent interment.

Q. Where was it buried ?

A. Under the sanctum sanctorum, or holy of holies of

King Solomon's Temple, over which they erected a marble monument with this inscription delineated thereon. A virgin weeping over a broken column, with a book open before her, in her right hand a sprig of cassia, in her left an urn, Time standing behind her with his hands unfolded in the ringlets of her hair.

Q. What do they denote?

A. The weeping virgin denotes the unfinished state of the Temple, the broken column that one of the principal supports of Masonry had fallen, the book open before her, that his memory was on perpetual record, the sprig of cassia, the timely discovery of his grave, the urn in her left hand, that his ashes are safely deposited under the *sanctum sanctorum* or holy of holies of King Solomon's Temple, and Time standing behind her with his hands infolded in the ringlets of her hair, that time, patience, and perseverance will accomplish all things.

SECTION THIRD.

Q. What does a Master's Lodge represent?

A. The *sanctum sanctorum* or holy of holies of King Solomon's Temple.

Q. How long was the Temple building?

A. Seven years, during which, it rained not in the day time, that the workmen might not be obstructed in their labour.

Q. What supported the Temple?

A. Fourteen hundred and fifty-three columns, and two thousand nine hundred and six Pilasters; all hewn from the finest Parian marble.

Q. What further supported it?

A. Three grand columns, or pillars.

Q. What are they called?

A. Wisdom, strength and beauty.

Q. What did they represent?

A. The pillar of wisdom represented Solomon King of Israel, whose wisdom contrived the mighty fabric; the pillar of strength, Hiram King of Tyre, who strengthened Solomon in his glorious undertaking; the pillar of beauty, Hiram Abiff the widow's son, whose cunning craft and curious workmanship beautified and adorned the Temple.

Q. How many were there employed in the building of King Solomon's Temple.

H2

A. Three Grand Masters, three thousand three hundred Masters, or overseers of the work, eighty thousand Fellow-Crafts, and seventy thousand Entered Apprentices; all those were classed and arranged in such a manner by the wisdom of Solomon, that neither envy, discord, nor confusion were suffered to interrupt that universal peace and tranquility that pervaded the work at that important period.

Q. How many constitutes an Entered Apprentice Lodge?

A. Seven; one Master and six Entered Apprentices.

Q. Where did they usually meet?

A. On the ground floor of King Solomon's Temple.

Q. How many constitutes a Fellow-Craft's Lodge?

A. Five; two Masters and three Fellow-Crafts.

Q. Where did they usually meet?

A. In the middle chamber of King Solomon's Temple.

Q. How many constitutes a Master's Lodge?

A. Three Master Masons.

Q. Where did they usually meet?

A. In the *sanctum sanctorum* or holy of holies of King Solomon's Temple.

Q. Have you any emblems on this degree?

A. We have several which are divided into two classes.

Q. What are the first class?

A. The pot of incense; the bee-hive; the book of constitutions guarded by the Tyler's sword; the sword pointing to a naked heart; the all-seeing eye; the anchor and ark; the forty-seventh problem of Euclid; the hour-glass; the scythe; and the three steps usually delineated on the Master's Carpet, which are thus explained:—The pot of *incense* is an emblem of a pure heart, which is always an acceptable sacrifice to the deity; and as this glows with fervent heat, so should our hearts continually glow with gratitude to the great and beneficent Author of our existence, for the manifold blessings and comforts we enjoy.—The *bee-hive* is an emblem of industry, and recommends the practice of that virtue to all created beings, from the highest seraph in heaven to the lowest reptile of the dust. It teaches us that as we came into the world rational and intelligent beings, so we should ever be industrious ones; never sitting down contented while our fellow creatures around us are in want, when it is in our power to relieve them, without inconvenieuce to ourselves. When we take a survey of nature, we behold man, in his infancy, more helpless and indigent than the brute creation: he lies languishing for days, weeks, months, and years, totally incapable of providing sustenane for himself; of guarding against the attacks of the willd beasts of the field, or shelterig himself trom the inclemencies of the weather. It might have pleased the great Creator of heaven and earth to have made man independent of all other beings; but, as dependence is one of the strongest bonds of society, mankind were made dependent on each other for protection and security, as they thereby enjoy better opportunities of fulfilling the duties of reciprocal love and friendship. Thus was man formed for social and active life, the noblest part of the work of God, and he that will so demean himself as not to be endeavourig to add to the common stock of knowladge and understanding may be deemed a *drone* in the *hive of* nature, a useless member of society, and unworthy of our protection as Masons.—The *book of constitution, guarded by the Tyler's sword*' reminds us that we should be ever watchful and guarded, in our thoughts, words, and actions, particularly when before the enemies of Masonry; ever bearing in rememberance those truly masonic virtues, *silence* and *circumspection*—The *sword, pointing to a naked heart*, demonstrates that justice will sooner or later overtake us; and although our thoughts, words, and actions may be hiden from the eyes of man; yet, that *all-seeing eye*, whom the *sun*, *moon*, and *stars*, obey, and under whose watchful care even comets perform their stupendious revolutions pervades the inmost recesses of the human heart, and will rewwrd us according to our merits.—The *anchor and ark*, are emblems of a well grounded *hope* and a well spent life. They are emblematical of that divine *ark* which safely wafts us over this tempestuous sea of troubles, and that *anchor* which shall safely moor us in a peaceful harbour, where the wicked cease from troubling, and the weary shall fiind rest.—The *forty-seventh problem of Euclid:* This was an invention of our ancient friend and brother, the great Pythagorus, who, in his travels through Asia, Africa, and Europe, was initiated into several orders of priesthoods and raised.

to the sublime degree of a Master Mason. This wise philosophor enriched his mind abundantly in a general knowledge of things, and more especially in geometry, or Masonry: on this subject he drew out many problems and theorems; and among the most distinguished he erected this, which, in the joy of his heart, he called *Eureca*, in the Grecian language signifying, *I have found it;* and upon the discovery of which he is said to have sacrificed a hecatomb. It teaches Masons to be general lovers of the arts and sciences.—The *hour-glass* is an emblem of human life. Behold! how swiftly the sands run, and how rapidly our lives are drawing to a close. We cannot without astonishment behold the little particles which are contained in this machine; how they pass away almost imperceptibly, and yet to our surprise, in the short space of an hour they are all exhausted. Thus wastes man! to-day, he puts forth the tender leaves of hope; to-morrow, blossoms. and bears his blushing honours thick upon him; the next day comes a frost, which nips the shoot, and when he thinks his greatness is still ripening he falls, like autumn leaves to enrich our mother earth.—The *scythe* is an emblem of time, which cuts the brittle thread of life, and launches us into eternity. Behold! what havoc the scythe of time makes among the human race; if by chance we should escape the numerous evils incident to childhood and youth, and with health and vigor arrive to the years of manhood, yet withal we must soon be cut down by the all-devouring scythe of time, and be gathered into the land where our fathers have gone before us.—The *three steps* usually delineated upon the Master's carpet, are emblematical of the three principal stages of human life. viz: youth, manhood and age. In youth, as Entered Apprentices, we ought industriously to occupy our minds in the attainment of useful knowledge: in manhood, as Fellow-Crafts, we should apply our knowledge to the discharge of our respective duties to God, our neighbours and ourselves; that so in age, as Master Masons, we may enjoy the happy reflections consequent on a well spent life, and die in the hope of a glorious immortality.

Q. What are the second class of emblems?

A. The spade, coffin, death-bead, marrow bones, and prig of cassia which are thus explaned; The *spade* opens the vault to receive our bodies where our active limbs will soon moulder to dust.—The *coffin death bed*, and *marrow bones*, are emblematical of the death and burial of our Grand Master Hiram Abiff, and are worthy of our serious attention.—The *sprig of casia* is emblematical of that immortal part of man which never dies—and when the cold winter of death shall have passed, and the bright summer's morn of the resurrection appears, the Son of righteousness shall descend, and send forth his angels to collect our ransomed dust; then, if we are found worthy, by his pass-word, we shall enter into the celestial Lodge above, where the Supreme Architect of the Univers presides, where we shall see the King in the beauty of holiness, and with him enter into an endless eternity.

Here ends the three first degrees of Masonry, which constitute a Master Mason's Lodge. A Master Masson's Lodge and a Chapter of Royal Arch Masons, are two distinct bodies, wholly independent of each other. The members of a Chapter are privileged to visit all Master Marons' Lodges when they please, and may be, and often are members of both at the same time; and all the members of a Master Mason's Lodge who are Royal Arch Masons, though not members of any Chapter, may visit any Chapter. I wish the reader to understrnd that neither all Royal Arch Masons nor Master Masons are members of either Lodge or Chapter: there are tens of thousands who are not members, and scarcely ever attend although priviledged to do so.

A very small proportion of Masons, comparatively speaking, ever advance any further than the third degree, and consequently never get the great word which was lost by Hiram's untimely death. Solomon, king of Israel, Hiram, king of Tyre, and Hiram Abiff, the widow's son, having sworn that they, nor neither of them would ever give the word except they three were present;' [and it is generally believed that there was not another person in the world at that time that had it,] consequently the word was lost, and supposed to be forever; but the sequel will shew it was found after a lapse of four hundred and seventy years, notwithstanding the word *Mah hah bon*, which was substituted by Solomon, still continues to be used by Master Masons, and no doubt will as long as Masonry attracts the attention of men; and the word which was lost is used in the Royal

Arch degree. What was the word of the Royal Arch degree before they found the Master's word which was lost at the death of Hiram Abiff, and was not found for four hundred and seventy years? Was there any Royal Arch Mason's before the Master's word was found?—I wish some masonic gentleman would solve these two questions.

The ceremonies, history, and the lecture, in the preceding degree, are so similar that, perhaps, some one of the three might have been dispensed with, and the subject well understood by most readers, notwithstanding, there is a small difference between the work and history, and between the history and the lecture.

I shall now proceed with the Mark Master's degree which is the first degree in the Chapter. The Mark Master's degree, the Past Master's, and the Most Excellent Master's, are called Lodges of Mark Master Masons, Past Masters, and Most Excellent Masters; yet, although called Lodges, they are a component part of the Chapter. Ask a Mark Master Mason if he belongs to the Chapter, he will tell you he does, but that he has only been marked. It is not an uncommon thing, by any means, for a chapter to confer all four of the degrees in one night, viz; the Mark Master, Past Master, Most Excellent Master; and Royal Arch Degrees.

APPENDIX 2

A Revelation of Free Masonry
(Rochester, New York, 1828)
Facsimile

A

REVELATION

OF

FREE MASONRY,

AS PUBLISHED TO THE WORLD

BY A

CONVENTION OF SECEDING MASONS,

HELD AT

LE ROY, GENESEE COUNTY, N. Y.

ON THE 4TH AND 5TH OF JULY, 1828:

CONTAINING A TRUE AND GENUINE DEVELOPEMENT OF

THE MODE OF INITIATION,

AND ALSO OF THE SEVERAL

LECTURES OF THE FOLLOWING DEGREES:

TO WIT:

IN THE CHAPTER,

MARK MASTER, PAST MASTER, MOST EXCELLENT MASTER, AND ROYAL ARCH.

IN THE ENCAMPMENT,

KNIGHT OF THE RED CROSS, KNIGHT TEMPLAR, KNIGHT OF THE CHRISTIAN MARK, AND GUARDS OF THE CONCLAVE, AND KNIGHTS OF THE HOLY SEPULCHRE.

IN THE ANCIENT COUNCIL OF THE TRINITY,

Denominated the Holy and Thrice Illustrious Order of the Cross,

THE ILLUSTRIOUS, MOST ILLUSTRIOUS, AND THRICE ILLUSTRIOUS DEGREES.

PUBLISHED BY

THE LEWISTON COMMITTEE.

ROCHESTER,

PRINTED BY WEED & HERON.

1828.

A REVELATION OF FREE MASONRY, &c.

FOURTH, OR MARK MASTER'S DEGREE.

Ceremonies used in opening a Lodge of Mark Master Masons.—One rap calls the Lodge to order—one calls up the Junior and Senior Deacons—two raps call up the subordinate officers—and three all the members of the Lodge. The Right Worshipful Master having called the Lodge to order, and all being seated, the Right Worshipful Master says to the Senior Warden, " Brother Junior, are they all Mark Master Masons in the south ?" Junior Warden answers, " they are Right Worshipful." R. W. M. " I thank you brother." R. W. M. " Brother Senior, are they all Mark Master Masons in the west ?" Senior Warden, " they are Right Worshipful." R. W. M. " they are in the east." At the same time gives a rap with the mallet, which calls up both Deacons. R. W. M. " Brother Junior, the first care of a Mason ?" " To see the Lodge Tyled, Right Worshipful." R. W. M. " attend to that part of your duty, and inform the Tyler that we are about to open a Lodge of Mark Master Masons, and direct him to tyle accordingly." Junior Deacon steps to the door and gives four raps, which are answered by four without by the Tyler—the Junior Deacon then gives one, which is answered by the Tyler with one—the door is then partly opened, and the Junior Deacon then delivers his message, and resumes his station, gives the due guard of a Mark Master Mason, and says, " the door is tyled, Right Worshipful." R. W. M. " by whom ?" Junior Deacon, " by a Mark Master Mason without the door, armed with the

B

three raps with the mallet, which calls up all the brethren, takes off his hat and says, "in like manner so do I, strictly prohibiting all profane language, private committees, or any other disorderly conduct, whereby the peace and harmony of this Lodge may be interrupted while engaged in its lawful pursuits, under no less penalty than the bye-laws enjoin, or a majority of the brethren present may see cause to inflict." "Brethren attend to giving the signs." The R. W. M. (all the brethren imitating him) extends his left arm from his body, so as to form an angle of about forty-five degrees, and holds his right hand transversely across his left, the palms thereof about an inch apart. This is called the first sign of a Mason—is the sign of distress in the first degree, and alludes to the position a candidate's hands are placed when he takes the obligation of an Entered Apprentice Mason; he then draws his right hand across his throat, the hand open with his thumb next his throat, drops it down by his side. This is called the due guard of an entered apprentice mason, and alludes to the penal part of the obligation. Next he places the palm of his open right hand upon his left breast, and at the same time throws up his left hand, and so extends his left arm as to form a right angle: from the shoulder to the elbow it is horizontal, from the elbow to the tip of the finger it is perpendicular. This is the sign and due guard of a Fellow Craft Mason, and also alludes to the penal part of the obligations, which is administered in this degree. After this the R. W. M. draws his right hand across his bowels, with his hand open, and the thumb next his body, and drops it down by his side. This is the sign or due guard of a master mason, and like the others allude to the penalty of this degree. He then throws up the grand hailing sign of distress: this is given by raising both hands and arms to the elbows perpendicularly, one on each side of the head, the elbows forming a square, his arms then drop by his side, he then clutches the third and little fingers of his right hand, with his thumb extends at the same time his middle and fore fingers, brings up his hand in such a manner as to have the side of the middle finger touch the rim of the right ear, then lets it drop, and as it falls brings the outward side of the little finger of the left hand across the wrist of the right, then lets them fall by his sides. This is the sign or due guard of a Mark Master Mason, and also alludes to the penal part of the obligation in this degree. Here it is proper to remark that in the opening of any Lodge of Masons, they commence giving the signs of an Entered Apprentice, and go through all the signs of the different degrees in regular gradation until they arrive to the one which they are opening, and commence at the sign of the degree in which they are at work, and descend to the last when closing. After going through all the signs as above described, the R. W. M. declares the Lodge opened in the following manner :—"I now declare this Lodge of Mark Master Masons duly opened for the despatch of business ;" the Senior Warden declare it to the Junior Warden, and he to the brethren. The R. W. M. then repeats a charge : " Wherefore, brethren, lay aside all malice and guile," &c. &c. [Monitor, page 76.]

The Lodge being opened and ready for business, the R. W. M. directs the Secretry to read the minutes of the last meeting, which generally brings to view the business of the present. If there are any candidates to be brought forward, that is generally the first business. A Master Mason wishing for further light in Masonry, sends a petition to the Chapter, and requests to be advanced to the honorary degree of Mark Master Mason : if there is no serious objection to the petition it is entered on the minutes, & a committee of several appointed to enquire into his character and report to the next regular communication : at that time, if the committee report in his favor and no serious objection is made against him otherwise, a motion is made that the ballot pass ; if carried, the Deacons pass the ballot boxes : these boxes are the same as in the preceding degrees. When the balls are received the box is presented to the Right Worshipful Master, Senior and Junior Wardens. R. W. M. "clear in the west brother Senior ?" S. W. "clear R. W." R. W. M. " clear in the south brother Junior ?" J. W. " clear Right Worshipful." R. W. M. says, " clear in the east." This being the case the candidate is accepted, but if there is one black ball in that end of the box which has the white tube, and the Senior Warden pronouncing " not clear" all stop, and inquiry is made, and the ballot passes again, and if blacked a third time the candidate is

B3

rejected. It being otherwise, the Senior Deacon, who is the candidate's cunductor, passes out of the Lodge into the adjoining room, where the candidate is in waiting, and there the conductor is furnished with a small oblong square, six inches long—the candidate is presented with a large white marble key stone, weighing probably twenty pounds, and is ordered by his conductor to take it by the little end, between his first and second fingers and thumb of his right hand. The door is then opened without ceremony, and they pass directly to the Junior Overseer's station at the south gate, which is nothing more than the Junior Warden's seat, and the conductor gives four raps with his block of timber on a pedestal in front of the Senior Overseer's station. J. O. "who comes here?" Conductor, "two brother Fellow-craft, with materials for the temple." J. O. "have you a specimen of your labor?" Conductor, "I have." J. O. "present it." The Conductor then presents the piece of timber before described: the Junior Warden receives it, and applys a small trying square to its different angles, and they agreeing with the angles of the square, he says, "this is good work, square work, such work as we are authorized to receive." Returns the block of timber, and turning his eye upon the candidate, asks, "who is this you have with you?" Conductor. "A Brother Fellow-craft." J. O. "have you a specimen of your labor." Con. "I have." J. O. "present it." The candidate then presents the key stone, the Junior Overseer receives it, and applies his square to all its angles, and they not agreeing with the angles of the square, he says, "what have you here brother? this is neither an oblong nor a square, neither has it the regular mark of the craft upon it, but from its singular form and beauty I am unwilling to reject it; pass on to the Senior Overseer, at the west gate for further inspection." They then pass on to the Senior Overseer's station at the west gate, which is the Senior Warden's seat, and gives four raps as before on the pedestal, which stands in front of the Senior Overseer. S. O. "who comes here?" Con. "two brother Fellow-crafts with materials for the the temple." Have you a specimen of your labor?" Con. "I have." S. O. "present it." The Conductor as before presents the block of timber, the Senior

Overseer applies his square to it, and finding it agrees with the angles of his square, says, "this is good work, square work, such work as we are authorized to receive: who is this you have with you?" Con. "a brother Fellow-Craft." S. O. "have you a specimen of your labour?" Con. "I have." S. O. "present it." The candidate then presents the key stone, and he applies it, but not fitting, he says, "this is neither an oblong nor a square, neither has it the regular mark of the craft upon it: it is a curious wrought stone, and on account of its singular form and beauty I am unwilling to reject it: pass on to the Master Overseer at the east gate for further inspection." They pass to his station at the east gate and give four raps. Master Overseer, "who comes here?" Conductor, "two Brethren Fellow Crafts with their materials for the temple." M. Overseer, "have you a specimen of your labor?" Con. "I have." M. Overseer, "present it." The conducter presents his billet of wood to him, and he applies his square to it, and like the other Overseer says, "this is good work, square work, such work as we are authorized to receive: who is this you have with you?" Candidate, "a brother Fellow Craft." M. Overseer, "have you a specimen of your labor?" Can. "I have." M. O. "present it." (It ought here to be remarked that when the candidate is presented with the key stone, and takes it between his thumb and two fingers it hangs suspended by his side, and he is requested to carry his work plumb, and the conducter taking good care to see that he does it, by the time he arrives at the Master Overseer's station at the east gate, and when the Master Overseer says, "present it," the candidate is extremely willing to hand over the key stone to him for inspection, for by this time it becomes very painful to hold any longer the stone which he has in charge. The Master Overseer having received the key stone, he applies his square to the different angles of it, and being found not to be square, he like the the other Overseer says, "this is neither an oblong nor a square, neither has it the regular mark of the craft upon it." He then looks sternly upon the candidate and demands, "is this your work?" Can. "it is not." M. Overseer, "is this your mark?" Can. "it is not." M. O. "where did you get it?" Can. "I pick-

B4

ed it up in the quarry." M. O. "picked it up in the quarry? this explains the matter: what! been loitering away your your time this whole week and now brought up another man's work to impose upon the Grand Overseers? this deserves the severest punishment; (motions the candidate to stand aside,) "Brothers Junior and Senior Overseers here is work brought up for inspection which demands a council." The Junior, Senior and Master Overseers then assemble in council. M. Overseer, presenting the stone, "did a Fellow Craft present this to you for inspection Brother Junior?" J. Overseer, "a Fellow Craft came to my office and presented this stone for inspection: I examined it and found it was neither an oblong nor a square, nor neither had it the regular mark of the craft upon it, but on account of is singular form and beauty I was unwilling to reject it, and ordered it to the Senior Overseeer at the west gate for further inspection." M. Overseer, "Brother Senior was this stone presented to you for inspection?" Senior Overseer, "It was—I know of no use for it in the temple—I tried it with the square, and observed it was neither an oblong nor a square, neither had it the regular mark of the craft upon it, but on account of its singular form and beauty I was unwilling to reject it, and therefore directed it to the Master Overseer at the east gate for further inspection." M. Overseer, "it was also presented to me for inspection, but I do not know of any use which it can be in the building." Sen. Overseer, "I know of no use for it." Jun. Overseer, "I know of no use for it." M. Overseer, "Brother Senior what shall we do with it?" S Overseer, "heave it over among the rubbish." the Master and Senior Overseers then take the stone between them, and after waving it backward and forward four times they heave it over in such a manner that the one letting go while the stone is arriving at the highest point it brings the stone in a quarterly direction over the other's left shoulder: the Junior Overseer being stationed in a suitable position at this moment receives the stone, and carries it away into the preparation room. R. W. M. "Brother Senior Warden assemble the craft to receive wages." At this command the brethren all arise and form a procession single file: the candidate is placed at the head of the procession and when stationed is told that "the last shall be first and the first last." The procession being formed they commence singing the following song: "Mark Masters all appear," &c. (see Monitor pa e 82) and at the same time commence a circular march (against the course of the sun) around the room, giving all the signs during their march, beginning with that of Entered Apprentice, and ending at that cf Mark Master. They are given in the following manner: the first revolution each Brother when opposite the R. W. M. gives the first sign in Masonry. The second revolution when opposite the Master the second, and so on until they give all the signs to that of Mark Master. While this ceremony is going on in the Lodge the Senior Grand Warden procures a sufficient number of cents and passes into the preparation room and opens a lattice window in the door which communicates to the lodge room, and when the craftsmen arrive to the Mark Master Mason's sign each one of them in their last revolution puts his hand through the window in the door and gives a token, (this is given by shutting the third and little fingers, extending the four and middle fingers, and placing the thumb over them in a suitable manner to receive the penny or cent,) and receives a penny or cent from the S. G. W. Matters are so timed in the march that when they come to that part of the song which says "caution them to beware of the right hand," it comes the turn of the candidate to put his hand through the aperture of the door and receive his penny, but not being able to give the token he is detected as an imposter, and the S. G. W. instead of giving him his penny seizes him by the hand and draws his arm full length through the door and holds him securely, exclaiming at the same time an imposter! an imposter! Others who are in the room with the S. G. W. cry out, "chop off his hand! chop off his his hand!" At this moment the conducter steps to the candidate and intercedes warmly in his behalf. Con. "spare him! spare him!" S. G. Warden. "he is an imposter. He has attempted to receive wages without being able to give the token. The penalty must be inflicted." Con. "he is a Brother Fellow Craft, and on condition that you will release him I will be responsible that he shall be taken before the Right Worshipful Master, where all the circum-

B5

stances shall be made known and if he condemns him I will see that the penalty is inflicted." S. G. Warden, "on these conditions I release him." The candidate is released and taken before the R. W. Master. Con. "this young Fellow Craft has brought up work for inspection which was not his own, and has attempted to receive wages for it; he was detected at the Senior Grand Warden's apartment as an imposter, and I became responsible on condition of his release that he should appear before the R. W. and if after a fair trial you should pronounce him guilty, that I should see the penalty of an impostor inflicted upon him." R. W. M. "Brother Jnnior Overseer did this man bring up work to your station for inspection?" J. Overseer. "he did. I inspected it, and observed that it was neither an oblong nor a square, neither had it the regular mark of the craft upon it, but on account of its singular form and beauty I was unwilling to reject it, therefore I ordered it passed to the Senior Overseer's station at the west gate for further inspection." R. W. M. "Brother Senior Overseer, did this young man bring up work to you for inspection?" S. O. "he did, and I for similar reasons offered by Brother Junior Overseer, was unwilling to reject it, and ordered it passed on to the Master Overseer at the east gate for further inspection." R. W. M. "Brother Master Overseer, did this young man bring up work to you for inspection?" "He did. I inspected the work, and observed that it was neither an oblong nor a square, neither had it the regular mark of the craft upon it: I then asked him if it was his work. He admitted that it was not. I asked him where he got it? he said he picked it up in the quarry. I rebuked him severely for his attempt to impose upon the Grand Overseers, and for loitering away his time, and then bringing up an other man's work for inspection. I then called a council of my Brother Overseers, and we knowing no use for the work hove it over among the rubbish." R. W. M. "Senior Grand Warden, did the young man attempt to receive wages at your apartment." S. G. W. "he did, and I detected him as an imposter, and was about to inflict the penalty, but the conductor becoming responsibe that if I would release him he would see the imposter taken before the R. W. and if found guilty that the penalty should be inflicted, I released him." R. W. M. "young man, it appears that you have been loitering away your time this whole week, and have now brought up another man's work for inspection, to impose upon the Grand Overseers, and what is more you have attempted to receive wages for labour which you never performed: conduct like this deserves prompt punishment. The penalty of an imposter is that of having his right hand chopped off. This young man appears as though he deserved a better fate, and as though he might be serviceable in the building of the temple. Are you a Fellow Craft? Candidate—I am. R. W. M. "can you give us any proof of it?" Candidate gives the sign of a Fellow Craft. R. W. M. "he is a fellow craft. Have you ever been taught how to receive wages?" Candidate, "I have not." R. W. M. "this serves in a measure to mitigate his crime. If you are instructed how to receive wages will you do better in future, and never again attempt to impose on the Grand Overseers, and above all never attempt to receive wages for labour which you never performed?" Candidate—I will. R. W. M. "the penalty is remitted." The candidate is then taken into the preparation room, and divested of his outward apparel and all money and valuables, his breast bare, and a cable tow four times round his body, in which condition he is conducted to the door, when the conductor gives four distinct knocks, upon the hearing of which the Senior Warden says to the R. W. "while we are peaceably at work on the fourth degree of Masonry, the door of our Lodge appears to be alarmed." R. W. M. "Brother Junior, see the cause of that alarm." The J. W. then steps to the door and answers the alarm by four knocks, the conductor and himself each giving another: the door is then partly opened, and the Junior Warden then asks, "who comes there?" Conductor, "a worthy brother, who has been regularly initiated as an Entered Apprentice Mason, served a proper time at such, passed to the degree of fellow craft, raised to the sublime degree of a master mason, and now wishes further light in Masonry by being advanced to the more honorable degree of mark master mason." J. W. "is it of his own free will and accord he makes this request?" Conductor, "it is." J. W. "is he duly and truly prepared?" Conductor—he is. J. W. "has he wrought in the quarry, and exhibited specimens of his skill in the preceding degrees?" J. W.—He has. J. W. "by what further right or benefit does he expect to obtain this favor?" J. W. "by the benefit of a pass word." R. W. M. "has he a pass word?" J. W. "he has not, but I have it for him." J. W. "give it me." J. W. (whispers in his ear) "JOPPA." J. W. "the pass word is right. You will let him wait until the R. W. M. is made acquainted with his request, and his answer returned." The Junior Warden returns him to the R. W. M. where the same questions are asked and answers returned, as at the door. The R. W. M. then says, "since he comes endowed with the necessary qualifications, let him enter in the name of the Lord, and take heed on what he enters. (Previous to the candidate's entering, one of the brethren who is best qualified for the station is selected and furnished with an engraving chisel and mallet, and placed near the door, so that when the candidate enters, it is on the edge of an engraving chisel, under the pressure of the mallet. As this is the business of no particular officer, we have for convenience styled him executioner.) Brother, it becomes my duty to put a mark on you, and such a one, too, as you will probably carry to your grave." Places the edge of the chisel near his left breast, and makes several motions with the mallet, as though he was about to strike upon the head of the chisel. Executioner, "this is a painful undertaking: I do not feel able to perform it," (turning to the R. W. M.) R. W. "this task is too painful: I feel that I cannot perform it: I wish the R. W. would select some other brother to perform it in my stead." R. W. M. "I know the task is unpleasant, and a painful one; but as you have undertaken to perform it, unless some other brother will volunteer his service and take your place, you must proceed." Executioner, "Brother, (calling the name) will you volunteer your service, and take my place?" Brother, "I cannot consent to do it," (after several solicitations and refusals.) Executioner, R. W. "no brother feels willing to volunteer his services, and I declare I feel unwilling and unable to perform it." R. W. M. "as no brother feels disposed to take your station, it becomes your duty to perform it yourself." Executioner, (taking his station,) "Brethren, support the candidate, (several take hold of the candidate,) Brother (naming some physician or surgeon) will you assist?" Doctor, (stepping up,) "Brethren, it becomes necessary that we have a bowl or some other vessel to receive the blood." A bowl is presented, having the appearance of blood upon it, and is held in a suitable position to receive the blood: the surgeon places his fingers on the left breast of the candidate, and gives council where it would be advisable to inflict the wound. The executioner then places the edge of the chisel near the spot, and draws back the mallet, and while making several false motions says, "operative masons make use of the engraving chisel and mallet to cut, hew, carve and indent their work; but we, as free and accepted masons, make use of them for the more noble and glorious purpose—we use them to cut, hew, carve, and indent the mind," giving, at the instant the last word is pronounced, a severe blow with the mallet upon the head of a chisel without the least injury to the candidate. The candidate is then conducted four times round the Lodge, and each time as he passes the station of the Master, Senior, and Junior Wardens, they each give one loud rap with their mallet: the Master in the mean time reads the following passages of scripture—Psalm 118, 22. "The stone which the builders refused is become the head stone of the corner." Math. 21, 42, "Did ye never read in the scriptures the stone which the builders rejected is become the head of the corner." Luke 20, 17, "What is this then that is written! The stone which the builders rejected, is become the head of the corner?" Acts 4, 11, "This is the stone which was set at nought of your builders, which has become the head of the corner." The reading of them is so timed as to be completed just as the candidate arrives at the Junior Warden's post: here he stops, and the same questions are asked, and answers returned, as at the door: the same passes at the Senior Warden and Master, who orders the candidate to be conducted back to the Senior Warden in the west, by him to be taught to approach the east, by four upright regular steps, his feet forming a square, and body erect at the altar: the candidate then kneels and receives the obligation, as follows:—

"I, A, B, of my own free will and accord, in presence of Almighty God, and this Right Worshipful Lodge of Mark Master Masons, do hereby and hereon, in addition to my former obligations, most solemnly and sincerely promise and swear that I will not give the degree of a Mark Master Mason to any one of an inferior degree, nor to any other person in the known world, except it be to a true and lawful brother or brethren of this degree, and not unto him nor unto them, whom I shall hear so to be, but unto him and them only whom I shall find so to be after strict trial and due examination, or lawful information given: Furthermore, do I promise and swear that I will support the constitution of the General Grand Royal Arch Chapter of the United States of America, also the Grand Royal Arch Chapter of this State, under which this Lodge is held, and conform to all the bye-laws, rules, and regulations of this or any other Lodge of Mark Master Masons, of which I may at any time hereafter become a member: Furthermore, do I promise and swear, that I will obey all regular signs and summonses given, handed, sent, or thrown to me from the hand of a brother mark master mason, or from the body of a just and legally constituted Lodge of such, provided it be within the length of my cable tow: Furthermore, do I promise and swear, that I will not wrong this Lodge, or a brother of this degree, to the value of his wages, (or one penny) myself knowingly, nor suffer it to be done by others if in my power to prevent it: Furthermore, do I promise and swear, that I will not sell, swap, barter, or exchange my mark, which I shall hereafter choose, nor send it a second time to pledge until it is lawfully redeemed from the first: Furthermore, do I promise and swear, that I will receive a brother's mark when offered to me requesting a favor and grant him his request if in my power, and if it is not in my power to grant his request I will return him his mark with the value thereof which is half a shekel of silver, or quarter of a dollar. To all of which I do most solemnly and sincerely promise and swear, with a fixed and steady purpose of mind in me to keep and perform the same, binding myself under no less penalty than to have my right ear smote off, that I may forever be unable to hear the word, and my right hand chopped off as the penalty as an imposter, if I should ever prove willfully guilty of violating any part of this my solemn oath or obligation of a Mark Master Mason. So help me God, and make me stedfast to keep and perform the same. Detach your hand and kiss the book."

The Master then produces the same key stone concerning which so much has already been said, and says to the candidate, "we read in a passage of scripture, Rev. 2--17. "to him that overcometh will I give to eat of the hidden manna, and give him a white stone and in the stone a new name written which no man knoweth save him that receiveth it." He then presents the stone to the candidate and says, "I now present you with a white stone on which is written a new name; we give the words that form this circle (the letters are so engraved on the stone as to form a circle) are the initials H. T. W. S. S. T. K. S. Hiram Tyran Widow's Son, sent to King Solomon. These placed in this form were the mark of our Grand Master Hiram Abiff. At present they are used as the general *mark* of this degree, and in the centre of them each brother places his own individual *mark*." The stone is then removed and the candidate still remains on his knees at the altar, the Master then takes the jewel containing his Mark from his neck and presents it to the candidate—requests of him some favor, such as the loan of five, ten, or twenty dollars. The candidate having left all his money and valuables in the preparation room, answers, "I cannot do it, I have no money about me:" and offers to return the *mark* to the Master, but he refuses to take it, and says to the candidate, "have you not just sworn that you will receive a Btrother Mark Master's mark when offered to you requesting a favor, and if not in your power to grant the favor, you would return him his mark with the value of it? is this the way you mind your obligations? Here I presented my mark with a request for a small favor; you say you cannot grant it, and offer to return my *mark* alone? Where is the quarter of a dollar you have sworn to return with it?" The candidate much embarrassed, answers, "I cannot do even that. I have no money about me. It was all taken from me in the preparation room." The Master asks, "are you quite sure you have none?" Candidate answers, "I am: it is all in the other room." Master, "you have not examined: perhaps some friend has in pity to your destitute situation supplied you with that amount unknown to yourself: feel in all your pockets, and if you find after a thorough search that you have really none, we shall have less reason to think that you meant wilfully to violate your obligation." The candidate examines his pockets and finds a quarter of a dollar, which some brother had slily placed there: this adds not a little to his embarrassment: he protests he had no intention of concealing it: really supposed he had none about him, and hands it to the Master with his mark. The Master receives it and says to the candidate, "Brother, let this scene be a striking lesson to you should you ever hereafter have a mark presented you by a worthy brother asking a favor; before you deny him make diligent search, and be quite sure of your inability to serve him: perhaps you will then find as in the present instance that some unknown person has befriended you, and you are really in a better situation than you think yourself." The candidate then rises and is made acquainted with the grips, words, and signs of this degree. The pass grip of this degree is made by extending the right arms and clasping the fingers of the right hands as one would naturally do to assist another up a steep ascent: the pass word is "Joppa:" the real grip is made by locking the little fingers of the right hand, bringing the knuckles together, placing the ends of the thumbs against each other: the word is, "Mark well." The signs have been described. After the grips, words and signs are given and explained, [see lectures] the Master says, "Brother, I now present you with the tools of a mark master, (here he points them out in the carpet, or in the chart,) which are the chisel and mallet: they are thus explained; the chisel morally demonstrates the advantages of discipline and education; the mind like the diamond in its original state, is rude and unpolished, but as the effect of the chisel on the external coat soon presents to view the latent beauties of the diamond, so education discovers the latent beauties of the mind, and draws them forth to range the large field of matter and space, to display the summit of human knowledge, our duty to God and man. The mallet morally teaches to correct irregularities, and to reduce man to a proper level, so that by quiet deportment, he may in the school of discipline, learn to be content. What the mallet is to the workmen, enlightened reason is to the passions; it curbs ambition, it depresses envy, it moderates anger, and it encourages good dispositions, whence arises among good Masons that comely order,

"Which nothing earthly gives, or can destroy,
The soul's calm sunshine, and the heartfelt joy."

The W. Master then delivers the following charge to the candidate, which completes the ceremony of advancement to this degree. [For the charge, see Monitor.]

CEREMONY OF CLOSING A LODGE OF MARK MASONS.

The Worshipful Master says, "Brother Junior Warden, assemble the brethren, and form procession for the purpose of closing the Lodge." The brethren then assemble and commence a circular march, singing the song, "Mark Masters all appear," [see Webb's Monitor, page 82,] with the same ceremony as described in another part of this degree. After the song is completed, the brethren compare the wages they have received, and finding that all have received alike, (one penny or cent) they begin to murmur among themselves, some pretending to think they ought to have more, as they have done all the labour—they finally throw down their wages upon the altar, declaring if they cannot be dealt justly with, they will have none. The Worshipful Master calls to order, and demands the cause of the confusion. Some brother answers, "Worshpful, we are not satisfied with the manner of paying the workmen; for we find for those who have done nothing, and even the candidate just received, is paid just as much as we, who have borne the heat and burden of the day. Master says, "it is perfectly right." Brother, "it cannot be right—it is very unreasonable." Master, "hear what the law says on this subject." He then reads the following parable, Mat. xx. 1, 16: "For the kingdom of heaven is like unto a man that is a householder, which went out early in the morning to hire labourers into his vineyard. And when he had agreed with the labourers for a penny a day, he sent them into his vineyard; and he went out about the third hour, and saw others standing idle in the market-place, and said unto them, go ye also into the vineyard; and whatsoever is right, I will give you; and they went their way. Again he went out about the sixth and ninth hour, and did likewise. And about the eleventh hour he went out, and found others standing idle, and saith unto them, why stand ye here all the day idle? They say into him, because no man hath hired us. He saith unto them, go ye also into the vineyard; and whatsoever is right, that shall ye receive. So when evening was come, the lord of the vineyard saith unto the steward, call the labourers, and give them their hire, beginning from the last unto the first. And when they came that were hired about the eleventh hour, they received every man a penny. But when the first came, they supposed they should have received more; and they likewise received every man a penny. And when they had received it, they murmured against the good man of the house, saying, these last have wrought but one hour, and thou hast made them equal unto us, which have borne the burden and heat of the day. But he answered one of them and said, friend, I do thee no wrong; didst thou not agree with me for a penny? Take that thine is, and go thy way; I will give unto this last, even as unto thee. Is it not lawful for me to do what I will with mine own? is thine eye evil because I am good? so the last shall be first, and the first last; for many be called, but few chosen." [We leave it for the public to judge, with what consistency King Solomon in his day, could introduce a passage of the New Testament, written long after, to settle a dispute arising among his workmen. They will observe that many passages of the New Testament are introduced in this and the following degrees, pretended to have been organized at the building of the Temple. We make no comments.] The brethren then declare themselves satisfied; the signs are given from Mark Master down to the Entered Apprentice, and the Master declares the Lodge closed.

Lectures on 4th, or Mark Master's degree.

SECTION FIRST.

Q. Are you a Mark Master Mason? A. I am: try me. Q. By what will you be tried? A. By the engraving chisel and mallet. Q. Why by the engraving chisel and mallet? A. Because they are the proper masonic implements of this degree. Q. On what was the degree founded? A. On a certain key stone which belonged to the principal arch of King Solomon's Temple. Q. Who formed this key stone? A. Our Worthy Grand Master Hiram Abiff. Q. What were the preparatory steps relative to your advancement to this degree? A. I was caused to represent one of the fellow-craft at the building of King Solomon's Temple, whose custom it was on the eve of every sixth day, to carry up their work for inspection. Q. Why was you caused to represent these fellow-crafts? A. Because, our worthy Grand Master Hiram Abiff had completed this key stone agreeable to the original plan, and before he gave orders to have it carried up to the Temple, was slain by three ruffians, as already represented in the preceding degrees; and it so happened that on the eve of a certain sixth day, as the craft were carrying up work for inspection, a young Fellow Craft discovered this stone in the quarry, and from its singular form and beauty, supposed it belonged to some part of the Temple, carried it up for inspection. Q. Who inspected it? A. The Grand Overseers, placed at the East, West and South gates. Q. How did they inspect it? A. On its being presented to the Junior Overseer at the south gate, he observed it was neither an oblong or a square, neither had it the regular mark of the craft upon it, but from its singular form and beauty was unwilling to reject it, therefore ordered it to be passed to the Junior Overseer at the west gate for further inspection, who for similar reasons suffered it to pass to the Master Overseer at the east gate, who held a consultation with his brother overseers, and they observed, as before, that it was neither an oblong or square, neither had it the regular mark of the craft upon it, and neither of them being Mark Master Masons, supposed it of no use in the building, and hove it over among the rubbish. Q. How many fellow crafts were there engaged at the building of the temple? A. Eighty thousand. Q. Were not the Master Overseers liable to be imposed upon by receiving bad work from the hands of such a vast number of workmen? A. They were not Q. How was this imposition prevented? A. By the wisdom of King Solomon, who wisely ordered that the craftsmen who worked should choose him a particular mark and place it upon all his work, by which it was known and distinguished when carried up to the building, and if approved, to receive wages. Q. What was the wages of a Fellow Craft ? A. A penny a day. Q. Who paid the craftsmen ? A. The Senior Grand Warden. Q. Was not the Senior Grand Warden liable to be imposed upon by impostors in paying off such a vast number of workmen ? A. He was not. Q. How was this imposition prevented ? A. By the wisdom of King Solomon, who also ordered that every craftsman applying to receive wages should present his right hand through a lattice window of the door of the Junior Grand Warden's apartment with a copy of his mark in the palm thereof, at the same time giving a token. Q. What was that token ? (This was before explained.) Q. What did it allude to ? A. To the manner of receiving wages, it was also to distinguish a true craftsman from an impostor. Q. What is the penalty on an impostor ? A. To have his right hand chopped off.

SECTION SECOND.

Q. Where was you prepared to be made a Mark Master Mason ? A. In the room adjoining the body of a just and lawfully constituted Lodge of such, duly assembled in a room or place representing a work-shop that was erected near the ruins of King Solomon's Temple. Q. How was you prepared ? A. By being divested of my outward apparel and all money, my breast bare, with a cable-tow four times about my body, in which situation I was conducted to the door of a Lodge, where I gave four distinct knocks. Q. What do these four distinct knocks allude to ? A. To the fourth degree of Masonry ; it being on that which I was about to enter. Q. What was said to you from without ? A. Who comes there ? Q. Your answer ? A. A worthy brother, who has been regularly initiated as an Entered Apprentice, served a proper time as such, passed to the Fellow Craft, raised to the sublime degree of a Master Mason, and now wishes further light in Masonry, by being advanced to the more honorable degree of a Mark Master Mason. Q. What further was said to you from within ? A. I was asked if it was of my own free will and accord I made this request, if I was duly and truly prepared, worthy and well qualified, had wrought in the quarries, and exhibited specimens of my skill and proficiency in the preceding degrees, all of which being answered in the affirmative, I was asked by what further right or benefit I expected to gain this favor. Q. Your answer? A. By the benefit of a pass word. Q. What was that pass word? A. *Joppa*. Q. What did it allude to? A. The city of Joppa, the place where the materials were landed for building King Solomon's Temple, after being prepared in the forest of Lebanon, and carried there on floats, (by sea.) [Masonic tradition informs us that the banks of this place are so perpendicular that it was impossible to ascend them without assistance from above, which was effected by brethren stationed there, with this strong grip, (this has been explained,) which, together with the word *Joppa*, has since been adopted as a proper pass to be given before entering any well regulated Lodge of Mark Master Masons.] Q. What further was said to you from within? A. I was bid to wait till the Right Worshipful Master in the east was made acquainted with my request, and his answer returned. Q. When his answer was returned, what followed? A. I was caused to enter the Lodge. Q. On what did you enter? A. On the edge of the engraving chisel, under the pressure of the mallet, which was to demonstrate the moral precepts of this degree, and make a deep and lasting impression on my mind and conscience. Q. How was you then disposed of? A. I was conducted four times regularly round the Lodge, and halted at the Junior Warden's in the south, where the same questions were asked, and answers returned as at the door. Q. How did the Junior Warden dispose of you? A. He ordered me to be conducted to the Senior Warden in the west, where the same questions were asked, and the same answers returned, as before. Q. How did the Senior Warden dispose of you? A. He ordered me to be conducted to the Right Worshipful Master in the east, where the same questions were asked, and answers returned, as before; who likewise demanded of me from whence I came, and whither I was travelling. Q. Your answer? A. From the west, and travelling to the east. Q. Why do you leave the west and travel to the

C2

east? A. In search of light. Q. How did the Right Worshipful Master dispose of you? A. He ordered me to be conducted back to the west from whence I came, and put in the care of the Senior Warden, who taught me how to approach the east, the place of light, by advancing upon four upright regular steps, to the fourth step, my feet forming a square, and my body erect at the altar, before the Right Worshipful Master. Q. What did the Right Worshipful Master do with you? A. He made a Mark Master Mason of me. Q. How? A. In due form. Q. What was that due form? A. Both knees bent, they forming a square; both my hands on the holy bible, square, and compass, my body being erect; in which posture I took upon me the solemn oath or obligation of a Mark Master Mason. Q. Have you that oath or obligation? A. I have. Q. Will you give it me? A. I will with your assistance. [Here, as in the preceding degree, you repeat after the Right Worshipful Master, I, A. B. &c. See obligation, page 14.] Q. After your oath or obligation what follows? A. Information was brought that the Temple was almost completed, but the craft was all in confusion for want of a certain key stone, which none of them had been instrumental to make. Q. What followed? A. King Solomon believing in confidence that our worthy Grand Master Hiram Abiff had completed this key stone agreeable to the original plan, ordered enquiry to be made among the Master Overseers, if a stone bearing a particular mark had been presented to them for inspection; and on enquiry being made it was found that there had. Q. What followed? A. King Solomon ordered search to be made for the stone, when it was found, and afterwards applied to its intended use. Q. What color was the stone? A. White. Q. What did it allude to? A. To a passage in scripture where it says, "To him that overcometh will I give to eat of the hidden manna, and I will give him a white stone, and in the stone a new name written, which no man knoweth saving him that receiveth." Q. What was that new name. A. The letters on the stone and the initials of the words for which they stand, viz—H. T. W. S. S. T. K. S. Q. Of what use is this new name to you in Masonry? A. It was the original mark of our worthy Grand Master Hiram Abiff, and is the general mark of this degree, and the letters form the circle in the centre, of which every brother of this degree places his particular mark, to which his obligation alludes. *Q.* What followed? A. I was more fully instructed with the secrets of this degree. *Q.* Of what do they consist? A. Of signs and tokens. *Q.* Have you a sign? A. I have. *Q.* What is it called? A. Heave over. *Q.* What does it allude to? A. To the manner of heaving over work that the overseers said was unfit for the Temple; also the manner the key-stone was hove over. *Q.* Have you any other sign? A. I have, (at the same time giving it.) *Q.* What is that? A. The due guard of a Mark Master Mason. *Q.* What does it allude to? A. To the penalty of my obligation, which is, that my right ear should be smote off, that I might forever be unable to hear the word, and my right hand be chopped off, as the penalty of an impostor, if I should ever prove wilfully guilty of revealing any part of my obligation. *Q.* Have you any further sign? A. I have. *Q.* What is that? A. The grand sign or sign of distress. *Q.* What does it allude to? A. To the manner fellow-crafts carry their work up to the temple for inspection; also the manner I was taught to carry my work on my advancement to this degree. *Q.* Have you any other sign? A. I have not, but I have a token, (gives it to him.) *Q.* What is this? A. The pass grip of a Mark Master Mason. *Q.* What is the name of it. A. "JOPPA." *Q.* What does it allude to? A The city of *Joppa*. *Q.* Have you any other token? A. I have. *Q.* What is this? A. The real grip of a Mark Master Mason. *Q.* What is the name of it? A. *Mark well.* *Q.* What does it allude to? A. To a passage of scripture where it says, "Then he brought me back the way of the gate of the outward sanctuary, which looketh toward the east, and it was shut; and the Lord said unto me, son of man, mark well, and behold with thine eyes, and hear with thine ears, all that I say unto thee concerning all the ordinances of the house of the Lord, and the laws thereof, and mark well the entering in of the house with every going forth of the sanctuary." *Q.* Who founded this degree? A. Our three ancient Grand Masters, viz—Solomon King of Israel, Hyram King of Tyre, and Hyram Abiff. *Q.* Why was it founded? A. Not only as an ho-

C3

norary reward to be conferred on all who have proved themselves meritorious in the preceding degrees, but to render it impossible for a Brother to suffer for the immediate necessities of life, when the price of his mark will procure them. *Q.* A Brother pledging his mark, and asking a favor, who does he represent? A. Our worthy Grand Master Hiram Abiff, who was a poor man, but on account of his great skill and mysterious conduct at the building of King Solomon's Temple, was most eminently distinguished. *Q.* A Brother receiving a pledge, and granting a favor, whom does he represent? A. King Solomon, who was a rich man, but renowned for his benevolence.

THE PAST MASTER'S DEGREE.

This degree is very simple, although Monitor writers say much about it. It is necessary that a Master Mason should take this degree, before he can constitutionally preside over a Lodge of Master Masons, as Master of it, and when a Master Mason is elected Master of a Lodge, who has not previously received the Past Master's degree, it is then confered upon him, often without any other ceremonies than that of administering the obligation.

This Lodge is opened and closed in the same manner that the Lodges of the first three degrees are: the candidate petitions, and is balloted for in the same manner, but he is received into the Lodge in a very different manner. He is conducted into the Lodge without any previous preperation, when the presiding officer rises and says, "Brethren, it is inconvenient for me to serve you any longer as Master of this Lodge. I wish you would select some other brother for that purpose." The candidate is nominated, the usual forms of ballotting for officers are then dispensed with, and a vote of the Lodge is taken by yeas and nays. The candidate is elected, and generally refuses to serve, but he is eventually prevailed on to accept, whereupon the presiding officer addresses the Master elect in the words following, viz. "Brother, previous to your investiture, it is necessary that you assent to those ancient charges and regulations, which point out the duty of a Master of a Lodge.

1. You agree to be a good man, and true, and strictly to obey the moral law.

2. You agree to be a peaceable subject, and cheerfully to conform to the laws of the country in which you reside.

3. You promise not to be concerned in any plots or conspiracies against government; but patiently to submit to the decisions of the supreme legislature.

4. You agree to pay a proper respect to the civil magistrate, to work diligently, live creditably, and act honorably by all men.

5. You agree to hold in veneration the orginal rules and patrons of Masonry, and their regular successors, supreme and subordinate, according to their stations, and to submit to the awards and resolutions of your brethren, when convened, in every case consistent with the constitution of the order.

6. You agree to avoid private piques and quarrels, and to guard against intemperance and excess.

7. You agree to be cautious in carriage and behaviour, cautious to your brethren, and faithful to your lodge.

8. You promise to respect genuine brethren, and discountenance impostors, and all dissenters from the original plan of Masonry.

9. You agree to promote the general good of society, to cultivate the social virtues, and to propagate the knowledge of the art.

10. You promise to pay homage to the Grand Master for the time being, and to his officer when duly installed, strictly to conform to every edict of the Grand Lodge or general assembly of Masons, that is not subversive of the principles and ground work of Masonry.

11. You admit that it is not in the power of any man, or

C4

body of men, to make innovations in the body of Masonry.

12. You promise a regular attendance on the committees and communications of the Grand Lodge on receiving proper notice, and to pay attention to all the duties of Masonry on convenient occasions.

13. You admit that no new lodge can be formed without permission of the Grand Lodge, and that no countenance be given to any irregular Lodge, or to any person clandestinely initiated therein, being contrary to the ancient charges of the order.

14. You admit that no person can be regularly made a Mason in, or admitted a member of, any regular Lodge without previous notice, and due inquiry into his character.

15. You agree that no visitors shall be received in your lodge without due examination and producing proper vouchers of their having been initiated into a regular Lodge."

The presiding officer then asks the Master elect (candidate) the following question, which he must answer in the affirmative. Q. "Do you submit to these charges and promise to support these regulations, as Masters have done in all ages before you? Ans. "I do." The presiding officer then addresses him. "Brother A. B. in consequence of your cheerful conformity to the charges and regulations of the order, you are now to be installed Master of this degree, in full confidence of your care, skill and capacity, to govern the same. But previous to your investiture it is necessary you should take upon yourself the solemn oath or obligation appertaining to this degree; if you are willing to take it upon you, you will please to kneel before the altar, when you shall receive the same." [Here Lodges differ very materially, but this is the most prevalent mode of proceeding.] The candidate then kneels on both knees, lays both hands on the Holy Bible, square, and compass, and takes the following oath or obligation:—"I, A. B. of my own free will and accord, in presence of Almighty God, and this Worshipful Lodge of Past Master Masons, do hereby, and hereon, most solemnly and sincerely promise and swear, in addition to my former obligations, that I will not give the degree of Past Master Mason, or any of the secrets pertaining thereto, to any one of an inferior degree, nor to any person in the known world, except it be to a true and lawful brother or brethren Past Master Masons, or within the body of a just and lawfully constituted Lodge of such, and not unto him or unto them whom I shall hear so to be, but unto him and them only whom I shall find so to be, after strict trial and examination, or lawful information. Furthermore, do I promise and swear, that I will obey all regular signs and summonses, sent, thrown, handed, or given, from the hand of a brother of this degree, or from the body of a just and lawfully constituted lodge of Past Masters, provided it be within the length of my cable-tow. Furthermore do I promise and swear, that I will support the constitution of the General Grand Royal Arch Chapter of the United States of America, also that of the Grand Chapter of the State of———under which this lodge is held, and conform to all the by-laws, rules, and regulations of this or any other lodge, of which I may at any time hereafter become a member, so far as in my power. Furthermore do I promise and swear, that I will not assist, or be present at the conferring of this degree upon any person, who has not, to the best of my knowledge and belief, regularly received the degrees of Entered Apprentice, Fellow-Craft, Master Mason, and Mark Master or been elected Master of a regular Lodge of Master Masons. Furthermore do I promise and swear, that I will aid and assist all poor and indigent Past Master Masons, their widows and orphans, wherever dispersed round the globe, they applying to me as such and I finding them worthy, so far as in my power without material injury to myself or family. Furthermore do I promise and swear, that the secrets of a brother of this degree delivered to me in charge as such, shall remain as secure and inviolable in my breast, as they were in his own before communicated to me, murder and treason excepted, and those left to my own election. Furthermore do I promise and swear, that I will not wrong this Lodge, nor a brother of this degree to the value of one cent, knowingly myself, nor suffer it to be done by others, if in my power to prevent it. Furthermore do I promise and swear, that I will not govern this Lodge, nor any other over which I may be called to preside, in a haughty, arbitrary or impious manner, but will

C5

at all times, use my utmost endeavours to preserve peace and harmony among the brethren. Furthermore, do I promise and swear, that I will never open a lodge of Master Masons, unless there be present three regular Master Masons beside the Tyler, nor close the same without giving a lecture, or some section or part of a lecture, for the instruction of the Lodge. Furthermore, that I will not knowingly set in any Lodge when any one presides, who has not received the degree of Past Master. [This last point is in many lodges entirely omitted. In some the two last.] All which I do most solemnly and sincerely promise and swear, with a fixed and steady purpose of mind to keep and perform the same, binding myself under no less penalty than to have my tongue split from tip to root, that I might forever thereafter be unable to pronounce the word, if ever I should prove wilfully guilty of violating any part of this, my solemn oath or obligation of a Past Master Mason. So help me God, and make me steadfast to keep and perform the same.

The obligation being administered, the candidate rises,* and the Master proceeds to give the sign, word, and grip of this degree, as follows. The sign (sometimes called the due guard) is given by laying the edge of the thumb of the right hand, in a vertical position on the centre of the mouth, high enough to touch the upper lip. The word is given by taking each other by the Master's grip, and pulling the insides of their feet together, when the Master whispers the word *Giblem*† in the ear of the candidate. They then clap their left hand on each other's right arms, between the wrist and elbow, disengaging (at the same moment) their right hand from the Master's grip; they each seize the left arm of the other with their right hands, between the wrist and elbow, and (almost at the same instant) yielding their left hand hold on each other's right arms, and moving their left

* In some lodges the Master takes the candidate by the Master's grip, and says, "Brother you will please rise," assisting him.

† There is much diversity of opinion among masons respecting this word: some insists that *Giblem* is the right word, others that *Gibelum* is the right word—the latter word was rejected because it was used by "Jachin and Boaz."

hands with a brisk motion, they clasp each other's right arm with their left hands above the elbow, pressing their finger nails hard against the arms: as they shift their hands from place to place, the Master says, (in union with these movements) "from grips to spans, and from spans to grips, a twofold cord is strong, but a threefold cord is not easily broken." The Master then conducts the candidate to the chair, and as he ascends the steps, the Master says, "Brother, I now have the pleasure of conducting you into the Oriental chair of King Solomon," places a large cocked hat on his head, and comes down to the front of the newly installed Master, and addresses him as follows, "worshipful Brother, I now present you with the furniture and various implements of our profession; they are emblematical of our conduct in life, and will now be enumerated and explained as presented."

"*The Holy Writings*, that great light in Masonry, will guide you to all truth; it will direct your path to the temple of happiness, and point out to you the whole duty of man. The *Square* teaches to regulate our actions by rule and line, and to harmonize our conduct by the principles of morality and virtue. The *Compass* teaches to limit our desires in every station: thus rising to eminence by merit, we may live respected, and die regreted. The *Rule* directs, that we should punctually observe our duty; press forward in the path of virtue, and neither inclining to the right nor to the left, in all our actions have *eternity* in view. The *Line* teaches the criterion of moral rectitude, to avoid dessimulation in conversation and action, and to direct our steps to the path that leads to *immortality*. The book of *Constitutions* you are to search at all times, cause it to be read in your lodge, that none may pretend ignorance of the excellent precepts it enjoins. Lastly, you receive in charge the by-laws of your Lodge which you are to see carefully and punctually executed.

"I will also present you with the mallet: it is an emblem of power. One stroke of the mallet calls to order, and calls up the Junior and Senior Deacons, two strokes calls up all the subordinate officers, and three the whole lodge. The following charge is then delivered to the newly installed Master (alias candidate) by the former Master.

"Worshipful Master, being appointed Master of this Lodge, you cannot be insensible of the obligations which devolve on you, as their head; nor of your responsibility for the faithful discharge of the important duties annexed to your appointment. The honour, usefulness, and reputation of your Lodge, will materially depend on the skill and assiduity with which you manage its concerns, while the happiness of its members will be generally promoted, in proportion to the zeal and ability with which you propagate the genuine principles of our institution. For a pattern of information, consider the luminary of nature, which, rising in the *east*, regularly diffuses light and lustre to all within its circle. In like manner it is your province to spread and communicate light and instruction to the brethren of your lodge. Forcibly impress upon them the dignity and high importance of Masonry, and seriously admonish them never to disgrace it. Charge them to practice out of the Lodge those duties which they have taught in it, and by amiable, discreet, and virtuous conduct, to convince mankind of the goodness of the Institution, so that when any one is said to be a member of it, the world may know that he is one to whom the burthened heart may pour out its sorrows, to whom distress may prefer its suit, whose hand is guided by justice, and his heart expanded by benevolence. In short, by a diligent observance of the by-laws of your lodge, the constitution of Masonry, and above all, the Holy Scriptures, which are given as a rule and guide of your faith, you will be enabled to acquit yourself with honor and reputation, and lay up a crown of rejoicing, which shall continue when time shall be no more."* The Master then says to the newly installed Master, "I now leave you to the government of your lodge." He then retires to a seat, and after a moment or two rises and addresses the candidate, (now in the chair as Master,) "Worshipful Master, in consequence of my resignation, and the election of a new Master, the seats of the Wardens

* This charge is frequently omitted when conferring the degree on a candidate but never when really installing a Master of a Lodge.

have become vacant. It is necessary you should have Wardens to assist you in the government of your Lodge. The constitution requires us to elect our officers by ballot, but it is common on occasions of this kind to dispense with those formalities, and elect by ayes and noes : I move we do so on the present occasion." The question is tried and carried in the affirmative.

The Master has a right to nominate one candidate for office and the brethren one. Here a scene of cofusion takes place which is not easily described. The newly installed *Worshipful* is made the but for every *worthy* brother to exercise his wit upon. Half a dozen are up at a time soliciting the Master to nominate them for Wardens, urging their several claims, and decrying the merits of others with much zeal: others crying out, order, Worshipful! keep order! others propose to dance, and request the Master to sing for them : others whistle, or sing, or jump about the room, or scuffle,and knock down chairs or benches. One proposes to call from labor to refreshment: another compliments the Worshipful Master on his dignified appearance,and knocks off his hat, or pulls it down over his face : another informs him that a lady wishes to enter. If the Master calls to order every one obeys the signal with the the utmost promptness, and drops upon the nearest seat; the next instant, before the Master can utter a word, all are on their feet again, and as noisy as ever : finally a nominal election is effected, and some prudent member, tired of such a ridiculous confusion, moves that the lodge be closed, which being done, the poor, (and if a stranger,) much embarrassed candidate, has his big hat taken from him, and is reduced to the ranks ; but for his consolation, the Worshipful Master informs him that the preceding scene, notwithstanding its apparent confusion, is designed to convey to him in a striking manner, the important lesson never to solicit, or accept, any office or station, for which he does not know himself amply qualified.

The LECTURE on the fifth or Past Master's degree is divided into five sections. The first section treats of the manner of constituting a Lodge of *M*aster *M*asons. The second treats of the ceremony of Installation, including the manner of receiving candidates to this degree as given above. The third treats of the ceremonies observed at laying the foundation stones of public structures. The fourth section—of the ceremony observed at the dedications of Masonic Halls. The fifth—of the ceremony observed at funerals, according to ancient custom, with the service used on the occasion. All the sections of this lecture are printed in full in Webb's Monitor, from the 83d to the 125th page, except such part of the second as relates to the induction of candidates, and the ceremony of opening and closing.

It ought to be here remarked, that the statement above is strictly correct. It includes all the ceremonies ever used in confering the degree of Past Master; but the ceremonies are more frequently shortened by the omission of some part of them: the presenting of the "various implements of the profession," and their explanations, are often dispensed with, and still more often the charge. By comparing this with the 2d section as described by Webb, the reader can see the whole ceremony of installing officers on all occasions.

MOST EXCELLENT MASTER'S DEGREE.

A Description of the Ceremonies used in opening a Lodge of Most Excellent Masters.

The Lodge being called to order, the Most Excellent Master says, "Brother Junior, are they all Most Excellent Masters in the south?" J. Warden, "they are, Most Excellent." Most Excellent Master, "Brother Senior, are they all Most Excellent Masters in the west?" S. W.

"they are Most Excellent." Most Excellent Master, "they are in the east," (gives one rap, which calls up both deacons.) "Brother Junior Deacon, the first care of a Mason?" J. D. "to see the door tyled, Most Excellent." M. E. M. "attend to that part of your duty, and inform the tyler that we are about to open this Lodge of Most Excellent Masters, and direct him to tyle accordingly." J. D. steps to the door and gives six knocks, which the tyler answers with six more: J. D. gives one more, which the tyler answers with one—the door is then partly opened, when the Junior Deacon informs the Tyler that a Lodge of Most Excellent Masters is about to be opened, and tells him to tyle accordingly, and then returns to his place in the Lodge, and says, "Most Excellent, the Lodge is tyled." M. E. M. "by whom?" J. D. "by a Most Excellent Master Mason without the door, armed with the proper implements of his office." M. E. M. "his duty there?" J. D. "to keep off all cowens and eves droppers, and see that none pass and repass without permission from the chair." M. E. M. "your place in the Lodge, Brother Junior?" J. D. "at the right hand of the Senior Warden in the west, Most Excellent." M. E. M. "your duty there, Brother Junior?" J. D. "to wait on the Most Excellent Master and Wardens, act as their proxy in the active duties of the Lodge, and take charge of the door." M. E. M. "the Senior Deacon's place in the Lodge?" J. D. "at the right hand of the Most Excellent Master in the east." M. E. M. "I thank you Brother. Your duty in the east, Brother Senior?" Senior Warden, "to wait on the Most Excellent Master and Wardens, act as their proxy in the active duties of the Lodge, attend to the preparation and introduction of candidates, and receive and welcome all visiting brethren." M. E. M. "the Secretary's place in the Lodge, Brother Senior?" S. D. "at the left hand of the Most Excellent Master in the east." M. E. M. "I thank you Brother. Your business there, Brother Secretary?" "The better to observe the Most Excellent Master's will and pleasure, record the proceedings of the Lodge, and transmit a copy of the same to the Grand Chapter if required, receive all monies and money bills from the hands of the brethren, pay them over to the Treaurer, and take his receipt for the same." M. E. M. "the Treasurer's place in the Lodge?" Sec'y, "at your right hand, Most Excellent." M. E. M. "I thank you, Brother. Your duty there, Brother Treasurer?" Treas. "the better to observe the Most Excellent Master's will and pleasure, receive all monies and money bills from the hands of the Secretary, keep a just and true account of the same, pay them out by the order of the Most Excellent Master and consent of the brethren." M. E. M. "the Junior Warden's place in the Lodge?" Treas. "in the south, Most Excellent." M. E. M. "I thank you Brother. Your business in the south, Brother Junior?" J. W. "as the sun in the south at high meridian is the beauty and glory of the day, so stands the Junior Warden in the south, the better to observe the time of high twelve, call the craft from labor to refreshment, superintend them during the hours thereof, see that none convert the hours of refreshment into that of intemperance or excess, call them again in due season, that the Most Excellent Master may have honor and they profit thereby." M. E. M. "the Senior Warden's place in the Lodge?" J. W. "In the west, Most Excellent." M. E. M. "I thank you, brother. Your duty in the west, Brother Senior?" S. W. "as the sun sets in the west to close the day, so stands the Senior Warden in the west to assist the Most Excellent Master in the opening his Lodge, take care of the jewels and implements, see that none be lost, pay the craft their wages if any be due, and see that none go away dissatisfied." M. E. M. "the Most Excellent Master's place in the Lodge?" S. W. "in the east, Most Excellent." M. E. M. "his duty in the east, Brother Senior?" S. W. "as the sun rises in the east to open and adorn the day, so presides the Most Excellent Master in the east to open and adorn his Lodge, to set his craft to work, govern them with good and wholesome laws, or cause the same to be done." [In some Lodges the foregoing ceremonies are omitted.] M. E. M. "Brother Senior Warden, assemble the brethren round the altar for the purpose of opening this Lodge of Most Excellent Master Masons." S. W. "Brethren, please to assemble round the altar for the purpose of opening this Lodge of Most Excellent Master Masons." In pursuance of this request, the brethren assemble around the altar and form a circle, and stand in such a position as to touch each other, leaving a space for the Most Excellent Mas er : they then all kneel on their left knee, and join hands, each giving his right hand brother his left hand, and his left hand brother his right hand, their left arms uppermost, and their heads inclining downward ; all being thus situated, the Most Excellent Master reads the follow ing portion of scripture : Psalm 24, "The earth is the Lord's, and the fulness thereof, the world and all that dwell therein. For he has founded it upon the seas, and established it upon the floods. Who shall ascend to the hill of the Lord ? and who shall stand in his holy place ? He that hath clean hands, and a pure heart ; who hath not lifted up his soul unto vanity, nor sworn deceitfully. He shall receive the blessing from the Lord, and righteousness from the God of his salvation. This is the generation of him that seek him, that seek thy face, O ! Jacob. Selah. Lift up your heads, O ye gates ! and be ye lift up, ye everlasting doors, and the King of Glory shall come in : who is this King of glory ? the Lord strong and mighty ! the Lord mighty in battle. Lift up your heads, O ye gates ! even lift them up, ye everlasting doors, and the King of glory shall come in." When the Most Excellent Master has read this much he leaves his seat and fills a space left him in the circle, which had been kept open for this purpose, and continues reading—"Who is this King of Glory ? the Lord strong and mighty, the Lord mighty in battle. Lift up your heads, O ! ye gates ! even lift them up, ye everlasting doors ! and the King of glory shall come in. Who is this King of glory. Selah." The reading being ended, the Most Excellent Master then kneels, joins hands with the others, which closes the circle, they all lift their hands as joined together up and down six times, keeping time with the words as the Most Excellent Master repeats them, one, two, three, one, two, three. This is masonically called balancing. They then rise, disengage their hands and lift them up above their heads with a moderate and somewhat graceful motion, cast up their eyes, turning at the same time to the right, they extend their arms and then suffer them to fall loose and nerveless against their sides. This sign is said by masons to represent the sign of astonishment made by the Queen of Sheba on first viewing Solomon's Temple. The Most Excellent Master now resumes his seat, and says, "Brethren attend to giving the signs;" The Most Excellent Master then gives all the signs from an Entered Apprentice Mason up to the degree of Most Excellent Master, in which they all join and imitate him. M. E. M "Brother Senior Warden, you will please to inform Brother Junior, and request him to inform the Brethren, that it is my will and pleasure that this Lodge of Most Excellent Master Masons be now opened for dispatch of business, strictly forbiding all private committees, or profane language, whereby the harmony of the same may be interrupted, while engaged in their lawful pursuits, under no less penalty than the by-laws enjoin, or a majority of the brethren may see cause to inflict. Senior Warden, "Brother Junior, it is the will and pleasure of the Most Excellent Master that this Lodge of Most Excellent Master Masons be now opened for dispatch of business, strictly prohibiting all private committees, or profane language, whereby the harmony of the same may be interrupted while engaged in their lawful pursuits, under no less penalty than the by-laws enjoin, or a majority of the brethren may see cause to infiict. J. W. "Brethren, you have heard the Most Excellent Master's will and pleasure as communicated to me by Brother Senior—so let it be done.

CEREMONIES OF INITIATION.

The Lodge being now opened, and ready for the reception of candidates, the Senior Deacon repairs to the preparation room, where the candidate is in waiting, takes off his coat, puts a cable-tow six times round his body, and in this situation conducts him to the door of the Lodge, against which he gives six distinct knocks, which are answered by the same number by the Junior Deacon from within; the Senior Deacon then gives one knock, and the Junior Deacon answers it by giving one more: the door is then partly opened by the Junior Deacon, who says, "who comes there?" Senior Deacon, "a worthy brother, who has been regularly initiated as an Entered Apprentice Mason, passed to the degree of Fellow-Craft, raised to the sublime degree of Master Mason, advanced to the honorary degree of a Mark Master Mason, presided in the chair as Past Master, and now wishes for further light in Masonry, by being received and acknowledged as a Most Excellent Master." Junior Deacon, "is it of his own free will and accord he makes this request?" Senior Deacon, "it is." J. Deacon, "is he duly and truly prepared?" S. Deacon, "he is." J. Deacon, "is he worthy and well qualified?" S. D. "he is." J. D. "has he made suitable proficiency in the preceding degrees?" S. D. "he has." J. D. "by what further right or benefit does he expect to obtain this favour?" S. D. "by the benefit of a pass word?" J. D. "has he a pass word?" S. D. "he has not, but I have it for him." J. D. "will you give it to me?" S. D. whispers in the ear of the Junior Deacon the word "RABONI." [In many Lodges the Past Master's word "GIBLEM," is used as a pass word for this degree, and the word "*Raboni*" as the real word.] J. D. "the word is right: since this is the case you will wait until the Most Excellent Master in the east is made acquainted with your request, and his answer returned." J. Deacon repairs to the Most Excellent Master in the east, and gives six raps as at the door. M. E. M. "who comes here?" J. D. "a worthy brother, who has been regularly initiated as an Entered Apprentice Mason, passed to the degree of Fellow Craft, raised to the sublime degree of a Master Mason, advanced to the honorary degree of Mark Master Mason, presided in the chair as Past Master, and now wishes for further light in masonry, by being received and acknowledged as a Most Excellent Master." M. E. M. "is it of his own free will and choice he makes this request?" J. D.—It is. M. E. M. "Is he duly and truly prepared?" J. D.—he is. M. E. M. "is he worthy and well qualified?" J. D. —he is. M. E. M. "has he made suitable proficiency in the preceding degrees?" J. D.—he has. M. E. M. "by what further right or benefit does he expect to obtain this favour?" J. D. "by the benefit of a pass word." M. E. M. "has he a pass word?" J. D. "he has not, but I have it for him." M. E. M. "will you give it to me?" Junior Deacon whispers in the ear of the Most Excellent Master the word "RABONI." M. E. M. "the pass is

D

right: since he comes endowed with all these necessary qualifications let him enter this Lodge of Most Excellent Masters, in the name of the Lord." The candidate is then conducted six times round the Lodge by the Senior Deacon, movin with the sun. The first time they pass round the Lodge, when opposite the Senior Warden, he gives one blow with the gavel, when opposite the Senior Warden he does the same, and likewise when opposite the Most Excellent Master. The second time round each gives two blows, the third three, and so on, until they arrive to six. During this time the Most Excellent Master reads the following passage of scripture: Psalm 122—"I was glad when they said unto me, let us go into the house of the Lord. Our feet shall stand within thy gates, O Jerusalem. Jerusalem is builded as a city that is compact together: Whither the tribes go up, the tribes of the Lord, unto the testimony of Israel, to give thanks unto the name of the Lord. For there are set thrones of judgment, the thrones of the house of David. Pray for the peace of Jerusalem: they shall prosper that love thee. Peace be within thy walls, and prosperity within thy palaces. For my brethren and companions' sakes, I will now say, Peace be within thee. Because of the house of the Lord our God I will seek thy good." The reading of the foregoing is so timed, as not to be fully ended until the Senior Deacon and candidate have performed the sixth revolution. Immediately after this the Senior-Deacon and candidate arrive at the Junior Warden's station in the south, when the same questions are asked, and the same answers returned, as at the door, (who comes here, &c.) The Junior Warden then directs the candidate to pass on to the Senior Warden in the west for further examination, where the same questions are asked and answers returned as before. The Senior Warden directs him to be conducted to the Right Worshipful Master in the east for further examination. The R. W. Master asks the same questions and receives the same answers as before. He then says, "please to conduct the candidate back to the west, from whence he came, and put him in the care of the Senior Warden, and request him to teach the candidate how to approach the east, by advancing upon six upright regular steps to the sixth step, and place him in a proper position to take upon him the solemn oath or obligation of a Most Excellent Master Mason. The candidate is conducted back to the west and put in care of the enior Warden, who informs him how to approach the east, as directed by the Most Excellent Master : The candidate kneels on both knees, and places both hands on the leaves of an opened Bible, square and compass. The Most Excellent Master now comes forward and says, " Brother, you are now placed in a proper position to take upon you the solemn oath or obligation of a Most Excellent Master Mason, which I assure you, as before, is neither to affect your religion or politicks. If you are willing to take it, repeat your name and say after me." The following obligation is then administered.

" I, A. B. of my own free will and accord, in presence of Almghty God, and this Lodge of Most Excellent Master Masons, do hereby and hereon, in addition to my former obligations, most solemnly and sincerely promise and swear that I will not give the degree of Most Excellent Master to any of an inferior degree, nor to any other person or persons in the known world, except it be to a true and lawful brother, or brethren of this degree, and within the body of a just and lawfully constituted lodge of such, and not unto him nor them whom I shall hear so to be, but unto him and them only whom I shall find so to be, after strict trial and due examination, or lawful information. Furthermore, do I promise and swear, that I will obey all regular signs and summonses, given, handed, sent, or thrown to me from a brother of this degree, or from the body of a just and lawfully constituted Lodge of such, provided it be within the length of my cable-tow, if in my power. Furthermore, do I promise and swear, that I will support the Constitution of the General Grand Royal Arch Chapter of the United States of America, also the Grand Royal Arch Chapter of the State of ———, under which this Lodge is held, and conform to all the by-laws, rules, and regulations, of this or any other lodge, of which I may at any time hereafter become a member. Furthermore, do I promise and swear that I will aid and assist all poor and indigent brethren of this degree, their widows and orphans, wheresoever dispersed around the globe, as far as in my power, without

D2

injuring myself or family. Furthermore, do I promise and swear, that the secrets of a brother of this degree given to me in charge as such, and I knowing them to be such, shall remain as secret and inviolable in my breast as in his own, murder and treason excepted, and the same left to my own free will and choice. Furthermore, do I promise and swear that I will not wrong this Lodge of Most Excellent Master Masons, nor a brother of this degree, to the value of any thing knowingly myself, nor suffer it to be done by others, if in my power to prevent it, but will give due and timely notice of all approaches of danger if in my power. Furthermore, do I promise and swear, that I will dispense light and knowledge to all ignorant and uninformed brethren at all times, as far as in my power, without material injury to myself or family. To all which I do most solemnly swear, with a fixed and steady purpose of mind in me to keep and perform the same, binding myself under no less penalty than to have my breast torn open, and my heart and vitals taken from thence, and exposed to rot on the dunghill, if ever I violate any part of this my solemn oath or obligation of a Most Excellent Master Mason, so help me God, and keep me steadfast in the due performance of the same." "Detach your hands and kiss the book."

The candidate is now requested to rise, and the Most Excellent Master gives him the sign, grip, and word appertaining to this degree. The sign is given by placing your hands one on each breast, the fingers meeting in the centre of the body, and jerking them apart as though you were trying to tear open your breast: it alludes to the penalty of the obligation. The grip is given by taking each other by the right hand, and clasping them so that each compress the third finger of the other with his thumb. [If one hand is large and the other small they cannot both give the grip at the same time.] It is called the grip of all grips, because it is said to cover all the preceding grips. The Most Excellent holds the candidate by the hand, and puts the inside of his right foot to the inside of the candidate's right foot, and whispers in his ear "RABONI." In some Lodges the word is not given in a whisper, but in a low voice. After these ceremonies are over, and the members seated, some noise is intentionally made by shuffling the feet,

M. E. M. "Brother Senior, what is the cause of this confusion?" S. W. "is not this the day set apart for the celebration of the Cape-stone, Most Excellent?" M. E. M. "I will ask Brother Secretary. Brother Secretary, is this the day set apart for the celebration of the Cape-stone?" Secretary, (looking in his book,) "it is, Most Excellent." M. E. M. "Brother Senior Warden assemble the brethren, and form a procession, for the purpose of celebrating the Cape-stone." The Brethren the nassemble, [the candidate stands aside, not joining in the procession,] form a procession double file, and march six times round the lodge, against the course of the sun, singing the following song, and giving all the signs from an Entered Apprentiee to that of Most Excellent Master: When opposite the Most Excellent Master, the first time they march round the lodge, each member gives the first sign of an Entered Apprentice, and preserves it until he nearly arrives opposite the Most Excellent a second time, then gives the second sign, and continues it in the same manner, and so of all others up to that of this degree, saying,

"All Hail to the Morning, that bids us rejoice:
The Temple's completed, exalt high each voice.
The Cape-stone is finished—our labour is o'er,
The sound of the gavel shall hail us no more.

To the power Almighty, who ever has guided
The Tribes of Old Israel, exalting their fame,
To him who hath governed our hearts undivided,
Let's send forth our vows to praise his great name.

Companions assemble on this joyful day,
(The occasion is glorious) the key-stone to lay:
Fulfilled is the promise, by the ANCIENT of DAYS,
To bring forth the cape-stone with shouting and praise.

[The key-stone is now produced and laid on the altar.]

There is no more occasion for level or plumb-line,
For trowel or gavel, for compass or square:*

* Here the brethren divest themselves of their jewels, sashes, aprons, &c.

D3

Our works are completed, the Ark safely seated,*
  And we shall be greeted as workmen most rare.

Names, those that are worthy our tribes, who have shared
And proved themselves faithful, shall meet their reward:
Their virtué and knowledge, industry and skill,
Have our approbation—have gained our good will.

We accept and receive them,† Most Excellent Masters,
  Trusted with honour and power to preside
Among worthy craftsmen, where'er assembled,
  The knowledge of Masons to spread far and wide.

ALMIGHTY JEHOVAH,‡ descend now and fill
This Lodge with Thy Glory, our hearts with good will:
Preside at our meeting, assist us to find
True pleasure in teaching good will to mankind.

Thy Wisdom inspired the great Institution;
  Thy strength shall support it till Nature expire—
And when the Creation shall fall into ruin,
  Its beauty shall rise through the mist of the fire.||

The members now all join hands as in opening; and while in this attitude the Most Excellent reads the following passage of scripture:—2d Chron. 7, 1, 4, "Now when Solomon had made an end of praying, the fire came down from Heaven, and consumed the burnt-offering and the sacrifices; and the glory of the Lord filled the house. And the priests could not enter into the house of the Lord, because the glory of the Lord had filled the Lord's house. And when all the children of Israel saw how the fire came

* The Ark which had been carried by two brethren in the procession is here placed on the altar.

† At these words the candidate is received into the procession.

‡ Here all kneel in a circle round the altar.

|| At the time the Ark is placed on the altar, there is also placed on it a pot of incense, to which fire is communicated by the Most Excellent Master just as the last line of the song is sung: this pot to contain incense is sometimes an elegant silver urn; but if the Lodge is too poor to afford that, a common tea-pot, with spout and handle broken off, answers every purpose—for incense some pieces of paper are dipped in spirits of turpentine.

down, and the glory of the Lord upon the house, they bowed themselves with their faces to the ground upon the pavement, and worshipped, and praised the Lord, saying, FOR HE IS GOOD,* FOR HIS MERCY ENDURETH FOREVER." The members now balance six times as before; in opening rise and balance six times more, disengaging themselves from each other, and take their seats: the Most Excellent Master then delivers the following charge to the candidate:—

"Brother, Your admittance to this degree of Masonry, is a proof of the good opinion the brethren of this lodge entertain of your masonic abilities. Let this consideration induce you to be careful of forfeiting, by misconduct and inattention to our rules, that esteem which has raised you to the rank you now possess.

"It is one of your great duties, as a Most Excellent Master, to dispense light and truth to the uninformed mason; and I need not remind you of the impossibility of complying with this obligation without possessing an accurate acquaintance with the lectures of each degree.

"If you are not already completely conversant in all the degrees heretofore conferred on you, remember, that an indulgence, prompted by a belief that you will apply yourself with double diligence to make yourself so, has induced the brethren to accept you.

"Let it therefore be your unremitting study to require such a degree of knowledge and information as shall enable you to discharge with propriety the various duties incumbent on you, and to preserve unsullied the title now conferred upon you of a Most Excellent Master."

After this a motion is made by some of the members to close the Lodge. This motion being accepted and received, the Most Excellent says, "Brother Junior Warden, you will please assemble the brethren round the altar, for the purpose of closing this Lodge of Most Excellent Mas-

* At the words for "he is good," the Most Excellent Master, who is High Priest of the chapter, kneels and joins hands with the rest: they all then repeat in concert the words, "for he is good, for his mercy endureth forever," six times, each time bowing their heads low towards the floor.

D4

ters." The Brethren immediately assemble round the altar in a circle, and kneel on the right knee, put their left arms over and join hands as before: while kneeling in this position, the Most Excellent reads the following psalm:—Psalm 134, "Beloved, bless ye the Lord! all ye servants of the Lord, which by night stand by the house of the Lord, lift up your hands in the sanctuary and bless the Lord! The Lord that made heaven and earth, bless thee out of Zion." The Most Excellent then closes the circle as in opening, when they balance six times, rise and balance six times more, disengage their hands, and give all the signs downwards, and declares the Lodge closed.

ROYAL ARCH DEGREE.

All legally constituted bodies of Royal Arch Masons are called Chapters, as regular bodies of Masons of the preceding degrees are called Lodges. All the degrees from Mark Master to Royal Arch are given under the sanction of Royal Arch Chapters. A person making application to a Chapter for admission, is understood as applying for all the degrees, unless he states in his application the particular degree or degrees he wishes to receive. If you ask a Mark Master if he belongs to a Chapter, he will answer yes, but has only been marked. If a person make application for all the degrees, and wishes to receive them all at one time, he is frequently balloted for only on the mark degree, it being understood that if accepted on that he is to receive tho whole. The members of Chapters who have received all the degrees, style each other companions; if they have not received the Royal Arch degree, brothers. It is a point of the Royal Arch degree "not to assist, or be present, at the conferring of this degree upon more or less than three candidates at one time." If there are not three candidates present, one or two companions, as the case may be, volunteer to represent candidates so as to make the requisite number, or a *team* as it is technically styled, and accompany the candidate or candidates through all the stages of exaltation. Every Chapter must consist of a High Priest, King, Scribe, Captain of the Host, Principal Sojourner, Royal Arch Captain, three Grand Masters of the Veils, Treasurer, Secretary, and as many members as may be found convenient for working to advantage. In the lodges for conferring the Preparatory degrees, the High Priest presides as Master, the King as Senior Warden, the Scribe as Junior Warden, the Captain of the Host as Marshal, or Master of Ceremonies, the principal Sojouner as Senior Deacon, the Royal Arch Captain as Junior Deacon, the Masters of the first, second and third Veils, as Junior, Senior and Master Overseers, the Treasurer, Secretary, and Tyler, as officers of corresponding rank. The Chapter is authorised to confer the degrees by a charter or warrant from some Grand Chapter.

The members being assembled, the High Priest calls to order and demands of the Royal Arch Captain if all present are R. A. Masons. The Royal Arch Captain ascertains and answers in the affirmative. The High Priest then directs him to cause the Tyler to be stationed, which being done the High Priest says, "Companions Royal Arch Masons, you will please to clothe, and arange yourselves for the purpose of opening the Chapter." The furniture of the Chapter is then arranged, the companions clothed with scarlet sashes and aprons, and the officers invested with the proper insignia of their respective offices, and repair to their proper stations. The High Priest then demands whether the Chapter is tyled, and is answered the same as in a lodge. The stations and duties of the offiices are then recited, (see lecture, sec. 1st.) After the duties of the officers are recited, the High Priest directs the Captain of the Host to assemble the Companions at the altar. The companions form a circle about the altar, all kneeling on the right knee, with their arms crossed, right arm uppermost and hands joined, leaving a space for the High Priest, who reads the following passage of Scriptures, 2d Thess. iii. 6—18. Now we com-

D5

mand you, brethren, that ye withdraw yourselves from every brother that walketh disorderly, and not after the tradition that ye received of us, for yourselves know, how ye ought to follow us, for we behaved not ourselves disorderly among you, neither did we eat any man's bread for nought, but wrought with labour and travail night and day that we might not be chargeable to any of you, not because we have not power, but to make ourselves an ensample unto you to follow us. For even when we were with you, this we commanded you that if any would not work, neither should he eat. For we hear that there are some, which walk among you disorderly, working not at all, but are busy-bodies. Now them that are such, we command and exhort, that with quietness they work and eat their own bread. But ye brethren be not weary in well doing. And if any man obey not our word, note that man and have no company with him, that he may be ashamed. Yet count him not as an enemy but admonish him as a brother. Now the Lord of Peace himself, give you peace always. The salutation of Paul, with mine own hand, which is the token, so I write." [The reader is requested to compare this with the Scripture—he will observe that the name of the Saviour is intentionally left out.] The High Priest then takes his place in the circle. The whole circle then balance with their arms three times three, that is, they raise their arms and let them fall upon their knees three times in concert, after a short pause three times more, and after another pause three times more. Then all break into squads of three, and raise the living arch. This is done by each Companion's taking his left wrist in his right hand, and with their left hands the three grasp each others right wrists, and raise them above their heads. This constitutes the living arch, under which the Grand Omnific Royal Arch word must be given, but it must also be given by three times three. In opening the Chapter this is done in the following manner. After the three have joined hands they repeat these lines in concert, and at the close of each line raise them above their heads, and say, " As we three did agree the sacred word to keep, " And as we three did agree the sacred word to search, " So we three, do agree, to raise this Royal Arch." At the close of the last line they keep their hands raised, while they encline their heads under them, and the first whispers in the ear of the second the syllable J A H, the second to the third, B U H, and the 3d to the 1st, L U N. The second then commences, and it goes round again in the same manner, then the third so that each Companion pronounces each syllable of the word.* They then seperate, each repairing to his station, and the High Priest declares the Chapter opened.

The LECTURE of the ROYAL ARCH degree is divided into two sections. The first section designates the appellation, number and station, of the several officers, and points out the purpose and duty of their respective stations.

Question. Are you a Royal Arch Mason ? Answer. *I am that I am.* Q. How shall I know you to be a R. A. Mason ? A. by three times three. Q. Where was you made a R. A. Mason ? A. in a just and legally constituted Chapter of R. A. Masons, consisting of Most Excellent, High Priest, King and Scribe, Capt. of the Host, Principal Sojourner, Royal Arch Captain, and the three Grand Masters of the Veils, assembled in a room or place representing the tabernacle erected by our ancient brethren, near the ruins of King Solomon's Temple. Q. Where is the High Priest stationed, and what are his duties? A. He is stationed in the Sanctum Sanctorum. His duty with the King and Scribe, to sit in the Grand Council, to form plans and give directions to the workmen. Q. The King's station and duty ? A. At the right hand of the High Priest, to aid him by his advice and counsel, and in his absence to preside. Q. The Scribe's station and duty ? A. At the left hand of the High Priest, to assist him and the King in the discharge of their duties, and to preside in their absence. Q. The Captain of the Host's station and duty ? A. At the right hand of the Grand Council, and to receive their orders,

* There is a great difference in the manner of giving the R. A. word in the different Chapters. Sometimes it is given at opening, as above stated, sometimes they commence with the word GOD, each one pronouncing a letter of it in succession, until they have each pronounced every letter of the word, then the word JEHOVAH, a syllable at a time, and then the word JAHBUHLUN, as described. There are also Chapters in which the latter word is not known, and there are others in which the word is not given at all at opening.

and see them duly executed. Q. The Principal Sojouner's station and duty? A. At the left hand of the Grand Council, to bring the blind by a way that they know not, to lead them in paths they have not known, to make darkness light before them, and crooked things strait. Q. The Royal Arch Captain's station and duty? A. At the inner Veil, or entrance of the Sanctum Sanctorum; to guard the same, and see that none pass, but such as are duly qualified, and have the proper pass-words and signets of truth. Q. What is the colour of his banner? A. White, and is emblematical of that purity of heart and rectitude of conduct, which is essential to obtain admission into the Divine Sanctum Sanctorum above. Q. The stations and duties of the three Grand Masters of the Veils? A. At the entrance of their respective Veils; to guard the same and see that none pass but such as are duly qualified and in possession of the proper pass-words and tokens. Q. What are the colours of their banners? A. That of the third, scarlet, which is emblematical of fervency and zeal, and the appropriate colour of the Royal Arch Degree. It admonishes us to be fervent in the exercise of our devotions to God, and zealous in our endeavours to promote the happiness of men. Of the second, purple, which being produced by a due mixture of blue and scarlet, the former of which is the characteristic colour of the symbolic, or three first degrees, and the latter that of the Royal Arch degree, is an emblem of union, and is the characteristic colour of the intermediate degrees. It teaches us to cultivate and improve that spirit of harmony between the brethren of the symbolic degrees, and the companions of the sublime degrees, which should ever distinguish the members of a society founded upon the principles of everlasting truth and universal philanthropy. Of the first, blue, the peculiar colour of the three ancient or symbolical degrees. It is an emblem of universal friendship and benevolence, and instruct us that in the mind of a Mason, those virtues should be as expansive as the blue arch of heaven itself. Q. The Treasurer's station and duty? A. At the right of the Captain of the Host; his duty to keep a just and regular account of all the property and funds of the Chapter placed in his hands, and exhibit them to the Chapter when called upon for that purpose. Q. The Secretary's place in the Chapter ? A. At the left of the principal Sojourner his duty to issue the orders and notifications of his superior officers, record the proceedings of the Chapter proper to be written, to receive all moneys due the Chapter, and pay them over to the Treasurer. Q. Tyler's place and duty? A. His station is at the outer avenue of the Chapter, his duty to guard against the approach of cowans and eaves-droppers, and suffer none to pass or repass but such as areduly qualified. The second section describes the method of exaltation to this sublime degree as follows : " Companion, you informed me at the commencement of this lecture, that you was made a R. A. Mason in a just and legally constituted Chapter of Royal Arch Masons.

Q. Where was you prepared to be made a R. A. Mason ? A. In a room adjacent to the chapter. Q. How was you prepared ? A. In a company of three I was hood-winked with a cable-tow seven times around our bodies ; in which condition we were conducted to the door of the Chapter, and caused to give seven distinct knocks, which were answered by a like number from within, and we were asked " Who comes there ? Q. Your answer ? Three brethren, who have been regularly initiated as Entered Apprentices, passed to the degree of Fellow Craft, raised to the sublime degree of Master Mason, advanced to the more honourable degree of Mark Master, presided as Masters in the chair, accepted and received as M. Excellent Masters, and now wish for further light in Masonry, by being exalted to the more sublime degree of Royal Arch Masons. Q. What was then said to you ? A. We were asked if we were duly and truly prepared, worthy and well qualified, had made suitable proficiency in the preceding degrees, and were properly avouched for. All which, being answered in the affirmative, we were asked by what further right or benefit we expected to obtain this favor ? Q. Your answer ? A. By benefit of a pass-word. Q. Had you that pass-word ? A. We had not, but our conducter gave it for us. Q. What was then said to you ? A. We were directed to wait with patience, till the Grand Council could be informed of our request and their pleasure known. Q. What answer was returned ? A. Let them enter under a living arch, and remember to stoop low, for he that humbleth himself shall be exhalted. Q. Did you pass under a living arch? A. We did. Q. How were you then disposed of? We were conducted to the altar, caused to kneel, and take upon ourselves the solemn oath or obligation of a Royal Arch Mason. Q. Have you that obligation? A. I have. Q. Will you give it me?

A. I, A. B. of my own free will and accord, in the presence of Almighty God and this Chapter of R. A. Masons, erected to God and dedicated to the holy order of St. John,* do hereby and hereon, most solemnly and sincerely promise and swear, in addition to my former obligations, that I will not give the degree of Royal Arch Mason to any one of an inferior degree, nor to any other being in the known world, except it be to a true and lawful companion Royal Arch Mason, or within the body of a just and legally constituted Chapter of such, and not unto him or unto them whom I shall hear so to be, but unto him or them whom I shall find so to be, after strict trial, due examination, or legal information received. Furthermore do I promise and swear that I will not give the Grand Omnific Royal Arch word, which I shall hereafter receive, neither in the Chapter nor out of it, except there be present two Companions Royal Arch Masons, who with myself make three, and then by three times three under a living arch not above my breath. Furthermore that I will not reveal the ineffable characters belonging to this degree, or retain the key to them in my possession, but destroy it whenever it comes to my sight. Furthermore do I promise and swear, that I will not wrong this Chapter, nor a Companion of this degree to the value of any thing, knowingly myself, or suffer it to be done by others, if in my power to prevent it. Furthermore do I promise and swear, that I will not be at the exaltation of a candidate to this degree, at a clandestine Chapter, I knowing it to be such. Furthermore do I promise and swear, that I will not assist or be present at the exaltation of a candidate to this degree, who has not regularly received the degrees of Entered Apprentice, Fellow Craft, Master Mason, Mark Master, Past Master, Most

* Or as it is at this time given in some Chapters, "to the honor of our ancient patron Zerubbabel."

Excellent Master, to the best of my knowledge and belief. Furthermore that I will not assist or see more or less than three candidates exhalted at one and the same time. Furthermore that I will not assist or be present at the forming or opening of a Royal Arch Chapter, unless there be present nine regular Royal Arch Masons. Furthermore do I promise and swear, that I will not speak evil of a companion Royal Arch Mason, neither behind his back nor before his face, but will apprise him of approaching danger if in my power. Furthermore do I promise and swear, that I will not strike a companion R. A. Mason in anger, so as to draw his blood. Furthermore do I promise and swear, that I will support the Constitution of the General Grand Royal Arch Chapter of the United States of America, also the constitution of Grand Royal Arch Chapter of the State under which this Chapter is held, & conform to all the by-laws, rules and regulations of this, or any other Chapter of which I may hereafter become a member. Furthermore do I promise and swear, that I will obey all regular signs, summonses, or tokens given, handed, sent, or thrown to me from the hand of a Companion Royal Arch Mason, or from the body of a just and lawfully constituted Chapter of such, provided it be within the length of my cable-tow. Furthermore do I promise and swear, that I will aid and assist a companion R. A. Mason, when engaged in any difficulty ; and espouse his cause, so far as to extricate him from the same if in my power, whether he be right or wrong. Also, that I will promote a Companion R. A. Mason's political preferment in preference to another of equal qualifications.* Furthermore do I promise and swear, that a companion R. A. Mason's secrets, given me in charge as such, and I knowing them to be such, shall remain as secure and inviolable in my breast as in his own, *murder and treason not excepted.*† Furthermore do I

* This clause is sometimes made a distinct point in the obligation in the following form, viz : Furthermore do I promise and swear, that I will vote for a companion R. A. Mason before any other of equal qualifications ; and in some Chapters both are left out of the obligation.

† In some Chapters this is administered. All the secrets of a companion without exception.

promise and swear, that I will be aiding and assisting all poor and indigent R. A. Masons, their widows and orphans, wherever dispersed around the globe, so far as in my power, without material injury to myself or family. All which I most solemnly and sincerely promise and swear, with a firm and steadfast resolution, to perform the same, without any equivocation, mental reservation, or self-evasion of mind in me whatever ; binding myself under no less penalty, than that of having my skull smote off, and my brains exposed to the scorching rays of the sun, should I ever knowingly, or willfully, violate or transgress any part of this my solemn oath or obligation of a Royal Arch Mason. So help me God, and keep me steadfast in the performance of the same.

Q. After receiving the obligation what was said to you ? A. We were told, that we were now obligated and received as R. A. Masons, but as this degree was infinitely more important than any of the preceding, it was necessary for us to pass through many trials and to travel in rough and rugged ways to prove our fidelity before we could be entrusted with the more important secrets of this degree. We were further told that though we could not discover the path we were to travel, we were under the direction of a faithful guide, who would "bring the blind by a way they know not, and lead them in paths they had not known, who would make darkness light before them, and crooked things straight, who would do these things and not forsake them." (see Isa. 42. 16.) Q. What followed ? A. We were caused to travel three times round the room, when we were again conducted to the altar, caused to kneel and attend to the following prayer. [See this prayer, Monitor, p. 134.] Supreme Architect of Universal nature, who by thine Almighty Word, didst speak into being the stupendous arch of heaven ! And for the instruction and pleasure of thy rational creatures, didst adorn us with greater and lesser lights, thereby magnifying thy power, and endearing thy goodness unto the sons of men : We humbly adore and worship thine unspeakable perfection ! We bless thee, that when man had fallen from his innocence and his happiness, thou didst leave him the powers of reasoning, and capacity of improvement and of pleasure. We thank thee, that amidst the pains and calamities of our present state, so many means of refreshment and satisfaction are reserved to us, while travelling the *rugged path* of life; especially would we at this time render thee our thanksgiving and praise for the institution, as members of which we are at this time assembled, and for all the pleasures we have derived from it. We thank thee that the few here assembled before thee, have been favored with new inducements, and been laid under new and stronger obligations of virtue and holiness. May these obligations, O Blessed Father! have their full effect upon us. Teach us, we pray thee, the true reverence of thy great, mighty and terrible name. Inspire us with a firm and unshaken resolution in our virtuous pursuits. Give us grace diligently to search thy word in the book of nature, wherein the duties of our high vocation are inculcated with divine authority. May the solemnity of the ceremonies of our institution be duly impressed on our minds, and have a happy and lasting effect on our lives! O thou who didst aforetime appear unto thy servant Moses *in a flame of fire out of the midst of a bush*, enkindle, we beseech thee, in each of our hearts, a flame of devotion to thee, of love to each other, and of charity to all mankind! May all thy *miracles and mighty works* fill us with thy dread, and thy goodness impress us with a love of thy holy name! May *Holiness to the Lord* be engraven upon all our thoughts, words and actions! May the incense of piety ascend continually unto thee, from the altar of our hearts, and burn day and night, as a sacrifice of a sweet smelling savour, well pleasing unto thee! And since sin has destroyed within us the first temple of purity and innocence, may thy heavenly grace guide and assist us in rebuilding a *second temple* of reformation, and may the glory of this latter house be greater than the glory of the former! Amen, so mote it be.

Q. After the prayer what followed? A. We were again caused to travel three times round the room, during which the following passage of scripture was read, and we were shown a representation of the bush that burned and was not consumed. (Exodus 3d, 1—6.) Now Moses kept the flock of Jethro his father-in-law, the Priest of Midian: and he led the flock to the back side of the desert, and came to

me ; give ear unto my voice. Let my prayer be set forth before thee as incense: and the lifting up of hands as the evening sacrifice. Set a watch, O Lord, before my mouth ; keep the door of my lips. Incline not my heart to any evil thing, to practise wicked works with men that work iniquity. Let the righteous smite me ; it shall be a kindness : and let him reprove me ; it shall be an excellent oil. Mine eyes are unto thee, O God the Lord : in thee is my trust ; leave not my soul destitute. Keep me from the snare which they have laid for me, and the gins of the workers of iniquity. Let the wicked fall into their own nets, whilst that I withal escape.

Psalm 142.—I cried unto the Lord with my voice ; with my voice unto the Lord did I make my supplication. I poured out my complaint before him ; I shewed before him my trouble. When my spirit was overwhelmed within me, then thou knewest my path. In the way wherein I walked have they privily laid a snare for me. I looked on my right hand, and beheld, but there was no man that would know me: refuge failed me ; no man cared for my soul. I cried unto thee, O Lord: I said, Thou art my refuge and my portion in the land of the living. Attend unto my cry, for I am brought very low ; deliver me from my persecutors ; for they are stronger than I. Bring my soul out of prison, that I may praise thy name.

Psalm 143.—Hear my prayer, O Lord, give ear to my supplications: in thy faithfulness answer me, and in thy righteousness. And enter not into judgment with thy servant: for in thy sight shall no man living be justified. For the enemy hath persecuted my soul ; he hath made me to dwell in darkness. Therefore is my spirit overwhelmed within me ; my heart within me is desolate. Hear me speedily, O Lord : my spirit faileth : hide not thy face from me, lest I be like unto them that go down into the pit. Cause me to hear thy loving kindness in the morning ; for in thee do I trust : cause me to know the way wherein I should walk ; for I lift up my soul unto thee. Bring my soul out of trouble. And of thy mercy cut off mine enemies ; for I am thy servant."

At length we arrived at Jerusalem, and presented ourselves at the first Veil of the Tabernacle.

Q. What was there said to you? A. The Master of the First Veil demanded of us, 'who comes there?' who dares approach this outer Veil of our sacred Tabernacle? who comes here? Q. Your answer? A. Three weary travellers from Babylon. They then demanded of us who we were, and what were our intentions. Q. Ycur answer? A. We are your own brethren and kindred, of the tribe of Benjamin: we are the descendants of those noble families of Giblimites, who wrought so hard at the building of the first Temple, were present at its destruction by Nebuchadnezzar, by him carried away captive to Babylon, where we remained servants to him and his sons, till the first year of Cyrus, King of Persia, by whose order we were liberated, and are now returned to assist in re-building the house of the Lord, without expectation of fee or reward? Q. What further was demanded of you? A. The password, "I am that I am." After giving which, the Master of the Veil, assured of his full confidence in us as worthy brethren, commended us for our zeal, and gave us the token and words to enable us to pass the second Veil. Q. What are they? A. The token is an imitation of that which Moses was commanded to exhibit to the children of Israel, casting his rod upon the ground it became a serpent, and putting forth his hand and taking it again by the tail, it became a rod in his hand. The words are these, "*Shem, Ham, and Japhet.*" Q. What followed? A. We were conducted to the second Veil, where the same questions were asked, and answers returned, as before, with the addition of the pass-words and token given at the First Veil? Q. What followed? A. The Master of the Second Veil told us that we must be true and lawful brethren to pass thus far, but further we could not go without his pass and token, which he accordingly gave to us. Q. What are they? A. The words are Shem, Japheth, and Adoniram. the Token is putting the hand in the bosom, plucking it out again, in imitation of the second sign which Moses was directed to make to the Israelites, when putting his hand into his bosom and taking it out again it became leprous as snow. Q. How were you then disposed of? A. We were conducted onwards to the Third Veil, when the same questions were asked, and answers returned, as before, with

E2

the addition of the token and words last received. Q. What followed? A. The Master of the Third Veil then gave us the sign, words, and signet, to enable us to pass the Fourth Veil, to the presence of the Grand Council. Q. What are the words, sign, and signet? A. The words are Japheth, Shem, Noah; the sign, pouring water upon the ground, in imitation of Moses, who poured water upon the ground and it became blood; the signet is called the signet of truth, and is Zerubbabel. It alludes to this passage, "In that day, I will take thee, O Zerubbabel, my servant, the son of Shealtiel, and will make thee as a signet: for I have chosen thee." [See Haggai, chap.2. ver.23.]

Q. What followed? A. We then passed to the Fourth Veil, where, after answering the same questions, and giving the sign, words, and signet, last received, we were admitted to the presence of the Grand Council, where the High Priest made the same demands as were made at the Veils, and received the same answers. Q. What did the High Priest further demand of you? A. The signs from Entered Apprentice to Most Excellent Master in succession. Q. What did he then say to you? A. He said we were truly three worthy Most Excellent Masters, commended us for our zeal and disinterestedness, and asked what part of the work we were willing to undertake. Q. Your answer? A. That we were willing to undertake any service, however servile or dangerous, for the sake of forwarding so great and noble an undertaking. Q. What followed? A. We were then furnished with a pick-axe, spade, and crow, and were directed to repair to the N. W. corner of the ruins of the old temple, and commence removing the rubbish, to lay the foundation of the new, and to observe and preserve every thing of importance and report to the Grand Council. We accordingly repaired to the place, and after labouring several days, we discovered what seemed a rock, but on striking it with the crow it gave a hollow sound, and upon closer examination we discovered in it an iron ring, by help of which we succeeded in removing it from its place, when we found it to be the key-stone of an arch, and through the aperture there appeared to be an immense vault curiously arched. We then took the stone, and repaired to the Grand Council, and presented it for their inspection. Q. What did the Grand Council then say to you? Q. They told us that the stone contained the Mark of our Ancient Grand Master Hiram Abiff; that it was truly a fortunate discovery, and that without doubt the vault contained things of the utmost consequence to the Craft. They then directed us to repair again to the place, and continue our researches. Q. What followed? A. We returned again to the place, and agreed that one of our number should descend by means of a rope, the middle of which was fixed firmly around his body, and if he wished to descend he was to pull the rope in his right hand, if to ascend, that in his left. He accordingly descended, and in groping about he found what appeared to be some ancient jewels, but the air becoming offensive he pulled the rope in his left hand, and was immediately drawn out. We then repaired to the Grand Council, made our report, and presented the articles found, which they pronounced the jewels of our three ancient Grand Masters, Solomon, Hiram, and Hiram Abiff. They commended us highly for our zeal and fidelity, assured us that it was a fortunate discovery, that it would probably lead to still more important ones, and that our disinterested perseverance should not go unrewarded. They directed us to repair again to the place, and make what further discoveries lay in our power. Q. What followed? A. We again returned to the place, and let down one of our companions as before. The sun having now reached its meridian height, darted its rays to the inmost recesses of the vault, and enabled him to discover a small chest or box curiously wrought, but the air becoming exceedingly offensive, he gave the sign and was immediately drawn out. We immediately repaired to the Grand Council, and presented our discovery. On examination the Grand Council pronounced it to be the *Ark of the Covenant*, which was deposited in the vault by our ancient Grand Master for safe keeping. On inspecting it more closely they found a key with which they opened it. The High Priest then took from it a book, which he opened, and read as follows: (Gen. 1—1, 3,) "In the beginning God created the heavens and the earth: and the earth was without form, and void and darkness was upon the face of the deep, and the

E3

spirit of God moved upon the face of the waters: and God said let there be light, and there was light. (Deut. 31—24, 26) And it came to pass when Moses had made an end of writing the words of this law in a book, until they were finished, that Moses commanded the Levites which bare the ark of the covenant of the Lord, saying, take this book of the law, and put it in the side of the ark of the covenant of the Lord your God, that it may be there for a witness against thee. [Ex. 25, 21.] And thou shalt put the mercy seat above, upon the ark, and in the ark thou shalt put the testimony that I shall give thee." He then declared it to be the Book of the Law, upon which the Grand Council, in an ecstacy of joy, exclaimed three times, "Long lost, now found, Holiness to the Lord." At the same time drawing their hands across their foreheads. Q. What further was found in the ark? A. A small vessel containing a substance, which, after the Council had examined, and the High Priest again read from the book of the law, (Ex. 16—32, 34,) he pronounced to be manna. "And Moses said, this is the thing which the Lord commandeth: fill an omer of the manna to be kept for your generations, that they may see the bread wherewith I have fed you in the wilderness, when I brought you forth from the land of Egypt. And Moses said unto Aaron, take a pot and put an omer full of manna therein, and lay it up before the Lord to be kept for your generations. As the Lord commanded Moses, so Aaron laid it up before the testimony, to be kept for a token." The High Priest then took a rod from the ark, which, after he had read the following passage, [Numb. 17—10.] "And the Lord said unto Moses, bring Aaron's rod again before the testimony to be kept for a token,' he pronounced to be Aaron's rod, which budded and blossomed as the rose. Q. Was there any thing further found in the ark? A. There was a key to the ineffable characters belonging to this degree, as follows: X beginning at top of this diagram at the left hand angle;

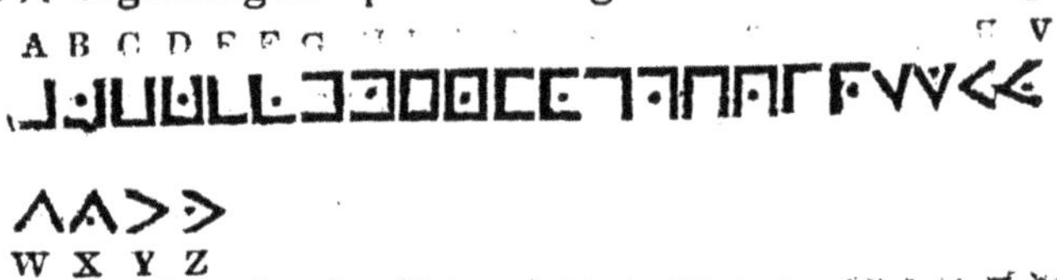

A B C D E F G … V

W X Y Z

The upper left hand angle without a dot is A; the same with dot is B, &c.

Q. What further was said to you? A. The High Priest read the following passage: (Exodus 6—2, 3,) "And God spake unto Moses, and said unto him, I am the Lord, and I appeared unto Abraham, unto Isaac, and unto Jacob, by the name of God Almighty, but by my name Jehovah was I not known to them." He then informed us that the name of Deity, the divine Logos, or word, to which reference is had in John 1st—1, 5. "In the beginning was the word, and the word was with God, and the word was God; the same was in the beginning with God: all things were made by him, and without him was not any thing made that was made: In him was life, and the life was the light of men: And the light shineth in darkness, and the darkness comprehendeth it." That this Logos, or word, was anciently written only in these sacred characters, and thus preserved from one generation to another. That this was the true masonic word, which was lost at the death of Hiram Abiff, and was restored at the re-building of the temple, in the manner we had at that time assisted to represent. Q. What followed? A. We were reminded of the manner in which we had sworn to give the R. A. word, were instructed in the manner and finally invested with the all-important word in due form. Q. What is the Grand Royal Arch word? A. JAH-BUH-LUN.* Q. How is it to be given? A. Under a living arch by three times three, in low breath, (see description of opening a chapter.) Q. What followed? A. We were presented with the signs belonging to this degree. Q. Will you give me those signs? Answered by giving the signs, thus: raise the right hand to the forehead, the hand and arm horizontal; thumb towards the forehead, draw it briskly across the forehead, and drop it perpendicularly by the side. This constitutes the due-guard of this degree, and refers to the penalty of the obligation. The grand sign is made by locking the fingers of both hands together, and carrying them to the top of the head, the palms upward, alluding to the manner in which the brother who descended into the

*This question and answer do not belong to the lecture, but are inserted to show the word plainly and unencumbered with ceremonies.

F4

vault, and found the ark, found his hands involuntarily placed to protect his head from the potent rays of the meridian sun. Q. What followed? A. The High Priest then placed crowns upon our heads, and told us that we were now invested with all the important secrets of this degree, and crowned and received as worthy Companions Royal Arch Masons. He then gives the charge. (see Masonic Chart, page **113**, or Webb's Monitor, **149**.)

The second section of the Lecture on this degree states minutely the ceremonies and forms of exaltation, (as the confering of this degree is styled,) but there seems to be some parts which require explanation. The principal sojourner conducts the candidates and is considered as representing Moses conducting the children of Israel through the wilderness. He is usually dressed to represent an old man, bowed with age, with a mask on his face, and long beard hanging down upon his breast; is introduced to the candidate in the preparation room by the name of Moses. On entering the Chapter, the candidates are received under a " living arch," that is, the companions arrange themselves in a line on each side of the door, and each joins hands with the one opposite to himself. The candidates entering, the Conductor says: " stoop low Brothers! we are about to enter the arches; remember that he that humbleth himself, shall be exalted; stoop low, Brothers, stoop low!" The candidates seldom pass the first pair of hands, or in other words the first arch, without being so far humbled as to be very glad to support themselves on all fours. Their progress may well be imagined to be very slow, for in addition to their humble posture, they are obliged to support on their backs, the whole weight of the living arches above. (Who would not go slow?) The Conductor to encourage them calls out occasionally, " stoop low, brothers, stoop low!" If they go too slow to suit the companions it is not unusual for some one to apply a sharp point to their bodies, to urge them on; the points of the pasteboard crown answers quite well for this purpose. After they have endured this humiliating exercise as long as suits the convenience of the companions, (and if they are not reduced to a more humble posture than all fours, they come off well,) they pass from under the living arches. Surely after this, they must *stay humbled for life.* The candidates next receive the obligation, travel the room, attend the prayer, travel again, and are shown a representation of the Lord appearing to Moses from the burning bush. This last is done in various ways. Sometimes an earthen pot is filled with earth, and green bushes set round the edge of it, and a candle in the centre ; and sometimes a stool is provided with holes about the edge, in which bushes are placed, and a bundle of rags, or tow, saturated with oil of turpentine, placed in the centre, to which fire is communicated. Sometimes a large bush is suspended from the ceiling, around the stem of which tow is wound wet with oil of turpentine. In whatever way the bush is prepared, when the words are read, "he looked and behold the bush burned with fire, &c." the bandage is removed from the eyes of the candidates, and they see the fire in the bush,* and at the words "draw not nigh hither ; put off thy shoes, &c." the shoes of the candidates are taken off, and they remain in the same situation while the rest of the passage is read to the words, "And Moses hid his face, for he was afraid to look upon God." The bandage is then replaced, and the candidates again travel about the room, while the next passage of scripture is read. (See Lecture.) At the words "and brake down the walls of Jerusalem" the companions make a tremendous crashing and noise, by firing pistols overturning chairs, benches and whatever is at hand, rolling cannon balls across the floor, stamping, &c. &c. and in the midst of the uproar the candidates are seized, a chain thrown about them, and they are hurried away to the preparation room. This is the representation of the destruction of Jerusalem, and carrying captive the children of Israel to Babylon. After a short time the proclamation of Cyrus is read, the candidates are unbound, and start to go up to Jerusalem, to assist in rebuilding the temple. The candidates, still hood-winked, are brought into the Chapter, and commence their journey over the rugged and rough paths. They are literally rough paths, sticks of timber framed across the path the candidate must travel, some inches from the floor, make no comfortable travelling for a person blindfold; but this is not always the

* This is frequently represented in this manner : When the person reading comes to that part where it says, "God called to him out of the midst of the bush, and said," &c. he stops reading, and a person behind the bushes calls out, "Moses, Moses," the conductor answers, 'here am I,' the person behind the bush then says, "Draw not nigh hither ; put off the shoes from thy feet, for the place whereon thou standest is holy ground : [his shoes are then slipped off :] Moreover, I am the God of Abraham, the God of Isaac, and the God of Jacob." The person first reading then says, "And Moses hid his face, for he was afraid to look upon God." At these words the bandage is placed over the candidate's eyes.

E5

way it is prepared;billets of wood singly,or in heaps,ladders,nets of cords, &c. &c. are all put in requisition to form the rough and rugged paths, which are intended as a trial of the *fidelity* of the candidates. If they escape with nothing more than bruised shins they do well. They have been known to faint away under the severity of the descipline, and occasion the *worthy* companions much alarm. After travelling the rugged paths till all are satisfied, they arrive at the first veil of the tabernacle, give the pass-word, and pass on to the second, give the pass-words, and present the sign. This it will be recollected is in imitation of the sign which Moses was directed to make to the children of Israel. He threw his rod upon the ground and it became a serpent; he put forth his hand and took it by the tail and it became a rod in his hand. The conductor is provided with a rod,made in the form of a snake, and painted to resemble one. This he drops upon the floor and takes up again. They then pass on to the next Veil,give the pass word, and make the sign, (put the right hand in the bosom and pluck it out again,) pass on to the next—gives the pass-words, and make the sign, (pour water upon the ground,)and are ushered into the presence of the *Grand Council*. The Veils are four in number, and of the same colour as the banners of the three Grand Masters of the Veils, and that of the Royal Arch Captain, blue, purple, scarlet and white, and have the same references and explanations. [see lecture.] The Grand Council consists of the M. E. High Priest, King and Scribe. The H. Priest is dressed in a white robe, with a breast plate of cut glass, consisting of twelve pieces to represent the twelve tribes of Israel, an apron, and a mitre. The King wears a scarlet robe, apron, and crown. The mitre and crown are generally made of pasteboard; sometimes they have them of the most splendid materials, gold and silk velvet, but these are kept for public occasions. The mitre has the words," Holiness to the Lord" in gold letters across the forehead. The Scribe wears a purple robe, apron, and turban. After having satisfied the Grand Council that they are true brethren, and stated their object in coming to Jerusalem,the candidates are directed to commence the labour of removing the rubbish of the old temple preparatory to laying the foundation of the new. For the purpose of performing this part of the ceremony, there is in or near the Chapter a narrow kind of closet, the only entrance to which is through a scuttle at the top; there is placed over this scuttle whatever rubbish is at hand, bits of boards, brick bats &c. and among them the key stone. After the candidates are furnished with the tools, (pick axe, spade and crow,) they are directed to this place, and remove the rubbish till they discover the key stone. This they convey to the Grand Council as stated in the Lecture. After the Grand Council have examined it they pronounce it to be the work of the Grand M. Hiram Abiff, and direct them to return and prosecute their researches, not doubting they will make many important discoveries. The candidates return and let down one of their number by a rope—he finds three squares, is drawn out, and all proceed with them to the Grand Council. The G. Council inspect them and pronounce them to be the three ancient jewels that belonged to the three ancient Grand Masters, Solomon, Hiram, and Hiram Abiff. The candidates then return to the vault and let down another of their number. Here let it be remarked, some Chapters, for the purpose of lightening the labours of the candidates, call in the aid of machinery. A pulley is suspended over the vault, and the candidate is *exalted* from the bottom at the tail of a snatch block: the one last let down finds at the bottom a small chest or box, upon which he gives the signal to be drawn out: he no sooner discovers the box, than the air in the vault, in the language of the lecture, "becomes exceedingly offensive." This is strictly true; for at the moment he takes up the box and is preparing to ascend, fire is communicated to a quantity of gun-powder at his feet, so that by the time he arrives at the top he is so completely suffocated with the fumes of the powder, that he is almost deprived of the power of respiration or motion. The box is carried to the G. Council and pronounced to be the Ark of the Covenant. It is opened and a Bible taken out, and some passages read from it. [see lecture.] One word respecting the representation of the Ark. It ought to be a splendid box covered with gold, and some of them are really elegant, but the Chapter must have such as it can afford; if it is too poor to procure splendid furniture, cheap articles are made to answer: for an ark, if the funds are low, a plain cherry or pine box will answer, and sometimes a cigar box is made the humble representation of the splendid ark, made, by divine command, of shiltin wood, and overlaid with pure gold. The H. Priest takes then from the ark a vessel containing something to represent manna. This vessel is of various forms and materials, from an elegant silver urn to a broken earthern mug; and the substance contained is as various as the vessels in which it is deposited, such as a bit of sugar, a piece of cracker, or a few kennels of wheat; whichever is used the H. Priest takes it out and gravely asks the King and Scribe their opinion of it: they say they think it is manna. The High Priest, then looks at it intently and says, "it looks like manna," smells it, and says, "it smells like manna," and then tastes it, and says, "it is manna!" The H. Priest then takes from the Ark a bit of an apple tree, sprout a few inches long, with some withered buds upon it, or a stick of a similar length with some artificial buds upon it, which, after consulting with the King and Scribe, he pronounces Aaron's rod. He then takes out the key to the ineffable characters and explains it. This key is kept in the Ark on four distinct pieces of paper. The key is marked on a square piece of paper, and the paper is then divided into four equal parts, thus, the outside lines represent the dimensions of the paper, the inside ones are the key, and the dotted ones the section that is made of the whole for the purpose of keeping it secret, should any *graceless cowan* ever get possession of the sacred Ark and attempt to rumage its contents. The other part of the key X is made on the back of the same piece of paper, so that on putting them together, it shows equally plain. It is said that these characters were used by Aaron Burr, in carrying on his treasonable practices, and by that means made public, since which time they have been written and read from left to right. After the ceremonies are ended the High Priest informs the candidates, in many or few words according to his ability, that this degree owes its orign to Zerubabel and his associates, who rebuilt the temple by order of Cyrus King of Persia. He informs them that the discovery of the secret vault and the inestimable treasures, with the long lost *Word*, actually took place in the manner represented in confering this degree, and that it is the circumstance upon which the degree is principally founded. The ceremony of closing a Chapter is precisely the same as at opening, to the raising of the living arch. The Companions join hands by threes in the same manner, and say in concert, with the same ceremony: "As we three did agree, the sacred word to keep." "as we three did agree, the sacred word to search," "so we three do agree, to close this royal arch." They then break without giving the word, as the H. Priest reads the following prayer: By the wisdom of the Supreme High Priest may we be directed, by his strength may we be enabled, and by the beauty of virtue may we be incited, to perform the obligations here enjoined upon us, to keep inviolable the mysteries here unfolded to us, and invariably to practice all those duties, out of the Chapter, which are inculcated in it. (Response.) So mote it be. Amen. The High Priest then declares the Chapter closed in due form.

KNIGHTS OF THE RED CROSS.

At the sound of the trumpet the line is formed. Master of Cavalry to the Sir Knight Warden, " when a Council of Knights of the Red Cross is about to be formed and opened, what is the first care?" Warden, " to see the Council chamber duly guarded." M. C. " please to attend that part of your duty, see that the sentinels are at their respective posts, and inform the Captain of the Guards that we are about to open a Council of Knights of the Red Cross for the despatch of business." Warden, "the Sentinels are at their respective posts, and the council chamber duly guarded." M. C. " are all present Knights of the Red Cross?" Warden, " they are." M. C. " attention, Sir Knights, count yourseves from right to left—right files handle sword—draw sword—carry sword—right files to the left double—second division forward, march, halt—right about face." Sir Kt. Master of Infantry, accompanied by the sword bearer and Warden, "please inform the Sovereign Master that the lines are formed waiting his pleasure." At the approach of the Council the trumpet sounds. M. C. " form aveneu : (the Council pass:) the Sovereign Master passes uncovered : recover arms, poise arms." Sovereign Master, " attention Sir Knights ; give your attention to the several signs of masonry : as I do so do you." [The Sir Knights give the sign from the first to the seventh degree.] Sov. M. " draw swords —take care to advance and give the Jewish countersign—recover arms : take care to advance and give the Persian countersign—recover arms." Sov. M. to Sir Kt. Master of the Palace, " advance, and give me the word of a Kt. of the Red Cross : the word is right—receive it on your left." The word is then passed around : when it arrives at the Chancellor he says, " Sov. M. the Red Cross word has arrived." Sov. M. " pass it on to me : [he gives it to the Sov. M.] Sir Kt. the word is right." Sov. M. to Sir Kt. Chancellor, " advance, and give me the grand sign, grip, and word, of a Kt. of the Red Cross : it is right—receive it on your left." [The word passes around as before, as will hereafter be explained, and when arrived at the Master of the Palace, he says] "Sov. M. the grand sign, grip and word have arrived." "Pass them on to me: Sir Kn't they are right. Left face—deposit helmets

—centre face—reverse arms—to your devotions: [the Sir Kt's all kneel and repeat the Lord's prayer:] recover arms—left face—recover helmets—centre face—right about face—to your posts—march."

FIRST SECTION OF LECTURES.

1st. Are you a Kt. of the Red Cross? That is my profession. 2d. By what test will you be tried? By the test of truth. 3d. Why by the test of truth? Because none but the good and true are entitled to the honors and privileges of this Illustrious order. 4th. Where did you receive the honours of this Illustrious order? In a just and regular council of Knights of the Red Cross. 5th. What number compose a Council? There is an indispensable number and a constitutional number. 6th. What is the indispensable number? Three. 7th, Under what circumstances are they authorized to form and open a Council of Knights of the Red Cross? Three Knt's of the Red Cross, being also Kt's Templars, and hailing from three different commanderies, may, under the sanction of a legal warrant from some regular Grand Encampment, form and open a Council of Knights of the Red Cross for the despatch of business. 8th. What is a constitutional number? A. 5, 7, 9, 11, or more. 9th. When composed of 5, 7, 9, 11, of whom does it consist? A. Sovereign Master, Chancellor, Master of the Palace, Prelate, Master of Cavalry, Master of Infantry, Master of Finance, Master of Despatches, Standard Bearer, Sword Bearer, and Warder. 10, Warder's station in the Council? A. On the left of the Standard bearer in the west. 11, His duty? A. To announce the approach of the Sov. Master, to see that the sentinels are at their respective posts, and the Council chamber duly guarded. 12. Sword Bearer's station in the Council? A. On the right of the Standard bearer in the West. 13. His duty? A. To assist in the protection of the banners of our order: to watch all signals from the Sov. Master, and see his orders duly executed. 14. Standard bearer's station? A. In the west.—15. His duty? A. To display, support and protect the banners of our order. 16. Why is the Standard bearer's station in the West? A. That the brilliant rays of the rising Sun, shedding their lustre upon the banners of our order, may encourage and animate all true and courteous

Knights,and dismay and confound their enemies. 17. Station of Master of Dispatches ? A. In front of the Master of the Palace. 18. His duty ? A. To observe with attention the transactions of the Council ; to keep a just and regular record thereof, collect the revenue, and pay the same over to the Master of Finance. 19. Station of the Master of Finance ? A. In Front of the Chancellor. 20. His duty ? A. To receive in charge the funds and property of the Council, pay all orders drawn upon the Treasurer, and render a just and regular account when called for. 21. Station of the Master of Infantry ? A. On the right of the second division, when separately formed ; on the left of the whole when formed in line. 22. His duty ? A. To command the second division or line of Infantry, teach them their duty and exercise ; also to prepare all candidates, attend them on their journey, answer all questions for them, and finally to introduce them into the Council Chamber. 23. Station of Master of Cavalry ? A. On the right of the first division when separately formed, and on the right of the whole when formed in line.—24. His duty ? A. To command the first divison or line of Cavalry, teach them their duty and exercise; to form the avenue at the approach of the Sov. Master, and prepare the lines for inspection and review. 25. Prelate's Station ? A. On the right of the Chancellor. 26. His duty ? A. To preside in the Royal Arch Council ; administer at the Altar ; to offer up prayers and adorations to Deity. 27. Station of Master of the Palace ? A. On the left of the Sov. Master in the East. 28. His duty ? A. To see that the proper officers make all due preparations for the several meetings of the Council ; to take special care that the Council Chamber is in suitable array for the reception of candidates, and the despatch of business ; to receive and communicate all orders issued by the Sov. Master, thro' the officers of the line. 29. Chancellor's station ? A. On the right of the Sov. Master. 30. His duty ? A. To receive and communicate all orders and petitions ; to assist the Sov. Master in the discharge of his various duties, and in his absence to preside in the Council. 31. Sovereign Master's station ? A. In the East. 32. His duty. A. To preside in the Council ; confer this order of Knighthood upon those whom his council may approve ; to preserve inviolate the laws and constitution of our order ; to dispense justice, reward merit, encourage truth, and diffuse the sublime principles of universal benevolence. Sov. Master " Sir Knight Chancellor, it is my will and pleasure that a Council of Knights of the Red Cross be now opened, and to stand open for the despatch of such business as may regularly come before it at this time, requiring all Sir Knights now assembled, or who may come at this time, to govern themselves according to the sublime principles of our order. You will communicate this to the Sir Kt. Master of the Palace, that the Sir Knights present may have due notice thereof, and govern themselves accordingly." [The Sir Knight Chancellor communicates it to the Sir Knight, Master of the Palace, and he to the Knights.] Sov. Master, " return arms ; right about face ; to your posts ; march ; centre face ; Sir Knights, this Council is now open for the despatch of business.

SECOND SECTION OF LECTURES.

1st, What were the preparatory circumstances attending your reception to this Illustrious Order ? A Council of Royal Arch masons being assembled in a room adjacent to the Council Chamber, I was conducted to the door, where a regular demand was made by 2, 3, and 2. 2d, What was said to you from within ? Who comes there. 3d, Your answer ? Companion A. B. who has regularly received the several degrees of Entered Apprentice, Fellow Craft, Master Mason, Mark Master, Past Master, Most Excellent Master, and Royal Arch degree, and now solicits the honor of being regularly constituted a Knight of the Red Cross. 4th, What was then said to you ? I was asked if it was of my own free will and accord that I made this request ; if I was worthy and well qualified ; if I had made suitable proficiency in the foregoing degrees, and was properly vouched for : all of which being answerd in the affirmative, I was asked by what further right or benefit I expected to gain admittance. 5th, Your answer ? By the benefit of a pass word. 6th, Did you give that pass word? I did with the assistance of my companions. [Here the Royal Arch word is given as described in the Royal Arch degree.] 7th, What was then said to you ? I was then directed to wait with patience till the Most Excellent Prelate should be informed of my request and his answer returned. 8. What was his answer? Let him be admitted. 9. What was you then informed? The Most Excellent Prelate observed, that the council there assembled, represented the Grand Council convened at Jerusalem in the second year of the reign of Darius King of Persia, to deliberate on the unhappy state of the fraternity during the reigns of Artaxerxes and Ahasueras, and to devise some means to obtain favor of the new Sovereign, and to gain his consent to proceed in rebuilding their new city and Temple. 10. What followed? The Most Excellent Prelate then informed me, that if I was desirous of attending the deliberations of the Council at this time, it was necessary that I should assume the name and character of Zerubabel, a Prince of the house of Judah, whose hands laid the foundation of the second Temple, and whose hands the Lord had promised should complete it. 11. What followed? The Most Excellent Prelate then read a lesson from the records of the Fathers, stating the impediments with which they were troubled by their adversaries, on the other side of the river, and the grievous accusations which were brought against them before the King. 12. What followed? My Conductor then addressed the Most Excellent Prelate, thus:—Most Excellent Prelate, our Sovereign Lord Darius the King, having now ascended the throne of Persia, new hopes are inspired of protection and support in the noble and glorious undertaking, which has been so long and so often interrupted by our adversaries on the other side of the river; for while yet a private man, he made a vow to God, that should he ever ascend the throne of Persia, he would send all the Holy vessels remaining at Babylon back to Jerusalem: Our Most Excellent and faithful Companion Zerubabel, who was formerly honored with the favorable notice and friendship of the Sovereign, now offers his services to encounter the hazardous enterprise of traversing the Persian dominions, and seeking admission to the presence of the Sovereign, where the first favorable moment will be seized to remind the King of his vow, and impress on his mind the almighty force and importance of truth; and from his known piety, no doubt can be entertained of gaining his consent, that our enemies be removed far hence, and that we be no longer hindered or impeded in our noble and glorious undertaking. 13. What was the Most Excellent Prelate's reply? Excellent Zerubabel, the Council accept with gratification and joy your noble and generous offer, and will invest you with the necessary passports, by means of which you will be enabled to make yourself known to the favor of one Council wherever you may meet them; but in an undertaking of so much importance it is necessary that you enter into a solemn obligation, to be faithful to the trust reposed in you.

14. What followed? The Most Excellent Prelate then invested me with a sword, to enable me to defend myself against my enemies, and said he was ready to administer the obligation.

15. Did you consent to that obligation? I did in due form.

16. What was that due form? Kneeling on my left knee, my right foot forming a square, my body erect, my right hand grasping the hilt of my sword, my left hand covering the holy Bible, Square and Compass, with two cross-swords thereon, in which due form I took upon me the solemn oath and obligation of Knight of the Red Cross.

17. Repeat the obligation.

"I, A. B. of my own free will and accord, in the presence of the Supreme Architect of the Universe, and these witnesses, do hereby and hereon, most solemnly and sincerely promise and swear, that I will always hale, forever conceal, and never reveal, any of the secret arts, parts or points of the mysteries appertaining to this Order of Knight of the Red Cross, unless it be to a true and lawful Companion Sir Knight of the Order, or within the body of a just and lawful Council of such; and not unto him or them, until by due trial, strict examinatian or lawful information, I find him or them lawfully entitled to receive the same.—I furthermore promise and swear, that I will answer and obey all due signs and regular Council of Knighrs of the Red Cross, or given to me from the hands of a Companion Sir Knight of the Red Cross, if within the distance of forty miles; natural infirmaties and unavoidable accidents only excusing me. I furthermore promise and swear, that I will not be present at the confering of this order of Knighthood upon any person, unless he shall have previously regularly received the several degrees of Entered Apprentice, Fellow Craft, Master Mason, Mark Master, Past Master, Most Excellent Master, and Royal Arch degree, to the best of my knowledge and belief. I furthermore promise aed swear, that I will not assist or be present at a forming and opening of a Council of Knights of the Red Cross, unless there be present at least five regular Knights of the Order, or the representatives of three different Encampments, acting under the sanction of a legal warrant. I further promise and swear, that I will vindicate the character of a Courteous Sir Knight of the Red Cross, when wrongfully traduced ; that I will help him on a lawful occsaion in preference to any Brother of an inferior degree, and so far as truth, honor and justice may warrant. I furthermore promise and swear, that I will support and maintain the by-laws of the Council of which I may hereafter become a member, the laws and regulations of the Grand Encampment under which the same may be holden, together with the constitution and ordinances of the General Grand Encampment of the United States of America, so far as the same shall come to my knowledge—to all which I do most solemnly promise and swear, binding myself under no less penalty than that of having my house torn down, the timbers thereof set up, and I hanged thereon ; and that when the last trump shall blow, that I be forever excluded from the society of all true and courteons Knights, should I ever wilfully or knowingly violate any part of this solemn obligation of Knight of the Red Cross ; so help me God, and keep me stedfast to kee and perform the same.

18. What followed ? The Most Excellent Prelate then directed me to rise and be invested with a countersign, which he informed me would enable me to make myself known to the friends of our cause wherever I should meet them, and would ensure me from them, succour, aid, and protection. [Here the Master of Infantry, who is the conductor, gives the candidate the Jewish conntersign : it is given under the arch of steel, that is, their swords elevated above their heads forming a cross, each placing his left hand upon the others' right shoulder, and whispering alternately in each others' ear;

F

the names of Judah and Benjamin.] 19. What followed The Most Excellent Prelate then invested me with a green sash, as a mark of our particular friendship and esteem : you will wear it as a constant memorial to stimulate you to the faithful performance of every duty, being assured that the memory of him who falls in a just and virtuous cause, shall forever flourish like the green Bay tree. 20. What followed ? I then commenced my journey, and was frequently accosted by guards, all of which, by means of the countersign I had received, I was enabled to pass in friendship, until I arrived at the bridge, which was represented to be in the Persian dominions: on attempting to pass this bridge, which I found strongly guarded, the Persian countersign was demanded, and being unable to give it, I was attacked, overpowered, and made prisoner. 21. What followed ? After remonstrating in vain against their violations, I told them I was a Prince of the House of Judah, and demanded an audiance with their Sovereign. 22. What was the answer ? You are a prisoner, and can obtain an audience with the Sovereign only in the garb of a captive and a slave. 23. Did you consent to this ? I did ; being firmly persuaded, that could I by any means gain access to the presence of the Sovereign, I should be able to accomplish the object of my mission. 24. What followed ? They then deprived me of my outward apparel, sash and sword, and having confined my hands and feet in chains, the links thereof were of a triangular form, they put sackcloth and ashes on my head. 25. Why were the links of the captives chain of a triangular form ? The Assyrians having learned that among the Jews the triangle was an emblem of the Eternal, caused the links of their chains to be made of a triangular form, thinking thereby to add to the miseries of their captives. 26. What followed? I was conducted to the door of the Council chamber, where the alarm being given by 4X3, the warder appeared and demanded, "Who comes there ?" 27. What answer was returned ? A detachment of His Majesty's guards having made prisoner of one, who reports himself to be Prince of the House of Judah. 28. What was then said to you ? I was asked from whence I came. 29. Your answer? From Jerusalem. 30. What was then demanded of you ? Who are you. 31. Your answer? The first among my equals, a Mason, and free by rank, but a captive and slave by misfortune. 32. What was you then asked ? My name. 33. Your answer? Zerubabel. 34. What were you then asked? What are your demands. 35. Your answer? To see the Sovereign if possible. 36. What was then said to you? I was then directed to wait with patience until the Sovereign Master should be informed of my request, and his answer returned. 37. What was that answer? That the necessary caution should be taken that I was not armed with any hostile weapons, and that I should then be admitted. 38. How were you then received? The guard being drawn up on the right and left of the throne, swords drawn, two of them placed at the door with swords crossed, under which I was permitted to enter, my face covered with my hands 39. How were you then disposed of? I was conducted in front of the Sovereign Master, who received me with kindness and attention, and listened with patience to my request. 40. What did the Sovereign Master then observe to the Council? That this Zerubabel was the friend of his youth, that he could neither be an enemy nor a spy. 41. What followed? The Sovereign Master thus addressed me, "Zerubabel, having now gained admittance into our presence, we demand that you immediately declare the particular motives which induced you, without our permission, and with force and arms, to pass the lines of our dominions?" 42. Your answer? Sovereign Master, the tears and complaints of my companions at Jerusalem, who have been so long and so often impeded in the noble and glorious undertaking in which they were permitted to engage by our late Sovereign Lord Cyrus the King; but our enemies having made that great work to cease by force and power, I have now come up to implore your Majesty's clemency, that you would be pleased to restore me to favor, and grant me employment among the servants of your household. 43. What was the Soverign's reply? Zerubabel, I have often reflected with much pleasure upon our early intimacy and friendship, and I have frequently heard, with great satisfaction, of your fame as a wise and accomplished mason, and having myself a profound veneration for that ancient and honorable institution, and having a sincere desire to become a member of the same, I will this moment grant your request, on condition that you will reveal to me the secrets of Free Masonry. 44 Did you consent to that? I did not? 45. What was your reply? Sovereign Master, when our Grand Master Solomon, King of Israel, first instituted the Fraternity of Free and Accepted Masons, he taught us that truth was a divine attribute. and the foundation of every virtue: to be good and true is the first lesson we are taught in Masonry. My engagements are sacred and inviolable: I cannot reveal our secrets. If I can obtain your Majesty's favor only at the expense of my integrity, I humbly beg leave to de-

F2

cline your royal protection, and will cheerfully submit to an honorable exile. 46. What was the Sovereign's reply? Zerubabel, your virtue and integrity are truly commendable, and your fidelity to your engagments, is worthy of imitation: from this moment you are free—my guards will divest you of those chains and that garb of slavery, and clothe you in suitable habiliments to attend me at the banquet hall. Zerubabel, you are free: guards, strike off those chains; and may those emblems of slavery never again disgrace the hands of a Mason, more particulary a Prince of the House of Judah. Zerubabel, we assign you a seat of rank and honor among the Princes and Rulers of our Assembly. 47. What followed? The guards being drawn up in the court yard, the warder informed the Sovereign Master that the guards were in readiness, waiting his pleasure. 48. What followed? He then ordered the guards to attend him to the banquet hall. 49. What occurred there? After having participated in a liberal entertainment, the Sovereign Master not being inclined to sleep, and many of the guard having retired, he amused himself by entering into conversation with some of his principal officers and friends, proposing certain questions to them, and offering a princely reward to such as should give the most reasonable and satisfactory answer. 50. What questions were proposed? Among others, "Which was the strongst, wine, the king, or women?" 51. What answers were returned? The Chancellor said wine was the strongest; the Master of the Palace said the king was the strongest; but I, being firmly persuaded that the time had arrived in which I could remind the king of his vow, and request the fulfilment of it, replied that women were stronger than either of the former, but above all things truth beareth the victory. 52. What followed? The King being deeply struck with the addition I had made to the question, ordered us to be preparad with proper arguments in support of our respective propositions on the day following 53. What followed? On the day following the Council being convened at the sound of the trumpet, the Chancellor was called upon for his answer, and thus replied, (see Templar's Chart.) 54. What followed? The Master of the Palace thus replied, (see Templars chart) 55. What followed? I then being called upon for my defence, answered as follows, [see Templar's chart.] 56. What followed? The King being deeply struck with the force of the arguments I had used, involuntarily exclaimed, "Great is truth, and mighty above all things: Ask what thou wilt, Zerubabel, and it shall be granted thee, for thou art found wisest among thy companions." 57. Your answer? [See Templar's Chart.] 58. What followed? The Sovereign Master thus addressed me, "Zerubabel, I will punctually fulfil my vow: letters and and passports shall be immediately issued to my officers throughout the realm, and they shall give you, and those who accompany you, safe conveyance to Jerusal m, and you shall be no longer hindered or impeded in rebuilding your City and Temple, until they shall be completed."

59. What followed? The Sovereign Master then invested me with a green sash, and thus addressed me, "This green sash, of which you were deprived by my guards, I now with pleasure restore to you, and will make it one of the insignia of a new order, calculated to perpetuate the remembrance of the event wich caused the renewal of our friendship; its colour will remind you that truth is a divine attribute, and shall prevail, and shall forever flourish in immortal green. I will now confer on you the highest honor in our power at this time to bestow, and will create you the first Knight of an order, instituted for the express purpose of inculcating the almighty force and importance of truth 60. What followed? The Sovereign Master then directed me to kneel, and said, by virtue of the high power in me vested, as the successor and representative of Darious, king of Persia, I now constitute you a Knight of the Illustrious order of the Red Cross—[at the same time laying the blade of his sword, first upon the right shoulder, then upon the head, and then upon the left shoulder of the Candidate.]— 61. What followed? The Sovereign Master then directed me to arise, and presenting me with a sword thus addressd me, "this sword, of which you were deprived by my guards, I now restore in your hands, as a true and courteous Knight: it will be endowed with three most excellent properties—its hilt be faith, its blade be hope, its point be charity it should teach us this important lesson, that when we draw our swords in a just and virtuous cause, having faith in God, we may reasonably hope for victory, ever remembering to extend the hand of charity to the fallen foe: sheathe it, and sooner may it rust in its scabbard, than be drawn in the cause of injustice or oppression." 62. What followed? The Sovereign Master then invested me with the Persian countersign. 63. Give it? This countersign is given like the Jewish, excepting this variation, it is given over instead of under the arch of steel. The words are Tatnia, Shetherboznia. 64. Who were they? They were Governors of Persian provinces, and enemies of the Jews. 65. What followed? The Sovereign Master then invested me with the Red Cross word. 66. Give it? [Each placing his left hand upon the others' right shoulder, at the same time bringing the point of the swords to each others' left side, in which position the word *Libertas* is given.] 67. What followed?—

F3

The Sovereign Master then invested me with the Grand sign, grip and word of Knight of the Red Cross. 68. Give them?—The grand sign is given by bringing the thumb and finger of the left hand to the mouth, and carrying it off in an oblique direction—the Grip is given by interlacing the fingers of the left hands—the word is veritas. The sign, grip and word s given under the arch of steel. 69. How do you translate the word? Truth. 70 To what does the sign allude? To the blowing of the Trumpet upon the walls and watch towers of the Council, but more particularly to' the obligation, "that whenthe last Trump shall sound, I shall be forever excluded from the society of all true and faithful Sir Knights." 71. What is the motto of our order? "Magna est veritas et prevalebit.

KNIGHT TEMPLAR AND KNIGHT OF MALTA.

Q. 1st. Are you a Knight Templar? A. that is my title Q. 2d. Where were you created a Knight Templar? A. In a just and lawful encampment of Knight Templars. 3d.

What number composes a just and lawful Encampment of Knight Templars? There is an indispensable number, and a constitutional number. 4th. What is an indispensable number. Three. 5th. Under what circumstances are they authorised to form and open an encampment of Knight Templars? Three Knight Templars, hailing from three different commanderies, may, under the sanction of a charter or warrant from some regular Grand Encampment, form and open an encampment for the despatch of business. 6th. What is a constitutional number? Seven, nine, eleven, or more. 7th. When composed of eleven, of whom does it consist? Warder, Sword bearer, Standard bearer, Recorder, Treasurer, Junior Warden, Senior Warden, Prelate, Captain General, Generalissimo, and Grand Commander. 8th. Warder's station? On the left of the Standard bearer, in the west, and on the left of the third division. 9th. His duty?—To observe the orders and directions of the Grand Commander; to see that the sentinels are at their respective posts; and that the encampment is duly guarded. 10th, Sword bearer's station? On the right of the Standard bearer in the west, and on the right of the third division. 11th. His duty? To assist in the protection of the banners of our order; to watch all signals from the Grand Commander, and see his orders duly executed. 12th. Standard bearer's station in the encampment? In the west, and in the centre of the third division. 13th. His duty? To display, support, and protect the banners of our order. 14th. Why is the Standard bearer's station in the west? That the brilliant rays of the rising sun, shedding their lustre upon the banners of our order, may encourage and animate all true and courteous Knights, and dismay and confound their enemies. 15th. Recorder's station in the encampment? In front of the Captain General. 16th. His duty? To observe with attention the order of the encampment, keep a just and regular record of the same, collect the revenue, and pay the same over to the Treasurer. 17th. Treasurer's station in the encampment? In front of the Generalissimo. 18. His duty? To receive in charge all funds and property of the Encampment, pay all orders drawn upon him, and render

F4

a just and faithful account when required. 19. Station of the Junior Warden in the Encampment? At the south west angle of the triangle, and on the left of the first division. 20. His duty? To attend to all poor and weary Pilgrims traveling from afar, to accompany them on their journey, answer all questions for them, and finally introduce them into the asylum. 21. Senior Warden's station in the Encampment? At the north west angle of the triangle, and on the right of second division. 22. His duty there? To attend on Pilgrim Warriors travelling from afar, to comfort and support Pilgrims penitent, and after due trial to recommend them to the hospitality of the Generalissimo. 23. Prelate's station in the Encampment? On the right of the Generalissimo. 24. His duty there? To administer at the altar, and offer up prayers and adorations to the Deity. 25. Captain General's station? On the left of the Grand Commander. 26. His duty? To see that the proper officers make all suitable preparations for the several meetings of the Encampment, and take special care that the asylum is in a suitable array for the introduction of candidates and despatch of business, also to receive and communicate all orders from the Grand Commanders to the officers of the line. 27. Generalissimo's station? On the right of the Grand Commander. 28. His duty? To receive and communicate all orders, signals and petitions, and assist the Grand Commander in the discharge of his various duties, and in his absence to govern the Encampment. 29. Grand Commander's station? In the east. 30. His duty? To distribute alms, and protect weary Pilgrims travelling from afar, to encourage Pilgrim Warriors, to sustain Pilgrims penitent, feed the hungry, clothe the naked, bind up the wounds of the afflicted, to inculcate hospitality, and govern his Encampment with justice and moderation.

SECOND SECTION OF LECTURES.

1. What were the preparatory circumstances attending your reception into this Illustrious Order? I was conducted to the chamber of reflection, where I was left in silence and solitude, to reflect upon three questions which were left with me in writing. 2. What were your answers? They were satisfactory to the Grand Com-

mander, but as a trial of my patience and perseverance he enjoined upon me the performance of seven years pilgrimage, clothed in pilgrim's weeds. 3. What followed? I was then invested with sandals, staff and scrip, and commenced my tour of pilgrimage, but was soon accosted by a guard, who demanded of me, "who comes there?" 4. Your answer? A poor and weary Pilgrim, travelling from afar, to join with those who oft have gone before, and offer his devotions at the holy shrine. 5. What said the guard? Pilgrim, I greet thee, gold and silver have I none, but such as I have, give I unto thee. 6. What followed? After having prticipated in the refreshments, (which is a glass of water and a cracker,) the guard took me by the hand and thus addressed me, "Pilgrim, hearken to a lesson to cheer thee on thy way and insure thee of success." 7. What followed? Lesson read. (See Templar's Chart.) The guard then took me by the hand and said, "fare thee well! God speed thee on thy way." 8. What followed? I still pursued my pilgrimage, but was often accosted by guards, from whom I received the same friendly treatment as from the first. 9. Where did your term of Pilgrimage end? At the door of the Asylum, where after giving the alarm by 3×3, the warder appeared and demanded, "Who comes there?" 10. Your answer? A poor and weary Pilgrim, travelling from afar, who having passed full three long years of Pilgrimage, now craves permission, if it shall please the Grand Commander, forthwith to dedicate the remaining four years to deeds of more exalted usefulness; and if found worthy his strong desire, is now to be admitted to those valiant Knights whose well-earned fame has spread both far and near for deeds of charity and pure beneficence. 11. What were you then asked? What surety can you offer that you are no imposter? 12. Your answer? The commendations of a true and courteous Knight, the Junior Warden, who recommends to the Grand Commander the remission of the four remaining years of Pilgrimage. 13. What followed? The Grand Commander then addressed the Most Excellent Prelate:—This being true, Sir Knight, our Prelate, you will conduct this weary Pilgrim to the altar, where having taken an obligation always to be faithlul to his vow, cause him forthwith to be invest-

F5

ed with a sword and buckler, that as a Pilgrim Warrior, he may perform seven years warfare, as a trial of his courage and constancy. 14. What followed? The Senior Warden then detached a party of Knights to escort me to the altar, where in due form I took upon me the obligation of a Knight Templar. 15. What was that due form? Kneeling on both knees upon two cross swords, my body erect, my naked hands covering the holy bible, square and compass, with two cross swords lying thereon, in which due form I received the solemn obligation of Knight Templar. 16. Repeat the obligation.

"I, A. B. of my own free will and accord, in the presence of Almighty God, and this Encampment of Knight Templars, do hereby and hereon, most solemnly promise and swear, that I will always hale, forever conceal, and never reveal, any of the secret arts, part or points, appertaining to the mysteries of this order of Knight Templars, or within the body of a just and lawful Encampment of such; and not unto him or them, until by due trial, strict examination, or lawful information, I find him or them lawfully entitled to receive the same: Furthermore do I promise and swear, that I will answer and obey all due signs and regular summonses, which shall be given or sent to me from regular Encampment of Knight Templars, if within the distance of forty miles, natural infirmities and unavoidable accidents only excusing me: Furthermore do I promise and swear, that I will help, aid and assist, with my counsel, my purse and my sword, all poor and indigent Knight Templars, their widows and orphans, they making application to me as such, and I finding them worthy, so far as I can do it without material injury to myself, and so far as truth, honor and justice may warrant: Furthermore do I promise and swear, that I will not assist or be present at the forming and opening of an Encampment of Knight Templars, unless there be present seven Knights of the order, or the representatives of three different Encampments, acting under the sanction of a legal warrant: Furthermore do I promise and swear, that I will go the distance of forty miles even barefoot and on frosty ground, to save the life and releive the distresses of a worthy Knight, should I know that his distresses required it, and my abilities permit:

Furthermore do I promise and swear, that I will wield my sword in defence of innocent virgins, destitute widows, helpless orphans, and the Christian Religion: Furthermore do I promise and swear, that I will support and main tain th bye laws of the Encampment of which I may hereafter become a member, the edicts and regulations of the Grand Encampment under which the same may be holden, together with the laws and constitution of the General Grand Encampment of the United States of America, so far as the same shall come to my knowledge: To all this I most solemnly and sincerely promise and swear, with a firm and steady resolution to perform and keep the same, without any hesitation, equivocation, mental reservation, or self-evasion of mind in me whatever, binding myself under no less penalty than to have my head struck off and placed on the highest spire in Christendom, should I knowingly or wilfully violate any part of this my solemn obligation of a Knight Templar. So help me God, and keep me stedfast to perform and keep the same."

17. What followed? The Most Excellent Prelate directed me to arise, and thus addressed me:—"Pilgrim, thou hast craved permission to pass through our solemn ceremonies, and enter the asylum of our Encampment: by thy sandals, scrip and staff, I judge thee to be a child of humility, and charity hospitality are the grand characteristics of this magnanimous order: in the characters of Knight Templars, you arebound to give alms to poor and weary pilgrims travelling from afar, to succour the needy, feed the hungry, clothe the naked, and bind up the wounds of the afflicted. We here wage war against the enemies of innocent virgins, destitute widows, helpless orphans, and the Christian Religion. If thou art desirous of enlisting in this noble and glorious warfare, lay aside thy staff and take up the sword, fighting manfully thy way, and with valour running thy course; and may the Almighty who is a strong tower and defence to all those who put their trust and confidence in him, be now and ever thy defence and thy salvation." 18. What followed? Having laid aside my staff and taken up the sword, the Most Excellent Prelate continued: "Having now taken up the sword, we expect you will make a public declaration of the cause in which you will wield it."

19. Your answer? I wield my sword in defence of innocent virgins, destitute widows, helpless orphans, and the Christian Religion. 20. What was the Prelate's reply? With confidence in this profession, our Senior Warden will invest you with the Warrior's pass, and under his direction, as a trial of your courage and constancy, we must now assign you seven years of warfare—success and victory attend you. (This pass-word is Maher-shalal-hash-baz, and is given under the arch of steel, as has been described.) 21. What followed? I then commenced my tour of warfare, and made professions of the cause in which I would wield my sword. 22. Where did your tour of warfare end? At the door of the asylum, where, on giving the alarm by 3X4, the warder appeared and demanded, "who comes there?" 23. Your reply? A Pilgrim Warrior, travelling from afar, who, having passed full three long years of warfare, is most desirous now, if it should please the Grand Commander, to be admitted to the honors and rewards that await a valiant Templar. 24. What was then demanded of you? What surety can you give that you are no imposter. 25. Your answer? The commendation of a true and courteous Knight, the Senior Warden, who recommends to the Grand Commander the remission of the four remaining years of warfare. 26th. What was then demanded? By what further right or benefit do you expect to gain admittance to the asylum.—27th. Your answer? By the benefit of a pass-word. 28th. Give it? [Here the Warrior's pass is given as before described] 29th. What was then said to you? I was directed to wait with courage and constancy, and soon an answer should be returned to my request. 30th. What answer was returned? Let him be admitted. 31st. What did the Grand Commander then observe? Pilgrim, having gained admittance to our asylum, what profession have you now to make in testimony of your fitness to be received a Knight among our number. 32d. Your answer? Most Eminent, I now declare in truth and soberness, that I hold no enmity or hatred against a being on earth, that I would not freely reconcile, should I find in him a corresponding disposition. 33d. What was the Grand Commander's reply? Pilgrim, the sentiments you

utter are worthy of the cause in which you are engaged; but still we must require some stronger proofs of your faithfulness: the proofs we demand are. that you participate with us in five libations; this being accomplished, we will receive you a Knight among our number. 34th.—What were the ingredients of the libations? Four of them were taken in wine and water, and the fifth in pure wine. 35th. What was the first libation? To the memory of Solomon, king of Israel. 36th. What was the second libation? To the memory of Hyram, King of Tyre. 37th. what was the third? To the memory of Hyram the widow's son, who lost his life in defence of his integrity. 38th. what followed? The Grand Commander then addressed me: Pilgrim, the order to which you seek to unite yourself is founded on the Christian religion; let us then attend to a lesson from the Holy Evangelest. 39th. What followed? The most excellent prelate then read a lesson relative to the apostacy of Judas Iscariot. [See Templar's chart.] 40th. What followed? The Grand Commander then addressed me, "Pilgrim, the twelve tapers you see around the triangle, correspond in number with the disciples of our Savior while on earth, one of whom fell by transgression, and betrayed his Lord and Master; and as a constant admonition to you always to persevere in the paths of honor, integrity, and truth, and as a perpetual memorial of the apostacy of Judas Iscariot, you are required by the rules of our order, to extinguish one of those tapers: and let it ever remind you, that he who can basely violate his vow, and betray his trust, is worthy of no better fate than Judas Iscariot." [The candidate extinguishes one of the tapers: the triangle is placed in the centre of the room, on which are twelve burning candles, between each candlestick a glass of wine, in the centre of the triangle is placed a coffin on which are the bible, scull, and cross-bones.] 41st. What followed? The relics were then uncovered, and the Grand Commander thus addressed me, "Pilgrim, you here behold an emblem of mortality resting on divinity, a human scull resting on the Holy Scriptures; it is to teach us that among all the trials and and vicissitudes which we are destined to endure while passing through the pilgrimage of this life, a firm reliance on divine protection, can alone afford us the consolation and satisfaction which the world can neither give nor take away. 42d. What followed? The Most Excellent Prelate then read a lesson to me with respect to the bitter cup. 43d. What followed? The Grand Commander took the scull in his hand, and pronounced the following Soliloquy: "How striking is this emblem of mortality, once animated like us, but now it ceases to act or think; its vital energies are extinct and all the powers of life have ceased their operations; and such, my brethren, is the state to which we are all hastening: let us, therefore, gratefully improve the remaining space of life, that, when our weak and frail bodies, like this memento, shall become cold and inanimate, and mouldering in sepulchural dust and ruins, our disembodied spirits may soar aloft to the blessed regions where dwells light and life eternal." 44th. What followed? The Most Excellent Prelate then read a lesson relative to the crucifixion. [See Templar's Chart.] 45th. What was the fourth libation? To the memory of Simon of Cyrene, the early friend and disciple of our Savior, who was compelled to bear his cross, and fell a martyr to his fate. 46th. What followed? The Grand Commander then addressed me: "Pilgrim, before you can be permitted to participate in the fifth libation, we must enjoin on you one year's penance as a trial of your faith and humility, which you will perform under the direction of the Junior and Senior Warden, with the scull in one hand and a lighted taper in the other, which is to teach you that with faith and humility you should cause your light to so shine before men, that they seeing your good works may glorify our father which is in heaven." 47th. What followed? I then commenced my tour of penance, and passed in a humble posture through the sepulchre, where the fifth lesson was read by the Senior Warden, relative to the resurrection. (Here the ascension of the Savior is represented on canvass, which the candidate is directed to look at: at the same time the Sir Knights sing a hymn.) After the hymn the prelate speaks as follows:

"I am the resurrection and the life, saith the Lord; he that believeth on me, though he were dead, yet shall he be made alive; and whosoever liveth and believeth on me shall never die. Pilgrim, the scene before you represents the splendid conclusion of the hallowed sacrifice, offered by the Redeemer of the world, to propitiate the anger of an offended Deity. This sacred volume informs us that our Savior, after having suffered the pains of death, descended into the place of departed spirits, and that on the third day he burst the bands of death, triumphed over the grave, and in due time ascended with transcendent majesty to heaven, where he now sits on the right hand of our heavenly father, a mediator and intercessor for all those who have faith in him. I now invest you with an emblem of that faith: (at the same time suspends from his neck a black cross:) it is also an emblem of our order, which you will wear as a constant memorial, for you to imitate the virtues of the immaculate Jesus, who died that you might live. Pilgrim, the ceremonies in which you are now engaged are calculated deeply to impress your mind, and I trust will have a happy and lasting effect upon your character. You were first, as a trial of your faith and humility, enjoined to perform seven years of pilgrimage; it represents the great pilgrimage of life through which we are all passing: we are all weary pilgrims, anxiously looking forward to that asylum, where we shall rest from our labors, and be at rest forever. You were then directed, as a trial of your courage and constancy, to perform seven years' warfare; it represents to you the constant warfare with the lying vanities and deceits of this world, in which it is necessary for us always to be engaged. You are now performing a penance as a trial of your humility.—Of this our Lord and Savior has left us a bright example. For though he was the Eternal Son of God, he humbled himself to be born of a woman, to endure the pains and afflictions incident to human nature, and finally to suffer a cruel and ignominious death upon the cross: it is also a trial of that faith which will conduct you safely over the dark gulph of everlasting death, and land your enfranchised spirit in the peaceful abodes of the blessed. Pilgrim, keep ever in your memory this awful truth, you know not how soon you may be called upon to render an account to that Supreme Judge, from whom not even the most minute act of your life is hid-

What was this obligation called? The sealed obligation. 69th. Why so? Because any obligation entered into, or promise ad in reference to this obligation, is considered by Knight Templars as more binding and serious than any other special obligation could be. 70th. What followed? The Most Excellent Prelate then read the sixth lesson, relative to the election of Matthias. [See chart.] 71st. What followed? The Generalissimo thus addressed the Grand ommander. "Most Eminent, by the extinguished taper on the triangle, I perceive there is a vacancy in our Encampment, which I propose should be filled by a choice from among those valiant Knights who have sustained the trials and performed the ceremonies required by our order." 72d. What followed? The Grand Commander then ordered the lots to be given forth, which being done, I was elected, and the Grand Commander thus addressed me, "In testimony of your election as a companion among us, and of your acceptance of that honor, you will re-light that extinguished taper; and may the Almighty lift upon you the light of his countenance and preserve you from falling." 73d. What followed? The Grand Commander then directed me to kneel, and said, by virtue of the high power in me vested as the successor and representative of Hugh De Paganis, and Geoffrey, of St. Omers, I now dub and create you, Knight Templar, Knight of Malta, of the ho y order of St. John of Jerusalem. [This is repeated three times, at the same time laying the blade of his sword first upon the right shoulder, then upon the head, and then upon the left shoulder of the candidate.] 74th. What followed? The Grand Commander then presented me a sword and thus addressed me, "this sword in your hand, as a true and courteous Knight, will be endowed with hree most excellent qualities; its hilt be justice impartial, its blade be fortitude undaunted, and its point be mercy; and let it teach us this important lesson, that we should ever be assured of the justice of the cause in which we draw our swords, and being thus assured, we should persevere with the most undaunted fortitude, and finally having subdued our enemies, we should consider them no longer such, but extend to them the most glorious attribute of God's mercy." 75. What followed? The Grand Commander then communicated to me the due guard, the penitent's pass, and the grand sign, grip and word of Knight Templars. 76. Give the due guard? (The sign is given by placing the *end* of the right thumb under the chin.) 77. To what does it allude? To the penalty of my obligation: to have my head struck off and placed upon the highest spire in Christemdom. 78. Give the penitent's pass? It is given as before described; the word is Golgotha. 79. What does this word allude to?

80. Give the grand sign? This sign is given by placing yourself in a situation, representing the Crucifixion of Christ. 81. To what does this sign allude? To the manner in which the Savior expired upon the Cross, and expiated the sins of the world. 82 Give the grip and word? The grip is given by interlacing the fingers of the right and left hand, with the fingers of the right and left hands of the Candidate, which forms a Cross. 83. What is the word? Immanuel. (This word is given at the time of giving the grip, and is the name of the grip.) 84 What does the grip teach us? That as our fingers are thus strongly interlaced, so should the hearts of Knight Templars be firmly interlaced in friendship and brotherly love. 85. What is the motto of our order? Rex regium et dominus dominonum. 86. How do you translate it? King of Kings, and Lord of Lords

---

KNIGHTS OF THE CHRISTIAN MARK
AND GUARDS OF THE CONCLAVE.

This conclave is governed by an Invincible Knight of the Order of St. John of Jerusalem, a Senior and Junior Knight, six Grand Ministers, Recorder, Treasurer, Conductor, and Guard

Opening.—" Sir Junior Knight, are all convened in a secret place, and secured from the prying eye of the profane?"

" We are, Invincible "

"Sir Senior Knight, instruct the Sir Knights to assemble in form for the purpose of opening this Invincible order."

The members kneel on both knees in a circle, each with his right hand on his heart, his left on his forehead.

Prayer.—" Eternal source of life, of light and perfection, Supreme God and Governor of all things, liberal dispenser of every blessing! we adore and magnify thy holy name for

G

the many blessings we have received from thy hands, and acknowledge our unworthiness to appear before thee; but for the sake and in the name of thy atoning Son we approach thee as lost and undone children of wrath; but through the blood of sprinkling, and the sanctification of the Holy Ghost, we come imploring a continuation of thy favors, for thou hast said that he who cometh to thee through faith in the son of thy love, thou wilt in no wise cast out; therefore at the foot of the cross we come, supplicating pardon for our past offences, that they may be blotted out from the book of thy remembrance, and be seen no more, and that the remainder of our days be spent as becometh the followers of the Holy One of Israel; and graciously grant that love, harmony, peace and unity may reign in this Council; that one spirit may animate us—one God reign over us, and one heaven receive us, there to dwell in thine adorable presence, for ever and ever. Amen."

The Invincible Knight takes the Bible and waves it four times over his head, saying, "REX REGNATIUM ET DOMINUS DOMINATIUM,"* kisses it and passes it on his right; it goes around until it comes again to the Invincible Knight, who opens and reads, Matthew, 5, 3—12, 16.

Always interlace the fingers of the left hand, draw your sword and present to the heart and say, "Tammuz Touliumeth: I pronounce this convention opened in ample form. Let us repair to our several stations, and strictly observe silence" *Preparation*—The candidate is shewn into the antichamber by the conductor, who clothes him in a gown of brown stuff, and leads him to the door of the council chamber where he knocks twice, six, and two, 2, 6, & 2 *Junior Knight*, "some one knocks for admission, Invincible Knight." *Invincible*, "see who it is, and make report" J. K. (goes to the door and reports) "one that is faithful in good works wishes admission here." *Inv.* "what good works hath he performed?" J. K. "he hath given food to the hungry, drink to the thirsty, and clothed the naked with a garment." *Inv.* "thus far he hath done well, but there is still much for him to do." 'To be faithful in my house, saith the Lord of Hosts, filled with love for my people.' If so, let him enter under the penalties of his symbolic obligation." He enters, makes signs until he arrives at the altar, there kneels. *Vow.*—"I, A. B. do promise and vow, with this same volume clasped in my hands,

---

*This phrase is probably intended to be translated "King of Kings and Lord of Lords." We infer this from its being subsequently thus written in plain English, although we know of no rules that would authorize a translation.—*Ed. Le Roy Gaz*

that I will keep secret the words, signs. tokens, and grips of this order of Knighthood from all but those Knights of St. John of Jerusalem, who have shewn a christian disposition to their fellow men, are professors of the christian faith, and have passed through the degrees of symbolic masonry; and that I will protect and support, as far as in me lies, the followers of the Lord Jesus Christ: feed them if hungry, give them drink if thirsty, if naked clothe them with garments, teach them if ignorant, and advise them for their good and their advantage. All this I promise in the name of the Father, of the Son and of the Holy Ghost; and if I perform it not, *let me be* ANATHEMA MARANATHA! ANATHEMA MARANATHA!!"*

The Invincible Knight interlaces the fingers of his left hand with those of the candidate, who lays his right hand on his heart. The Invincible Knight draws his sword; the Senior Knigt does the same; they cross them on the back of the candidate's neck, and the Invincible Knight says, "by virtue of the high power in me vested by a bull of *His Holiness, Pope Sylvester*, I dub you a Knight of the Christian Mark, member of the Grand Council, and Guard of the Grand Conclave." The Invincible Knight then whispers in his ear, "Tammuz Touhumeth." The Knights come to order: the Senior Knight takes his seat, the candidate continues standing the Conductor brings a white robe; the Senior Knight says, "thus saith the Lord, he that believeth and endureth to the [illegible] " overcome, and I will cause his iniquities to pass from h[illegible] he shall dwell in my presence for ever and ever Take away his filthy garments from him and clothe him with a change of raiment. For he that overcometh, the same shall be clothed in white raiment, and his name shall be written in the book of life, and I will confess his name before my father and his holy angels. He that hath an ear to hear let him hear what the Spirit saith unto the true believer. Set ye a fair mitre upon his head, place a palm in his hand, for he shall go in and out and minister before me, saith the Lord of Hosts, and he shall be a disciple of that rod taken from the branch of the stem of Jesse. For a branch has grown out of his root, and the Spirit of the Lor[d] hath rested upon it; the spirit of his wisdom and might and righteousness is the girdle of his loins, and faithfulness the girdle of his vine, and he stands as an *Insignia* to the people, and him shall the Gentiles seek, and his rest shall be glorious. Cause them that have charge over the city to draw near, every one with the destroying weapon in his hand."

**Anathema Maranatha* is a phrase used once in the Scriptures. It signifies "accursed at the aiming of the Lord."—*Ed. Gaz.*

G2

The six Grand Ministers come forward from the north with swords and shields The first is clothed in white, and has an ink-horn by his side, and stands before the Invincible Knight, who says: "Go through the city; run in the midst thereof and smite; let not thine eye spare, neither have pity, for they have not executed my judgments with clean hands, saith the Lord of Hosts" The candidate is instructed to exclaim: "Woe is me, for I am a man of unclean lips, and my dwelling has been in the tents of Kedar and among the children of Meshec." Then he that has the inkhorn by his side takes a live coal with the tongs from the altar, and touches the lips of the candidate and says, "If ye believe, thine iniquities shall be taken away, thy sins shall be purged: I will that these be clean with the branch that shall be given up before me. All thy sins are removed and thine iniquities blotted out. For I have trodden the wine press alone, and with me was none of my people For behold I come with dyed garments from Bozrate, mighty to save. Refuse not therefore to hearken; draw not away thy shoulders; shut not thine ear that thou shouldst not hear." The six ministers now proceed as if they were about to commence the slaughter, when the Senior Knight says to him with the inkhorn: "Stay thine hand, proceed no further until thou hast set a mark on those that are faithful in the house of the Lord, and trust in the power of his might. Take ye the signet and set a mark on the forehead of my people that have passed through great tribulation and have washed their robes, and have made them white in the blood of the Lamb, which was slain from the foundation of the world." The Minister takes the signet and presses it on the candidate's forehead. He leaves the mark in red letters, "*King of Kings and Lord of Lords.*" The Minister opens the scroll and says, "Sir Invincible Knight, the number of the sealed are one hundred and forty and four thousand." The Invincible Knight strikes four, and all the Knights stand before him. He says, "Salvation belongeth to our God which sitteth upon the throne and unto the Lamb." All the members fall on their faces and say, "Amen. Blessing, honor, glory, wisdom, thanksgiving and power, might, majesty, and dominion, be unto our God, forever and ever, Amen." They all cast down crowns and palm branches, and rise up and say: "Great and numberless are thy works, thou King of saints. Behold the star which I laid before Joshua, on which is engraved seven eyes, as the engraving of a signet, shall be set as a seal on thine arm—as a seal on thine heart; for love is stronger than death; many waters cannot quench it: If a man would give all the treasures of his house for love he cannot obtain it : It is the gift of God through Jesus Christ our Lord."

Charge.—Invincible Knight, I congratulate you on your having been found worthy to be promoted to this honorable Order of Knighthood. It is highly honorable to all those worthy Knights, who with good faith and diligence perform its many important duties. The honorable situation to which you are now advanced, and the illustrious office which you now fill, is one that was much desired by the first noblemen of Italy, but ambition and jealousy caused his Highness, *Pope Alexander*, to call on his ancient friend, the Grand Master of the Knight of St. John of Jerusalem, to guard his person and the Holy See,as those Knights were known to be well grounded in the faith, and zealous followers of the Lord. The members of the guard were chosen *by their countenances*, for it is believed that a plain countenance is an indication of the heart ; and that no stranger should gain admission and discover the secrets of this august assembly, this Order of *Christian Mark* was conferred on those who went about doing good,and following the example of their Illustrious Master, Jesus Christ. Go thou and do likewise."

Motto.—" Christus regnat, vincit, triumphat.* Rex regnantium et Dominus dominantium."

Israel on the left breast, a triangular plate of gold, seven eyes engraved on one side, on the other the letter G in the five points.

---

* Christ rules, conquers, triumphs.—*Ed. Le Roy Gaz.*

KNIGHTS OF THE HOLY SEPULCHRE.

History.—St. Helena, daughter of Caylus, King of Britain, consort of Constantine, and Mother of Constantine the Great, in the year 296 made a journey to the Holy Land in search of the Cross of Jesus Christ. After levelling the hillocks and destroying the temple of Venus, three Crosses were discovered. It was now difficult to discover which of the three was the one sought for by her. By order of his holiness, Pope Marcellinus, they were borne to the bed of a woman who had long been visited by sickness and lay at the point of death : she placed her hands upon the second Cross first, which rendered her no service, but when she laid her l and upon the third, she was

G3

restored to her former health. She instantly arose, giving glory to God, saying he was wounded for our transgressions, he was bruised for our iniquities, the chastisement of sin was upon him, and with his stripes we are healed, and God hath laid on him all our iniquities. On the spot where the Crosses were found, St. Helena erected a stately Church, one hundred paces long and sixty wide, the east end takes in the place where the Crosses stood, and the west of the Sepulchre; by levelling the hills the Sepulchre is above the floor of the Church, like a grotto which is twenty feet from the floor to the top of the rock: there is a Superb Cupola over the Sepulchre, and in the aisle are the tombs of Godfrey and Baldwin, Kings of Jerusalem. In 302 St. Helena instituted the Order of Knights of the Holy Sepulchre of our Lord and Saviour Jesus Christ. This Order was confirmed in 304 by his Holiness, Pope Marcellinus: they were bound by a sacred vow to guard the Holy Sepulchre, protect pilgrims, and fight Infidels, and enemies of the Cross of Christ. The city of Jerusalem was rebuilt and ornamented by Ælias Adrian, Emperor of Rome, and given to the Christians in 120. The Persians took it from them in 637, and in 1008 it fell into the hands of the Turks, under whose oppressions it long groaned, until Peter the Holy steered the western Princes to release the distressed Church, and in 1096 Godfrey and Baldwin unfurled the banner of the Cross and expelled the Turks. He was to have been invested with the royal wreath of majesty, but he thought it not meet to wear a crown of laurel when his blessed Saviour had worn a crown of thorns. Yet for the common good he suffered himself to be called the King of Palestine.

DESCRIPTION, &c.

The Council must represent a Cathedral Church, the altar covered with black, upon which must be placed three large candles, a Cross, and in the centre a scull and cross bones. The Principal stands on the right side of the altar, with a Bible in one hand, and a staff in the other; soft music plays, and the Vail is drawn up, and discovers the altar: the Choir say:

"Hush, hush, the heavenly choir,
They cleave the air in bright attire:
See, see, the lute each angel brings,
And hark divinely thus they sing:

"To the power divine,
All glory be given,
By man upon earth,
And angels in heaven."

The Priest stops before the altar and says: "Keyric Elieson, Christe Elieson, Keyric Elieson, Amen: Gloria Sibi Domini! I declare this Grand Council opened, and ready to proceed to business." The Priests and Ministers take their severa stations and observe order. The candidates being prepared, he alarms at the door by seven raps, and the Prelate says to Verger, "see the cause of that alarm and report." Verger goes to the door and reports: "Right Reverend Prelate, there are seven brethren who solicit admission to this Grand Council." Prelate says, "On what is their desire founded?" Verger, "On a true christian principle, to serve the church and its members, by performing the seven corporeal works of mercy, and to protect and guard the holy Sepulchre, from the destroying hands of our enemies." Prelate, "Admit them that we may know them, if you please." They are then admitted: Prelate says to them, "Are you followers of the Captain of our salvation?" Verger says, "We are Right Reverend Prelate." P. "Attend then to the sayings of our Master Jesus Christ" Thou shalt love the Lord thy God with all thy heart, with all thy mind, with all thy soul, and with all thy might. This is the first great commandment and the second is like unto it: thou shalt love thy neighbor as thyself: on these two commandments hang all the law and the prophets. The Verger and Beadle hold the bible on which the candidates place their right hands. Vow: I, A. B. in the name of the high and undivided Trinity, do promise and vow to keep and conceal the high mysteries of this noble and invincible order of Knights of the Holy Sepulchre, from all but such as are ready and willing to serve the Church of Christ, by acts of valor and charity, and its members by performing all the corporal works of mercy; and that as far as in me lies I will defend the Church of the Holy Sepulchre from pillage and violence, and guard and protect pilgrims on their way to and from the Holy Land; and if I perform not this my vow, to the best of my abilities, let me become *Inanimatus*. Interlace your fingers with the candidate, cross your arms and say, "De mortuis nil nisi bonum." Prelate says, "Take the sword and travel onward—guard the Holy Sepulchre—defeat our enemies—unfurl the banner of our Cross—protect the Roman Eagle—return to us with victory and safety The candidates depart—go to the south where they meet a band of Turks, a desperate conflict ensues, the Knights are victorious; they seize the crescent, and return to the Cathedral in triumph, and place the Banner, Eagle and Crescent before the altar, and take their seats. (22d chap. St. John, read by Prelate.) Then the Choir sing,

G4

"Creator of the radiant light,
Dividing day from sable night;
Who with the light bright origin,
The world's creation didst begin."

Prelate then says, "Let our prayer come before thee, and let our exercises be acceptable in thy sight." The seven candidates kneel at the foot of the altar. The Prelate takes the bread and says, "Brethren, eat ye all of this bread in love, that ye may learn to support each other." He then takes the cup and says, "Drink ye all of this cup to ratify the vow that ye have made, and learn to sustain one another." The Prelate then raises them up by the grip, (interlace the fingers)and says, "1st, Sir, I greet thee a Knight of the Holy Sepulchre;: go feed the hungry : 2d. Give drink to the thirsty. 3d. Clothe the naked with a garment. 4th Visit and ransom the captives. 5th. Harbor the harborless, give the orphan and widow where to lay their heads. 6th. Visit and relieve the sick. 7th. Go and bury the dead." All make crosses and say, "In nomini;patria filio et spiritus sancto, Amen. Prelate says, "Brethren, let us recommend to each other the practice of the four cardinal virtues ; Prudence, Justice, Temperance, Fortitude." Closing. The Knights all rise, stand in circle, interlace their fingers and say, "Sepulchrum" Prelate then says, "Gloria Patria et filio et spiritus sancto." Brethren answer, "Senet erat in principio et nunc et semper et in secule seculovuem. Amen.

Benediction.—"Blessed be those, oh Lord our God! Great first cause and Governor of all things! thou createst the world with thy bountiful hand, and sustained it by thy wisdom, by thy goodness and by thy mercy! It cometh to pass that seed time and harvest never fail! It is thou that givest every good and perfect gift! Blessed be thy name for ever and ever!" To examine a Knight of the Holy Sepulchre. he holds up the first finger of the right hand, Knight holds up the second. you then hold up the third, and he shuts up his first: this signifies three persons in one Godhead.

THE HOLY AND THRICE ILLUSTRIOUS ORDER OF THE CROSS, CALLED A COUNCIL

Diploma of a Comp. of the ancient Council of the Trinity.

Anno Cr. seu Covt. 896.

C F M C S C A O P	THE ANCIENT COUNCIL OF THE TRINITY, BY THEIR SUCCESSORS IN THE UNITED STATES OF AMERICA.

ST ALBERT, To Every Knight Companion of the Holy and Thrice Illustrious ORDER OF THE CROSS: Be it known unto you, that, with regard to unquestionable vouchers, we have confirmed the Induction of the Knight Templar Mason into the Councils of the said Order of Knighthood, and herein do warrant him as a worthy and ILLUSTRIOUS Companion thereof: and hoping and confiding that he will ever so demean himself as to conduct to the Glory of I. H. S., the Most Holy and Almighty GOD, and to the honor of his MARK, we do recommend and submit him to the confidence of all those throughout the world, who can truly and deservedly say, "I am a Christian:" and that no unwarrantable benefits shall arise from this Diploma, and we charge all concerned, cautiously and prudently to Mark the bearer on the mystic letters therein contained, and to regard only the result, in its application and privileges.

Done out of Council, at Le Roy, in the county of Genesee, and State of New-York, of these U. S. A. *August* 1st, 1827.

	Sir——————
COMMENDATIONS,	SOVEREIGN PREFECT.
SIR KNIGHTS COMP'NS.	SIR J. H. C. MILLER,
	ACT'G PREF.

The officers and Council all in their places. The Most Illustrious Prefect addresses the Most Worthy Provost thus: "Most Worshipful Provost, what is the o'clock?" Most Worshipful Provost says, rising and facing the east, at the same time rising his Mark in his right hand, "Most Illustrious Prefect, it is now the first hour of the day, the time when our Lord suffered and the veil of the Temple was rent asunder, when darkness and consternation [illegible] spread over the earth, when the confusion of the old Covenant was made light in the new, in the Temple of the Cross. It is, Most Illustrious Prefect, the third watch, when the implements of Masonry were broken—when the flame, which led the wise men of the east, re-appeared—when the cubick stone was broken, and the word was given. Most Illustrious Prefect,

G5

says to Worthy Herald: "It is my will that this house of God be closed, and the remembrance of those solemn and sacre events, be here commemorated: make this, Worthy Herald, known to the Most Worshipful Provost in due and ancient form." The Worthy Herald bows and approaches the Most Worshipful Provost, where he bows thrice, faces about and gives a blast with his horn, and after the Knights have filed out by threes without the door, except the worthy Senior Inductor, he does his errand, viz: "Most Worshipful Provost, it is the Sovereign will of Count Albertus, of Pergamus, that this house of God be closed, and that those solemn and sacred events in the new Covenant be here commemorated; you will observe this." The Worthy Herald bows, and the Most Worshipful Provost rises and addresses the Worthy Sen. Inductor thus, "It is the will of the Most Illustrious Prefect that here now be opened a Council of Knights of the Cross: what therein becoms your duty?" Worthy Senior Inductor says, "to receive the commands of my superiors in the order, and pay obedience thereto—to conduct and instruct my ignorant pass-brethren; and to revere, and inculcate reverence in others, for the Most Holy and Almighty God." The Most Worshipful Provost rises fiercely and says, "by what right do you claim this duty?" Worthy S. Inductor says, "by the right of a sign, and the mark of a sign." Most Worshipful Provost says, "will you give me a sign?" Worthy Sen. "I could if I should." The Most Worshipful Provost then partly extends both arms, pointing downwards to an angle of 39°, with the palms open, and upwards, to shew they are not sullied with iniquity and oppression, and says, "Worthy Sen. Inductor, you may give it." The Worthy S Inductor then looks him full in the face, and with his fore finger touches his right temple, and lets fall his hand and says, "this is a sign" Most Worshipful Provost says, "a sign of what?" Worthy S. Inductor says, "aye, a sign of what?" Wor. Pro. says, "a penal sign." Worthy S. Inductor says, "your sign is—" Most Worthy Pro. says, "the last sign of my induction." Most Worthy Pro. says, "but you have the mark of a sign" Worthy S. Inductor says, "the sign whereof my mark is a mark, I hope is in the Council above." Most Worthy Pro. says, "but the mark—" Worthy S Inductor says, "is in my bosom." Thereupon he produces his mark in his left hand, and with the fore finger of his right on the letter S on the cross, asks, "what's that?" Most Wor. Pro. says, "Lisha." Wor. Pro. puts his finger on the letter H; and asks, "what is this?" Worthy S. Inductor says, "Sha." Worthy S. Inductor then puts his finger on the letter I, and asks, "what is this?" Most Wor. Pro. says, "Baal." What then is your Mark? Worthy S. Inductor says, "Baal, Sha, Lisha, I am the Lord." The Most Worshipful Provost then says, "you are my brother, and the duty is yours of ancient right: please announce the council open." The worthy Senior Inductor steps to the door and gives three raps, and is answered by some Knight from without, who is then admitted, and the worthy S. Inductor gives the *conditional* sign, (which is by partly extending both arms, as before described,) the Knight answering by putting his finger to his right temple, as before. The worthy S. Inductor then addresses the chair, thus: "Most Illustrious Prefect, a professing brother is within the council by virtue of a sign." Most Illustrious Prefect says to Worthy Herald, "go to this professing brother, and see him marked before the chair of the Most Worshipful Provost: conduct him thither, Worthy Herald." The Worthy Herald says to the Knight, "worthy Sir, know you the sacred cross of our council?" Knight says, "I am a Christian." The Worthy Herald then says, "follow me." When arrived before the Most Wor Pro. the Worthy Herald says, "Most Worthy Provost, by order of the Most Illustrious Prefect, I here bring you to be marked a professing brother of the cross." The Most Wor. Pro. says, "worthy sir, know you the cross of our council?" Knight says, "I am a christian." The Most Worthy Pro. says, "no more."

OBLIGATIONS OF THRICE ILLUSTRIOUS KNIGHTS OF THE CROSS.

FIRST OBLIGATION.

You, Mr.—, do now by your honor, and in view of the power and union of the Thrice Illustrious Order of the Cross, now first made known to you, and in the dread presence of the most holy and almighty God, solemnly and sincerely swear and declare, that to the end of your life you will not, either in consideration of gain, interest, or honor, nor with good or bad design, ever take any the least step or measure, or be instrumental in any such object, to betray or communicate to any person or being, or number of the same, in the known world, not thereto of cross and craft entitled, any secret or secrets, or ceremony or ceremonies, or any part thereof appertaining to the order and degree known among Masons as the Thrice

Illustrious Order of the Cross.—That you will not, at any time or times whatever, either now or hereafter, directly or indirectly, by letter, figure or character however or by whoever made, ever communicate any of the information and secret mysteries heretofore alluded to.—That you will never speak on or upon, or breathe high or low, any ceremony or secret appertaining thereto, out of council, where there shall not be two or more Knights companions of the order present, besides yourself, and that in a safe and sure place, whereby any opinion even of the nature and general principles of the institution can be formed by any other person, be he Mason or otherwise, than a true Knight companion of the cross: nothing herein going to interfere with the prudent practice of the duties enjoined by the order, or any arrangement for their enforcement.

2. You further swear that should you know another to violate any essential point of this obligation, you will use your most decided endeavors, by the blessing of God, to bring such person to the strictest and most condign punishment, agreeable to the rules and usages of our ancient fraternity; and this by pointing him out to the world as an unworthy vagabond; by opposing his interest by deranging his business, by transferring his character after him wherever he may go, and by exposing him to the contempt of the whole fraternity and the world, but of our Illustrious order more especially, during his whole natural life: nothing herein going to prevent yourself or any other, when elected to the dignity of Thrice Illustrious, from retaining the ritual of the order, if prudence and caution appear to be the governing principle in so retaining it, such dignity authorising the elected to be governed by no rule but the dictates of his own judgment, in regard to what will best conduce to the interest of the order; but that he be responsible for the character of those whom he may induct, and for the concealment of the said ritual.

3. Should any Thrice Illustrious Knight or acting officer of any council which may have them in hand, ever require your aid in any emergency in defence of the recovery of his said charge, you swear cheerfully to exercise all assistance in his favor which the nature of the time and place will admit, even to the sacrifice of life, liberty and property. To all and every part thereof we then bind you, and by ancient usage you bind yourself, under the no less infamous penalty than dying the death of a traitor, by having a spear or other sharp instrument, like as our divine Master, thrust in your left side, bearing testimony even in death of the power and justice of the mark of the holy cross.

SECOND OBLIGATION.

"Mr.——before you can be admitted to the light and benefit of this Thrice Illustrious order, it becomes my duty, by ancient usage, to propose to you certain questions, not a thing vainly ceremonial; but the companions will expect true answers: they will concern your past life, and resolutions for the future. Have you given me without evasion or addition your baptismal and family names, and those of your parents, your true age as far as within your knowledge; where you were educated, where you were born, and also where was your last place of residence? or have you not? 'I have.' It is well.

2d Were your parents free and not slaves? had they right and title in the soil of the earth? were they devoted to the religion of the cross, and did they so educate their family? have you searched the spiritual claims of that religion on your gratitude and your affections? and have you continued steadfast in that faith from choice and a conviction of your duty to heaven, or from education? 'From duty and chice.' This also is right.

3d. Have you ever up to this time lived according to the principles of that religion by acting upon the square of virtue with all men, nor defrauding any, nor defamed the good name of any, nor indulged sensual appetites unreasonably, but more especially to the dishonor of the matrimonial tie, nor extorted on, or oppressed the poor. 'I have not been guilty of these things.' You have then entitled yourself to our highest confidence by obeying the injunctions of our Thrice Illustrious Prefect in heaven, 'of doing to all men even as you would that they should do unto you.' Mr.—can you so continue to act, that yearly on the anniversary of St. Albert, you can solemnly swear for the past season you have not been guilty of the crimes enumerated in these questions? 'By the help of God I can.' Be it so, then, that annually. on the anniversary of St. Albert, you swear to these great questions; and the confidence of the Knights Companions of the Order in you, rests on your being able so to do.

4th. For the future then, you promise to be a good man, and to be governed by the moral laws of God and the rules of the Order, in always dealing openly, honorably, and above deceit, especially with the Knights Companions of the Order. 'I do.'

5th You promise so to act with all mankind, but especially with the fraternity, as that you shall never be justly called a bad paymaster, ungrateful, a liar, a rake, or a libertine, a man careless in the business of your vocation, a drunkard, or a tyrant. 'I do.'

6th. You promise to lead a life as upright and just in relation to all mankind as you are capable of, but in matters of difference to preserve the interest of a companion of the order, of a companion's friend for whom he pleads, to any mere man of the world. I 'do.'

7th. You promise never to engage in mean party strife, nor conspiracies against the government or religion of your country, whereby your reputation may suffer, nor ever to associate with dishonorable men even for a moment, except it be to secure the interest of such person, his family or friends, to a companion, whose necessities require this degradation at your hands. 'I do.'

8th. You promise to act honorably in all matters of office or vocation, even to the value of the one third part of a Roman penny, and never to take any advantage therein unworthy the best countenance of your companions, and this, that they shall not, by your unworthiness, be brought into disrepute. I 'do.'

THIRD OBLIGATION.

"I do now, by the honor and power of the mark of the Holy and Illustrious Order of the Cross, which I do now hold to heaven in my right hand as the earnest of my faith, and in the dread presence of the most holy and almighty God, solemnly swear and declare, that I do hereby accept of, and forever will consider the cross and mark of this order as my only hope: that I will make it the test of faith and fellowship; and that I will effect its objects and defend its mysteries to the end of my days with my life and with my property—and first, that in the state of collision and misunderstanding impiously existing among the princes and pilgrims, defenders and champions of the holy cross of Jesus our Lord, now assembled in the land and city of their peace, and considering that the glory of the Most High requires the greatest and strictest unanimity of measures and arms, the most sacred union of sentiment and brotherly love in the soldiers who there thus devote themselves to his cause and banner, I swear strictly to dedicate myself, my life and my property forever hereafter to his holy name and the purposes of our mark, and to the best interest of all those who thus with me become Knights of the Cross: I swear forever to give myself to this holy and illustrious order, confiding fully and unreservedly in the purity of their morals and the ardor of their pious enthusiasm, for the recovery of the land of their fathers, and the blessed clime of our Lord's sufferings, and never to renounce the mark of the order nor the claims and welfare of my brethren.

2nd. And that the holy and pious enthusiasm of my brethren may not have slander or disgrace at my hands, or the order be injured by my unworthiness, I swear forever to renounce tyranny and oppression in my own person and place, whatever it may be, and to stand forth against it in others, whether public or private: to become the champion of the cross; to observe the common good; be the protector of the poor and unfortunate; and ever to observe the common rights of human nature without encroachment or permitting encroachment thereon, if in my power to prevent or lessen it. I will moreover act in subordination to the laws of my country, and never countenance any change in the government under which I live, without good and answerable reasons for so doing, that ancient usages and immemorial customs be not overturned.

3d I swear to venerate the mark as the wisdom and decree of Heaven, to unite our hands and hearts in the work of the holy crusade, and as an encouragement to act with zeal and efficacy; and I swear to consider its testimonies as the true and only proper test of an Illustrious brother of the Cross.

4th. I swear to wear the mark of this order, without any the least addition except what I shall be legally entitled to by *Induction*, forever, if not without the physical means of doing so, or it being contrary to propriety; and even then, if possible, to wear the holy cross; and I swear to put a chief dependence for the said worthy and pious objects therein.

5th. I swear to put confidence unlimited in every Illustrious brother of the Cross, as a true and worthy follower of the blessed Jesus, who has sought this land not for private good, but pity, and the glory of the religion of the Most High and holy God.

6th. I swear never to permit my political principles nor personal interest to come counter to his, if forbearance and brotherly kindness can operate to prevent it; and never to meet him if I know it, in war or in peace, under such circumstances that I may not in justice to myself, my cross and my country, wish him unqualified success; and if perchance it should happen without my knowledge, on being informed thereof, that I will use my best endeavors to satisfy him, even to the relinquishing my arms and purpose. I will never shed a brother's blood nor thwart his good fortune, knowing him to be such, nor see it done by others if in my power to prevent it.

7th. I swear to advance my brother's best interest, by always supporting his military fame and political preferment in opposition to another; and by employing his arms or his aid in his vocation, under all circumstances where I shall not suffer more by so doing, than he, by my neglecting to do so, but this never to the sacrifice of any vital interest in our holy religion, or in the welfare of my country.

8th. I swear to look on his enemies as my enemies, his friends as my friends, and stand forth to mete out tender kindness or vengeance accordingly: but never to intrude on his social or domestic relations to his hurt or dishonor, by claiming his privileges, or by debauching or defaming his female relations or friends.

9th. I swear never to see calmly nor without earnest desires and decided measures to prevent the ill treatment, slander or defamation, of any brother Knight, nor ever to view danger or the least shadow of injury about to fall on his head without well and truly informing him thereof; and if in my power to prevent it, never to fail by my sword or counsel, to defend his welfare and good name.

10th. I do swear never to prosecute a brother before those who know not our order, till the remonstrances of a council shall be inadequate to do me justice.

11th. I swear to keep sacred my brother's secrets, both when delivered to me as such, and when the nature of the information is such as to require secrecy for his welfare.

12th I swear to hold myself bound to him, especially in affliction and adversity, to contribute to his necessities my prayers, my influence and my purse.

13th I swear to be under the control of my council, or, if belonging to none, to that which is nearest to me, and never to demur to, or complain at any decree concerning me, which my brethren, as a council, shall conceive me to deserve, and enforce on my head, to my hurt and dishonor.

14th. I swear to obey all summonses sent from any council to me, or from any Most Illustrious Knight, whether Illustrious Counsellor for the time being, or by *Induction*, and to be governed by the constitution, usages and customs of the order without variation or change.

15. I swear never to see nor permit more than two Candidates, who with the Senior Inductor, will make three, to be advanced at the same time in any Council where I shall be; nor shall any Candidate, by suffrage, be inducted without a unanimous vote of the Illustrious Brethren in Council; nor shall any Council advance any member, there not being three Illustrious Knights, or one Most Illustrious and four Illustrious Kt's of the Cross present, which latter may be substituted by Most Illustrious Induction; nor yet where there shall not be a full and proper mark of the Order, such as usage has adopted to our Altar, of metal, or other durable and worthy material, contained within the apartment of Council, as also the Holy Bible: nor will I ever see a Council opened for business, without the ceremony of testing the mark, exercised on the character of every Brother, prayers, and the reading of the 35th Psalm of David

nor will I ever see, consent to, or countenance, more than two persons of the same business or calling in life, to belong to, or be inducted and advanced, in any one Council of which I am a member, at the same time ; nothing therein going to exclude members from other parts of the country or from foreign parts, from joining us, if they consent formally and truly to stand in deference and defence, first, of their special *bar-brethren* in the Council, nor to prevent advancements to fill vacancies, occasioned by death or removal To all this, and every part thereof, I do now as before, by the honor and power of the Mark, as by an honorable and awful oath, which confirmeth all things in the dread presence of the most Holy and Almighty God, solemnly and in truth, bind and obligate my soul ; and in the earthly penalties, to wit, that for the violation of the least matter or particle of any of the here-taken obligations, I become the silent and mute subject of the displeasure of the Illustrious Order, and have their power and wrath turned on my head, to my destruction and dishonor, which like the *Nail of Jael*, may be the sure end of an unworthy wretch, by piercing my temples with a true sense of my ingratitude—and for a breach of silence in case of such an unhappy event, that I shall die the infamous death of a traitor, by having a spear or other sharp weapon, like as my Lord, thrust in my left side—baring testimony even in death of the power of the Mark of the Holy and Illustrious Cross, before I. H. S. our thrice Illustrious Councillor in Heaven, the Grand Council of the Good.—To this I swear.

END.

INDEX

Prepared by S. Brent Morris, 33°, G∴C∴

T

U

V

W, X, Y, Z

Arturo de Hoyos, the Magician.
Original painting by Bro. Ivan D. Ivanov, Bulgaria

His Previous Books Include:

The Cloud of Prejudice: A Study in Anti-Masonry (1992)
Rituals of the Masonic Grand Lodge of the Sun, Bayreuth, Germany (1992)
Liturgy of Germania Lodge No. 46 F&AM (1993)
The Book of the Words—Sephir H'Debarim: With an Introduction by Art de Hoyos (1999)
Albert Pike's Esoterika: The Symbolism of the Blue Degrees of Freemasonry (2005)

The Rituals of the Swedish System of Freemasonry: The German Große Landesloge (2005)
The Scottish Rite Ritual Monitor and Guide (2007)
Light on Masonry: The History and Rituals of America's Most Important Masonic Exposé (2008)
Masonic Formulas and Rituals Transcribed by Albert Pike (2010)
Albert Pike's Morals and Dogma: Annotated Edition (2011)
Freemasonry's Royal Secret (2014)
Reprints of Rituals of Old Degrees (2016)

In Collaboration with S. Brent Morris:
Is It True What They Say About Freemasonry? The Methods of Anti-Masons (1994)
Freemasonry in Context: History, Ritual, Controversy (2004)
Committed to the Flames: The History and Rituals of a Secret Masonic Rite (2008)
The Most Secret Mysteries of the High Degrees of Masonry Unveiled (2011)
Allegorical Conversations Arranged by Wisdom (2012)

As Editor and/or Author of Introduction/Preface:
(ed.) *Collectanea* (Grand College of Rites, 1994–2017)
(ed.) *Miscellanea* (Grand Council, Allied Masonic Degrees, 2001)
(ed.) C. F. Kleinknecht, *Forms and Traditions of the Scottish Rite* (2001)
(ed.) L. P. Watkins, *Albert Pike's String of Pearls* (2008)
(ed.) L. P. Watkins, *International Masonic Collection*, 1723–2011 (2012)
(intro.) S. Dafoe, Morgan: *The Scandal the Shook Freemasonry* (2009)
(intro.) A. Bernheim, *Un certaine idée de la franc-maçonnerie* (2009)
(ed./intro.) R. L. Hutchens, *A Bridge to Light: A Study in Masonic Ritual & Philosophy* (2010)
(preface) A. de Keghel, *Le défi Maçonnique Américain* (2015)
(preface) D. L. Harrison, *The Lost Rites of Freemasonry* (2017)

Forthcoming:
With S. Brent Morris, *Early Masonic Sources: Catechisms, Rituals, and Pamphlets, 1563–1735* (2020 est.)
With Josef Wäges, *Eccosais Masonry: A History of the High Degrees from the Scots Master to the Order of the Royal Secret* (2021 est.)

Designed by Arturo de Hoyos and S. Brent Morris
Composed in InDesign CS5 using Minion Pro, IM Fell English Pro, & Symbol.

Related Titles from Westphalia Press

Ancient Mysteries and Modern Masonry: The Collected Writings of Jewel P. Lightfoot, Edited by Billy J. Hamilton Jr.

Jewel P. Lightfoot. Former Attorney General of the State of Texas. Past Grand Master of the Masonic Grand Lodge of Texas. From humble beginnings in rural Arkansas, he worked to become an educated man who excelled in law and Freemasonry. He was a gentleman of his time, well-known as a scholar, public speaker, and Masonic philosopher.

Essay on The Mysteries and the True Object of The Brotherhood of Freemasons
by Jason Williams

This isn't a reprint of a classic. It's a new rendition with new life breathed into it, to be enjoyed both by the layperson trying to understand the Craft and Masonic scholars taking a deeper dive into the fraternity's golden years—when the concepts of liberty and equality were still fresh.

Female Emancipation and Masonic Membership: An Essential Collection
By Guillermo De Los Reyes Heredia

Female Emancipation and Masonic Membership: An Essential Combination is a collection of essays on Freemasonry and gender that promotes a transatlantic discussion of the study of the history of women and Freemasonry and their contribution in different countries.

Freemasonry, Heir to the Enlightenment
by Cécile Révauger

Modern Freemasonry may have mythical roots in Solomon's time but is really the heir to the Enlightenment. Ever since the early eighteenth century freemasons have endeavored to convey the values of the Enlightenment in the cultural, political and religious fields, in Europe, the American colonies and the emerging United States.

Freemasonry: A French View
by Roger Dachez and Alain Bauer

Perhaps one should speak not of Freemasonry but of Freemasonries in the plural. In each country Masonic historiography has developed uniqueness. Two of the best known French Masonic scholars present their own view of the worldwide evolution and challenging mysteries of the fraternity over the centuries.

Worlds of Print: The Moral Imagination of an Informed Citizenry, 1734 to 1839
by John Slifko

John Slifko argues that freemasonry was representative and played an important role in a larger cultural transformation of literacy and helped articulate the moral imagination of an informed democratic citizenry via fast emerging worlds of print.

Why Thirty-Three?: Searching for Masonic Origins
by S. Brent Morris, PhD

What "high degrees" were in the United States before 1830? What were the activities of the Order of the Royal Secret, the precursor of the Scottish Rite? A complex organization with a lengthy pedigree like Freemasonry has many basic foundational questions waiting to be answered, and that's what this book does: answers questions.

The Great Transformation: Scottish Freemasonry 1725-1810
by Dr. Mark C. Wallace

This book examines Scottish Freemasonry in its wider British and European contexts between the years 1725 and 1810. The Enlightenment effectively crafted the modern mason and propelled Freemasonry into a new era marked by growing membership and the creation of the Grand Lodge of Scotland.

Getting the Third Degree: Fraternalism, Freemasonry and History
Edited by Guillermo De Los Reyes and Paul Rich

As this engaging collection demonstrates, the doors being opened on the subject range from art history to political science to anthropology, as well as gender studies, sociology and more. The organizations discussed may insist on secrecy, but the research into them belies that.

The Great Transformation: Scottish Freemasonry 1725-1810 by Dr. Mark C. Wallace

This book examines Scottish Freemasonry in its wider British and European contexts between the years 1725 and 1810. The Enlightenment effectively crafted the modern mason and propelled Freemasonry into a new era marked by growing membership and the creation of the Grand Lodge of Scotland.

Getting the Third Degree: Fraternalism, Freemasonry and History Edited by Guillermo De Los Reyes and Paul Rich

As this engaging collection demonstrates, the doors being opened on the subject range from art history to political science to anthropology, as well as gender studies, sociology and more. The organizations discussed may insist on secrecy, but the research into them belies that.

Freemasonry: A French View by Roger Dachez and Alain Bauer

Perhaps one should speak not of Freemasonry but of Freemasonries in the plural. In each country Masonic historiography has developed uniqueness. Two of the best known French Masonic scholars present their own view of the worldwide evolution and challenging mysteries of the fraternity over the centuries.

Étienne Morin: From the French Rite to the Scottish Rite by Arturo de Hoyos and Josef Wäges

Explore the symbolic rituals worked throughout the life of the colony and understand exactly how the most widespread symbolic masonic ritual, the Scottish Rite craft ritual was created and from what sources.

Why Thirty-Three?: Searching for Masonic Origins by S. Brent Morris, PhD

What "high degrees" were in the United States before 1830? What were the activities of the Order of the Royal Secret, the precursor of the Scottish Rite? A complex organization with a lengthy pedigree like Freemasonry has many basic foundational questions waiting to be answered, and that's what this book does: answers questions.

A Place in the Lodge: Dr. Rob Morris, Freemasonry and the Order of the Eastern Star
by Nancy Stearns Theiss, PhD

Ridiculed as "petticoat masonry," critics of the Order of the Eastern Star did not deter Rob Morris' goal to establish a Masonic organization that included women as members. Morris carried the ideals of Freemasonry through a despairing time of American history.

Brought to Light: The Mysterious George Washington Masonic Cave
by Jason Williams MD

The George Washington Masonic Cave near Charles Town, West Virginia, contains a signature carving of George Washington dated 1748. This book painstakingly pieces together the chronicled events and real estate archives related to the cavern in order to sort out fact from fiction.

Dudley Wright: Writer, Truthseeker & Freemason
by John Belton

Dudley Wright (1868-1950) was an Englishman and professional journalist who took a universalist approach to the various great Truths of Life. He travelled though many religions in his life and wrote about them all, but was probably most at home with Islam.

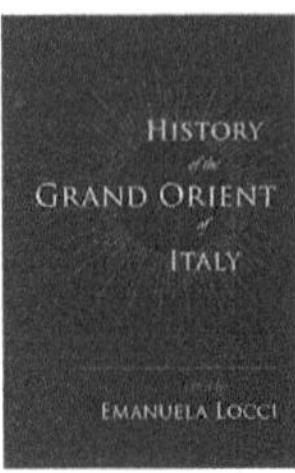

History of the Grand Orient of Italy
Emanuela Locci, Editor

No book in Masonic literature upon the history of Italian Freemasonry has been edited in English up to now. This work consists of eight studies, covering a span from the Eighteenth Century to the end of the WWII, tracing through the story, the events and pursuits related to the Grand Orient of Italy.

westphaliapress.org

www.ingramcontent.com/pod-product-compliance
Lightning Source LLC
Chambersburg PA
CBHW071959260326
41914CB00004B/859
9781637235317